Gadamer's Century

Gadamer's Century

Essays in Honor of Hans-Georg Gadamer

edited by Jeff Malpas, Ulrich Arnswald, and Jens Kertscher

The MIT Press
Cambridge, Massachusetts
London, England

This book was set in Baskerville by Achorn Graphic Services, Inc., and was printed and bound in the United States of America.

Library of Congress Cataloging-in-Publication Data

Gadamer's century : essays in honor of Hans-Georg Gadamer / edited by Jeff Malpas, Ulrich Answald, and Jens Kertscher.
  p. cm. — (Studies in contemporary German social thought)
 Includes bibliographical references and index.
 ISBN 0-262-13403-9 (alk. paper) — ISBN 0-262-63247-0 (pbk. : alk. paper)
 1. Gadamer, Hans Georg, 1900– 2. Philosophy. 3. Hermeneutics. I. Gadamer, Hans Georg, 1900– II. Malpas, J. E. III. Arnswald, Ulrich von, 1940– IV. Kertscher, Jens. V. Series.
B3248.G34 G36   2002
193—dc21

                                                                 2001044170

Contents

Contents

Acknowledgments

The editors would like to give special thanks to Lawrence Kennedy Schmidt for his invaluable assistance during the preparation of this volume.

The idea for this collection of essays in honor of Gadamer's one-hundredth birthday emerged during Jeff Malpas's time as a Humboldt Research Fellow in the Philosophisches Seminar of the University of Heidelberg during 1998–1999. The volume itself came together under the auspices of the University of Heidelberg, the University of Tasmania, and the European Institute for International Affairs, Heidelberg. We would like to thank each of these institutions, including the Alexander von Humboldt Foundation, for their assistance and support. Our gratitude also extends, of course, to all the contributors to this volume for having accepted the invitation to philosophize with Gadamer and to Larry Cohen at MIT Press for giving his support to the project at an early stage in its development. In addition, we would like to thank Bert Peeters, Stefano Franchi, and Michael Isenberg (for their translations of the essays by Ricœur, Albert, Kertscher, and Vattimo) and Cynthia Townley (for editorial assistance). Special thanks are due to Eilidh St. John for her work in proofing and compilation of the index.

This volume is a project of the European Institute for International Affairs, Heidelberg. The European Institute for International Affairs is an independent, nonprofit and nonpartisan scientific organization whose main task is to encourage the exchange of ideas and research results in the domains of the social sciences and the humanities.

Introduction

Jeff Malpas, Ulrich Arnswald, and Jens Kertscher

When reviewing his life as an old man, Johann-Wolfgang Goethe wrote: "Es wäre nicht der Mühe wert, siebzig Jahre alt zu werden, wenn alle Weisheit der Welt Torheit wäre vor Gott."[1] ("It would not be worth the trouble to live to seventy years of age were all the wisdom of the world but foolishness before God.") Hans-Georg Gadamer, whose life work is honored in this collection of essays, has long surpassed Goethe's "seventy years," but there seems little doubt, whatever perspective is adopted, that the wisdom that has been accrued and articulated in the course of that life amounts to a great deal more than "foolishness."

Few, if any, philosophers now living have had an involvement and influence in philosophy over the last century to compare with that of Hans-Georg Gadamer. He has been responsible for major contributions to aesthetic theory, to the study of Plato and Hegel, to humanistic studies, and to the philosophy of history and the *Geisteswissenschaften*. As a one-time student of Martin Heidegger, Gadamer has taken up and developed a number of central Heideggerian insights in new and important ways, while his engagement with his contemporaries such as Habermas, Betti, and others have been memorable events in themselves. Moreover, as Gianni Vattimo points out in his essay here, the shape of contemporary hermeneutics is itself almost entirely due to Gadamer's influence, while his magnum opus, *Truth and Method,* has attained the status of one of the great philosophical works of the last century.[2]

Yet how to honor a philosopher who has already become a classic in his own lifetime? An answer to this question may be found in Gadamer's own work. In *Truth and Method,* Gadamer comments on the classical as something that has an ongoing significance and meaning that preserves itself even in the face of the eroding and decaying influence of time.[3] As Gadamer writes: "What we call 'classical' does not first require the overcoming of historical distance, for in its own constant mediation it overcomes this distance by itself. The classical, then, is certainly 'timeless,' but this timelessness is a mode of historical being. . . . This is just what the word 'classical' means: that the duration of a work's power to speak directly is fundamentally unlimited."[4] The surest testament to the status of Gadamer's work as indeed "classical" in this way must be its continuing ability to speak to us—and not just to a select few. An ability to speak that is itself given testament by our own capacity to respond to the work, to take up the ideas it presents to us, and to find in it a source of insight, inspiration, and challenge. The aim of this collection is not merely to provide a marker of Gadamer's one-hundredth birthday (in 2001, his one hundred and first) but to provide a measure of the truly classical character of Gadamer's work through exhibiting something of the breadth of engagement that his work has provoked and the extent to which that work does indeed speak to us even across differences of culture, style, and philosophical tradition.

In pursuit of this aim, the essays assembled here range across a number of topics and approaches, including contributions from those who have direct and well-acknowledged interest in Gadamer and Gadamerian hermeneutics as well as those for whom Gadamer might otherwise be thought to be a less central influence. Moreover, while all of these essays, in one way or another, take Gadamer's work as an important point of departure, none of them are concerned merely with issues of Gadamerian scholarship or exegesis. The emphasis is thus on the moment of *applicatio* rather than *explicatio* as it might apply in the encounter with Gadamer's own work.

Of course, not only is this emphasis on "application" in keeping with the idea of the "classical" as it has been spelled out here, but it also reflects what might be termed the "classical" temper of Gadamer's style of philosophizing—"classical" in just the sense that it has always exhibited a commitment to ongoing engagement with others and to the openness that is a necessary part of such engagement. As Gadamer writes: "In human relations the important thing is . . . not to overlook his [i.e., the other's] claim but to let him really say something to us. Here is where openness belongs. But ultimately this openness does not exist only for the person who speaks; rather anyone who listens is fundamentally open. Without such openness to one another there is no genuine human bond."[5] Although Gadamer has had an enormous personal effect on twentieth-century thought, he has never been a solitary or self-obsessed thinker. Indeed, not only have the ideas of dialogue and conversation been central themes in Gadamer's philosophical writings, but they also have been central features of his philosophical practice. In this respect, it is only fitting that Lawrence Schmidt's sketch of Gadamer's life, with which this collection properly begins, should itself begin with the account of a conversation in a Freiburg Weinstube in 1974.

No less than in Gadamer's own life and work, dialogue and "conversation" figure as important themes in almost all of the essays contained in this collection. In some cases the focus is explicitly on some aspect of the dialogic structure of understanding or on issues that arise directly from it. Charles Taylor and Jay Garfield both address issues of understanding as they apply across cultures and traditions—and in Garfield's case, as they arise in relation to contemporary philosophical practice itself; Ulrich Arnswald examines similar issues from the perspective of the ideas of forms of life and language games; Gerald Bruns considers the way in which rationality is itself always worked out within the realm of everyday practical engagement—within a dialogue that is always socially and linguistically mediated; John Connolly examines the exegetical practice of Meister Eckhart and the possibility that it might be grounded in something like a Gadamerian account of the necessary connection between *explicatio* and *applicatio;* Alasdair MacIntyre explores the working out of that dialogue in relation to the reading of philosophical texts; Jeff Malpas looks to dialogue or "play" as indicative, not merely of the character of understanding, but also of its essential ground. Elsewhere the focus is less on the dialogue of understanding as such and more on the way in which that dialogue plays itself out in particular cases or with respect to particular issues: issues of relativism; of race, gender, and social identity; of historical distance and historical engagement; of philosophical interpretation and scientific inquiry.

Many of the essays that make up this volume are, of course, themselves continuations of conversations that have already been long underway—conversations that represent a continuation of the authors' own engagement with Gadamer's thought and, in the case with Ulrich Arnswald's, Robert Holub's, and Robert Pippin's contributions in particular, a continuation of an ongoing dialogue with the philosophical names of the past, in these cases, Wittgenstein, Nietzsche, and Hegel. Moreover, in keeping with Gadamer's own breadth of philosophical erudition and interest, it is not only modern thought that figures in these pages, but also that of the ancients and medievals. In Stanley Rosen's essay, for instance, it is the age-old quarrel between poetry and philosophy, or as one might also put it, between the humanistic and scientistic impulses within philosophy itself, that takes center stage. Although Rosen presents Gadamer as adopting a mediating role in this quarrel, Hans Albert's contribution suggests a different view with Gadamer's hermeneutics counterposed to the "critical rationalism" of Karl Popper. In Albert's essay, it is the ongoing engagement between himself and Gadamer that is the main focus of discussion, and the dialogue between Gadamer and other recent and contemporary figures, including Derrida, Habermas, and Heidegger, also figures as an important element in many of the contributions. But new conversations, or conversations that have a relatively short history to them, are also opened up here.

In this latter respect, John McDowell's essay is particularly important, inasmuch as it develops further the connection between McDowell and Gadamer that was already evident in McDowell's *Mind and World*. Moreover, McDowell also brings the work of Davidson into the picture, and the question of the relation (or, indeed, the contrast) between Davidson's work and that of Gadamer is not only a feature of McDowell's contribution, but also figures in a number of other essays, most notably in those of Taylor and Malpas. Here it is not merely a dialogue between individuals that comes to the fore, but a dialogue between different philosophical traditions—although just how different remains a point deserving further exploration.

The space that is opened up in the encounter with another is one that is always animated by language—the importance of conversation in Gadamer's life and work is thus a reflection, not only of the dialogue that lies at the heart of understanding, but of the way in which that dialogue stands in an essential relation to the linguistic, even though it encompasses more than merely that which can be spoken. Just as dialogue and conversation take a central role in many of the discussions here, so too is it a role that is for the most part shared with language as well as with the temporal and sociohistorical dimension in which language itself moves. For Jens Kertscher in particular, the role of language in understanding—and the famous Gadamerian pronouncement that "Being that can be understood is language"[6]—is his main concern, while for Paul Ricœur and Alasdair MacIntyre it is the medium of history and tradition, and, in Ricœur's case, the role played there by temporal distance, and so also by death.

Yet inasmuch as the essays contained here do indeed encompass a remarkable diversity of philosophical perspectives, interests, and styles, so they are also indicative of the ever-present possibility of dialogue not only within, but also across language and tradition, and of the formation of new modes of discourse, new traditions, new modes of philosophizing. If one of the aims of this collection is to provide testimony to Gadamer's own remarkable capacity to engender philosophical and human engagement, then another aim is to hold open the possibility of a mode of philosophical thinking that would be adequate to the challenge that Gadamer's own energy, insight, and openness presents to us—a mode of thinking that would not remain enclosed within the narrow confines of its own specialized vocabulary and canon, but one that would indeed be capable of encompassing more of that broad range of problems and approaches that is characteristic of contemporary philosophy. It is perhaps the pursuit of just such an ambition that is the most fitting way of honoring and celebrating the one hundred years of Hans-Georg Gadamer.

Notes

1. Johann-Wolfgang Goethe, *Maximen und Reflexionen*, in *Goethes Werke, Hamburger Ausgabe in 14 Bänden*, Band 12 (Munich: C. H. Beck, 1982), 515.

2. In his own contribution to this volume, Alasdair MacIntyre asserts his confident expectation that both *Truth and Method* (*Wahrheit und Methode*, first published, 1960) and *The Idea of the Good in Platonic-Aristotelian Philosophy* (*Die Idee des Guten zwischen Platon und Aristoteles*, first published 1978) will be counted as classics of twentieth-century thought.

3. The classical, writes Gadamer, "epitomizes a general characteristic of historical being: preservation amid the ruins of time" (*Truth and Method*, translated by Joel Weinsheimer and Donald Marshall [New York: Continuum, 2nd rev. ed., 1989], 289).

4. Hans-Georg Gadamer, *Truth and Method*, 290.

5. Ibid., 361.

6. Ibid., 475.

1

Hans-Georg Gadamer: A Biographical Sketch

Lawrence Schmidt

At the end of the 1974 summer semester, Professor Hans-Georg Gadamer traveled the short distance from his home in Heidelberg to the University of Freiburg to entertain questions concerning hermeneutics from students in Professor Werner Marx's seminar. I attended that seminar, where we had studied *Wahrheit und Methode*. Professor Marx had collected questions and forwarded them to Gadamer. To read an important work in philosophy and then have the opportunity to converse with the philosopher is a rare and invigorating experience. The intensity of the conversation grew when we retired to a cozy *Weinstube* in the old town. Although he walked with a slight limp, Gadamer struck me as a man in his prime: his power of concentration, the sparkling eyes as another interjected a further question, his willingness to graciously entertain and even improve upon a critical comment before delving into an answer, his enthusiasm to pursue the subject matter, and his stamina, which outlasted most of us. This is but one of innumerable encounters that attest to Gadamer's humanity and delight in conversation, which continue today, even at one hundred.

Hans-Georg Gadamer was born on February 11, 1900, in Marburg, Germany.[1] His immediate roots were Silesian; his mother, Emma Gewiese, and father, Johannes Gadamer, were born in Waldenburg near Breslau. In 1891 Johannes Gadamer moved to Marburg where he studied pharmacology and began his academic teaching career at the university. In 1902 Johannes Gadamer followed a call to become professor at the University of Breslau, so Hans-Georg grew up in Breslau, a professor's child. His childhood was not without incident. His one-year younger sister died when not yet five months old, his two-year older brother, Willi, suffered from chronic epilepsy, his mother died in 1904, and his father remarried, to Hedwig Hellich, in 1905. Gadamer describes his father as authoritarian, though with good intentions. Yet, as a young boy he enjoyed hiking in the mountains, playing soldier during the yearly summer vacations on the Baltic Sea, and, after moving in 1909, playing in a fine, large backyard, where he learned how to ride a bicycle. His youthful reactions to the sinking of the Titanic and the beginning of World War I brought a stern word from his father. Hans-Georg attended the *Heiligen Geist Gymnasium* (grades 6–13) where he learned French well and enjoyed literature but read no philosophy. He did read and was deeply impressed by the poetry of Stefan George. After graduation Gadamer began his university studies in the summer semester of 1918 at the University of Breslau; he tried several different humanistic disciplines and reports reading his first work in philosophy, Kant's *Critique of Pure Reason*. In Professor Hönigswald, Gadamer found his first philosophy teacher.

In 1919 the Gadamers moved back to Marburg; Gadamer senior had received the professorship of his former teacher. Hans-Georg entered the University of Marburg, studying philosophy (with Paul Natorp and Nicolai Hartmann), German literature, history, and art history. Gadamer recounts that the atmosphere of his first years at Marburg was marked by a general loss of orientation among the students. Gadamer's first friend, Oskar Schürer, belonged to the circle around Richard Hamann, all critical of modern bourgeois society. Another circle centered around Wolters, a close friend of Stefan George, to which Gadamer did not belong but heard about through Hans Anton. Professor Hartmann appears to have exerted the most influence on Gadamer. Following Hartmann's suggestion, Gadamer traveled to the University of Munich for the summer semester of 1921 where he first heard of the Heidegger phenomenon in Freiburg. The phenomenology classes in Munich were of little interest, so he concentrated on art history, attending lectures by Heinrich Wölflin. On this trip he was accompanied by Frida Kratz and they

enjoyed hiking in the Alps.[2] Gadamer's studies progressed well and
he was in the inner circles of Hartmann and Ernst Curtis (Romance
languages). In 1922 his father was elected Rektor (president) of the
university. In May Gadamer's doctoral dissertation, *Das Wesen der
Lust nach den platonischen Dialogen,* supervised by Paul Natorp, was
accepted. Just a few months later, in August, Gadamer was infected
with polio, which was moving through the city. Because of the danger of further infection, Gadamer was confined to his room for several months, reading Husserl and a manuscript of Heidegger's that
presented a sketch of his Aristotle interpretation. Heidegger's analysis of the "hermeneutic situation" in this manuscript so deeply impressed Gadamer ("like an electric shock,")[3] that he resolved to go
to Freiburg and study with him.[4] Gadamer was able to fight off the
polio, recovering slowly. On April 20, 1923, Gadamer married Frida
Kratz.

The young couple moved to Freiburg for the beginning of the
1923 summer semester. In his first personal meeting with Heidegger,
Gadamer was struck by Heidegger's stature, so impressive had Heidegger loomed in Gadamer's imagination. That semester Gadamer
attended all of Heidegger's classes, including one on Aristotle's
Ethics VI and one on ontology that presented the hermeneutics of
facticity. In the class on Kant's religious writings, co-taught by
Ebbinghaus, Gadamer noticed the inner connection of philosophy
and religion in Heidegger. That summer the inflation crises reached
dramatic proportions. The Gadamers were invited by Heidegger to
join him in his hut in Todtnauberg for four weeks in August. During
this stay Gadamer developed a close relationship with Heidegger;
he said it was like a "practical introduction to hermeneutics."[5] In the
fall of 1923, Heidegger received an associate professorship at the
University of Marburg, and the Gadamers followed Heidegger back
to Marburg. The Gadamers moved into a two-room apartment.
There was a good deal of activity in their home. Friends, including
Karl Löwith and Walter Bröcker (Heidegger's assistants from Freiburg), Gerhard Krüger, and Jacob Klein, would come over after
Heidegger's early morning lecture, buying food along the way
to eat breakfast together and holding discussions until noon.[6] Eve-
nings were often spent reading books to each other aloud. Knowing

Marburg, Gadamer assisted Heidegger in settling in, helping him with errands. Another reading circle of Gadamer, Schlier, and Krüger, and later Bornkamm and Dinkler, met at Professor Bultmann's home to read classical Greek texts. In 1924 Gadamer published his first two articles, both on Hartmann and unmistakably influenced by Heidegger. The university president's son was progressing well.

By the beginning of 1925, however, Heidegger appeared no longer pleased with Gadamer's progress. At least Gadamer interpreted a letter from Heidegger in this manner. So Gadamer decided to begin to study classical philology under Paul Friedländer, working toward a teaching certificate that could provide for the future. After a relatively short period, Gadamer took the examination in classical philology on July 20, 1927. In addition to Friedländer, Heidegger, who had just published *Being and Time,* was the other examiner. Gadamer did well and apparently Heidegger was now favorably impressed with Gadamer's work, for the next day he offered Gadamer the possibility of writing his habilitation with him. Gadamer joined Löwith and Krüger, who were also working under Heidegger. Gadamer had to hurry, since Heidegger was leaving Marburg to occupy Husserl's chair in Freiburg. Gadamer was under pressure, and the situation worsened when his father's health deteriorated leading to his death from cancer on April 15, 1928. Gadamer was able to submit his manuscript during the summer of 1928, entitled "Interpretation des platonischen Philebos," and first published in 1931 as *Platos dialektische Ethik.*[7]

Heidegger and Friedländer were quite satisfied with Gadamer's habilitation. Academically Gadamer had succeeded, but he now entered the German academic's no-man's-land. Although officially sanctioned to teach at the university, he had no permanent position. Further, to retain this qualification, the *venia legendi,* Gadamer had to teach each semester and he was paid according to the number of students attending. Gadamer also applied for and received a small amount of money to investigate Greek philosophy of nature. For the next years the Philosophy Department tried to attain a teaching contract for him for ethics and aesthetics but was unsuccessful because of the world financial situation. In the summer semester of

1929 Gadamer delivered his first lecture course, concerning ethics. Gadamer continued in this position of limbo for several years, teaching at first one and then up to three classes per semester, primarily on Greek philosophy.

On January 30, 1933, Hitler became chancellor. On August 21, Heidegger became president of the University of Freiburg, aligning himself with National Socialism. On August 24 the Philosophy Department was finally able to get funding for the position in ethics and aesthetics for Gadamer, who became a temporary professor. In November Gadamer, as most German professors, signed in an unclear manner[8] the document in which the professors declared their commitment to Hitler and the National-Socialist State. In January 1934 Gadamer's *Platon und die Dichter* (Plato and the Poets)[9] was published; it is a shorter version of a longer manuscript that was refused for publication.[10] He was invited in May to temporarily fill the position of Richard Kroner in Kiel, who had been suspended because of Jewish blood. For the winter semester of 1934–35 Gadamer continued in Kiel. In 1934 the faculty at Marburg attempted to obtain the official title of professor for Gadamer, but this proposal was rejected, as Gadamer said, because of his Jewish friends and anti-Nazi position.[11] Since Gadamer would not join the party, nor emigrate, and since he wanted to preserve his academic career, he voluntarily entered a training camp for aspiring academics basically for Nazi indoctrination, called the Academy for Professors. In the winter semester of 1935–36 and the summer semester of 1936, he was given the position in Marburg replacing the suspended Erich Frank. In the fall of 1936, Gadamer traveled to Frankfurt to hear Heidegger's lecture, *Der Ursprung des Kunstwerkes*. Finally, in April 1937, Gadamer received the title of a *nichtbeamteter außerordentlicher* professor at the University of Marburg, that is, a lower-level non-civil-service professorship. In October Gadamer, with Krüger and Bröcker, traveled to the Black Forest to visit Heidegger for two weeks. In March 1938 Gadamer received an invitation temporarily to fill Arnold Gehlen's chair in philosophy at the University of Leipzig. Gadamer had hopes of receiving a permanent position, since Gehlen had received an invitation to Königsberg. Finally, on January 1, 1939, he became a full professor and chair of the Department of Philosophy in Leipzig.

He now had a permanent and respectable position, and on April 15 the rest of the family joined him in Leipzig.

On July 8, 1939, at the age of 39, Gadamer presented his inaugural lecture for his professorship in Leipzig, entitled "Hegel und der geschichtliche Geist." In a letter to Löwith, Gadamer compared the situation in Germany to Hegel's master and slave dialectic, where Germany and Italy were characterized as the poorer slave.[12] Grondin notes that there are only some small hints in Gadamer's publications that he agreed with some of the aims and achievements of the "new" Germany, for example, the fate of the German people and using Hegel, on whom he was then working, to see the path of Germany in relation to the moral substance of the people. But as Grondin states Gadamer never identified with the Führer, the party, or its institutions.[13]

Gadamer taught his classes without using prepared manuscripts. In addition to almost regular classes on Greek philosophy, other subjects included Hegel, Kant, Nietzsche, modern philosophy, and one on the question of principles in the humanities. In August 1939, after a vacation in southern Germany, Gadamer visited Heidegger when they heard of Hitler's agreement with Stalin; Gadamer remembers Heidegger's enthusiasm.[14] He also visited Jaspers in Heidelberg, a philosopher whom Gadamer valued and supported during the trying war years. One lecture from this period needs to be mentioned. It was delivered in Paris, May 29, 1941, and it concerned Herder. It has been discussed by Orozco and Grondin, due to the changes made when it was printed after the war, leaving out phrases which Orozco interprets as indicating a leaning toward fascism but which Grondin defends, saying Gadamer never names the ideology or party and argues rather for Herder's humanism.[15]

The center of Leipzig was bombed on December 4, 1943, destroying much of the university, so classes were held in a room without heating, lighting, or windowpanes. Gadamer escaped from the destruction in Leipzig, delivering a series of lectures in Portugal in March and April of 1944. There he met and traveled with Carl F. von Weizsäcker. Upon returning to Leipzig, Gadamer learned of his brother Willi's death. Gadamer belonged to a circle around Goerdeler in Leipzig, but he did not know of the plot against Hitler.

Goerdeler's daughter was a friend of Käte Lekebusch, who was Gadamer's regular student and assistant. From July 15 to July 25 Gadamer was on a trip to Breslau to convince Viktor von Weizsächer to join the department in Leipzig when the plot to kill Hitler failed on July 20. Many people then lost their lives and many feared for their family's and their own lives. Käte Lekebusch was denounced during this terror, but she was acquitted for lack of evidence by the civil court. The Gestapo was not finished with her, however, so she was transferred to their jail in Berlin. Orders for her transportation to the concentration camp, Ravensbrück, had already been received, when at the last minute the jailer opened the jail as the Russians advanced.[16] As the war slowly closed in over Leipzig, Gadamer was inducted into the defensive army (*Volksstrum*), but because of his polio he only had to report on Sundays. The U.S. troops entered Leipzig on April 18, 1945, capitulation came in May, and by July the Russians had replaced the Americans. The Gadamers had survived World War II.

After a short stint as dean of the Philosophical-Historical Faculties, Gadamer was elected president of the University of Leipzig on January 21, 1946. As president, Gadamer's aim was to rebuild the university and reestablish its political independence as a place of higher education. The university reopened in February and Gadamer's inaugural address warned of education only for technology and affirmed the independence of research. Differences and tensions with Soviet ideology made progress slow. When there was time to read, Gadamer indulged in lyric poetry. As the year progressed, Gadamer came to see that a new ideology threatened the university. On June 18, 1946, he responded to Jaspers that he would consider a position in the West. Gadamer bowed to political pressure in 1947 and opened a new department for the study of Marxism. Gadamer found a position in Frankfurt am Main beginning in October 1947. At the end of October Gadamer returned to Leipzig to officially transfer the president's title. While in Leipzig, Gadamer was arrested and interrogated on November 7; after three days he was released.[17] As Gadamer left the East for the West, he rode in the train car with his household goods and library, armed with cigars, cigarettes, and liquor. It still took four days to reach the border,

Lawrence Schmidt

where his provisions enabled a quicker passage without a Russian inspection.

In Frankfurt Gadamer was able to return primarily to teaching. Their living situation was poor: they had little fuel, little food, and little money to spend. His marriage fell apart. In late April 1948, Gadamer visited Heidegger. In May he finally received his title as professor in Frankfurt. In late March 1949, Gadamer traveled with seven other German professors to an international philosophy congress in Argentina.[18] There, for the first time since the war, he met several old friends, including Löwith and Helmut Kuhn. Gadamer says that during this international congress he was impressed by what one can learn if one enters into a true conversation with others.[19] Upon returning to Frankfurt, he received a call to the University of Heidelberg to assume Jaspers's chair in philosophy.

Gadamer moved to Heidelberg in June 1950, where he continues to reside. He married Käte Lekebusch in Frankfurt on July 8, 1950. Between April 1949 and February 1951, Gadamer taught in both Frankfurt and Heidelberg. Although Gadamer's relation to Jaspers was good before he received the call to Heidelberg, their relationship cooled from that time onward.[20] In Heidelberg Gadamer dedicated himself to teaching in the Department of Philosophy, declining a position as dean. His students of this period included Reiner Wiehl, Konrad Cramer, Friedrich Fulda, Wolfgang Wieland, and Dieter Henrich. Gadamer returned to his lectures on art and history in order to develop these into a book, but time for this existed only in the vacations. Recognizing the importance of conversation to philosophizing, Gadamer developed three projects. He conducted his own introductory classes in philosophy, instead of turning them over to assistants. He invited a small group of select students, at most twelve, to meet with him for a three-hour discussion of major texts in philosophy. He also instituted the practice of inviting well-known philosophers to come to the department to give lectures. In 1953 Gadamer was able to entice Löwith, then in New York, to join the Philosophy Department in Heidelberg. Gadamer and Kuhn established the *Philosophische Rundschau;* Käte Gadamer-Lekebusch was responsible for the publication, having experience in this area.

During the 1950s Gadamer slowly, slowly wrote his magus opus, *Wahrheit und Methode* (*Truth and Method*). For him writing was tortuous; he felt Heidegger peering over his shoulder, and writing lacked the give and take present in a conversation. Hints of the development can be found in Gadamer's courses and lectures. In Leipzig, Frankfurt, and Heidelberg (summer semester 1955) one of Gadamer's lectures was on art and history, an introduction to the humanities. In May 1951 he was invited to join the Heidelberg Academy of Sciences, presenting a lecture "Theorie der Hermeneutik" (The Theory of Hermeneutics), which succinctly presented the basis for philosophical hermeneutics. In the winter semester of 1951–52 he lectured on the Enlightenment and Romantics, moving from Nicholas of Cusa to Leibniz. For Krüger's fiftieth birthday (January 30, 1952), Gadamer presented the direction of his investigation.[21] Gadamer's lecture in Bremen in May 1953 was entitled "Wahrheit in den Geisteswissenschaften"[22] and that summer his lecture traced the movement in philosophy from Hegel to Heidegger. In 1955 Gadamer delivered "Was ist Wahrheit?" (What is Truth?)[23] to a student association of the University of Frankfurt, and that summer he lectured on the humanities and held a seminar on Kant's third critique. Gadamer wrote the original eighty-page sketch of *Truth and Method* during the years of 1955 and 1956.[24] For the winter semester 1955–56 there was a seminar on the problem of language, in the summer semester 1956 a lecture on Aristotle, and in the winter semester 1956–57 a lecture on aesthetics. On September 27, 1956, Gadamer's daughter Andrea was born. In 1957 Gadamer was invited to the University of Loewen where he presented, in French translation, a lecture on the problem of historical consciousness. Finally Gadamer received a research semester for the winter semester 1958–59 and was able to complete the manuscript. *Truth and Method* was published by J. C. B. Mohr (Paul Siebeck) in 1960.

After the publication of *Truth and Method,* interest in philosophical hermeneutics grew slowly. The introduction to the second edition written in 1963 and published in 1965, indicates that some questioned the universality of hermeneutic understanding, while others, especially Emilio Betti, thought the application of Gadamer's theory of understanding in the humanities would sacrifice objectivity. It was the debate with Jürgen Habermas and K.-O. Apel that catapulted hermeneutics to the center of attention in the late 1960s. Although Habermas agreed with Gadamer's critique of positivism, he believed Gadamer had gone too far in limiting the capacities of reason and so prevented ideology critique. Their debate was published by Suhrkamp, in 1971, as *Hermeneutik und Ideologiekritik.*

During the 1960s Gadamer continued his regular topics in his classes. First in the winter semester 1969–70, he conducted a seminar entitled "Hermeneutik und Dialektik." In 1961 he visited Betti while on a trip to lecture in Italy. Gadamer founded the *Hegel Vereinigung* (Hegel Society) in 1962. As director of the German Philosophical Society, he organized a conference in Heidelberg on the problem of language in 1966. The first of the four volumes of Gadamer's collected essays (*Kleine Schriften*) was published in 1967. Gadamer officially retired on February 14, 1968, but he continued to fill his vacant position until a replacement was appointed in 1970. In February 1968 Gadamer embarked on the first of many trips to the United States and Canada, having been invited to the Schleiermacher Conference at Vanderbilt University in Tennessee. Professor Charles Scott at Vanderbilt organized a series of lectures at several other universities after the conference for Gadamer; the following year Gadamer returned to North America. Richard Palmer's 1969 book, entitled *Hermeneutics: Interpretation Theory in Schleiermacher, Dilthey, Heidegger, and Gadamer,* introduced Gadamer and hermeneutics to the English speaking world. In June 1969 Gadamer organized a conference on Heidegger for his eightieth birthday in Heidelberg to which Heidegger came. For Gadamer's seventieth birthday, his former students Bubner, Cramer, and Wiehl edited a two-volume commemorative collection of essays entitled *Hermeneutik und Dialektik.*

Gadamer actually retired in 1970 and began to travel extensively, although he continued to present one lecture during the summer semesters in Heidelberg. For the next several years during part of the fall, Gadamer was a guest professor at the Catholic University in Washington (1969), Syracuse University (1971), McMaster University (Canada 1972–75), and at Boston College (1974–86). In 1971 Gadamer was honored with the *Bundesverdienstkreuz* and became a member of the *Ordens pour le mérite* (Order of Merit). In 1972 Gianni Vattimo translated *Wahrheit und Methode* into Italian and in 1975 the English translation, *Truth and Method,* was published (French in 1976 and Spanish in 1977). Heidegger died on May 26, 1976, and Gadamer participated in the Freiburg commemoration in December, reading "Sein Geist Gott" (Being Spirit God).[25] In 1977 Gadamer published his autobiography, *Philosophische Lehrjahre* (*Philosophical Apprenticeships*). Gadamer received the Hegel prize from the city of Stuttgart in 1979.

In the 1980s Gadamer held only two lecture courses in Heidelberg, but he traveled extensively, in addition to the United States, going to South Africa and Yugoslavia; Naples, Italy (1981 and almost yearly thereafter until 1997); Breslau, Poland (1982); as well as many trips in the western European nations. I met Gadamer again in the summer of 1980 when he traveled to Perugia, Italy, for the *Collegium Phaenomenologium,* an annual four-week graduate and postgraduate seminar, whose topic that year was hermeneutics. In 1981 Gadamer encountered Jacques Derrida in Paris at the Goethe Institute.[26] In 1985 the first of the ten volumes of his *Gesammelte Werke* (*Collected Works*) was published. In May 1986 he attended the meetings of the Heidegger Society in Messkirch for the first time. The late 1980s seemed to me an opportune time to bring those interested in Gadamer's thought to Heidelberg to discuss their ideas with Gadamer. To this end, with the help of Professor Reiner Wiehl (Heidelberg) and Professor James Risser (Seattle), I organized a larger international conference on *Wahrheit und Methode* in 1989 at the *Wissenschaftsforum* in Heidelberg. Beginning in 1991 this conference evolved into a smaller, annual international symposium meeting in July at the *Philosophisches Seminar* in Heidelberg.

In the 1990s, Gadamer continued to travel but less and less as the long-term effects of his bout with polio made walking more and more difficult. He continued to exercise on his training bicycle at home, however, and he would go almost twice weekly to his office in the *Philosophisches Seminar,* climbing the stairs to Frau Hornung's office where he would dictate letters and conduct business. Afterward he would retire to his office to prepare his next publication or to receive an inquisitive scholar, who could come from any corner of the world, and engage that person in a conversation. Often they would then retire to a nearby restaurant for a glass of wine or dinner. On February 11, 2000, scholars and admirers from around the world came to Heidelberg to celebrate Gadamer's centennial with him.

Notes

1. This sketch would not have been possible without Jean Grondin's, *Hans-Georg Gadamer—eine Biographie* (Tübingen: Mohr Siebeck, 1999), which is currently being translated into English. Those of Gadamer's autobiographical works that are currently available in English are *Philosophische Lehrjahre* (Frankfurt am Main: Vittorio Klostermann, 1977), translated as *Philosophical Apprenticeships* (Cambridge: MIT Press, 1995) and "Reflections on my Philosophical Journey," in *The Philosophy of Hans-Georg Gadamer,* edited by Lewis Edwin Hahn (LaSalle: Open Court, 1997), 3–64.

2. Grondin, *Hans-Georg Gadamer,* 84.

3. Gadamer, *Philosophische Lehrjahre,* 212.

4. Gadamer, *Gesammelte Werke,* 3 (Tübingen: J. C. B. Mohr [Paul Siebeck], 1987), 286.

5. Gadamer, *Gesammelte Werke,* 2 (Tübingen: J. C. B. Mohr [Paul Siebeck], 1986), 486.

6. Grondin, *Hans-Georg Gadamer,* 132, quotes a letter from Löwith to the effect that they met at Gadamer's while Gadamer speaks of meeting at Krüger's (*Philosophische Lehrjahre,* 35).

7. Gadamer, *Plato's Dialectical Ethics. Phenomenological Interpretations Relating to the Philebus,* translated by Robert M. Wallace (New Haven: Yale, 1991).

8. Grondin, *Hans-Georg Gadamer,* 184.

9. Gadamer, In *Dialogue and Dialectic: Eight Hermeneutical Studies on Plato,* translated by Christopher Smith (New Haven: Yale, 1980), 39–72.

10. See Grondin, *Hans-Georg Gadamer,* 189ff and also Teresa Orozco, *Platonische Gewalt* (Hamburg: Argument Verlag, 1995), 32ff concerning the debate about this text.

11. Grondin, *Hans-Georg Gadamer,* 204ff.

12. Ibid., 229.

13. Ibid., 232.

14. Ibid., 237.

15. See Grondin, *Hans-Georg Gadamer,* 241ff and Teresa Orozco, *Platonische Gewalt,* 105ff.

16. See Grondin, *Hans-Georg Gadamer,* 250–253.

17. Grondin, *Philosophische Lehrjahre,* 133ff.

18. Gadamer places this trip in February (*Gesammelte Werke,* 2, 492), but Grondin, *Hans-Georg Gadamer,* 310, cites the proceedings, which give the dates as 30 March to 9 April.

19. Grondin, *Hans-Georg Gadamer,* 310 n. 46.

20. See Grondin, *Hans-Georg Gadamer,* 304ff.

21. Ibid., 318.

22. "Truth in the Humanities," in Brice Wachterhauser, ed., *Hermeneutics and Truth* (Evanston, Ill: Northwestern University Press, 1994), 25–33.

23. In Wachterhauser, ed., *Hermeneutics and Truth,* 33–47.

24. See Grondin's discussion of this manuscript in the translation of his book *Sources of Hermeneutics* (Albany: SUNY, 1995), 83ff.

25. Gadamer, *Heidegger's Ways* (Albany: SUNY, 1994), 181–197.

26. See *Dialogue and Dialectic,* edited by Diane Michelfelder and Richard Palmer (Albany: SUNY, 1989).

2

Critical Rationalism and Universal Hermeneutics

Hans Albert

Hans-Georg Gadamer may well be considered one of the most influential German philosophers of our time, perhaps even the most
influential of them all. Although invited to contribute to this volume
in his honor, however, I do not assume that the editors imagine I
have revised my views concerning the ways of German philosophical
thinking as represented by him.

Three primary reasons motivate my contribution here. First, the
fact that Gadamer's thinking continues to exercise such a vast influence upon so many people. Second, there is a tendency to misconstrue the differences between his views and mine in a way that is
obstructive to the solution of like problems. And third, notwithstanding my sometimes harsh attacks upon his views, Gadamer has always
shown a kind disposition toward me that cannot be taken for granted
and that I am bound to respect. There remains a happy reminis-
cence of a conference, held in Dublin by the "International Association for Cultural Freedom" in September 1977, when I regularly had
breakfast with him and his charming wife and was granted the opportunity to listen to his amusing tales. His farewell lecture, in February
1969 in Heidelberg, at which Heidegger, among others, was present,
stamped itself most vividly upon my memory.[1] I also remember a
correspondence that involved an exchange of ideas that demonstrated Gadamer's willingness to practice that kind of dialogue with
"dissenters" that certainly dominates his philosophical outlook. It is

for this reason as well that I wish to congratulate him on his one-hundredth birthday.

As to the philosophy developed by Gadamer in his work *Wahrheit und Methode* (*Truth and Method*), I always have taken it to be a continuation of Heidegger's thinking, but with different premises.[2] As to the difference between Gadamer's and the Messkirch philosopher's views, Jürgen Habermas is not incorrect when he states that the merit of "having urbanized the Heideggerian province" belongs to Gadamer. Yet Gadamer may well be given credit, even by those at variance with his universal hermeneutics, for not having taken up his teacher's later philosophy. For it seems that Heidegger's path of thought leads into a blind alley and it would not have been a promising enterprise to follow him there.[3]

Heidegger's political escapades at the opening period of the Third Reich seem to have struck Gadamer as strange enough. It is true that Gadamer identified himself with the then aims of German foreign policy, and he admired its successes, but unlike many of his colleagues, he betrayed no attachments to the ruling ideology of the period.[4] As for the rest, he had cherished sundry illusions about the general situation of that time as well as about future developments then quite common in Germany. His having recourse to Hegel upon entering into the contemporary historical situation is not at all incomprehensible.

I still remember having entertained similar illusions myself. I used to judge the situation according to Oswald Spengler's views which I had accepted after reading his book *Jahre der Entscheidung* (*Decisive Years*) and other writings of his. Gadamer, obviously, had been influenced by certain diffuse ideas of catastrophe emerging after World War I that are expressed in Spengler's works and elsewhere. And no less do the views and approaches opposed to the philosophy of enlightenment found in the works of Spengler and others seem to have been in accord with Gadamer's own tendencies and to have shaped his mind.[5]

In the centenarian's biography, Jean Grondin has mapped out the trajectory of his philosophical development in a way that should arouse interest, above all, for its chapter on the "Marburg Demons." In this chapter, Grondin gives an account of the change in Gadamer's philosophical thinking that made him turn from Nicolai Hartmann's critical realism, to which he had first adhered, to a Heidegger-inspired "hermeneutically radicalized phenomenology."[6] Grondin, in this context, writes of a "changing of the guard from Hartmann to Heidegger in Gadamer's galaxy of stars." "Heidegger's appearance in Marburg," he states, "was like an earthquake awesomely shaking almost all of Hartmann's former students."

At that time Heidegger, by his appearance, rhetoric, and revolutionarily resounding tone, obviously had a capacity to draw the attention of almost every student to him. Nowadays, the fascination he had as a teacher, not surprisingly, is almost lost to those of us who have to proceed from his texts alone. The "dark clouds of his sentences" with "lightnings flashing" are evidently less impressive as reading matter—especially if you keep the necessary distance from their "begetter" and are given the time to analyze them.

Gadamer, albeit fascinated at first by Heidegger's conceptions, established a philosophy of his own at quite a distance from Heidegger's. According to Grondin, *Wahrheit und Methode* "is a pensive and productive answer to Heidegger's philosophical incentive, felicitously avoiding those interdependent models of Heideggerian scholasticism and inquisition respectively"[7]—as any such response must be if it is not to be merely a reiteration of Heidegger's views. In this respect, Grondin is right in pointing to "important alternations as to Heidegger's ontological philosophy and to Gadamer's striking vindication of humanistic tradition."[8] Heidegger, in his turn, apparently declared "hermeneutic philosophy" to be Gadamer's own cause, thereby expressing his own distance from it.

From the 1960s onward I have been observing Gadamer's philosophical views.[9] Time and again I submitted these views to criticism, and the facts noted above give me reason to comment on them again. The hermeneutical change in twentieth-century philosophy that is due, in the main, to Heidegger's philosophical efforts, and to those of his most influential student, Gadamer, has led to consequences apt to reinforce those problematical features of German tradition that are opposed to enlightenment. There can be little doubt that this holds especially true for Heidegger's attempts to undermine occidental rationalism. His endeavors to overcome objective thinking have finally led to that kind of philosophical expressionism that may rightly be defined as a farewell to the project of knowledge.[10]

Gadamer did not follow him there. But in developing his universal hermeneutics, he allowed himself to be influenced by Heidegger's philosophy in such a way as to incorporate certain features of Heidegger's thought into his own position. His "urbanization of the Heideggerian province" involves less a return to tradition—which Heidegger was intent on destroying—than a continuation of a project nascent in Heidegger's philosophy coupled with a departure from the Messkirch philosopher's jargon.

Let us here consider some aspects of Gadamerian thought that I find somewhat disturbing.[11] In the first place, Gadamer has attempted—using the model of the text as a reference point—to characterize knowledge, in general, as interpretation. In asking how understanding can be possible at all, he attempts to surpass the transcendental question put forth by Kant, presenting his universal hermeneutics as an alternative to the modern scientific outlook, but without ever submitting this to any closer scrutiny. When Gadamer does discuss this issue, however, his presentation verges on caricature.

As to that radical historism, advocated in many passages in Gadamer's works, the kind of reasoning offered in its support shows that he does not take into consideration the theses and arguments of naturalism that may well be an alternative to his own views. Moreover, his thesis of a universality of understanding imputes, by way of implication, an ontological position altogether incompatible with his own version of historism. Antinaturalism, as adopted from Heidegger, forces Gadamer to reject the idea that any general insights into human nature could be conclusive about the problem of understanding.

The rehabilitation of prejudice that Gadamer proposes, following in Heidegger's footsteps, has the extreme consequence for textual interpretation of a sort of immunization of interpretation from all relevant criticism whatsoever. Grondin has observed, quite correctly, points of contact between Gadamer's treatment of the problems of prejudice and elements in Popper's writings.[12] It is something that I myself realized when reading Gadamer's *Wahrheit und Methode* (*Truth and Method*) for the first time in February 1967,[13] and I was, as Grondin states, quite baffled by it. But Gadamer's dealing with those problems is itself embedded in a general outlook that gives to his rehabilitation of prejudice a turn quite contrary to the methodological revisionism found in Popper.

Grondin maintains that, in this respect, there had been some "solidarity to begin with" between Popper, Albert, and Gadamer respectively that had been revoked by us later. This was not, however, a matter of "solidarity" between people in the common meaning of the term, but merely of agreement in particular views. On reading the passage from Popper quoted by Grondin, the differences are immediately apparent. Moreover, if Grondin had quoted the relevant passage of my letter to Paul Feyerabend, it would have been obvious that I had then already, in 1967, pointed out the difference which later, in 1994, is given a more thorough consideration in my *Kritik der reinen Hermeneutik* (*Critique Of Pure Hermeneutics*). It is out of the question, then, that I could have altered my views in the way maintained by Grondin.

Within the scope of an elaboration of his ontological views, as inspired by Humboldt, Gadamer advocates a certain kind of epistemological relativism, but the fatal consequences this has for his own position seem to elude his attention. It is a relativism that is paralleled by an analytical relativism, partly due to the influence of Ludwig Wittgenstein's later philosophy as well as Gadamer's own thinking, that is the outcome of a certain view on the role of language in relation to human thought.

On the classical tradition of hermeneutics that developed from the eighteenth century onward as a general instruction for expounding texts as such, Gadamer contributed nothing to the understanding of its significance. On the contrary, proceeding from his own philosophical premises, he attempted to overcome that tradition altogether and to prove its ambitions to be unattainable and irrelevant. Such are, in brief, several of the objections I have advanced against Gadamer's universal hermeneutics. The incompatibility of the elements of Gadamer's thinking, at which these objections are directed, with the ideas emerging from critical rationalism needs no further explication.

My own views in relation to the problems of knowledge and hermeneutics and also, in this context, my criticism of pure hermeneutics have been themselves subject to objections from several authors, while Gadamer, too, has objected to some of my views discussed here.[14] Essentially these objections depend, as I have attempted to show elsewhere, on obvious misunderstandings.[15] In turning against "pure" hermeneutics, I mean to reject hermeneutics of a kind that seeks shelter from the methods and results of factual science and endeavors to appear immune from any external criticism based on such methods and results.

As it turns out, we are dealing here with different kinds of objection that are, nevertheless, interrelated. There are those who aim to defend Gadamer's philosophical hermeneutics against realism and naturalism, but who show little interest in the Gadamerian "craft" of understanding. Then there are those critics who also reject naturalism, although they give more attention and respect to Gadamer's own body of work, and some even consider the pretensions of pure hermeneutics to be somewhat strained. A common feature of all these critics, however, is their way of dealing with what I have written, namely, that they reinterpret my ideas in such a way as to render their own objections plausible. As a result, they impute to me ideas that are obviously at variance with what I have explicitly written on the issues in question. This hermeneutical way of proceeding seems to me to be a consequence of the fact that these authors have already accepted the view that, in expounding a text, it matters little what their authors actually meant to say.[16]

In this respect, Jean Grondin, above all others, deserves special mention. He has attempted to prove the consistency of pure hermeneutics with critical rationalism and, at the same time, to demonstrate the deficient character of the Popperian approach.[17] To render his own interpretation plausible, Grondin is bound to neglect important differences between the two philosophical positions at issue and to misconstrue the view he criticizes in a way that results in some quite unacceptable judgments of the relation between those positions. I have elsewhere commented on Grondin's inquiries.[18] If one takes account of those aspects of the Gadamerian approach that I have undertaken to criticize, then Grondin's claim that critical rationalism "carried through consistently . . . will eventually result in hermeneutics" is seen to lack sufficient support.

As is well known, Karl-Otto Apel and Jürgen Habermas have firmly positioned the Gadamerian account within the discussion of social scientific method. Both these philosophers set forth a transcendental philosophy inspired by universal hermeneutics that was meant to overcome the "scientism" and "objectivism" of analytical thinking—the latter being said to be incapable of reflecting on its own foundations. Within the framework of transcendental hermeneutics, they set forth an account of knowledge as divided into three modes that is reminiscent of Max Scheler's sociology of knowledge and in which Gadamer's hermeneutics stands as godfather to one such mode.[19]

Although Apel characterizes his view as a "realism critical of meaning," it may well be viewed as belonging to that range of positions, including Putnam's "internal realism," that are essentially derivatives of transcendental idealism. These contemporary versions of idealism proceed from the metaphysical assumption that, so far as knowledge is concerned, we always find ourselves confronted with a reality "constituted," or, as is preferably stated nowadays, "language-impregnated." These positions thereby face difficulties similar to those that also arise in relation to Kant's development of the notion of constitution—difficulties that, at the beginning of the nineteenth century led to the transition to transcendental realism.

Meanwhile, the different versions of modern antirealism have been submitted to severe criticisms that cannot adequately be dealt with here.[20] Metaphysical realism as well as the notion of truth going along with it has proven to be a tenable position. Moreover, the question about the conditions of possible knowledge has turned out to be a problem that can be handled within the framework of a realistic conception.[21] And it need not be stressed, within the scope of critical rationalism, that, to arrive at a realistic analysis of the human ways of knowledge and their possible outcome, language as a tool of human intellectual effort as well as of an examination of social and institutional conditions is indispensable.

Moreover, as a form of rational instruction in the art of interpretation conceived in the eighteenth century, hermeneutics has its legitimate place within this scheme. It is, however, just this kind of hermeneutics that has been rejected as inadequate by Gadamer in *Wahrheit und Methode*.

It is quite clear to me that my criticism of universal hermeneutics, and of the linguistically oriented idealism influenced by it, will make no impact whatsoever on international discussion, since German contributions will hardly come into question here. Moreover, modern Anglo-Saxon philosophers seem to have an attraction to German philosophy just inasmuch as its products are unmistakably marked by Hegel, Heidegger, or Gadamer. This is true even for exponents of economic thought whose reception of German hermeneutics occasionally begets almost grotesque consequences.[22] Karl Popper's critical rationalism has had much less chance of having an explicit impact on discussions within the range of philosophy or social science than, for instance, neoclassical empiricism or Ludwig Wittgenstein's later philosophy—both of which are more closely related to American pragmatism.[23] On the other hand, Popper's ideas are time and again being adopted on the quiet, without their source being revealed. When they do appear in an analytical or hermeneutical makeup they seem to be more appealing than in their original state. But they nonetheless appear, at least to some extent, to have already become part and parcel of philosophical "common sense."

Translated by Michael Isenberg

Notes

1. See *Paul Feyerabend—Hans Albert. Briefwechsel*, edited by Wilhelm Baum (Frankfurt: Fischer, 1997), 96, where I reported on this. Jean Grondin, in his biography on Gadamer has misunderstood this report. In the absence of any prior assumptions, one cannot deduce from that report that I, "for all my ironical distance," exhibited "a certain reverence for Heidegger." See Jean Grondin, *Hans-Georg Gadamer—eine Biographie* (Tübingen: J. C. B. Mohr, 1999), 331. The point was rather that, unless one knew Heidegger in those earlier days, the spell cast by the Messkirch philosopher upon several of his students may be beyond comprehension.

2. Hence the title of the Gadamer-chapter: *Im Banne Heideggers* (*Spell-bound by Heidegger*) in my book: *Kritik der reinen Hermeneutik. Der Antirealismus und das Problem des Verstehens*

Critical Rationalism and Universal Hermeneutics

(*Critique Of Pure Hermeneutics. Antirealism and the Problem of Understanding*) (Tübingen: J. C. B. Mohr, 1994), 36–77.

3. See the third chapter of my book: *Kritischer Rationalismus. Vier Kapitel zur Kritik illusionären Denkens* (*Critical Rationalism. Four Chapters Concerning Criticism of Illusionary Thinking*) (Tübingen: J. C. B. Mohr, 2000).

4. See Grondin, *Hans-Georg Gadamer,* 230ff.

5. Ibid., 62ff, 67–68.

6. Ibid., 91ff.

7. Ibid., 301–302.

8. Ibid., 327ff.

9. At first in my *Traktat über kritische Vernunft* (Tübingen: J. C. B. Mohr, 1991, 5th ed.), 166–170, 252ff; English translation, *Treatise on Critical Reason* (Princeton: Princeton University Press, 1986), and in further detail in *Kritik der reinen Hermeneutik.*

10. See my criticism in chapter I of *Kritik der reinen Hermeneutik,* 6–35.

11. For a more detailed examination see *Kritik der reinen Hermeneutik.*

12. See Grondin, *Hans-Georg Gadamer,* 336.

13. See my *Briefwechsel* with Feyerabend, 30.

14. See the afterword of *Truth and Method,* 551ff.

15. See my *Kritik der reinen Hermeneutik,* 74ff.

16. See my essay, "Der Naturalismus und das Problem des Verstehens," in *Hermeneutik und Naturalismus,* edited by Bernulf Kanitscheider and Franz Josef Wetz (Tübingen: J. C. B. Mohr, 1999), 3–20, where I comment on several contributions of that kind.

17. See Jean Grondin, *Die Hermeneutik als Konsequenz des kritischen Rationalismus,* in Kanitscheider and Wetz (eds.), 38–46.

18. See "Der Naturalismus und das Problem des Verstehens," 17–20.

19. See Karl-Otto Apel, *Transformation der Philosophie, Band I: Sprachanalytik, Semiotik, Hermeneutik* (Frankfurt am Main: Suhrkamp, 1973), and Jürgen Habermas, "Erkenntnis und Interesse," *Merkur* 19 (1965), 1145 (Habermas's inaugural lecture of June 28, 1965); for criticism see: Hans Albert, *Transzendentale Träumereien* (Hamburg: Hoffmann und Campe, 1975); "Kritischer Rationalismus. Vom Positivismusstreit zur Kritik der Hermeneutik," in *Renaissance der Gesellschaftskritik?* edited by Hans Albert, Herbert Schnädelbach and Roland Simon-Schäfer (Bamberg: Universitätsverlag, 1999), 15–43.

20. See Michael Devitt, *Realism and Truth* (Oxford: Blackwell, 1991); Richard Schantz, *Wahrheit, Referenz und Realismus. Eine Studie zur Sprachphilosophie und Metaphysik* (Berlin/ New York: De Gruyter, 1996); *Kritischer Rationalismus und Pragmatismus,* edited by Volker

Hans Albert

Gadenne (Amsterdam/Atlanta: Rodopi, 1998); Alan Musgrave, *Essays on Realism and Rationalism* (Amsterdam/Atlanta: Rodopi 1999).

21. See my book, *Kritik der reinen Erkenntnislehre. Das Erkenntnisproblem in realistischer Perspektive* (Tübingen: J. C. B. Mohr, 1987).

22. See my essay, "Hermeneutics And Economics," *Kyklos* 41 (1988); also the fifth chapter of *Kritik der reinen Hermeneutik,* 136–163.

23. William Warren Bartley, in his latest book, *Unfathomed Knowledge, Umeasured Wealth. On Universities and the Wealth of Nations* (LaSalle: Open Court, 1990), has attempted to explain this.

3

On the Certainty of Uncertainty: Language Games and Forms of Life in Gadamer and Wittgenstein

Ulrich Arnswald

Forms of life can only be understood as human ways of acting. To understand the meaning of a form of life, we have to understand the human way of acting *in action,* which is to understand the meaning of a certain form of life as a certain *way of acting.* Action reflects back on what human beings take for granted, in so far as the individual reflects upon his action when acting. Thus certainty is not based on any kind of conviction but rather on action. In *On Certainty*[1] Ludwig Wittgenstein raises the issue that we might want to ask *why* we act in a certain way. The answer he delivers, however, is as straightforward as it is inevitable: we just do it. We act and that we do so is simply self-evident. To try to answer the question why we act in the way we do would mean nothing other than to try and explain why we are human in one way rather than another. But it makes no sense to ask such a question. If we can respond at all, we can say no more than that we do so because we are human beings.

I

Forms of life are subject to constant change, but they nevertheless stand within a framework that is relatively static—as the waters of a river are in constant motion relative to the more or less stable river-bed.[2] Wittgenstein employs the *river-bed* metaphor as a suggestive picture for different forms of human life or different human behaviors, which themselves are in permanent flux. The idea that human behavior basically flows makes Wittgenstein's concept rather distinctive. In the strongest sense, the shaping of forms of life are then generated by a system of forces or a structure, which is the river-bed, external not only to the minds of each individual actor but also to the minds of all actors. In this picture the river-bed is a shared form of life that belongs to all forms of life and all communities as a whole. This mutual aspect that all forms of life have language makes us aware of the fact that we also share some kind of common tradition and history across all forms of life. This encompassing background is constituted by what Wittgenstein terms *natural history* (*Naturgeschichte*). At the same time, the *river-bed* metaphor has embedded within it a commonsense conviction of holism, insofar as one single form of life will have to conform to the river-bed just as the whole requires it to.

For the moment, let us assume that there are two different ways in which we can talk about forms of life.[3] One is the concept of a form of life from the perspective of the individual actor, who aims to explain his own being in the world. Such a concept determines a form of life as essentially singular and need make no reference to anything beyond just that one form of life that is at stake. The other alternative is a collective concept of a form of life. It is concerned with belonging to a river where the different forms of life float, so that the river itself is nothing other than the inside of the social realm. The idea of a single form of life that an individual actor might have in mind is meant to signify the individual form of life manifested in the action of each individual actor; whereas an individual who understands himself as part of a collectively shared form of life is concerned with the social realm and the interaction within. He may seek to understand the various forms of life within this social realm, but he does not aim for a full understanding of the individual's particular actions. It might be appealing to suppose that these two different ways of thinking about forms of life or these two forms of life themselves (forms that correspond to the individual and the social), could be simply combined. At the social level the idea of a form of life provides an indication of the way in which, while conflict is always possible as a result of misunderstanding, ignorance, arrogance, or foolishness, such conflict is nevertheless preventable or can be overcome if we reflect on the broader context of our action. By contrast, at the more narrowly focused "individual" level, the idea of a form of life directs us toward a method for explaining and accounting for human action as it is determined by "human nature" and the larger framework of human life as such.

The desire always to be able to provide an explanation of individual behavior is essentially the expression of a desire always to understand things scientifically. The very concept of scientific explanation can itself be viewed as a unifying scheme among human beings, yet it is precisely this call for a scientific approach to human life and action that Wittgenstein, in *On Certainty*, puts in question. Wittgenstein has a much more radical objection to the entire supposition that science gives reasons for what we presume to *know*. He disagrees with the conviction that we *know* when we can predict or explain what is happening, provided that we can identify the regularities occurring in nature. This point is potentially radical. For Wittgenstein there is a limit to the scientific approach when it comes to human life and action. Our actions are not based on some ultimate set of reasons, nor does knowledge consist merely of the capacity to predict and explain. In contrast to G. E. Moore's insistence that what we know can be seen as based on certain uncontestable and absolutely basic beliefs—"I know that here is one hand"—Wittgenstein argues that we cannot have any reasons for trusting in our knowledge, and also cannot imagine the reverse, namely *not* to *know* what we presume to *know*. We take the presumption to *know* for granted without being able to give any reasons for it.[4]

It is this trust in our knowledge that makes us act. The foundation of our action is, according to Wittgenstein, action itself. And when we act we often just do so because we have no choice in the matter given that we are. However, the most important fact about our own acting is that any kind of action has a particular meaning for the individual so that when we act in a certain way we do not stop to ask ourselves why we do so. For instance, we follow rules, obey orders, punish certain actions, give commands, make reports, describe colors, take an interest in the feelings of others, practice mathematical propositions, or monitor religious rules, and so forth, and actually even do so without having knowledge about them, in other words, without *knowing* them. The fact that such rules, propositions or orders are *unknowable* is the crucial and important point. Wittgenstein does not conclude from the fact, however, that we take things for granted that we cannot justify, that we therefore have to assume some kind of essentialism.

Yet given that there is a kind of certainty that is always present when we act, we might at least wish to ask where our certainty in acting comes from. For Wittgenstein, the certainty or security of how to act is part of our *natural history,* which means that by acting the way we do, we coincide with the action of others. This coincidence then produces the feeling of security or certainty, which then again gives us the feeling that our action was ex post facto justified. Our whole acting is based on these ultimate conditions and they do not allow for any further justifications. Action is instead a *praxeologically* founded concept. Yet for our action to coincide with others and for us to be able to interact with others in this way is for us to share a form of life with others. This means, however, that it is only in the context of the other, with whom we interact, that a form of life can become a concept in its own right. If there were no others, then the concept of a form of life could not exist, since no single form of life would be distinguishable as such, and we would be unable to realize the distinct concept of a form of life at all. Thus we cannot have knowledge of only one form of life, but, if we possess knowledge of a form of life at all, we always have knowledge of more than one such form. This is not to say that the idea of a singular form of life must be abandoned, but only that we cannot understand any particular form of life independently of other such forms and of the differences between them.

Forms of life are thus always multiple, such that even the idea of a single form of life implies other such forms too. Different individuals may contribute different forms of life and associated with those different forms are different "world-pictures" (*Weltbilder*). Although each individual may well have such a different picture of the world, this need not undermine the possibility of discourse between individuals. Indeed, differences between world-pictures cannot be so great that they are mutually incomprehensible, or "incommensurable," since if such incomprehensibility were to obtain, then we would be unable to recognize even those images as other world-pictures or as associated with other forms of human life. There is, therefore, a real limit to possible differences, not only between world-pictures but also between forms of life, at least to the extent that they remain comprehensible as forms of life. Even the fact that we might not share similar criteria for our actions—which means that our certainty in acting will be based upon different motives—would not lead to incomprehension of each other's point of view. As long as some form of discourse is possible, insofar as there is a chance to persuade the other by dialogue and argumentation, we still have something in common. This commonality is already presupposed by the possibility of coincidence in action—by the very fact that we can somehow interact with one another. The possibility of communication across different world-pictures or between different forms of life rests on just such interaction or coincidence of action. We may say, more directly perhaps, that it is our action and capacity for action that provides the authentic background that allows us to bridge the difference between ourselves and others.

Since language is the primary vehicle of expression, linguistic meaning becomes a crucial component of social life. The problem of understanding the other, and of coming to an appreciation of the other's form of life, thus comes to center on the problem of understanding other's use of language. Although differences between languages or language games may well complicate our understanding of the other, the fact of such linguistic difference does not affect the foundations of comprehension in a way that would make understanding impossible from the start. Yet this immediately raises the question of the precise nature of the foundations that are at issue here and it is at this point that Gadamerian hermeneutics must enter the equation. Before moving on to consider matters from such a hermeneutic perspective, however, some further clarification of the Wittgensteinian idea of a "language game" must first be provided.

II

A language game is, for Wittgenstein, an interwoven complex of verbal and of nonverbal action from which neither the verbal nor the nonverbal component can be separated out. It is, moreover, a structure that by its very nature resists any attempt at systematization or abstraction. Thus, if one is to learn the meaning of a word within a language game, or the significance of a particular instance of behavior within that game, one has no choice but to participate and learn to play the game. "The essence of the language game," we read in *Causes and Effect*, "is a practical method (a way of acting), not speculation, empty talk."[5] In this respect, language games have a character that mirrors the character of forms of life, namely, that they can only be understood as human ways of acting. Indeed, one might say that language games and forms of life are parallel concepts. In *Philosophical Investigations* Wittgenstein summarizes this point by saying that to imagine a language means nothing other than to imagine a form of life.[6] Of course, this raises another question: what then is the difference between a language game and a form of life?

One way of capturing the difference at issue is to focus on what is involved in understanding both of a form of life and a language game. Each encompasses verbal and nonverbal components. Whereas understanding a form of life can be developed and expressed (and it must be possible to arrive at an understanding of the language associated with it), in the case of the *language game,* arriving at an understanding of the game requires that we learn how to play along with it. It is the nonverbal that takes precedence here— a matter of learning to play the game rather than learning the language itself. The fundamental question that arises is, of course, whether there has to be a minimum degree of commonality in language games between two individual actors in order to enable differences in forms of life or, indeed, conflict between them, to come into focus. I rule out such a minimum requirement, because neither side in such a discourse has to take an impartial or external view to understand the other's form of life. Rather, both sides can enter the discourse from their respective points of view and on the basis of their respective language games.

This particular point is very clear in Wittgenstein's later thought, for there he explicitly takes account of the possibility of learning new language games and of movements between language games— something that naturally stands as a necessary prerequisite for any transition or understanding between different forms of life. Language games are thus not neatly closed systems, but quite the opposite; they are open to movements between various articulations that allow for reaching an understanding with the other.[7]

At the core of a language game is a successful common action performed by at least two actors that leads to the opportunity of expanding the common base of action and so toward understanding each other more. Successful common action relies upon a language game, where our propositions rest on others "beyond any doubt." It is not sufficient to assume that such openness toward the other is a deficit of our linguistic competence. In contrast, I argue that it is one of the main features of our linguistic ability to accommodate a degree of openness that allows us to discover new opportunities for acting and therefore new forms of life along with it.

A peculiarity of Wittgenstein's philosophy of language is the fact that he does not consider language as based merely on rules, but rather on a language competence that can be understood as consisting of human freedom to formulate such rules again and again. Thus no language rules are simply imposed on us, although we are following some generally accepted rules and only sometimes make use of our ability to formulate new rules. In Wittgenstein's words: "new types of language, new language games, as we may say, come into existence, and others become obsolete and get forgotten."[8] This ability to formulate rules is a kind of linguistic core competence peculiar to human beings, and it is this competence that allows us to make transitions between two language games without having to go first via a *tertium comparationis*. Indeed, change in language is essentially linked to the concept of language games. Hence, as Haller writes, "language games must then be regarded as variable, mutable, and transitory. More precisely, one ought to say that human societies and communities invent, maintain and even forget language games."[9]

Whenever the inherited context changes, questions arise about the relation between language and the reality of the world emerging from the ground of language and recurring again and again in ever new language games. The relation between language and the world, which is at the ground of every language game, can therefore be understood as the *leitmotif* of Wittgenstein's philosophy of language. Philosophy derives from the "deep disquietudes,"[10] which in the *Philosophical Investigations* Wittgenstein also says are as "deep as the forms of language."[11] Moreover, since human beings are drilled in language exercises such that language comes to be a kind of taken-for-granted second nature, so language gives rise to a complex set of behavioral patterns that conceal our understanding of how language works. To figure out how language works then, we have to begin with a deed, an action, that is, with a language game, which gives us a particular ground of certainty in the form of a particular mode of practice. As Wittgenstein remarks: "The primitive form of the language game is certainty, not uncertainty. For uncertainty could never lead to action. . . . I want to say: it is characteristic of our language that the foundation on which it grows consists in steady ways of living, regular ways of acting."[12]

Since a language game is based on interplay within the social realm, it depends on our own action and on the action of others. The language game is not performed in a vacuum, but always within a particular form of life. Moreover, a form of life is again bound to a communal aspect of language that makes us aware of the fact that we are part of a tradition, members of a language community. The form of life that we have acquired is rooted in that community. This community follows certain rules and customs, as well as certain habits and regularities, which shape and mold both language games as well as forms of life. As members of a community we come to realize that the tradition and presuppositions of that community already shaped and molded our language and action from the very first day we entered into it, since in fact "the rule-governed nature of our languages permeates our lives."[13]

Our knowledge and language are precisely grounded on the same fact, on the same hard ground out of which our ability to play language games grows. This "nature," which is often called our *natural history*, is nothing more than the having of a form of life. It is based on the fact that human beings are part of a social realm, which makes it possible to come to some common judgments and common ways of acting, and thus to be capable of understanding the other. Consequently, we could say, with Wittgenstein, aiming for an understanding of other forms of life is "simply what we *do*. This is use and custom among us, or a fact of our natural history."[14] The modest form of linguistic relativism that is implied here can be taken as indicative of the essentially "praxeological foundation" that lies at the very base of every language game. It excludes the possibility of adopting some neutral "point of view" that could be taken up by philosophers. Clearly, the transition from one language game to another is something we are familiar with. The fact that we do not have any "objective" criteria or a kind of "outside" view does not cause any problems for the movement between language games and is therefore no barrier to understanding. Wittgenstein therefore states: "You must bear in mind that the language game is so to say something unpredictable. I mean: it is not based on grounds. It is not reasonable (or unreasonable). It is there—like our life."[15]

The shaping and molding of forms of life is not something that occurs in any direct fashion, but instead occurs by means of the particular language games in which individual actors participate. It is also only within such language games that conflict between forms of life emerges. Given that the ability to play language games is a presupposition of a conflict of forms of life, we can assume that conflicts of forms of life are also always conflicts between different articulations of such forms. As such, they are not insolvable. Therefore whenever we face a conflict of forms of life, this does not necessarily lead to one form being found superior to another, but actually could also lead to an enrichment of both forms of life by way of analogy. Moreover, it does not follow from a conflict of different forms of life that either of them has to remain in the same kind of *status quo ante*. Although there is no kind of justification for favoring one form of life *over* another, Wittgenstein understands individual judgments even to be justified when they are used unjustifiably. In situations of conflict, therefore, individual judgments possess a right in themselves. As Wittgenstein remarks: "To use a word without a justification does not mean to use it without right."[16] But then what we ought to do is to exchange experience and facts with others. The exchange should lead us to new concepts and help us to find a common base for understanding. Given that we do have common agreements in action as well as a shared context of common language, it is possible for us to develop new concepts, and thus new forms of life. In *Zettel*, Wittgenstein writes: "It is a fact of experience that human beings alter their concepts, exchange them for others when they learn new facts."[17]

My understanding of Wittgenstein is that he stresses the importance of our *natural history,* which is the background composed of our customs, traditions, rules, social institutions, our inherited form of life as well as the certainty we presume to have when *acting.* From this ground, or *river-bed,* our language emerges. Without this inherited context, language would not be possible and neither would changes in our judgments and forms of life. I do not wish to claim that Wittgenstein resolved our problems about forms of life and language games; far too much remains too imprecise after all. He certainly did help us to find a corner stone from which to build an understanding of conflicts.[18] But how can we reiterate again and again this needed human practice that helps us gain some clarity along the lines of Wittgenstein's "praxeological foundationalism"?

III

Here Gadamer jumps in. In *Truth and Method*[19] he emphasizes the importance of hermeneutical dialogue in order to come to an understanding (*Verständigung*) with the other. This provides an approach with which we can understand a text or event. Like Wittgenstein, Gadamer agrees that understanding (*Verstehen*) can never be final. Through an exchange of different views and perspectives, different forms of life, and different world-pictures, we can enrich our own understanding and knowledge.

From the immense contribution Gadamer has made to philosophy and thought of the twentieth century, his single most important insight may turn out to be a conceptual scheme that allows us to overcome cultural conflicts as well as clashes of different forms of life. Gadamer develops a scheme that may be applicable to those parts of philosophy where meaning remains ambiguous, that is to say, those areas which resist systematization. Surely this is the case when we talk about forms of life or language games. Here we only gain understanding when we make use of inherited background, including inherited language. By using our own language, by using our own form of life, we can overcome difficulties and extend the language game until we understand the point made by the other. For Gadamer, through language we *form a horizon* to other languages. By doing so, we already express a certain degree of openness toward these other or new worlds.

Both Gadamer and Wittgenstein agree that we inherit particular *parameters of interpretation,* or a particular background, through the history of the society and culture we belong to. The Gadamerian hermeneutical approach, however, requires not only that we understand the history or knowledge of the past but that we face the encounter with the other. The aim of this process is not to control the other, but rather to reach a common agreement in one form or another, to develop a common ground for further redefining one's own objectives and to reach further understanding and knowledge. Georgia Warnke points out: ". . . it is rather characteristic of it [genuine conversation] that all participants are led beyond their initial positions towards a consensus that is more differentiated and articulated than the separate views which the conversation-partners began."[20]

It must be stressed that hermeneutical understanding is party-dependent. As such, it is always linked to the subjectivity of the human being and therefore cannot lead to "objective knowledge" in an epistemic sense. Therefore Gadamer maintains that it does not make sense to believe in a concept of "objective knowledge," since objective knowledge can neither be reached in human affairs nor in science. For present purposes, the impossibility of objective knowledge in human affairs is the pertinent issue. But what makes

Gadamer not believe in objective knowledge? There are two major strands of arguments: on the one hand, such objective knowledge would not take into sufficient consideration the importance of culture within our lives. Culture makes things indefinable; it is an ever-new source for creativity, inspiration, and innovation. On the other hand, such objective knowledge would have to be based on the possibility that human knowledge and experience could be transcended from one human being to another in an intergenerational transfer, but this is—we presume to be certain—impossible. Given that our lives are finite we can only collect knowledge and experience in our own lifetime. Thus what we consider to be knowledge, according to Gadamer, always has some contingency built into it. As Gadamer remarks: "In fact history does not belong to us; we belong to it."[21]

At this point, another of Gadamer's themes becomes relevant: the theme of *experience*. Gadamer understands the *coming-to-be-in-language* of the subject matter of the referent as *experiencing*. He agrees with Humboldt that the linguistic perspective (*Sprachansicht*) of each individual also represents a perspective of the world as such (*Weltansicht*). As a result the expression of the subject matter in language can only be partial, since the entire "world-perspectives" (*Weltansichten*) cannot be captured in language.[22] Nevertheless, only when we figure out the right words to express the experience, do we recognize, according to Gadamer, the experience for what it is. This is owing to the fact that experiencing is a language-influenced process and therefore finding the adequate wording is part of our experience.[23] An interesting parallel with Wittgenstein can be drawn here. When Wittgenstein argues that to have a language is already to participate in a form of life he agrees with Gadamer in the sense that it is imaginable that a linguistic perspective (*Sprachansicht*) could be the same as a perspective of the world (*Weltansicht*). What is the rule for Gadamer, however, is only an exceptional case for Wittgenstein. And second, Wittgenstein assumes that it is a fact of experience that humans learn from others and change their concepts when they learn new facts. These new facts are, of course, expressed in language via new language games and articulations. For Gadamer, experience lies in finding the right words since only then do we realize experience as such. If we understand finding the adequate wording as finding a new fact, then it is quite obvious that the two are in accord here.

When discussing different forms of life earlier, Wittgenstein's *river-bed* metaphor was mentioned. There I made explicit why forms of life are generated by a system of forces or a structure, which is the river-bed, external not only to the mind of each actor but also external to the minds of all actors. This surrounding environment, which also can be called the social realm, does not directly shape our forms of life but does so indirectly, via language and its articulation. Language and its articulation shape our forms of life by triggering further reactions because in language games our language mirrors our own action and the actions of others. A form of life is tied to a communal aspect of language. This communal aspect of language makes us aware of the fact that we are part of a tradition, members of a language community. Furthermore, I have shown that a community follows certain rules and customs, as well as certain habits and regularities, which are shaping both language games as well as forms of life. As members of a language community, we come to realize that the tradition of our community has shaped our language and action from the first day we entered the world. In Gadamer, a rather similar concept is found. Although many heavily contest this concept, it can be understood in a similar fashion to Wittgenstein's concept of embeddedness in "the regularity of our language." What we inherit when entering the world and learning a language Gadamer understands as an inherited set of prejudices, which we receive in a passive manner, since it is part of the inherited tradition that we call our background. What Wittgenstein says of our *natural history,* therefore, also holds true for Gadamer: we do inherit prejudices through culture. Most of the culture we inherit in a passive way by being born into a certain society. We are part of a tradition in so far as we have inherited a set of prejudices, which embeds us within the tradition.[24]

In full agreement with Wittgenstein, however, "for hermeneutic understanding it follows that we are not limited to the premises of our tradition but rather continually revise them in the encounters with and discussions we have about them. In confronting other cultures, other prejudices and, indeed, the implications that others draw from our own traditions, we learn to reflect on both our assumptions and our ideas of reason and to amend them in the direction of a *better* account."[25] In Wittgenstein we find such a view, for instance, in the preface to *Philosophical Investigations* where he compares himself to a draughtsman drawing a landscape from various points of view, which are to be compared with one another. This runs through his efforts to introduce new ways of seeing things.[26] Naturally, the view of others is one way for Wittgenstein to revise his own view, although it has to be noted that it is true that his "praxeological" point of view comes across quite often as being purely self-centered. The difference remains, however, that it is Gadamer who delivered a conceptual scheme or a tool that helps give meaning to those parts of philosophy that remain ambiguous; whereas Wittgenstein solely aimed to show what human practice is needed in order to gain a degree of clarity about philosophical problems in the first place.

It makes sense that Gadamer places much more emphasis on how we should treat an interlocutor and how we should proceed in a dialogue. Here are just a few examples: the acknowledgment of another person's view as a serious truth claim that has to be assumed to be correct. In this way, one's own view can be questioned by the other and voluntary acceptance of arguments stands against one's own point of view. This does not mean, however, that one automatically follows blindly what the other might wish to demand.[27] Another case is when Gadamer demands that each interlocutor must have the "good will" to listen and acknowledge what the other has to say.[28] We cannot find in Wittgenstein at all such *explananda* of how to behave in a dialogue. This is owing to the fact that Gadamerian hermeneutics depends on the application of a hermeneutic scheme in a certain situation. Both the investigator and the one who understands are part of that situation and involved in the application. It is essential that particular understandings have an effect on one's own being.[29] The essential point of comparison is that both the investigator and the one who understands are involved in the same situation where understanding depends upon the application of a general scheme to a specific situation and where that particular understanding affects one's own being. The way to understand each other occurs via the unveiling of our implicit understanding, which conceals the view of the other in our form of life and culture. By understanding the other we learn to allow for his or her difference and at the same time allow ourselves to be questioned. This hermeneutic scheme is doubly party-dependent and should finally lead us to the *fusion of horizons,* which is a Gadamerian term for the integration of differing views toward an improved understanding and a correction of previous misunderstandings or distortions. The result will still be far from perfect. It is rather an ongoing process toward a true understanding of the other, which is rather slow and can only be achieved with difficulties. In overcoming different contexts of understanding, we must take into account the opinions, views, and beliefs of others when discussing a subject matter with them on an equal footing.

We gain in many ways from such an effort. Even if we finally do not change our view, we can nevertheless learn from the objections, counterexamples, and considerations that the other proposes. We can even strengthen our position by improving our own point of view and defending it against criticism. We can also incorporate the other's position into our view. It does not matter if we accept the criticism or not, in any case we will find ourselves much better informed about the other and his point of view. Therefore, whatever that criticism means for our initial point of view, we will find our own view more developed than the one with which we began. And given that this is the case for everybody involved in this process, the result is consequently *pareto-optimal.*

This *fusion of horizons* occurs along with the extension of our language competence by playing ever-new language games. For Wittgenstein, the creation of ever-new language games is a core competence of human beings and it is this competence that allows us to make transitions between two language games. As a result, we bring into existence "new types of language, new language games" and therefore forget others, which then become obsolete. For Gadamer, it is also in language games where the interlocutors are absorbed into the conversation with otherness and open themselves for questioning by the other. As Gadamer claims, it is "the

Ulrich Arnswald

[language] game itself that plays, for it draws the players into itself and thus itself becomes the actual subjectum of the playing."[30] Again, we can see how similar the views of the two thinkers are on this point. Both rule out the need for a *tertium comparationis* for the transition from one language game to another. For Wittgenstein, however, change in the language games occurs through change in the inherited background, which then again has its impact on the questions about the relation between language and the reality of the world, and finally leads to the emerging of new language games out of the ground of language, whereas change in Gadamer is the result of change in the horizons. Horizons evolve and a horizon describes the world of a human being, and as such always has to be in motion. As Gadamer remarks: "A horizon is not a rigid boundary but something that moves with one and invites one to advance further."[31] One might want to add that language games are then promptly mirroring the change of the horizons of individual human beings. Further, Gadamer's concept of "horizons" has a kind of "inner" movement that is essential when trying to understand the problem of distortions in understanding and communication, given that there is nothing like a "stable" horizon.

IV

What this essay claims to have shown is twofold: first, the number of similarities that exist between Gadamer and Wittgenstein when it comes to playing language games, overcoming conflicts of different forms of life, and trying to understand the other.[32] Wittgenstein can be read as in quite astonishing accordance with Gadamer in some of his main philosophical arguments. Second, I endeavored to explain why Gadamerian hermeneutics have to be used as an extension to the discussion of forms of life and language games in Wittgenstein in order to come to an understanding of the other. Nobody has expressed this sentiment more elegantly than Georgia Warnke when she states: "To the extent that individuals and cultures integrate this understanding of others and of the differences between them within their own self-understanding, to the extent, in other words, that they learn from others and take a wider, more differentiated view, they can acquire sensitivity, subtlety and a capacity for discrimination."[33] In this specific aspect I am inclined to add that here Gadamer could help us achieve an "urbanization" of Wittgenstein's idea of tolerance and understanding the other.

Apart from the mere philosophical challenge of trying to make use of two great thinkers of the twentieth century, Gadamer and Wittgenstein, I also had an eye on one of the great challenges ahead of us in the twenty-first century: to overcome cultural differences and to accept and appreciate other forms of life as an enrichment to our own lives in a world of globalization, which tends to make the world an ever smaller planet. As Gadamer already claimed years ago, it is becoming more and more urgent

to see the common in the other and in otherness. In our contracting world quite different cultures, religions, customs, and values come into contact with one other. It would be an illusion to believe that only a rational system of utilitarian thinking so to speak, a kind of religion of the world economy, could regulate the social existence on this ever shrinking planet" ("im Anderen und in der Andersheit das Gemeinsame erkennen zu lernen. In unserer eng zusammenrückenden Welt begegnen sich zutiefst verschiedene Kulturen, Religionen, Sitten, Wertschätzungen. Es wäre eine Illusion zu meinen, daß nur ein rationales System der Nützlichkeiten, sozusagen eine Art Religion der Weltwirtschaft, das menschliche Zusammenleben auf diesem immer enger werdenden Planeten regulieren könnte").[34]

While "our historical situatedness does not only limit what we can know with certainty; it can also teach us how to remember and integrate what we must not forget."[35] By the same token, we always have to run up against the prison of our *uncertainty* and we might then again find comfort in our inherited background that, in the end, constitutes for us *a kind of certainty*.

Acknowledgments

While I was researching this paper in the summer of 1999, I was also a visiting scholar at St. Catharine's College, University of Cambridge, and I am deeply indebted to Dr. C. J. R. Thorne and to the college for his and its generosity. Furthermore thanks are due to the University of Heidelberg, and especially to Professor Peter-Christian

Müller-Graff for supporting my work on Wittgenstein and allied matters by providing me with a Cambridge scholarship. My debts to the philosophy of Hans-Georg Gadamer go well beyond the points that are already evident in my citations of his work. I have found continuous inspiration in his cultivation of a style of dialogue that seems not to be present any longer in contemporary philosophy.

Notes

1. Ludwig Wittgenstein, *On Certainty*, edited by G. E. M. Anscombe and G. H. von Wright, translated by G. E. M. Anscombe (Oxford: Basil Blackwell, 1969).

2. See *On Certainty*, §97ff. Wittgenstein notes, of course, that the division here is not a sharp one.

3. I do not wish to give here an account of the discussion of a "form of life" or "forms of life" between Newton Garver, *This Complicated Form of Life* (Chicago and Lasalle, Illinois: Open Court, 1984) and Rudolf Haller, *Questions on Wittgenstein* (London: Routledge, 1988). The reader will easily see that I side with Haller on this matter.

4. This view is sometimes called the "nonepistemic" interpretation. It has lately appeared, for instance, in the work of Peter Strawson, *Skepticism and Naturalism: Some Varieties* (London: Methuen, 1985), Hilary Putnam, *Renewing Philosophy* (Cambridge, MA: Harvard University Press, 1992), Hans Julius Schneider, *Phantasie und Kalkül* (Frankfurt am Main: Suhrkamp, 1992), Matthias Kroß, *Klarheit als Selbstzweck* (Berlin: Akademie Verlag, 1993), and Anja Weiberg, *"Und die Begründung hat ein Ende"—Die Bedeutung von Religion und Ethik für den Philosophen Ludwig Wittgenstein und das Verständnis seiner Werke* (Wien: WUV-Universitätsverlag, 1998).

5. Ludwig Wittgenstein, *Causes and Effect: Intuitive Awareness*, 405, *Philosophia* 6 (1976), 409–424.

6. See Ludwig Wittgenstein, *Philosophical Investigations*, translated by G. E. M. Anscombe (Oxford: Basil Blackwell, 1953), §19, 8.

7. See Hans Julius Schneider, *Wittgenstein und die Grammatik*, 28–29, in *Mit Sprache spielen*, edited by Hans Julius Schneider and Matthias Kroß (Berlin: Akademie Verlag, 1999), 11–29.

8. See Wittgenstein, *Philosophical Investigations*, §23, 11.

9. Rudolf Haller, *Questions on Wittgenstein*, 117–118.

10. See Wittgenstein, *Philosophical Investigations*, §111, 47.

11. See Wittgenstein, *Philosophical Investigations*, §111, 47.

12. Wittgenstein, *Causes and Effect: Intuitive Awareness*, 20–21.

On the Certainty of Uncertainty

13. Ludwig Wittgenstein, *Remarks on Colour,* edited by G. E. M. Anscombe, translated by Linda L. McAlister and Margarete Schättle (Oxford: Basil Blackwell, 1977) §303, 57.

14. Ludwig Wittgenstein, *Remarks on the Foundation of Mathematics,* edited by G. H. von Wright, R. Rhees, and G. E. M. Anscombe, translated by G. E. M. Anscombe (Oxford: Basil Blackwell, 1956), I, §63, 20.

15. Wittgenstein, *On Certainty,* §559, 73.

16. Wittgenstein, *Philosophical Investigations,* §289, 99.

17. Ludwig Wittgenstein, *Zettel,* edited by G. E. M. Anscombe and G. H. von Wright, translated by G. E. M. Anscombe (Oxford: Basil Blackwell, 1967) §352, 64–65.

18. Cf. Matthias Kroß, *Klarheit als Wahrheit,* 163, in *Die ungewisse Evidenz,* edited by Gary Smith and Matthias Kroß (Berlin: Akademie Verlag, 1998) 139–171.

19. Hans Georg Gadamer, *Truth and Method,* translated by Joel Weinsheimer and Donald Marshall (New York: Continuum, 2nd rev. ed., 1989).

20. Georgia Warnke, *Gadamer: Hermeneutics, Tradition and Reason* (Stanford: Stanford University Press, 1987), 169.

21. Gadamer, *Truth and Method,* 276.

22. See Gadamer, *Truth and Method,* 442.

23. See Gadamer, *Truth and Method,* 417.

24. See Gadamer, *Truth and Method,* 277.

25. Warnke, *Gadamer: Hermeneutics, Tradition and Reason,* 170.

26. Wittgenstein, *Philosophical Investigations,* preface, ix.

27. See Gadamer, *Truth and Method,* 361.

28. See Hans-Georg Gadamer, *Text und Interpretation,* 343, in *Gesammelte Werke,* Band 2, *Hermeneutik II* (Tübingen: Mohr Siebeck, 1986) , 330–360.

29. See Gadamer, *Truth and Method,* 312.

30. Ibid., 490.

31. Ibid., 245.

32. Here I must contradict Gianni Vattimo, who argues in *Beyond Interpretation: The Meaning of Hermeneutics for Philosophy* (Stanford: Stanford University Press, 1997, 60) that: "According to a programme that is still in fact very much alive in recent thinking (inspiring, for example, the Wittgensteinian idea of linguistic therapy via the careful distinction of the specific rules of different linguistic games) progress in philosophy and in rationality is achieved by throwing the spotlight on various dimensions of experience and clarifying

Ulrich Arnswald

their specificity, which is then taken as a normative basis for judgment and choice." It seems Vattimo is falling into the trap of a common misunderstanding of Wittgenstein. This being said, I acknowledge that most recently more and more people are reading Wittgenstein differently (see also note 5 above referring to the so-called nonepistemic interpretation of Wittgenstein).

33. Warnke, *Gadamer: Hermeneutics, Tradition and Reason,* 174.

34. Hans-Georg Gadamer, *Bürger zweier Welten,* 125, in *Das Erbe Europas* (Frankfurt am Main: Suhrkamp, 1989), 106–125.

35. Warnke, *Gadamer: Hermeneutics, Tradition and Reason,* 174.

4

The Hermeneutical Anarchist: *Phronesis*, Rhetoric, and the Experience of Art

Gerald Bruns

Reason exists for us only in concrete, historical terms—i.e., it is not its own master but remains constantly dependent on the circumstances in which it operates.
—*Gadamer*, Truth and Method

Complex Systems (Historicity)

One of the basic projects of philosophical hermeneutics is to give an account of the rationality of everyday life. The thesis is that rationality, like understanding, is as much a mode of being as it is a state of consciousness.[1] Fair enough, but a mode of what sort of being and at what stage of development? This thesis runs up against the idea that associates rationality with modernity as a condition toward which each individual (or history, or totality of human cultures) must advance as if from more primitive states of awareness. Poetry, for example, is still understood by almost every philosopher—as Vico understood it and Hegel as well—as a premodern or prelogical condition in which cognition remains embedded in images, narratives, and the immediacy of feeling, whereas reason means emancipating cognition through projects of enlightenment, bringing the world and ourselves in it under conceptual control. Likewise the philosophical view of everyday life, still very much in place, is that the everyday occurs at the level of poetry—the level of pictures, ideology, myth, and unexamined talk (*Gerede*). The everyday is the routinized and unreflective par excellence. One can only speak of the rationality of everyday life as something tacit or embedded. At this level rationality becomes at best an anthropological concept like Peter Winch's: "to say of a society that it has a language is also to say that it has a concept of rationality."[2]

Anthropology, however, is never a bad place to begin. We need an account of everyday rationality because we are, as the social theorist Zygmunt Bauman reminds us, inhabitants of complex systems.[3] The model of complex systems captures succinctly the human experience of historicity or finitude, because such systems are temporal rather than mechanical or cybernetic (not so much in time as made of it). This means that they are turbulent and unpredictable in their workings and effects. Complex systems are not governed by factors of any statistical significance (for example, a single imperceptible event can produce massive changes in a given system), and therefore they cannot be described by laws, rules, paradigms, causal chains, deep structures, or even a finite, canonical series of narratives. What anthropologists call thick descriptions are needed because a complex system cannot be comprehended as a totality but only piecemeal, detail by irreplaceable detail.

It follows that nothing that occurs within a complex system is capable of being calculated in advance or controlled by concepts and procedures, because there is no position within the system from which the whole can be observed, and no satellite provides an Archimedean perspective. No agency can view more than its own small area, and no area can be controlled from a single site. Thus complex systems are unmanageable; they are structured like the weather. So history will more closely resemble the history of art than the history of Spirit. The model of strategic reasoning favored by rational-choice theory thus has little application here. There is no possibility of building or sustaining any top-down order of things that would enable power to circulate through the system to the advantage of any single actor. Efforts to do so (say through the manufacture of "technically mediated life forms") will only produce more complex systems or in the end bring catastrophe, which is basically the moral of modernity's project of rationalizing the world.[4]

The trick is to understand that complex systems, however anarchic, are not irrational. This is because they are inhabited by multiple, heterogeneous, mostly single-purpose agents whose actions are autonomous (that is, uncontrollable), whose goals are irreducible to all-embracing purposes, and whose talents include responsiveness, flexibility, improvisation, readiness for revision, and the imagination (in detail) of infinite possible worlds (what we used to think of as literature). A good memory helps when coupled by hermeneutical experience with the power of forgetting. Above all resilience in defeat (the motto of comedy). These virtues make it possible to introduce order into complex systems.[5] Moreover, they do so from below and without trying to exceed the finite dimensions of local, temporary, micropolitical arrangements that are more likely to resemble movements than institutions, organizations, or settled communities. At ground level the idea is to make the right next move rather than to determine universals, justify positions, or apply means to ends in predictably profitable ways. The introduction of such finite deposits of order is not just one task of reason; it is arguably the only rational task that reason could have, given the reality of complex systems, which is (from the standpoint of philosophical hermeneutics, among other radical historicisms) the only kind of reality there is.

Phronesis

The idea of a rationality from below has always been a basic theme of hermeneutical research, most prominently in its efforts to reconstruct the conditions of rhetorical culture, or what P. Christopher Smith has called a culture of "original argument,"[6] but also, and more interestingly, in Hans-Georg Gadamer's analysis of aesthetic experience as a form of participation in the event of art, or play for short.[7] I want to try to work out here Gadamer's suggestion that there is an internal coherence between rhetoric and aesthetics, or between the dialectical give-and-take that defines the rationality of rhetorical culture and the experience of art, even (and perhaps especially) that of modern art, with its genius for frustrating every expectation of meaning.[8]

The starting point in both cases, as Gadamer has indicated in a number of contexts, is Aristotle's distinction between *techne* and *phronesis* as alternative modes of practical reasoning, where *techne* is understood as a species of rule-governed behavior, whereas *phronesis* is a condition of moral knowledge at the level of particular situations—call it a mode of responsiveness to what is singular and irreducible and therefore refractory to rules, categories, models, advanced pictures of the good life, and the whole idea of totality or an order of things as such. Beneath knowing what something is or what something is for or how to make something, there is knowing what a situation calls for in the way of right action, even when the situation is so complex and unprecedented that one experiences the shortfall of one's principles, beliefs, or patterns of conduct, or even one's sense of how things should go if they are to go right. As Gadamer says, "we are always already in the situation of having to act," but courses of action (unlike rules for conceptual construction or the production of goods) are never given in advance.[9] *Phronesis* is reason at home in the anarchy of complex systems—reason that shows itself in timeliness, improvisation, and a gift for nuance rather than in the rigorous duplication of results.

The difficulty has always been how to clarify *phronesis* conceptually (or even how to translate it: prudence, practical wisdom, reasonableness, and discernment are among the customary alternatives, but there are probably a half-dozen others).[10] Gadamer remarks that Aristotle's definitions (*Nichomachean Ethics*, VI) are notoriously vague, but perhaps that is because *phronesis* inhabits the indeterminate and untheorizable, and paradoxically loses definition the moment one tries to grasp it.[11] In *Die Idee des Guten zwischen Plato und Aristoteles* (*The Idea of the Good in Platonic-Aristotelian Philosophy*), however, Gadamer shows how Plato expanded the customary Greek usage of *phronesis* to include dialectical thinking; that is, on Gadamer's reading, Plato identifies the dialectic with *phronesis*.[12] Dialectical thinking in Plato is, Gadamer says, not a *techne* or art—not "an ability or knowledge"— but "a way of being": namely, being "reasonable."[13]

This way of being belongs to language; it emerges dialectically in human life as speech. Not speech in the way Socrates speaks in *The Republic*, proceeding according to a principle of internal necessity that allows him to say only what he *must* be said—in other words, conceptual construction governed by the law of noncontradiction. Of course it is not *not* that, not *not* systematic reasoning, but prior to such reasoning, and as a condition of its possibility, it is speech as social practice in which people facing a dilemma gather together to talk things out. Dialectic does not presuppose a world of ideas that we must try to reach by means of consecutive reasoning; it is aimed rather at life on the ground, amid situations where universals and possibly even examples cannot reach. How to respond to such situations? There is nothing for it but, given one's experience, deliberation as to the best one can do under the circumstances. That's Plato's dialectic, which aims, says Gadamer, "not at the idea of the good but the question of the good in human life," or "the good for us" in our finite condition, the good that is feasible here and now.[14] Dialectic at this level belongs to the perspective of rhetoric; it defines a culture of rhetoric in Gadamer's sense of this term, where rhetoric "from oldest tradition has been the only advocate of a claim to truth that that defends the probable, the *eikos,* and that which is convincing to reason, against the claim of science to accept as true only what can be demonstrated and tested."[15]

The Principle of Insufficient Reason

A "claim to truth that . . . is convincing to ordinary reason" takes us back from Plato's ideal *polis* to the *polis* of Protagoras, where Protagoras is not the windbag that Plato makes him out to be but Hans Blumenberg's anthropological Protagoras, the theorist and champion of Prometheus who sees human beings as metaphysically deficient in comparison with other creatures in nature and for whom rhetoric is the transcendental fire that will make human culture and therefore survival possible. Blumenberg writes:

In the language of modern biological anthropology, man is a creature who has fallen back out of the ordered arrangements that nature has accomplished, and for whom actions have to take the place of the automatic controls that he lacks or correct those that have acquired erratic inaccuracy. Action compensates for the "indeterminateness" of the creature man, and rhetoric is the effort to produce the accords that have to take the place of the "substantial" base of regulatory processes in order to make action possible. From this point of view, language is a set of instruments not for communicating information or truths, but rather, primarily, for the production of mutual understanding, agreement, or toleration, on which the actor depends. This is the root of "consensus" as a basis for the concept of what is "real."[16]

Gerald Bruns

Rhetoric is a way of improvising moments of order in the absence of a standing order of things. It differs from philosophy and science in the sense that it belongs to a world of complex systems where there isn't time to determine definitive truths. It presupposes a world of randomness and contingency where events come rushing at you and survival requires immediate action. Rhetoric is, Blumenberg writes, "a technique for coming to terms in the provisional state prior to all definitive truths and ethics. Rhetoric creates institutions where evident truths are lacking."[17] Philosophy and science have all the time in the world: long, intricate arguments can be worked out, tests can be run and double-, triple-, or quadruple-checked; counterfactuals can be introduced and alternative models constructed. We can wait for "the best theory so far," and then of course for the one after that. In the end we may get it right. But rhetoric belongs to the world where all the information that you need, the divine view from above or the prophetic view of the end of history that would be necessary to determine without doubt the best course of action, is just metaphysically lacking. "Philosophy's program succeeds or fails," Blumenberg writes, "but it does not yield any profit in installments. Everything that remains, this side of definitive evidence, is rhetoric; rhetoric is the vehicle of the *morale par provision* (i.e., Descartes's provisional morality, meant to help him get along in the world until he completed the construction of his cybernetic system)."[18] The objection that rhetoric deals with mere appearances or with "reality-effects," however true the objection might appear on paper, is, in effect, empty: "The antithesis of truth and effect is superficial, because the rhetorical effect is not an alternative that one can choose instead of an insight that one could *also* have, but an alternative to a definitive evidence that one *cannot* have, or cannot have yet, or at any rate cannot have now."[19] It is wrong to think of the enthymeme as merely a short and easy form of argument—argument for dummies, as Aristotle put it; it is rather the only form of argument possible within the finitude of complex systems.

Rhetoric is the work of *phronesis* in contrast to the *episteme* of science and the *techne* of rational-choice theories of strategic calculation. "To see oneself in the perspective of rhetoric," Blumenberg writes, "means to be conscious both of being compelled to act and of the lack of norms in a finite situation."[20] The "circumstance of being compelled to act . . . determines the rhetorical situation."[21] Rhetoric in this sense is a mode of responsibility rather than, purely and simply, a mode of knowledge; it responds to the need for action by producing a consensus in the absence of sufficient (that is, self-evident) reasons. As Blumenberg writes, "The axiom of all rhetoric is the principle of insufficient reason (*principium rationiis insuffi-cientis*). It is a correlate of the anthropology of a creature who is deficient in essential respects. If man's world accorded with the optimism of the metaphysics of Leibniz, who thought that he could assign a sufficient reason even for the fact that anything exists at all, rather than nothing (*'cur aliquid potius quam nihil'*), then there would be no rhetoric, because there would be neither the need nor the possibility of using it effectively."[22] Plato's *Republic* is an attempt to construct, or imagine, a world of sufficient reason—a world in which rhetoric and poetry would be, at best, gratuitous, nonproductive expenditures of energy, mere *epideixis* or "show," at all events outside the order of reason. But Blumenberg's thesis is that rhetoric is a real-world construction of a provisional order of reason, a practical construction of what is reasonable in a world where randomness and contingency cannot be eliminated, at least not now, or not without great cost. Here one should cite Gadamer's wonderful essay, "Notes on Planning for the Future," with its argument that we ought to think of our relation to the world on "the model of piloting" rather than in terms of theoretical construction and instrumental control.[23]

Accordingly, Blumenberg emphasizes that "the principle of insufficient reason is not to be confused with a demand that we forgo reasons, just as 'opinion' does not denote an attitude for which one has no reasons but rather one for which the reasons are diffuse and not regulated by method. One has to be cautious about making accusations of irrationality in situations where endless, indefinitely extensive procedures have to be excluded; in the realm of reasoning about practical activities in life, it can be more rational to accept something on insufficient grounds than to insist on a procedure modeled on that of science."[24] Blumenberg at all events wants "to hold to the idea of seeing in [rhetoric] a form of rationality itself—a rational way of coming to terms with the provisionality of reason."[25]

The accusation that rhetoric is irrational or a *pseudos* of reason belongs, Blumenberg notes, to the history of Cynicism: the accusation
is an assertion that the social and historical world (that is, the everyday human world) in which one is compelled to act for provisional
reasons is not a world worth living in.[26]

The Rationality of Rhetoric

But then what form, exactly, does the rationality of rhetoric take? One
answer is to be found in Gadamer's account of the essentially metaphorical structure of Plato's dialectic. The dialectic, Gadamer writes,
is not "a method of systematic, universal development of all determinations of thought" but an inconclusive or open-ended movement of
the One and the "indeterminate Two." The indeterminacy of the
"dyad" makes the conceptual determination of anything *as such* impossible: "the logos always requires that one idea be 'there' together
with another. Insight into one idea *per se* does not yet constitute knowledge. Only when the idea is 'alluded' to in respect to another does
it display itself *as* something."[27] But this indeterminacy is productive;
it is the logos tuned to the singularity and irreducibility of things—
things on the hither side of the concepts and distinctions that we use
to produce large-scale or top-down pictures of how things are. The
dialectic of the One and the Many enables us to take up "the multiplicity of respects in which a thing may be interpreted in a language."

Recall the first hypothesis in Plato's *Parmenides:* there that multiplicity was not a burdensome ambiguity to be eliminated, but an
entirety of interrelated aspects of meaning which articulate a field
of knowing. The multiple valences of meaning that separate from
one another in speaking about things contains a productive ambiguity, one pursued not only by the academy but also by Aristotle with
all his analytic genius. The productivity of this dialectic is the positive
side of the ineradicable weakness from which the procedure of conceptual determination suffers. That ever contemporary encounter
with the *logoi* of which Plato speaks is found here in its most extreme
form. It is displayed here as the experience we have when the conventional meaning of single words gets away from us. But Plato
knows full well that this source of all *aporia* is also the source of *eupho-*

ria which we achieve in discourse. He who does not want the one will have to do without the other. An unequivocal, precise coordination of the sign world with the world of facts—of the world of which we are the master with the world we seek to master by ordering it with signs, is not language. The whole basis of language and speaking, the very thing which makes it possible, is ambiguity or "metaphor," as the grammar and rhetoric of a later time will call it.[28]

The *logos*, in other words, is not a form of subsumptive reasoning; it is a way of taking something now this way, now that, in all of its irreducible singularity, as if moving horizontally, piloting on the ground toward endlessly opening horizons, rather than vertically by means of noncontradictory statements toward a pyramid of ideas. Our concepts do not underlie and shape our discourse; they evolve *in* our discourse through the transference of meanings that occur in taking something in its aspects, now one way, now another. This lateral dialectical process underlies the hierarchical movement of logic and makes it possible.

The dialectic, taken simply in its deep metaphorical structure, however, remains entirely abstract unless it is historicized within the social and historical world in which human beings are compelled to act; that is, unless it is realized or read back into the human lifeworld *as rhetoric*. The dialectic derives from and has its only reality in *dialegesthai* (as *sumbouleuesthai*), that is, speech as speaking-together, taking counsel with one another, working out an agreement as to what must be done. So the form taken by the rationality of rhetoric is not only dialectical in the metaphorical sense of taking or understanding one thing in terms of another or in terms of a "multiplicity of respects"—for example, in terms of the complex circumstances of our involvement with the thing in the everyday lifeworld; it is also socially as well as logically argumentative: it implies human beings in a face-to-face relation with one another. (As Emmanuel Levinas says, solidarity is face-to-face before it is side-by-side.)

As such, rhetorical argument runs deeper than the propositional style of philosophical argument, so deep that it is not too much to say (as Christopher Smith does) that it originates somatically or pathologically in the human body, where *êthos* and *pathos*, character and feeling, provide the conditions that make the *logos* possible. That rhetorical argument is (literally) *embodied* argument is what Smith wants to argue by reading Aristotle's *Rhetoric* along the lines opened up by Heidegger's recuperation of Aristotle, and particularly the *Rhetoric*, as part of his development of a "hermeneutics of facticity," with its emphasis on mood (*Stimmung*) and attunement (*Befindlichkeit*) as fundamental conditions of everyday existence.[29] Here the question of how things sound and how they look—how a speaker strikes us, how true or false what he says "rings"—is not (or is not reducible to) the sophistic manipulation of appearances; it has rather to do with argument's deepest (prelogical or rhetorical) structure. And this is a structure of feeling as well as of cognition.

The idea here is to follow Heidegger and Gadamer in understanding the priority of listening over seeing. Smith does this in a provocative way by insisting on the fundamentally *acoustical* nature of rhetorical deliberation. Beneath the dialectical *form* of the argument—understanding one thing as another, taking it now this way, now that, as the "multiple respects" in which we find ourselves with it in our everyday lifeworld—beneath these formal or tropical operations there is the question of how we are meant to *hear* the argument, how it is meant to strike us in our specific and perhaps critical situation.[30] Walter Ong once argued that the rhetorical culture of antiquity and the Middle Ages, out of which the culture of metaphysics or of objectifying rationality slowly emerged, is now lost to us because its imagination was fundamentally oral-aural in character, whereas in modernity we are conditioned to think of everything in terms of spatial and visual analogies.[31] We are resolutely "ocularcentric," to use David Levin's term.[32]

Christopher Smith brings an argument of roughly this sort to bear on his reading of Plato, in particular the *Phaedrus,* proposing that Plato's critical and even dismissive attitude toward writing in fact conceals and disguises a deep commitment to the silent world of mathematical demonstration, making all things transparent to view and seeing the deep structure of things. This is a world that can only be brought about in writing.[33] Plato's own monumental achievements as a writer are not a paradox or a performative contradiction but are the fullest expression of his philosophical project, which (whatever its final form was to be) was designed to overthrow the acoustical culture of rhetoric, the culture of original argument. To the silencing of the oracles and the expatriation of the poets there is to be added the silencing of rationality itself, the reconceptualization of *dialegesthai* away from *sumbouleuesthai* toward monological (private), taxonomic reasoning—a movement that, essentially, describes the plot of the *Phaedrus*. The critique of writing, so far as *that* goes, resolves itself into a critique of mediation as such, as the Seventh Letter suggests, for the aim of reason now is to free itself from any world in which it has to depend on mediation, and this means (for a start) transcending the ungrounded everyday "narrative-historical" world in which human beings are compelled to act on less than self-evident reasons. Here is where the history of philosophy properly begins: namely, with the substitution of the dialogical character of original argument by a monological form of argument that produces demonstrations of what is so and cannot be otherwise.

Underlying Aristotle's conception of demonstrative reasoning, for example, is the need for relief from the anarchy and interminability of rhetorical argument, which always starts out from prior accomplishments of discourse rather than from unshakable first principles, and which is inconclusive, or which stops from time to time but never ends, owing to the historicity or finitude of human existence. This makes the culture of original argument seem vulnerable to the machinations of Sophistic rhetoric. In *Metaphysics* 4 Aristotle seems to side with mathematical reason as the only alternative to the anarchy and indeterminacy that bedevils human judgment. But the point of the *Nichomachean Ethics* and the *Rhetoric* is to mitigate this commitment to deliberation from above and to show the possibility of rational argument within the limits of human finitude—an *anarchic rationality*. A dialectic that has to live with contingencies, contradictions, and open-endedness is not helpless against the sophistical *techne* of power. Smith's idea is that what saves rhetorical deliberation from the machinations of Sophistic argument is the ethical matrix in which it actually lives. To feel the force of rhetoric's rationality:

[W]e must get beneath the *logos* or logic of an argument to the *êthos* and *pathos* in which this *logos* was originally embedded. We must get back . . . to the character of the speaker and the feeling that we undergo about the speaker and the subject matter he or she is presenting for our decision. For in the end, deliberation's

defense against sophism, and hence the securing of any dialectical argumentation, cannot lie in securing first principles or *archai* from which to infer unassail-
able conclusions. Rather, *it lies in recovering for argument the ethical predisposition
or* hexis *of the speakers who engage in it.* . . . It lies in recourse to their consequent
reasonableness, virtue, and goodwill or lack of these.[34]

As if rationality depended on how we are with one another—how
attuned we are to what is being said, whatever the logical form of
the argument.

Gadamer reads Plato as recognizing from the start that demonstrative reasoning from first principles is possible only in mathematics
and cannot be transported to the human lifeworld, where it is just
the case that everything can always and perhaps always should be
otherwise. Randomness and contingency, after all, are conditions
of human freedom. At ground level rhetorical argument, with its
dialectical structure of taking something now one way, now another,
must take the place of ultimate foundations by constructing bases
on which to stand or starting points from which to act. There is no
blueprint here. So if we ask, with Georgia Warnke, "what guarantees
the rationality of the dialogic arena?"—that is, what underwrites the
rationality of rhetoric—the answer is: nothing, or anyhow nothing
fixed, at any rate nothing that does not have to be got up on the
spot.[35] An argument cannot be guaranteed by its form. In "The Hermeneutics of Suspicion," Gadamer had asked about "the relation of
the rationality of science to the rationality of life," and his answer was
that whereas the first has to be methodically produced, the second is
given in language as a dialogue structured according to the interplay
of the one and the indeterminate dyad. This givenness is not an
ultimate foundation, however, because it is possible only in virtue
of our participation in the give and take of the argument as it occurs
in the situations in which we find ourselves. In life, Gadamer writes,
participation, being-with or being-together, must do the work of
Letztbegründungen.[36]

The Conditions of Social Reason

The conditions that make the rationality of life possible are not logical but historical and cultural. One could say that the history of everyday rationality is like the history of art in which not everything is

possible at every moment. This seems to be the upshot of Gadamer's idea that dialogue presupposes *eros*, friendship, and good faith on the transcendental argument that any other set of conditions (suspicion, methodical doubt, the standard seminar-room philosophical distrust of rhetoric) would be fatal to any relation to the other. Hence the attempt to distinguish a higher rhetoric from the culture of the Sophists—distinguish, that is, between an erotic culture (as in the *Phaedrus*) in which the task of conversation is to win someone over, and an eristic culture (as in the *Gorgias* or the *Protagoras*) in which the goal of dialogue is to win by reducing one's interlocutor to silence. A good question is how, on the evidence, to distinguish between these two cultures, since of course in all of his so-called erotic discourses Socrates inevitably reduces his adversaries to silence. In most of the Socratic dialogues Socrates does not win over his interlocutor but simply defeats him. Presumably one has to distinguish between the silence of wonder and the silence of the outwitted. But where, when one thinks of it, does Socrates produce wonder? Bewilderment, to be sure, but wonder?

Christopher Smith's reconstruction of the original argument of rhetoric is useful because it is an archeology of reason that takes us back from theory to practice and in turn beneath practice to the conditions of existence or forms of life that must be in place for there to be anything like rational practice at all. On Smith's analysis these conditions are (*pace* Plato) democratic. Rhetoric is an alternative to tyranny: that is, everyday rationality presupposes something like a *polis* or public sphere in which social and political deliberation is freely possible. The rationality of everyday life is just this original social and political culture of argument, *sumbouleuesthai*, taking counsel together in a public space, airing and resolving disagreements, doing so out loud, not brokering in the back room but coming in open forum to a shared or at least acceptable agreement as to what is to be done. Moreover, only from *sumbouleuesthai* can one learn *bouleuesthai*, taking counsel with oneself. Ethical deliberation or ethical reasoning is a derivation from the sociality of original argument.

The difficulty is in locating this sociality historically. It is interesting that Smith takes recourse to the Homeric and tragic background of rhetorical culture as a way of describing in its pure form the

embodied nature of original argument whose traces are still percep-
tible in Aristotle's *Rhetoric*. Homer here means Homeric psychology,
in which there are no words for mind or soul but a good many instances of dialogical reasoning, as when Odysseus takes counsel with
his *thumos,* an emphatic case of the original unity of *pathos, ethos,*
and *logos,* knowing in one's gut what is right, trusting one's *kradie,*
heart or instinct. *Phronesis* derives from Homeric *phrenes,* the organ
of intellection. Smith stresses the embodied, patho/logical character of such rationality. But in Homer none of these "organs" of determination is called upon or has any life except in situations of
struggle. Struggle is the mode of existence of the heroic world; struggle gives the definition of Homeric ontology. The question is: struggle for what? Here I think of the inconclusive way in which Homer's
Odyssey ends. Remember that Odysseus is facing the families of the
suitors whom he has just annihilated. They rise up against him, inspired by the speech of Eupeithes (whose name means "good per-
suader"). Odysseus could retaliate and obliterate them at a stroke,
but Athena intervenes to say, "Ithacans, hold off from war, which is
disastrous"—thus thrusting Odysseus into what one can rightly call
the original and originary rhetorical situation. It is not a situation
of *philia, eros,* good faith, or solidarity. It is a situation in which these
things are called for, but not given; it is the task of Odysseus to produce them. But how?

How to proceed from the heroic world of power or dependence
on superior strength to a culture of original argument? This must
be the foundational question of politics. On this point conservative
Gadamerians would perhaps say that solidarity cannot be produced,
and that what Odysseus lacks is precisely the backdrop of tradition
that would provide the common matrix for himself and others;
whereas a more radical view would be that Athene is simply the
stand-in and interpreter of tradition, with its reservoirs of experience concerning, among other things, the consequences of revenge.
In any case the meaning of *phronesis* lies in the situation in which
Odysseus now finds himself. There's no blueprint for him. Either
he has it in him, or he doesn't, to intervene in the situation in light
of what Athene suggests and to make the future (including himself
in it) different from the past. The task is to construct from his own

resources what Gadamer calls "the decisive condition and basis of all social reason."[37] (He may fail.)[38]

Not surprisingly, the conditions of social reason (like forms of justice) are most visible when they are absent. Thucydides' history offers a picture of a culture of original argument under actual conditions, for example, as in the Corcyrean debate in which appeals to justice occur precisely where one would expect arguments from expediency and self-interest. Thucydides shows the rhetorical culture of Athens in all of its richness and complexity, both how it works and how, as the war progresses, it deteriorates as questions of justice give way to self-assertion and the displacement of rhetoric by naked will-to-power, as (famously) in the Melian dialogues, which read in part as follows:

Athenians. On our side we will use no fine phrases saying, for example, that we have a right to our empire because we defeated the Persians, or that we have come against you now because of the injuries you have done us—a great mass of words that nobody would believe. And we ask you on your side not to imagine that you will influence us by saying that you, though a colony of Sparta, have not joined Sparta in war, or that you have never done us any harm. Instead we recommend that you should try to get what it is possible for you to get, taking into consideration what we both really do think; since you know as well as we do that, when these matters are discussed by practical people, the standard of justice depends on the equality of power to compel, and that in fact the strong do what they have the power to do and the weak accept what they have to accept.

Melians. Then in our view (since you force us to leave justice out of account and to confine ourselves to self-interest)—in our view it is at any rate useful that you should not destroy a principle that is to the general good of all men— namely, that in the case of all who fall into danger there should be such a thing as fair play and just dealing, and that such people should be allowed to use and to profit by arguments that fall short of a mathematical accuracy. And this is a principle which affects you as much as anybody, since your own fall would be visited by the most terrible vengeance and would be an example to the world.[39]

Notice that the Athenian speech is an instance of plain speaking so simple and straightforward that argument has been abandoned altogether, whereas the Melians invoke the norms of original argument, namely, the freedom to argue their case on its merits according to the principle of justice, and to do so with arguments "that fall short of mathematical accuracy." Interestingly, the Melians are reduced to appealing to the Athenians in the Rawlsian language of rational choice: justice is in your interest, Athenians; you'll discover in the long run, but probably too late, that fairness pays. Interminable argument is the only alternative to tragedy's interminable cycle of vengeance; talk is the basic mode of public safety. The Athenian refusal to listen will define their future, namely the reversion to savagery that Greek tragedy explores. In this situation the significance (as well as the limits) of *phronesis* could not be more self-evident.

The Hermeneutical Experience of Art

Gadamer's idea is that the point of the game is to play it.[40] This applies to art as well as to social and political relations (art for Gadamer is internal to these relations). In our experience of the work of art, particularly a modernist or avant-garde work—for example, a Cubist collage or, more radically, one of John Cage's compositions like *4'33"* in which a pianist sits silently at the piano for four minutes thirty-three seconds—we are apt to find ourselves in a situation not so much different from the one to which Odysseus must respond when confronted by the family of suitors: that is, how he is to proceed is not self-evident; what is self-evident, or at all events incumbent upon him, is that he cannot proceed as usual or simply according to custom. He now finds himself, without knowing it or without realizing its full dimensions, in something like a new world or an alien culture, one which is nevertheless continuous with his own so that he cannot simply exempt himself from the task at hand.

Likewise, to paraphrase Blumenberg, to see ourselves in the perspective of the work of art is to be conscious both of being compelled to respond and of the lack of norms that might serve as a guide or would justify our decision. The axiom of art history, like the axiom of rhetoric, is "the principle of insufficient reason." How to live with this principle is the task of *phronesis,* or everyday reason, which is as indispensable to the experience of art as it is to ethical reasoning and moral action. But what does the experience of art look like, exactly? Is it merely bewildering (as Cage is always bewildering), or has it its own mode of intelligibility even in aleatory avant-garde circumstances?

Start with Gadamer's phenomenological thesis, derived from Heidegger (but also perhaps from his own reading of Plato's dialogues), that the work of art is an event as well as an object, in which case the main question to ask about the work is not "what is it?" but "how does it occur?" The answer is that it occurs in our encounter with it, that is, what is encountered is the coming-into-appearance of the work, which is not an event that merely reproduces an original production; it is the emergence of the original itself. As Gadamer writes, "presentation [*Darstellung*] is the mode of existence of the work of art";[41] that is, its mode of being consists in its being played like a drama or a work of music: "it is in the performance and only in it . . . that we encounter the work itself."[42] Or again: "the presentation or performance of a work of literature or music is something essential, and not incidental to it, for it merely completes what the works of art already are—the being there of what is presented in them."[43] Performance is not something added to the work or a rendition or version of it; it is an appearance of the thing itself.[44] The point to grasp is that the thing itself exists in no other way. Its mode of appearance is its mode of being.

On this theory it is a mistake to think of the work as a self-contained formal object that merely persists in time and retains its identity as a relic that fills up museums and standard editions. The work of art is not (or not just) an aesthetic object. Or, as Gadamer sometimes expresses it, "the temporality of the aesthetic" is neither the timelessness of the museum, nor is it the Hegelian temporality of supercession in which the present subsumes the past and leaves behind what is merely over and done with (namely, the history of art, which Hegel famously sees as *Vergangen*). On the contrary, for Gadamer the work of art belongs to the temporality of the festival in which a singular event comes around again.[45] The festival is not a commemorative event nor an altogether different festival but the occurrence of the once and future thing itself in its own "autonomous time."[46] It is the arrival of what has come to pass. Likewise our encounter with the work of art is an event in which what Gadamer calls "the hermeneutic identity" of the work shows itself in all of its uniqueness and originality.[47] Hermeneutic identity is not something to be construed like a meaning, but something to be constructed as the form that occasions the event of the work. In *Warheit und Methode* (*Truth and Method*) Gadamer calls this event "transformation into structure [*die Verwandlung ins Gebilde*],"[48] a taking shape in which the work materializes as the thing it is in our experience of it—something that happens again and again each time we experience the work, and where "every repetition is as original as the work itself."[49] But what is the nature of this experience?

In Gadamer's theory the experience of art is not a contemplative experience, but an experience of play in which we are caught up and carried away in the self-presentation of the work. In contrast to the Kantian account of aesthetic experience, which presupposes a model of perception, this self-presentation is not something we stand apart from as observers but something in which we participate—and this is true whether the work is a Renaissance portrait or an avant-garde provocation. Indeed, the virtue of the model of play is that it emancipates the work of art, not to say ourselves, from universal concepts and ready-to-wear experiences; it has a hermeneutical application of universality. The point is that participation must do the work of principles and rules. When Duchamp sets up a snow shovel in his studio, pronouncing it his latest composition, he lays down a challenge that we may not know how to take up. What is the "transformation into structure" that turns the mere snow shovel into the avant-garde work? The temptation is to seek some alchemical process that transforms base matter into significant form, since something like this surely occurs (Arthur Danto calls it a "transfiguration of the commonplace").[50] Gadamer's counsel is to hold to the model of the game. If we do not know how to respond to Duchamp's challenge, how do we go about learning? No differently from the way one learns to play any game. As we know from Wittgenstein, it is not enough to learn rules or to follow explanations; one has to enter a form of life. What is required in this event is something like *phronesis,* the more so since clearly here is a game without rules and without precedent and whose end or return cannot be calculated in advance.

Indeed, one is tempted to say, tautologically, that what the experience of art requires is, basically, *experience;* that is, as Aristotle said, *phronesis,* knowing what a situation calls for in the way of right action, is not a virtue of the young but the condition of "being experienced" that comes from living through things themselves, like friendship, falling in love, or being a father. Here stories rather than concepts and rules provide the conditions that make experience possible, because they give us, in a way rules and concepts never can, the conditions in which experience actually takes place. Recall what Gadamer writes in *Truth and Method* about the negativity of hermeneutical experience (*Erfahrung*)—experience that does not confirm but rather surpasses and even overturns what we had thought, which is why experience can never be codified as science:

> Experience stands in an ineluctable opposition to knowledge and to the kind of instruction that follows from general theoretical or technical knowledge. The truth of experience always implies orientation toward new experience. That is why a person who is called experienced has become so not only *through* experiences but is also open *to* new experiences. The consummation of his experience, the perfection that we call "being experienced," does not consist in the fact that someone already knows everything and knows better than anyone else. Rather, the experienced person proves to be, on the contrary, someone who is radically undogmatic; who, because of the many experiences he has had and the knowledge he has drawn from them, is particularly well equipped to have new experiences and to learn from them. The dialectic of experience has its proper fulfillment not in definitive knowledge but in the openness to experience that is made possible by experience itself.[51]

It follows that, on Gadamer's theory, the hermeneutical experience of art would not result in connoisseurship or expertise—nor, for all of that, in either philosophy of art, or art criticism, or the self-understanding artistry (*techne*) of the maker—but simply in a capacity for experiencing art that is free from the dogmatisms that are attached as a matter of course to conventional forms of aesthetic knowledge or sophistication. Indeed it is not too much to see an internal link between hermeneutical experience and modernism itself, given that any experience of the modernist work at all presupposes the kind of reversal of consciousness (*Umkehrung des Bewußtseins*) that characterizes the emancipatory character of hermeneutical experience. "Every experience worthy of the name," Gadamer writes, "thwarts an expectation. . . . [It] implies a fundamental negativity that emerges between experience and insight"—

where insight (*Einfall*) "is more than the knowledge of this or that situation. It involves an escape from something that had deceived us and held us captive."[52]

It is not difficult to see how this works in Gadamer's case. In *Die Aktualität des Schönen* (The Relevance of the Beautiful), Gadamer, the classicist, takes up, among other examples of modernist art, a Cubist painting, and he writes that our relation to the work is a relation of "playing along with it"—entering into the "autonomous time" of the work, which is to say its movement of self-presentation. This means tracing its construction piece by piece, playing along with the dissonance of its elements, experiencing its unity, even if this unity can no longer be understood in terms of an aesthetics of harmony.[53] But for this to happen the classicist must have already made him or herself at home in the culture of the avant-garde—must already have made this culture his or her own.[54] This is a crucial point. To enter into the autonomous time of the work also means entering into the movement of the art world in which the Cubist work emerges as a work of art according to its own theory of what counts as art. Constructing the hermeneutic identity of the Cubist work is not just an aesthetic or "constructivist" process. One does not follow the design of construction in Duchamp's shovel as if it were a sculpture. The fact is there is no knowing beforehand, as if by an appeal to genre, what makes Duchamp's thing a work. Vexation is perhaps part of the experience of the work. Why is there any experience at all? Recall the motto of art history: not everything is possible at every moment.

In this view, constructing the hermeneutic identity of the work would mean entering—historically and hermeneutically—into the complex moment of its possibility in which the work gives itself the definition of art, in defiance of prevailing markets and the history of taste. This experience of possibility is what modernism is. So the idea is how to enter into the modernist conditions of the work's possibility. This means, at the very least, opening oneself to new possibilities of experience, not to say new concepts of art. Doubtless it is the task of aesthetic norms to define possibilities of experience. But aesthetic norms are never simply given. They evolve within the event or history of art itself in the way that, in a rhetorical culture, ethical norms evolve within the give-and-take of deliberation under the exigency of action. They are in any case *not* presiding universals; they emerge in the hermeneutic identity of the singular, irreplaceable work itself. It is in this respect that the experience of art should be thought of as a work of *phronesis,* a judgment based not on universals but on our understanding and responsiveness to the complex historical situation in which the work comes into appearance—a situation in which our schemes and categories almost certainly have to change if anything is to occur at all. Being historical in this event means being able to change—and isn't this what modernism teaches? As Gadamer says, "the work of art has its true being in the fact that it becomes an experience that changes the person who experiences it."[55] The crucial point to mark is that this is not just a change in one's private outlook; it is a change in one's world.

In Gadamer's aesthetics the event of the work of art is not a museum event in which we simply gape at the thing, or regard it knowingly from a disinterested standpoint; it is an event in which the work claims a place in the world *we* inhabit—indeed, it is right to say that the work claims a piece of us and insists on belonging to our lives.[56] Gadamer's idea is that the event of art is not a tree falling in the forest but an event of witness, testimony, and appropriation. The idea is not to restore an eminent text to its original condition, or to experience it as a timeless work of art at the level of the universal. The point is that the original can only come into being *when I make it my own.* This means encountering the thing itself not under the description of historical documentation, much less by way of received ideas of aesthetic form, but as a kind of epiphany within my own historical and cultural environment. This is what Gadamer calls the "event of tradition." Historically (as the example of the avant-garde shows quite dramatically) the work is not a passive object but an interruption or alteration in the schemes by which I make sense of things. The fact that appropriation conditions the event of art and makes it possible is the reason why, to borrow Jean-Luc Nancy's expression, "art can never be addressed from the [transcendental] horizon of a *kosmos* or a *polis*" but only from below at the level of the singular and irreducible.[57]

Appropriation is also why art can never be for us, as for Hegel, "a thing of the past" (*Ein Vergangenes*). The work that is merely over and done with is no longer art. The transcendence of art is always here and now, but this transcendence is our (my) responsibility. This is what Gadamer means when he writes, "The work of art cannot simply be isolated from the 'contingency' of the chance conditions in which it appears, and where this kind of isolation occurs, the result is an abstraction that reduces the actual being of the work. The work of art itself belongs to the world to which it presents itself. A drama really exists only when it is played, and ultimately music must resound."[58] Appropriation lifts the work out of its afterlife so that even in a museum it is no longer a museum piece.[59] In this respect it makes sense to say that we are responsible for the life of the work. The difficulty lies in being able to articulate what this means.

Appropriation does not mean taking possession of the thing as if at an auction. Paul Ricœur thinks of appropriation as a project in which I take up the work as a projection of my own possibilities.[60] The work breaks open a new world for me to inhabit. But precisely for this reason it calls into question my world as it is given. Thus for Adorno the work is always essentially critical of the world in which it makes its appearance. Gadamer would say that the experience of the modernist work is hermeneutical rather than strictly aesthetic because of the way the work resists and subverts the concepts and categories that structure the horizon of the present (not to say of philosophy). This is how the history of art moves—as if in complete disregard of the history of taste. Duchamp's Readymades are simply a lucid and radical instance of this movement, which exposes us to the insufficiency of our reasons (or as Gadamer would say, to our historicity). In terms of aesthetics, what we experience is the fact that we no longer know what art is.[61]

It is as if the experience of art deprived us of our aesthetic concepts. In fact this is the main thesis of "The Relevance of the Beautiful." In a way Hegel could never have foreseen, modernism brings the history of art to an end by "making all previous art appear as something belonging to the past in a different and more radical sense [than Hegel's]."[62] As Gadamer writes, we cannot avoid "the fact that when we visit a museum and enter the rooms devoted to the most recent artistic developments, we really do leave something behind us."[63] "A new social force [gesellschaftliches Agens] is at work in the claim of the modern artist."[64] Modernism entails the thesis of historical difference and epistemological break. Yet it is precisely this thesis that makes its appearance within the historical and cultural environment to which we belong. It is an event in *our* history, it confronts *us,* and the confrontation conditions and shapes our self-understanding in the nature of the case. This is the whole idea of *Wirkungsgeschichte* as an exigency of self-understanding. There is no question of understanding ourselves and our world unless we come to terms with this event. So the idea is to start the history of art up again by means of acknowledgment and appropriation. Gadamer puts this by writing that "historical consciousness and the new self-conscious reflection arising from it combine with a claim that we cannot renounce: namely, the fact that everything we see stands before us and addresses us directly as if it showed us ourselves."[65] Gadamer's idea would be that modernist or avant-garde art requires us to come to terms with our modernity. This is not an easy assignment, as one can see from Heidegger's "The Origin of the Work of Art," which characterizes the *work* of the work of art in explicitly modernist terms of "starting history all over again," yet the work that Heidegger takes as his example is the Greek temple—a work whose time has passed and whose work no longer has any force in our world, since our temporality is no longer defined by the work of art but, as Heidegger thinks, by technology.

At the time of writing and revising "The Origin of the Work of Art," Heidegger thought that art history was a history of the decline of art (see the Nietzsche lecture, "Six Basic Developments in the History of Aesthetics").[66] Heidegger seems to have created for himself an imaginary world of the Greeks. But this is just where Gadamer thinks Heidegger was mistaken. Indeed, "The Relevance of the Beautiful" is clearly written against Heidegger's rejection of modernism. What if, as Adorno thought, what defines our culture is not technology but the opaque modernist work, whose resistance to conceptualization and control opens up an alternative social space within the rationalization of the world—not a space of aesthetic differentiation but an alternative mode of being? It is just the possibility of such an alternative that motivates Gadamer's aesthetics with its emphasis on the festive and performative experience of the work of art. In his essay on "The Play of Art" Gadamer writes: "Insistence on the opposition between life and art is tied to the experience of an alienated world."[67] But unlike Adorno, Gadamer does not set the modernist work against the world. On the contrary, appropriation means working out a place for the work within the situation in which we find ourselves. If this means reshaping the world so as to overcome the opposition between art and life, or between then and now, or between the familiar and the strange, then we must count this task as just what the experience of art finally entails.

Here is the place to put the question: What is it to be addressed by a modernist or avant-garde work of art? What form could this address take? For Gadamer the claim of the modernist work has an ethical as well as aesthetic dimension, that is, a dimension of responsibility in which one takes up the work as a task in relation to one's time and place (and others in it). As said, the work is not simply a cultural product available for consumption in the marketplace of the art world that one can pick up or not as one chooses. Nor is it simply a philosophical problem of aesthetics that one can work out through conceptualization and theory. Gadamer's idea is that the claim of the artwork is deeper than any claim upon our taste or aesthetic interest, deeper than our profession of values or philosophical outlook. Gadamer's way of formulating this deeper claim is to understand the work as addressing us as a Thou, that is, as an Other whose approach to us is transcendent in the way Emmanuel Levinas uses this term. The work addresses *me* not as a logical subject who responds to the work through the mediation of ready-made concepts; it addresses *me* as a "who," that is, someone situated here and now—someone not interchangeable with others—whose task is to bring the work into being in this here and now by making it my own. A good example of this is to be found in Gadamer's encounter with Paul Celan's poetry. This is not a project in which I develop principles that transform my relation to the work into a judgment of universal validity. On the contrary, in this event my relation to the work is one of proximity rather than one of theory. There is no engaging the work at a distance or at the level of what is universal and necessary. To experience the work at all I must take responsibility for it, taking it upon myself and staking myself on its claim. In this event the work can be said to expose me to my world and to others in it. How do I address them?

The philosopher Stanley Cavell gives an example of what this might entail in an essay on "Music Discomposed" (1967) in which Cavell (who trained as a composer) addresses the problem of how a composer of music in the 1960s could come to terms with the New York avant-garde in which the question of what counts as music is suddenly completely open and highly conflicted. Here is a situation in which criteria are no longer available for defining, much less legitimating, one's practice as a composer. What young composers are trying to compose proves unintelligible not only to audiences but also to one's fellow composers, so that no one can say who legitimately belongs to the music world and who does not. This shortfall of criteria—this insufficiency of reason—is the fundamental feature of twentieth-century art. Cavell calls it the "burden of modernism":

Painting still grows, as it always has, in particular cities; apprenticeship and imitation are still parts of its daily life. Writers do not share the severe burden of modernism which serious musicians and painters and sculptors have recognized for generations: a writer can still work with the words we all share. . . . My impression is that serious composers have, and feel they have, all but lost their audience, and that the essential reason for this . . . has to do with crises in the internal, and apparently irreversible, developments within their own artistic procedures. This is what I meant by "the burden of modernism": the procedures and problems it now seems necessary to composers to employ and confront to make a work of art at all *themselves* insure that their work will not be comprehensible to an audience.[68]

The problem of the audience is not just a problem of connoisseurship. Cavell says that composers themselves "do not quite know who is and who is not rightly included among their peers, whose work counts and whose does not. No wonder, then, that we outsiders do not know."[69] So what are outsiders to do? The conditions of aesthetic experience have shifted out from under our feet, so much so, says Cavell, "that the possibility of fraudulence, and the experience of fraudulence, is endemic [to] the experience of contemporary music; that its full impact, even its immediate relevance, depends upon a willingness to trust the object, knowing that the time spent with its difficulties may be betrayed, I do not see how anyone who has experienced modern art can have avoided such experiences."[70] It is just a fact of the matter that "the dangers of fraudulence, and of trust, are essential to the experience of art."[71] These are difficulties that concepts of aesthetic experience can no longer address. The issues here are no longer merely aesthetic; they are also ethical.

For example, Cavell writes: "In emphasizing the experiences of fraudulence and trust as essential to the experience of art, I am in effect claiming that the answer to the question, 'What is art?' will in part be an answer which explains why it is we treat certain objects, or how we *can* treat certain objects, in ways normally reserved for treating persons."[72] Of course, the work is not a person or any sort of subjective communication. The point is rather how we are with the work (one could call it a relation of being-with): we can in any case no longer address it as an object in a relation of disinterest or aesthetic judgment. Cavell's thought is, remarkably, that we put ourselves up as hostages to the work, as if our relation to the work were one of accepting it, taking it upon ourselves, without being able (try as we might) to justify our action on the basis of concepts or criteria of judgment. As if my relation to the work now had to take the form of responsibility—what Cavell likes to call, "taking responsibility for one's experience":

This seems to be to suggest why one is anxious to communicate the experience of such objects. It is not merely that I want to tell you how it is with me, how I feel, in order to find sympathy or to be left alone, or for any other of the reasons for which one reveals one's feelings. It's rather that I want to tell you something I've seen, or heard, or realized, or come to understand, for the reasons for which *such* things are communicated (because it is news, about a world we share, or could). Only I find that I can't tell you; and that makes it all the more urgent to tell you. I want to tell you because the knowledge, unshared, is a burden—not, perhaps, the way having a secret can be a burden, or being misunderstood; a little more like the way, perhaps, not being believed is a burden, or not being trusted. It matters that others know what I see, in a way it does not matter whether they know my tastes. It matters, there is a burden, because unless I can tell what I know, there is a suggestion (and to myself as well) that I do *not* know. But I *do*—what I see is *that* (pointing to the object). But for that to communicate, you have to see it too. Describing one's experience of art is itself a form of art; the burden of describing it is like the burden of producing it.[73]

Isn't Cavell in much the same situation as the Melians confronting the Athenians or as Odysseus vis-à-vis the families of the suitors? One could say that the experience of art places us in the condition of original argument in which one cannot reflect oneself out of the argument by claiming to speak from a transcendental standpoint. One speaks not from above but from below on the basis of intimacy and as if passing along something to be shared, and which, in the nature of the case, could be rejected. But in this event what would be refused would be an experience, not a judgment; or, by extension, it would be the refusal of a world.

Notes

1. See Hans-Georg Gadamer, "The Philosophical Foundations of the Twentieth Century," in *Philosophical Hermeneutics,* translated by David E. Linge (Berkeley: University of California Press, 1976), 125.

2. "Understanding a Primitive Society," in *Rationality,* edited by Brian Wilson (New York: Harper & Row, 1970), 99.

3. Zygmunt Bauman, *Intimations of Postmodernity* (London: Routledge, 1992), 191–192. Compare Gilles Deleuze and Félix Guattari, "1933: Micropolitics and Segmentarity," *A Thousand Plateaus,* translated by Brian Massumi (Minneapolis: University of Minnesota Press, 1987), 208–231.

4. See Gadamer, "What Is Practice? The Conditions of Social Reason," *Reason in the Age of Science,* translated by Frederick G. Lawrence (Cambridge: MIT Press, 1981), 73.

5. See Michel de Certeau on "the clandestine forms taken by the dispersed tactical, and makeshift creativity of groups or individuals caught in the nets of discipline" (de Certeau, *The Practice of Everyday Life,* translated by Steven Rendell [Berkeley: University of California Press, 1984], xiv–xv).

6. P. Christopher Smith, *The Hermeneutics of Original Argument* (Evanston, Ill.: Northwestern University press, 1997), 3.

7. See also Christopher Smith's claim that that "rhetoric underlies logic, not the other way around" (Smith, "Plato as Impulse and Obstacle in Gadamer's Development of a Hermeneutical Theory," in *Gadamer and Hermeneutics,* edited by Hugh Silverman [New York: Routledge, 1991], 32). This, in a sentence, is the thesis of *The Hermeneutics of Original Argument,* which is something like an archeology of everyday rationality. It attempts "to 'lay bare' and 'lay out' the structure and nature of argument as it originally occurs in existence," but this laying-bare and laying-out requires going behind and beneath the

Gerald Bruns

systematization of reason in which philosophy received its first definition as the attempt or at least desire to know what things like justice and the good are in themselves apart from our efforts to negotiate a just, right, or good-enough state of affairs by choosing one course of action over another.

8. See Gadamer, "Reflections on My Philosophical Journey," translated by Richard E. Palmer, in *The Philosophy of Hans-Georg Gadamer*, edited by Lewis Edwin Hahn (LaSalle: Open Court, 1997), 41–44.

9. *Wahrheit und Methode, Gesammelte Werke* 1 (Tübingen: J. C. B. More [Paul Siebeck], 1986), 322; *Truth and Method*, translated by Joel Weinsheimer and Donald Marshall (New York: Continuum, 2nd rev. ed., 1989), 317.

10. See James Risser's discussion of *phronesis* in *Hermeneutics and the Voice of the Other: Re-reading Gadamer's Philosophical Hermeneutics* (Albany: SUNY Press, 1997), 105–110. Risser's idea is that "the best word for *phronesis* in English is in fact 'judgment'; it is the determination of the good that cannot be done by rules" (110). See also Rod Coltman's discussion of Gadamer's appropriation of Heidegger's retrieval of Aristotle's notion of *phronesis* in *The Language of Hermeneutics: Gadamer and Heidegger in Dialogue* (Albany: SUNY Press, 1998), 19–24.

11. See Gadamer's "Praktisches Wissen," written in 1930, but unpublished until its inclusion in his *Gesammelte Werke*, 5 (Tübingen: J. C. B. More [Paul Siebeck], 1985), 230–248.

12. *Gesammelte Werke*, 7 (Tübingen: J. C. B. More [Paul Siebeck], 1991), 147–148; *The Idea of the Good in Platonic-Aristotelian Philosophy*, translated by Christopher Smith (New Haven: Yale University Press, 1986), 35–37.

13. *Gesammelte Werke*, 7, 148–149; *The Idea of the Good*, 38–39.

14. *Gesammelte Werke*, 7, 144; *The Idea of the Good*, 30–31. In *Life without Principles* (Oxford: Basil Blackwell, 1996), Joseph Margolis argues that as "historied or historicized" beings the most we can hope for is a "second-best morality" modeled on Plato's conception in the *Statesman* of the "second-best state" (*Life without Principles*, 207–219). Margolis writes: "There are no moral principles, I say, just as there are no laws of nature or rules of thought. Or, whatever we offer in the way of principles or laws or rules are artifactual posits formed within a changing *praxis*. . . . 'Principles' are no more than the idealized 'necessities' of the observed *sittlich* regularities of our world (or invented 'improvements' of the same). They are the instruments of effective ideology" (*Life without Principles*, 206).

15. "The Scope and Function of Hermeneutical Reflection," in *Philosophical Hermeneutics*, 24.

16. Hans Blumenberg, "An Anthropological Approach to the Contemporary Significance of Rhetoric," in *After Philosophy: End or Transformation*, edited by Kenneth Baynes, James Bohman, and Thomas McCarthy (Cambridge, MA: MIT Press, 1987), 433.

17. Ibid., 435.

18. Ibid.

19. Ibid., 436.

73

The Hermeneutical Anarchist

20. Ibid., 437.

21. Ibid.

22. Ibid., 447.

23. *Gadamer on Education, Poetry, and History: Applied Hermeneutics,* translated by Lawrence Schmidt and Monica Reuss (Albany: SUNY Press, 1992), 174–175.

24. Hans Blumenberg, "An Anthropological Approach to the Contemporary Significance of Rhetoric," 448.

25. Ibid., 452.

26. See Blumenberg, "Sophists and Cynics: Antithetical Aspects of the Prometheus Material," *Work on Myth,* translated by Robert M. Wallace (Cambridge, Mass.: MIT Press, 1985), 328–349.

27. *Dialogue and Dialectic: Eight Hermeneutical Studies on Plato,* translated by Christopher Smith (New Haven: Yale University Press, 1980), 152.

28. Ibid., 111.

29. *The Hermeneutics of Original Argument,* 23–25.

30. In *The Hermeneutics of Original Argument,* Smith writes: "Aristotle has made it clear . . . that in rhetorical conviction [*pistis*] the argument or *logos* itself does not stand on its own; on the contrary, in any successful rhetorical argument it is conjoined with *êthos* and *pathos,* with the character of the speaker and the appropriate feelings or *pathê* that are to be communicated in the argument or *logos.* Consequently, we, who are uncovering and explicating the structure of argument as it originally takes place in rhetoric, can no longer be concerned solely with what is *shown* in the argument, with what its language brings into the open for us to *see,* rather we must consider what the argument gives us to *hear.* From now on . . . we must pay attention to the tone of what is said, for *êthos* and *pathos* are both communicated acoustically" (82).

31. See, for example, Walter J. Ong, S.J., "System, Space, and Intellect in Renaissance Symbolism," *The Barbarian Within* (New York: Macmillan, 1962), 68–87.

32. See David Michael Levin, "Decline and Fall: Ocularcentrism in Heidegger's Reading of the History of Metaphysics," in *Modernity and the Hegemony of Vision,* edited by David Michael Levin (Berkeley: University of California Press, 1993), 186–217.

33. See Jack Goody's *The Domestication of the Savage Mind* (Cambridge: Cambridge University Press, 1977), 36–51, on writing as a condition for the development of critical thinking and mathematical reason.

34. *The Hermeneutics of Original Argument,* 214.

35. See Georgia Warnke, "Walzer, Rawls, and Gadamer: Hermeneutics and Political Theory," in *Festivals of Interpretation: Essays on Hans-Georg Gadamer's Work,* edited by Kathleen Wright (Albany: SUNY, 1990), 156.

36. See Gadamer, "The Hermeneutics of Suspicion," in *Hermeneutics: Questions and Prospects*, edited by Gary Shapiro and Alan Sica (Amherst: University of Massachusetts Press, 1984), esp. 62–65.

37. *Reason in the Age of Science*, 87.

38. In *Radical Hermeneutics: Repetition, Deconstruction, and the Hermeneutic Project* (Bloomington: Indiana University Press, 1987), 110–115, John Caputo argues that Gadamer stresses the continuity of tradition but cannot cope with the possibility of a tradition in crisis or going to pieces. But this leaves out of account a Gadamerian understanding of *phronesis* as that which is called into play in extreme situations like the one Odysseus finds himself in, where the norms of heroic culture have to be appropriated in a radically new (and decisively critical) way in order to address the claim that Athene introduces. The poem encourages us to think of Odysseus as a figure of *phronesis* whose task is to reconstruct heroic tradition in light of the catastrophe of war and suffering. He may fail, but if anyone is up to the task, Odysseus is.

39. Thucydides, *The Peloponnesian War*, V, 89–90.

40. *Wahrheit und Methode*, 112; *Truth and Method*, 106.

41. *Wahrheit und Methode*, 120; *Truth and Method*, 115.

42. *Wahrheit und Methode*, 121; *Truth and Method*, 116.

43. *Wahrheit und Methode*, 139; *Truth and Method*, 134.

44. Gadamer goes so far as to say that "however much [the work] is transformed or distorted in being presented, it still remains itself. . . . Every repetition is as original as the work itself" (*Wahrheit und Methode*, 127–128; *Truth and Method*, 122).

45. In *Truth and Method* Gadamer writes: "As a festival it is not an identity like a historical event, but neither is it determined by its origin so that there was once the 'real' festival—as distinct from the way in which it later came to be celebrated. From its inception . . . the nature of a festival is to be celebrated regularly. Thus its own original essence is always to be something different (even when celebrated in exactly the same way). An entity that exists only by always being something different is temporal in a more radical sense than everything that belongs to history. It has its being only in becoming and return [*es hat nur im Werden und im Wiederkehren sein Sein*]" (*Wahrheit und Methode*, 128; *Truth and Method*, 123).

46. *Gesammelte Werke*, 8 (Tübingen: J. C. B. More [Paul Siebeck], 1993), 132–133; RB, 42.

47. *Gesammelte Werke*, 8, 117; *The Relevance of the Beautiful and Other Essays*, translated by Nicholas Walker, edited by Robert Bernasconi (Cambridge: Cambridge University Press, 1986), 26–27.

48. *Wahrheit und Methode*, 116; *Truth and Method*, 110.

49. *Wahrheit und Methode*, 128; *Truth and Method*, 122.

50. See Danto, *The Transfiguration of the Commonplace: A Philosophy of Art* (Cambridge, MA: Harvard University Press, 1981), esp. 1–32.

The Hermeneutical Anarchist

51. *Wahrheit und Methode*, 361; *Truth and Method*, 355.

52. *Wahrheit und Methode*, 362; *Truth and Method*, 356.

53. *Gesammelte Werke*, 8, 118; *The Relevance of the Beautiful*, 27–28.

54. See Diane Michelfelder, "Gadamer on Heidegger on Art," in *The Philosophy of Hans-Georg Gadamer*, edited by Hahn, 451–452.

55. *Wahrheit und Methode*, 108; *Truth and Method*, 102.

56. *Wahrheit und Methode*, 28–31; *Truth and Method*, 126–128.

57. "The Vestige of Art," *The Muses*, translated by Peggy Kamuf (Stanford: Stanford University Press, 1996), 85.

58. *Wahrheit und Methode*, 121; *Truth and Method*, 116.

59. *Wahrheit und Methode*, 126; *Truth and Method*, 120. See Adorno, "The Valéry Proust Museum," (*Prisms*, translated by Samuel and Shierry Weber [Cambridge, MA: MIT Press, 1981]), where Valéry takes the objectivist view that the work of art, in virtue of its formal integrity, is what it is in itself apart from anyone's experience of it, in contrast to Proust, for whom "works of art are from the outset something more than their specific aesthetic qualities. They are part of the life of the person who observes them; they become an element of his consciousness. He thus perceives a level in them very different from the formal laws of the work. It is a level set free only by the historical development of the work, a level which has as its premise the death of the living intention of the work ("The Valéry Proust Museum," 181). Like Adorno, Gadamer seeks an account of the experience of the work that embraces both Valéry's formalism ("transformation into structure") and Proust's aestheticism, which is a mode of performance that one might think of calling "being-with the work."

60. See Paul Ricœur, "Appropriation," *Hermeneutics and the Human Sciences*, translated by John B. Thompson (Cambridge, MA: MIT Press, 1981), 182–193.

61. In "A Matter of Meaning It," Stanley Cavell describes his experience of Anthony Caro's sculptures, which he cannot simply dismiss as absurd, but which he cannot integrate into his prior experiences of what sculpture (or, indeed, art) is. "The problem is that I am, so to speak, struck with the knowledge that this is sculpture, in the same sense that any object is. The problem is that I no longer know what sculpture is, why I call *any* object, the most central or traditional, a piece of sculpture. How *can* objects made this way elicit the experience I had thought confined to objects made so differently? And that this is a matter of experience is what needs constant attention." See *Must We Mean What We Say? A Book of Essays* (Cambridge: Cambridge University Press, 1969), 218. See also Thierry de Duve, *Kant after Duchamp* (Cambridge, MA: MIT Press, 1996).

62. *Gesammelte Werke*, 8, 97; *The Relevance of the Beautiful*, 6.

63. *Gesammelte Werke*, 8, 100; *The Relevance of the Beautiful*, 8–9.

64. *Gesammelte Werke*, 8, 101; *The Relevance of the Beautiful*, 10.

65. *Gesammelte Werke*, 8, 102; *The Relevance of the Beautiful*, 11.

Gerald Bruns

66. *Nietzsche: The Will to Power as Art*, translated by David Farrell Krell (New York: Harper & Row, 1979), 77–91. See Robert Bernasconi, "The Greatness of the Work of Art," *Heidegger in Question: The Art of Existing* (Atlantic Highlands, NJ: Humanities Press, 1993), 99–116.

67. *Gesammelte Werke*, 8, 92; *The Relevance of the Beautiful*, 30.

68. Cavell, *Must We Mean What We Say?* 187.

69. Ibid., 188.

70. Ibid.

71. Ibid., 188–189.

72. Ibid., 189.

73. Ibid., 192–193.

5

Applicatio and *Explicatio* in Gadamer and Eckhart

John M. Connolly

I

In his epoch-making treatise on philosophical hermeneutics, *Truth and Method,* Gadamer undertook a rehabilitation of the element of what he calls "application" in the concept of understanding a text, that is, putting the text to *practical use* in the work of interpretation. The hermeneutical theorists of the German Romantic era, he tells us, had corrected the reigning and overly intellectual conception that depicted understanding (the *subtilitas intelligendi*) and explication (*subtilitas explicandi*) as separate mental acts, the former an interior achievement, the latter a kind of logically distinct externalization of it. The Romantics realized that the two belong together. We might capture the point by saying, with Wittgenstein, that someone's capacity to explicate a text is a *criterion* for saying of her that she understands it, hence is a part of the grammar of "understands."

Gadamer saw it as his own contribution to carry this work one step further and to resuscitate the element of application in the forms of interpretation about which he has written so much. He recognizes that this insight is to some extent an old one, already present among eighteenth-century Pietists such as Rambach (who spoke of the *subtilitas applicandi*), but they too missed the inner or logical connections among understanding, explication, and application. For Gadamer, to understand a text *is* to be able to explicate it *and thus* to apply it to oneself in one's particular historical situation. With an eye especially toward literary, artistic, and philosophical interpretation, he urges on his philosophical audience the relevance of more obviously practical branches of hermeneutics such as are involved in legal decisions and preaching based on a scriptural text.[1]

Legal and scriptural exegesis can be said (albeit not without controversy) to have an important feature, to wit, that at the hands of the exegete (e.g., a constitutional court, or a preacher) the original text undergoes an *expansion* of its meaning:

> A law does not want to be understood historically. . . . And a text of religious revelation wants just as little to be taken as a mere historical document, rather it should be so understood that it exercises its salvific effect. This means in both cases that the text, whether a law or a message of salvation, must, if it is to be appropriately understood, i.e. in accord with the text's own claims, be understood new and differently. Understanding is in these cases always application.[2]

Examples might be the extension by the U.S. Supreme Court in the 1960s of the idea of a constitutional privacy right to cover sexual matters; or the utilization by Martin Luther King, Jr., in the same era of scriptural texts to attack institutionalized segregation in the southern United States.

Gadamer notoriously goes on to argue that the same element of application is at work in *all* forms of interpretation, even in the humanities with their apparent detachment from anything like the normative or action-oriented context of courtroom or pulpit. And, he claims further, it is precisely this unavoidable element of application that makes the process of understanding an *unending* one: each new situation of interpretation requires a new concretization of the meaning-potential in the text: "It is enough to say that one understands *differently* when one understands at all."[3]

The point of Gadamer's insistence on the element of *applicatio* in the interpretive understanding that is central to humanistic disciplines, such as history and literary criticism, is to reject the applicability to them of a certain ideal of disciplinary knowledge. Drawn from the apparent success of the natural sciences at producing objective knowledge capable of seemingly endless elaboration by succeeding generations of researchers, this ideal exercised a powerful attraction on humanities scholars from the early nineteenth century on. The

German Historical School, for instance, spoke of its aim to depict the past "as it actually happened."[4] While undoubtedly a great deal was gained by the energetic gathering of long-forgotten primary texts, the careful deciphering of these texts, and their scrupulous rendering in critical editions (as was originally done in this same ethos by Pfeiffer and Denifle for the works of Meister Eckhart), in Gadamer's view "a myth of method" was simultaneously developed that threatened to obscure the vital connection of these texts to the *interests,* and hence to the historical situatedness and finitude of their interpreters. History and literature are necessarily situated; they are the products of the practitioners' *application* of the historical or literary data to their own historical situation.

I shall ask here about the relationship of *applicatio* and *explicatio* in the German sermons of Meister Eckhart (ca. 1260–1328?). Eckhart, a member of the Order of Preachers (Dominicans) and a successor of Thomas Aquinas on the Dominican chair of philosophy in Paris, achieved renown and some notoriety for his learned and daring homiletic work. He himself said his sermons and exegetical treatises often seemed at first glance "monstrous" or "false," and that they contained "novelties and rarities." They are marked by an open and urgent concern for the spiritual well-being of his listeners as well as by apparent indifference to the literal sense of the scriptural texts which provide their starting points, with the master instead developing strongly allegorical readings. This same tendency was present in Eckhart's earlier and more academic Latin works, consisting largely of learned commentaries on books of the Bible (*Genesis, the Book of Wisdom, the Gospel according to John,* etc.), but here the allegorical method was more moderately, even traditionally, used.

Although Eckhart's Latin writings were well regarded in his day and are indeed of high quality, it was the later, Middle High German sermons and treatises which became the basis both of Eckhart's lasting fame and of his prosecution by the Inquisition. Twenty-eight propositions from these works were labeled either heretical or suspicious in the Papal Bull, *In agro dominico,* of March 1329. It is clear that Eckhart's more radical views, though rooted in Christian traditions stretching back to Origen and Augustine, were seen by his fourteenth-century critics as dangerously close to, if not identical with, proscribed doctrines held by beguines, beghards, and others suspected of proclaiming "liberty of the spirit" in those turbulent decades.[5]

The disputed theology which Eckhart proclaims in the German sermons is hard to separate from their exegetical daring. To an unusual extent he eschews *literal* readings, instead favoring vivid, sometimes startling allegorical renditions. Thus it has been tempting for some to fault Eckhart on hermeneutical grounds, that is, for having abandoned the established medieval tradition of exegesis which had spoken, since Patristic times, of the "fourfold meaning" of Scripture: literal, allegorical, moral and anagogical (or mystical). Whereas Origen in the third century had strongly preferred allegorical exegesis, in which the historical events, persons, and objects spoken of in the text are themselves taken as denoting spiritual realities, most leading authorities gave priority to the *sensus literalis.* For example, Eckhart's great fellow Dominican, Thomas Aquinas, claimed that "all the senses [of Scripture] are founded on one—the literal—from which alone can any argument be drawn."[6] Against this backdrop it is thus not surprising that in his detailed study of Eckhart's hermeneutics Eberhard Winkler wrote that "in the German sermons one can hardly talk of 'interpretation.' True, the literal sense is presupposed and occasionally touched on, but in fact it plays no role. Mostly the [scriptural] text serves only as a springboard for allegorical expositions that circle around the theme of 'God and the soul.' "[7]

The question is: when one looks squarely at Eckhart's allegorical attempts to connect scriptural texts about the distant past to the spiritual present of his listeners, must one conclude, with Winkler and others, that in Eckhart's German sermons this manifest *concern* for *applicatio,* for a practice-oriented connection to the spiritual needs of the congregation, has crowded out the element of *explicatio,* of bringing out the text's own inherent meaning, with the result that "one can hardly talk of 'interpretation'" here at all? Or has Winkler overlooked Gadamer's point that "understanding is in these cases always application"? To get at an answer—and indeed to come to a deeper understanding of Gadamer's own claim—I shall first take a closer look at a case of Eckhart the Preacher at work; then I shall ask about the relationship between *applicatio* and *explicatio* in this example of Eckhart's exegesis; and I shall close with some general reflections on the notion of scriptural interpretation.

II

For illustrative purposes, I select a German sermon (Quint 2) on a passage in the Gospel of St. Luke, "[Jesus] entered into a certain village: and a certain woman named Martha received him into her house" (10:38).[8] This is the start of the familiar story of Martha and Mary, but Eckhart is here not interested in the central features of the narrative (about which he preaches extensively elsewhere), he instead remains with this opening sentence. Remarkably he translates the Latin verse ("intravit [Jesus] in quoddam castellum et mulier quaedam Martha nomine excepit illum in domum suam") thus: "Our Lord Jesus Christ went up to a citadel and was received by a virgin who was a wife."[9]

The Latin *mulier* (woman) is occasionally used by classical authors to mean "wife," but nowhere in the original is there a literal warrant for "virgin." This daring translation, however, is crucial for the substance of the sermon, for Eckhart immediately continues: "Well, now mark this word carefully: it must necessarily be that she was a virgin, this person by whom Jesus was received. 'Virgin' means a person free of all alien images, as free as s/he was when s/he did not yet exist. . . ."[10]

The term "virgin" is thus not to be taken biologically in this context, but rather in a spiritual sense denoting an emptiness of the soul akin to that sought in certain forms of meditation. In another sermon (Quint 1) Eckhart takes the famous episode in which Jesus drove the merchants and money-changers from the temple to mean that Jesus wants the temple—*the soul*—to be empty "so that nothing further shall dwell within it than God alone."

In this sermon Eckhart goes on to argue that the emptiness, receptivity, and freedom from distraction of the virginal soul are not enough, for "If a person were always a virgin, no fruit would come of it. If s/he is to be fruitful, it is also necessary to be a *wife*."

"Wife" too is given an allegorical reading as denoting the fertility, fruitfulness, or productivity of the soul. In another famous sermon on the Martha and Mary story in Luke (Quint 86), Eckhart stands on its head what at first blush seems the obvious—and is certainly the common—reading of the Scripture and claims that Jesus is praising the busy, caring work of Martha over Mary's preference for sitting rapt at his feet. For in Eckhart's view it is Martha who has achieved the goal of accepting *and then acting from* the divine will, thus bearing fruit in her deeds.

Returning to the sermon, there follows an important criticism of monastic ascetic practices (fasting, vigils, self-chastisement, etc.) as a kind of *distracting attachment to works*. Eckhart says that it "deprives one of the freedom to be available to God in the present moment and to follow Him alone in the light with which He would show you what to do and to avoid, free and new in every moment as if you neither had nor wanted nor could do anything else." *This* is the fruitfulness of a (spiritual) "wife," female or male, who follows not her own will, but the indwelling guidance of the Holy Spirit. Such a person "bears much fruit, and the fruit is as large as God, neither less nor more."

Later in the sermon, after a learned discourse on the powers of the soul (possibly interpolated from another Eckhart fragment by a later editor), Eckhart expands allegorically on the *citadel* into which Jesus entered: "Behold, now mark how singular and simple is this "citadel" in the soul of which I speak and which I have in mind, elevated above every modality. . . ." The "citadel" is that highest part of the soul, which Eckhart sometimes refers to as the "little spark" or the "ground" or the "light of the spirit." It has nothing to do with time or space, and Eckhart more than once referred to it as *uncreated,* a claim that brought upon him the wrath of the Inquisition, which cited this very text in its indictment. In this sermon he is above all concerned to stress the *indescribability* of this part of the soul and how its union with God is beyond all understanding. Strikingly the phrase, "a Something which is neither this nor that," often used by Eckhart and others in the tradition of negative theology to point at the ineffable Divine Reality is here attached also to the citadel of the soul: "I have sometimes said that there is a power in the soul which alone is free. Sometimes I have called it the guardian of the spirit, sometimes I have called it a light of the spirit, sometimes I have said that it is a little spark. But now I say it is neither *this* nor *that;* and yet is a *something* that is more exalted over 'this' and 'that' than are the heavens above the earth."

At the end of the sermon Eckhart goes so far as to state that "in *this* part the soul is the same as God (*gote glîch*) and not otherwise." Clearly aware of the audacity of this claim Eckhart cites an unusual authority for it: "What I tell you is true: I call the Truth as a witness and offer my soul as a pledge."

Clearly, the sermon is itself an allegory of the soul, stating that if the soul wishes to attain its highest goal it must be both virginal and wifely, admitting Jesus into its highest part, its "citadel," and there bearing divine fruit (a process otherwise referred to by Eckhart as "the birth of God's Son in the soul") by surrendering its attachments to works and being wholly open to the divine guidance. At the same time the sermon ends with a peculiar, seemingly contradictory disclaimer about its own status: it is "the Truth," yet what it describes is said to be beyond both description and comprehension. This point will loom large in the fourth and final section, below, which discusses the logical status of scriptural interpretations. But first a fuller description of Eckhart's exegetical approach in sermons is presented, such as the one just looked at.

III

The key to understanding Eckhart's daring sermonic approach lies in seeing it as motivated by a combination of two factors: on the one hand his sermons, at least in cases where for various reasons we can reconstruct their context, display a strong element of addressing the particular needs of the congregation in question, and doing so in a manner that is deliberately provocative: this is homiletic *applicatio,* and it is this which we can connect with Winkler's complaint about arbitrariness. On the other hand, I will try to show that Eckhart's preaching is guided by a form of the principle of the "hermeneutic circle": the individual scriptural interpretations he gives are arguably not arbitrary, but instead are derived from his conviction about the fundamental meaning of the whole of the Christian Revelation, a meaning which in its turn is of course largely constructed from the various parts: this is Eckhart's use of the standard part-whole *explicatio*. And so far from these two elements being in conflict with one another, from Eckhart's point of view they are essentially interconnected. As Gadamer might put it, genuine understanding always involves *both* explication of the text *and* its application to the reader's own situation: for the preacher this entails the question how best to bring home the text's meaning to the congregation.

Recall Winkler's charge that an interpretation such as the one studied here is little better than a capricious leap from the Gospel text into the preacher's views on "God and the soul." Perhaps we can understand the charge this way: that in these sermons, in an attempt to effect a spiritual conversion in his audience, Eckhart abandons the craft or science of *explicatio* in favor of unbridled *applicatio,* thus making the text say whatever he wants it to say (e.g., *mulier* as "virgin/wife").

Can we recover elements of Eckhart's *applicatio* in this sermon? Much work has been done in recent decades to reconstruct the setting of many of Eckhart's sermons. Consider the following. First, in the turbulence of the early fourteenth century there were a series of repressive measures aimed by the Archbishop of Strasbourg toward communities of religious women, both the lay communities known as beguines and religious houses such as those of the Dominicans. In the midst of this turbulence Eckhart, who was among the most prominent German Dominicans, and whose teaching bore a resemblance to that of some of the more renowned and suspect beguines, was sent by the Dominicans to Strasbourg, presumably to bring order into a potentially dangerous situation. He often preached to communities of nuns (and perhaps beguines). And further, a variety of sources note that these women (particularly those in the cloistered religious orders) were sometimes drawn to (extreme) ascetic and/or mystical practices, and that Eckhart, renowned as a mystic, nonetheless takes a critical stance toward such practices in both of his surviving sermons based on Luke 10:38.

Given all this background, it is at least quite plausible to find in the text specific elements of *applicatio:* in *that* historical situation and in the hands of Eckhart, Luke 10:38 is claimed to have a mystical but antiascetic meaning which might easily have been missed were it not for the challenge represented by monastic rigorism to the notion of Christian perfection, perhaps especially for women. In Gadamerian terms, Eckhart attempts to concretize the partly latent meaning-potential of the scriptural text by bringing it to bear on the particular situation in which he and his listeners found themselves. In so doing he sought to render the text relevant and instructive to their lives. As to what *they* made of his words we can only speculate.

Can one also find in these sermons evidence of the constraints of *explicatio,* that is, the use by Eckhart in his allegorizing sermons of something like rules, or a principled hermeneutic approach? The elements of a positive answer to this question might look like this:

1. Jesus himself and the New Testament authors frequently claimed that his person and life were prophesied and prefigured in the Old Testament. This practice of allegorical reading was elaborated by church fathers such as Origen, Augustine, and others. In a further step they explicitly applied it to the New Testament itself: if Jesus could be presented in the New Testament as the fulfillment of the covenant God made with Abraham and hence as the hidden meaning of the Old Testament, so too might the events of his life recorded in the Gospels be construed to have a hidden level of meaning reinforcing his teaching.

2. This allegorical method brings to light in a suggestive *and hence,* for the listener, in a potentially effective way the deepest truths about "God and the soul," which are themselves presented in a variety of ways in the Scriptures and are arguably the essence of its teaching.

3. Finally, since these truths fundamentally defy human comprehension, their *indirect* (allegorical, metaphorical, parabolical) presentation may arguably be the most effective, or even the only possible one, both in Scripture and in sermon.[11]

The constraint of *explicatio* is just this: to be plausible as a reading, the hidden meaning Eckhart uncovers in Luke 10:38 must conform to the overall structure of the teaching of the New Testament, *and* it must have the symbolic "fit" ferreted out by the allegorical method of reading: the symbol must be clearly decipherable as such, since (as in poetry) it was presumably *meant* to be understood.

Scriptural hermeneutics is not a single, uniform practice, even within Christianity. One familiar kind of New Testament interpretation, for example, focuses on the *ethical* dimension of Jesus' teaching, its message of universal love and forgiveness: this is the Jesus of the Sermon on the Mount and the parable of the Good Samaritan. Here the preacher's task is to adapt or apply those teachings to the situation of the congregation. This can admittedly be a daunting task, since the message has to contend not only with transposition across time, space, and cultures but also with the resistance from the less benign and often dominant aspects of human nature. In this confrontation the original message itself is modified, sometimes fairly drastically.[12] One might call this "the homiletics of morality," but it presents no greater challenge in principle than is involved in interpreting the ethical teachings of Aristotle or the Stoics.

This approach is decidedly *not* Eckhart's, who regarded it as relatively superficial and secondary to a related and more profound hermeneutical challenge. Certainly Jesus gives moral instruction in the Gospels, but he does so, on Eckhart's view, in deliberately parabolical form, and it is the mark of a parable that it partially *hides its meaning.* Far more important than the surface is what lies beneath, as Eckhart declares in the prologue to one of his Latin commentaries on the Hebrew Bible:

Christ, the Truth Himself, in parabolical fashion in the Gospels both gives moral instruction and also transmits *the general roots of profound, hidden truths to those who have "ears to hear"* [emphasis added]. . . . No one can be thought to understand the scriptures who does not know how to find its hidden marrow—Christ the Truth. Hidden under the parables we are speaking of are very many of the properties that belong to God alone, the First Principle, and that point to his nature. [My] mode of proceeding in this work is this. First the text itself will always be literally interpreted. Second, the things that seem to be hidden in parabolical fashion under the words of each text will be treated.[13]

In Eckhart's view the moral teaching of Jesus is inextricably embedded in these profound but hidden truths about "God and the soul," hence it is the preacher's task to help his audience understand these, if only allegorically, since a literal understanding is out of the question.

In most of the German sermons Eckhart's interest in the literal or surface meaning *per se* as a topic for commentary, always modest, all but disappears. Indeed, the focus on the parabolical, hidden, or mystical meaning imposes on his preaching an entirely different task from that which confronts the "homiletics of morality," a task that is in a sense, insuperable: like a koan, the parable—whether it be Jesus' own or an allegory the preacher composes (as in the sermon on Luke 10:38)—is both necessary and also necessarily incomplete, for its task is to point us in the direction of a truth that is in a sense humanly unattainable. On Eckhart's view, to be effective, *applicatio*—itself a criterion of the preacher's own understanding—demands allegorization, but even so the truth to be communicated will resist clear formulation.

In a noteworthy passage (in Quint 53) Eckhart gives a succinct description of his goals in preaching. He writes of his own work:

> When I preach it is my wont to speak about detachment, and of how we should rid ourselves of self and all things. Secondly, that we should be informed (*ingebildet*) back into the simple good which is God. Thirdly, that we should remember the great nobility God has put into the soul, so that we may come miraculously to God. Fourthly, of the purity of the divine nature, for the splendor of God's nature is *unspeakable. God is a word, an unspoken word* [emphasis added]. Augustine says: "All scripture is vain. If we say God is a word, He is spoken; if we say God is unspoken, He is ineffable." Yet He is something, but who can utter this word? None can do so but He who is this Word. . . .[14]

Eckhart describes here in striking brevity a *homiletic program*. It is not a mechanical schema per se, rather it represents a general framework to be applied to the text and derived from Eckhart's overall view of what the Scripture *as a whole* is communicating: the need for the soul to awaken from its slumber of distracted attachment and return to its divine origin, of which a spark (*vünkelîn*) or citadel *(bürgelîn)* is present *in* the soul itself; and yet both this divine spark/citadel and its Author are equally indescribable, so that both Scripture and sermon are, in a sense, as paradoxically futile as they are necessary. We might call this "the homiletics of the mystical ground."[15] All of these elements are to be found in the sermon examined in section II (as well as in many others). Hence that particular interpretation can and should be viewed as *guided by* this overall programmatic framework, an instance of the whole-part dynamic of the hermeneutic circle, and thus an example of Eckhartian *explicatio*.[16]

John M. Connolly

In another sermon (Quint 29) Eckhart complains of the restrictive hermeneutical approach practiced by certain unnamed clerics: "I marvel at how some priests, learned men with pretensions to eminence, are so easily satisfied and are misled by these words that our Lord spoke, 'All that I have heard from my Father, I have revealed to you' (John 15:15). They want to understand this as meaning that He has revealed to us [only] as much as we need 'on our journey' to our eternal bliss. I do not accept this interpretation, for it is not the truth." This laconic rejoinder—"it is not the truth"—is itself not unproblematic, since this "truth" is not one that is directly describable. Still, the intent is clear: Eckhart's critique of the specific interpretation rests on his overall understanding of the entire Christian revelation.

Having explored in Eckhart's sermonic practice his mixture of *applicatio* and *explicatio,* this section addresses the peculiar twist he often gives to his sermons with respect to the concept of truth. As in sermon 2 discussed above, he not infrequently implores his listeners to believe him, for "what I tell you is true: I call the Truth itself as a witness and offer my soul as pledge." But to *understand* this truth manifestly requires more than that one simply listen or to weigh the merits of an argument. Elsewhere (in a sermon—Quint 52—on the text "Blessed are the poor in spirit") Eckhart identifies poverty in spirit with detachment and states: "Now I beg you to be poor in this way in order to understand this sermon: for by the eternal Truth I tell you that unless you are *like this truth* (*glîch dirre wârheit*) we are about to speak of, you will not be able to understand me" (emphasis added).

Here Eckhart appears to be saying that to understand him one must have already come to accept—even more, to *live*—the point of view he presents in his sermons. But is it fair to claim that only the converted, the insider, *can* understand? I turn to this question next.

IV

This concluding section draws some general lessons about scriptural exegesis from the foregoing. I begin with the point just alluded to, Eckhart's apparent insistence on *agreement* with his views as a condition for understanding them. This brings to mind a similar (and initially surprising) claim of Gadamer's, that "the goal of all communication and all understanding is *agreement* [with one's interlocutor] in the matter at hand."[17] What Gadamer (with Quine and Davidson, et al.) means is that in everyday communication we have no choice but to begin with a general acceptance—within limits—of what an interlocutor tells us. (Gadamer calls this attitude the "anticipation of perfection," but it has also been called the "principle of charity.") It is only when such acceptance or agreement proves impossible that we pause to ask whether we might in fact *not* be understanding what the other means by his or her words. When we find ourselves unable to accept the truth-value of the other's claims, we have reached what is, in Gadamer's view, potentially the most fruitful point in such interactions, where our own prejudices, normally invisible, can emerge from hiding and be called into question. The encounter with eminent texts: historical, literary, and so forth, repeatedly forces us into this situation, a situation Gadamer characterizes as one of *openness*. It is here that we are in a position to learn something new, about ourselves and the world.

Reading Eckhart's German sermons one quickly gets the sense that the preacher is trying to induce such openness in his listeners because he feels they do *not* in fact understand the Christian message, though—and this is the greatest barrier—they *think* they do. Again and again in his sermons Eckhart warns that his listeners will not understand what he is saying. Confronted with this situation, his tactic to break through this prejudice is apparently to confront the audience with what he called, in a Latin work, *nova et rara,* the novel and unusual. The point of his approach is to shock and create a reaction of disagreement, though not a permanent one. His goal of course is to achieve in his congregation—whether too readily complacent (recall his critique of the "learned clerics" in sermon 29), or inclined to deviations from orthodoxy (e.g., of the "free spirit" variety)—a lively sense of the *true peculiarity* of the Christian revelation, its utter strangeness when compared with our everyday views of the world, and yet its incontestable origins in the teachings of Jesus.

Stepping back, Eckhart offers his hearers *interpretations of scriptural passages,* statements that purport to show the hidden meaning of familiar-yet-distant texts. Quite commonly, in dealing with these texts scriptural exegetes and preachers have claimed to be interpreting by giving the *intent of the author,* a typical understanding of all textual interpreting ("author-intentionalism"). The special mark of the Christian Scripture, however, is its claim to be divinely inspired and hence to have *both* a human *and* a divine author.[18]

The human authors of the Scripture, even in Eckhart's time, were temporally and culturally remote, more so—we now realize—than was appreciated in the Christian tradition, which tended to take far too much at face-value, for example the texts' own claims about who wrote them, or to assume in what now seems a simplistic way what the genre of a given scriptural text is. Thanks to the efforts of those scholars alluded to above who since the nineteenth century have subjected all such documents to critical scrutiny, we today recognize the gulf that separates us from the cultures that produced them. In the case of the New Testament texts, coming as they did from a small, splinter community of dissident Jews and some Gentile converts, the obscurity of the human authors is far greater than with most Greek and Roman writings contemporary to them. To verify the meaning of a contested passage in one of the Pauline letters, by independently determining the author's intent, is a daunting task in practice.

As if that were not enough, the *real* challenge for a philosophically grounded and mystically aware exegete such as Eckhart is the traditional claim of divine co-authorship of the Scripture. It is *this* Author who is primary and crucial, the Inspirer of the text and the focus of Christian faith, and yet it is He who is *inaccessible in principle* (in one of many different formulations for this mystery, Eckhart paradoxically calls God "an unspoken Word"). To paraphrase the prophet Isaiah, His ways are not our ways, that is, He is *totally* other, and yet at the same time He is closer than the air we breathe. Indeed for Eckhart in the depth and ground of the soul the union is so complete that we cannot find any distinction at all: "In *this* part the soul is the same as God and not otherwise." Yet neither God nor this "citadel of the soul" can be described or even properly named, they are "neither *this* nor *that.*"

It follows that whatever Eckhart's own understanding of his undertaking, he has denied his right to base his Biblical exegesis on author-intentionalism, that is, on the view that to explain the meaning of the text is to identify what the author *intended* to say. For author-intentionalists the *de facto* unavailability of the author, one who is long-since dead, means that their interpretations have the logical form of *hypotheses*, that is, claims that perhaps cannot be confirmed in the present state of knowledge, but which *have a truth-value*, though we are not (or not presently) in a position to establish it. In the case of the Scripture, however, author-intentionalism is pushed over the edge into a kind of unintelligibility, since here the exegete's "interpretive hypothesis" is one which *in principle* cannot be verified by human minds.

Eckhart is fully aware of this paradox. In the sermon Quint 51 he writes: "I have often said: the shell must break, and that which is within must come out; for if you want to have the kernel, you have to break the shell. And accordingly: if you want to find nature unveiled, *all likenesses must break*, and the further one penetrates, the closer one is to being" (emphasis added). The principle on which all allegorical interpretation rests is that of *likeness*, and for allegorical interpreters such as Eckhart it is precisely the use of likenesses which allows one to break the shell of the literal and penetrate to the hidden meaning, the kernel. What Susanne Köbele has called "the unexpected twist" in the passage just quoted from sermon 51 is that the allegorizing Eckhart here states his conviction that, as Köbele puts it, "the absolutely incommensurable divine word cannot be attained by means of proportionalities" or likenesses.[19]

If author-intentionalism is out of the question for the Christian exegete, what alternative is there to the conclusion that interpretation of the Scripture is impossible in principle? In an earlier work Thomas Keutner and I argued that Gadamer gave us sufficient reason to conclude that author-intentionalism is inadequate as an account of the work done by ordinary *literary* (as well as by psychoanalytic) interpreters. In particular we endorsed Gadamer's claim that the meaning of an eminent literary text is never exhausted, and instead unfolds itself over time in the various interpretations given it by succeeding generations of readers as *in grasping it* they apply the text to their own times and circumstances. In a different idiom, we described this as a "constructivist" view of literary

John M. Connolly

meaning: meaning is not "found" ready made in a text; nor is it arbitrarily invented by the reader. Rather, it is always a joint product of text and interpreter, hence to understand the text requires its construal (*explicatio*) by readers who cannot but bring to the text a cast of mind marked by their historical situations (*applicatio*).

Can this approach cast light on Eckhart's hermeneutics? I believe so. For Christians the Scripture vibrates with deep levels of meaning that at once point to the (partly) ineffable *and* impart teachings essential for the reader's (or listener's) salvation. The latter fact means that the message of the text concerns *each* person who becomes aware of it, and not merely the people of the first century C.E. who were the original addressees; thus *applicatio* is as necessary here as it is in juridical contexts, in which a law passed, say, in 1900 is applied to a case in the year 2000. But how are we to tell *what* the Scripture is telling us, if the message is ineffable? How is *explicatio*, much less *applicatio*, to have any grip at all in this situation?

Though the message may be shrouded in mystery, the method of its proclamation is not. By Eckhart's time New Testament exegesis had unfolded within the various Christian communities for thirteen centuries. Succeeding interpretations were judged in part by their conformity to the exegetical tradition and in part by their overall consonance with what one may call the Christian forms of life. New, even radically new exegeses were permitted provided they could be supported by persuasive argumentation (and, on occasion, the force of arms, as for example in the Reformation).

What is special in the situation of an Eckhart is that, with a philosopher's intensity and a mystic's optimism, he presses his line of interpretation to its logical conclusion. In effect he says:

We have it *on the best evidence* (i.e. from the Scripture itself, properly read, *and* from the Fathers such as Augustine, as well as from the philosophers, and—especially?—from my own and others' deepest experience) that in our everyday "take" on the world we are radically mistaken. For instance, we think that all sorts of things matter that in fact do not matter; and we insist on having our own way when the path to happiness is to step back, listen to the will of God, and follow it. And yet to make this clear to others we have only the words of our ordinary experience, words which are at home in precisely the sorts of situations which reinforce the ordinary but erroneous view of things.

What is the preacher to do in such a bind? Like Plato's Socrates he is convinced that we are all prisoners in a cave of our illusions. Socrates' way out was to confront people with philosophic demonstrations of the insufficiency of their everyday beliefs. Eckhart does some of the same, but his more characteristic answer in the German sermons is to use images and metaphors in a deliberately provocative, indeed shocking way (*nova et rara*), and repeatedly to admonish his audience to "see for themselves" by the practice of detachment.[20] Given the resilience of what is called common sense, we should perhaps not wonder that both he and Socrates wound up on trial for their lives.

Hilary Putnam and Thomas Tymoczko have argued that even if our reality were radically different from what we believe it to be, for instance if we *really* were "brains in a vat" being fed electronically the experiences we take to be genuine, we could not even coherently formulate a statement of this fact, since our words have their meaning and reference from their everyday contexts.[21] Does this rule out as incoherent the claims of an Eckhart that our true reality is ineffable? Not necessarily, for we can accept the Putnam-Tymoczko view and consistently with it hold that we *could,* in ways we cannot imagine, someday come to see that we were mistaken: the familiar is not *guaranteed* to be correct (if it were, we could speak of "linguistic idealism").[22] Like an honest classical physicist converted to quantum physics, we can—given the right circumstances—come to see that we had the *wrong concepts.*

Eckhart's position has a certain formal resemblance also to that of Freud and Jung. He proposes a way of looking at the world very different from the ordinary one, from which follows a very different mode of interpretation. To an outsider neither the worldview nor the mode of interpretation initially make much sense; and the adherents of the novel paradigm cannot produce an *experimentum crucis* to compel belief—far from it! By definition a Freudian cannot *demonstrate* the reality of the unconscious, yet Freudian interpretations (of dreams, symptoms, slips of the tongue, etc.) can—to adherents—be both convincing and therapeutic. They can lead one to see his or her life in a different way, a way that may well involve the laying aside of neuroses, compulsions, symptoms, and the like. The

John M. Connolly

individual interpretations of dreams, slips, and so forth by the thera-
pist or the patients themselves cannot be properly understood in an
author-intentionalist manner, since the "author" (i.e., the unconscious workings of the mind) cannot be accessed; and still an interpretation can be assessed for its plausibility, within the framework
of the paradigm, in terms both of its conformity to the canons of
Freudian theory and its efficacy in the life of the patient.[23]

Similarly in Eckhart's case, the preacher's exegesis cannot be held
up against the Author's intention in order for us to judge its adequacy, but this does not mean that all such interpretations are by
definition inadequate. The tests here are the interpretation's conformity to the canons of scriptural exegesis (*explicatio*) and its success
in reaching its audience, i.e. for Eckhart: awakening a sense of the
depth of the mystery of our lives as revealed in the Bible and the
writings of the Fathers and the philosophers (*applicatio*).[24] Within
this framework a given interpretation can be judged more or less
accurate, appropriate, inspiring. Eckhart's accusers, of course,
found his exegeses erroneous and dangerous.

In this sense, from Eckhart's point of view the whole of the Scripture itself and all the works of Christian preachers are a vast web of
retellings of the same "simple Truth," retellings that literally speaking
are all vain, but which in the context of the lives of the participants
can be profoundly meaningful. And the strands from which that
meaningfulness is woven are, necessarily in equal parts, spun from
explicatio and *applicatio*.

Acknowledgments

My work in this essay has benefited from the critical comments of
my colleagues Jay Garfield and Harold Skulsky.

Notes

1. Hans-Georg Gadamer, *Wahrheit und Methode, Gesammelte Werke* 1 (Tübingen: J. C. B.
Mohr [Paul Siebeck], 1986); 312–316; *Truth and Method*, translated by Joel Weinsheimer
and Donald Marshall (New York: Continuum, 2nd rev. ed., 1989), 307–312. All the translations are my own.

2. *Wahrheit und Methode*, 314; *Truth and Method*, 275.

Applicatio and *Explicatio* in Gadamer and Eckhart

3. *Wahrheit und Methode,* 302; *Truth and Method,* 264.

4. This famous phrase was coined by the historian Leopold von Ranke in 1824. Ranke was later professor at what was then the world's leading center of research, the University of Berlin.

5. The beguines and beghards were religious communities of lay women and men, respectively. They attained notoriety in Eckhart's lifetime when one of them, Marguerite Porete, was burned at the stake by the Inquisition.

6. *Summa Theologiae* I Q. 1 *art. ad* 1. This translation is from the *Introduction to St. Thomas Aquinas,* edited by Anton Pegis (New York: Random House, 1948).

7. Eberhard Winkler, *Exegetische Methoden bei Meister Eckhart* (Tübingen: J. C. B. Mohr [Paul Siebeck] 1965), 112, my translation.

8. I quote here the well-known King James Version, which has "village" where the Latin Vulgate, cited directly by Eckhart, has *castellum* (citadel).

9. I use the German texts in *Meister Eckhart Werke I–II, Bibliothek des Mittelalters,* vols. 20–21, *Texte und Übersetzungen von Josef Quint, Herausgegeben und kommentiert von Niklaus Largier* (Frankfurt: Deutscher Klassiker Verlag, 1993), hereinafter referred to as "Quint 1" (or 2, etc.). This sermon and others are available in a reliable recent translation by M. O'C. Walshe, *Meister Eckhart: Sermons & Treatises,* 2 vols. (London and Dulverton: Watkins, 1979 and 1981). This particular sermon was one of those cited by the inquisitors at Eckhart's Cologne trial, and his response has also been preserved.

10. English versions cannot reproduce a play-on-words in the German that supports the allegory; in the translation Eckhart gives of the Gospel citation it is said that Martha "*empfängt*" Jesus, a word that means both "received" and "conceived."

11. This last point about Eckhart's approach is persuasively elaborated by Niklaus Largier in his essay, "*Figurata Locutio:* Hermeneutik und Philosophie bei Eckhart von Hochheim und Heinrich Seuse," in *Meister Eckhart: Lebensstationen—Redesituationen,* edited by Klaus Jacobi (Berlin: Akademie Verlag, 1997).

12. A good example is the way in which medieval Benedictine thinkers worked to Christianize the modes of behavior that the warrior caste brought with it from Germanic paganism, the result being the code of chivalry, a peculiar development for followers of Jesus, who had admonished Peter in the Garden of Gethsemane to *put away* his sword.

13. *The Book of the Parables of Genesis,* in Edmund Colledge, O.S.A. and Bernard McGinn, *Meister Eckhart: The Essential Sermons, Commentaries, Treatises, and Defense* (New York: Paulist Press, 1981), 94.

14. See Augustine, *De Doctrina Christiana* I, 6, 6.

15. I am indebted for the term to recent and still unpublished work of Bernard McGinn.

16. I am not of course endorsing either the overall framework or its use by Eckhart to explicate *Luke* 10:38. My concern is rather to show that there is an exegetical method at work here.

John M. Connolly

17. *Wahrheit und Methode,* 297; *Truth and Method,* 260, emphasis added.

18. There are also other hermeneutical approaches than the author-intentionalist one, for example, what is sometimes called "text-intentionalism." See the distinctions drawn in *Hermeneutics versus Science? Three German Views,* edited by J. Connolly and T. Keutner (Notre Dame: University of Nore Dame Press, 1988), introduction, 1–67, esp. 1–8.

19. S. Köbele, "*Primo aspectu monstruosa:* Schriftauslegung bei Meister Eckhart," *Zeitschrift für deutsches Altertum und deutsche Literatur* 122, 1 (1993), 65.

20. The *need* to shock, to awaken his audience from its "dogmatic slumbers," perhaps explains his interpolation of "virgin/wife" into *Luke* 10:38. He could as easily have explained that while the text literally says "woman" (*mulier*), we also know that to receive Christ into our souls requires that this woman (allegorically, the soul) be a virgin. But putting the point as he did, by *translating* the Latin *mulier* as "virgin who was a wife," he gets the extra mileage of *applicatio* by startling his audience (presumably cloistered nuns who were both virgins and "wives of Jesus").

21. Hilary Putnam, *Realism and Reason* (Cambridge: Cambridge University Press, 1983); and Thomas Tymoczko, "In Defense of Putnam's Brains," *Philosophical Studies* 57 (1989), 281–297.

22. See Ludwig Wittgenstein, *On Certainty* (Oxford: Basil Blackwell, 1969), §§638–669, esp. §§643–646; and the commentary in G. E. M. Anscombe, "The Question of Linguistic Idealism," in Anscombe, *From Parmenides to Wittgenstein, The Collected Philosophical Papers of G. E. M. Anscombe,* vol. 1 (Minneapolis: University of Minnesota Press, 1981), 131–133.

23. This way of construing psychoanalytic interpretation has been persuasively argued by Ernst Konrad Specht, for instance in Specht, "Literary-Critical Interpretation—Psychoanalytic Interpretation," in *Hermeneutics versus Science?* edited by Connolly and Keutner, 153–169.

24. On this latter issue we have only sketchy evidence of Eckhart's success in his own day, but to judge by the verdict of history and the fact that his writings have perhaps never been more avidly read and studied than at present, there is reason to think he made, and continues to make, his point.

6

Philosophy, Religion, and the Hermeneutic Imperative

Jay L. Garfield

1 Introduction

This is an essay about the meaning of life. It is hence about our hermeneutical self-understanding. The word "meaning" notoriously has many meanings, and indeed in at least two senses in its primary occurrence in the preceding sentence. And it might be that when we seek the meaning of a text and the meaning of our life, we are seeking not simply different meanings, but different kinds of things entirely—that the first inquiry is properly hermeneutical and that the second is perhaps religious, or at least phenomenological. Among Gadamer's great achievements is to show that this is not so— that in coming to understand our lives as meaningful we apply the same hermeneutical considerations to ourselves that we apply when understanding texts. That insight might seem to resolve the notoriously difficult problem of understanding the meaning of life into the *prima facie* easier problem of textual semantics. Unfortunately, however, it goes the other way around: the apparently unproblematic encounter with ink on the page or sound waves in the air turns out to be fraught with all of human being.

This essay is also about a curious hermeneutical and political phenomenon in the contemporary academy, one I will approach from personal experience, and experience I only came to understand through reflection on Gadamer's hermeneutic theory: I was brought up in the Western philosophical tradition, and more narrowly,

Jay L. Garfield

primarily on what gets called somewhat polemically and mislead-ingly "Anglo-American" philosophical literature. Throughout my education and early professional career, I never questioned, nor was encouraged to question the presupposition that philosophy is a European phenomenon. (Nor, I might add, did I consciously assert that it is—the issue simply never arose.) Never did a Chinese, Japanese, Indian, Tibetan or African philosopher or text enter my philosophical horizon until I began my teaching career and was led in that direction by the interests of my students. As it happens, my research interests have drifted eastward and now a consider-able portion of my professional time is spent working on Indo-Tibetan Buddhist philosophy and in collaboration with Tibetan philosophers.

The fact that I often work in this area has occasioned a number of interactions in which my Western colleagues say things like, "When you were still doing philosophy . . ." or "Now that you are working in religious studies . . ." Now the questions I address when I work on texts and with scholars in this tradition are often much like those I address when I work on Western texts and with Western colleagues, give or take a bit—problems concerning the nature of causation, the nature of mind and intentionality, moral psychology, logic, the theory of justification, and so forth. Given that this is the case, and that it is no secret that it is the case, these encounters with Western colleagues suggest a peculiar attitude toward this work. This attitude is more peculiar still given the fact that without exception those who preface their remarks in this way never read either my work in this area or the literature it addresses. But they know that it is not philosophy. And despite their epistemological sophistica-tion, the juxtaposition of this knowledge claim with the manifest lack of evidence for it does not trouble them. Nor, I hasten to add, is this attitude somehow peculiar to my immediate acquaintances. One sees it reflected in philosophical curricula throughout the West, and in the fact that the vast majority of Western scholars of Asian philoso-phy are located not in departments of philosophy but in depart-ments of religious studies, Asian studies, and so forth.

I find that it does not trouble most Western philosophers that they have never so much as glanced at a text written in Asia, or entered into dialogue with an Asian philosopher (*mutatis mutandis* for Africa, the Islamic world, etc.). Nor does it trouble many in our profession that academic departments in the West are often called "philosophy departments" when their academic coverage is limited to the Western philosophical tradition. Why not?

There are two comfortable answers that I hear most often when I raise this challenge. The first is this: there is a world of difference between philosophy and religion, and what passes for "Eastern philosophy" is in fact religion misnamed. Western philosophy is independent of religion, and is a rational, religiously disinterested inquiry into fundamental questions about the nature of reality, human life, and so forth. But this distinction is supposed to deliver the result that St. Thomas Aquinas's *Summa Theologica,* Descartes's *Meditations,* including the proofs of the existence of God, and Leibniz's discussion of theodicy are philosophical, while Dharmakīrti's investigations of the structure of induction and of the ontological status of universals, Tsong khapa's account of reference and meaning, and Nāgārjuna's critique of essence and analysis of the causal relation are religious. Anyone who has a passing familiarity with all of the relevant texts will agree that something has gone seriously wrong if this distinction is taken seriously.

The second reply is this: Western philosophers simply plead their lack of familiarity with the Asian texts and inability to approach them, let alone to teach them or to use them in research. Those who offer this reply sometimes piously lament the presumably irremediable lacunae in their own philosophical training or their lack of competence in the relevant canonical languages. Better for the shoemaker to stick to his last, they say, then to lapse into charlatanism. This argument—however noble the scholarly sentiments to which it appeals—of course must rely on at least one of the following suppressed premises: (1) Asian philosophy is unreadable by anyone with European ancestry; (2) one should never read anything one has not already read or teach anything one has not been taught in graduate school; and (3) one must never rely on a translation in teaching and research, and Asian languages are impossible to learn. I am not sure which of these options is more implausible, but many seem unembarrassed by reliance on at least one.

I find this second reply hard to take seriously as a theoretical position, though to be sure it demands political and rhetorical attention as a late moment in postcolonial racism. My real concern is with the first reply—that Asian philosophy, so-called, is in some deep sense different in kind from Western philosophy—that it is religious in a sense that Western philosophy is not—and so with the relation between philosophy and religion and the connection of that relation with our understanding of the intellectual and geographical bounds of philosophy.

2 The Meaning of Life

Human self-understanding is always hermeneutical. It is by now a commonplace, thanks to the work of Hans-Georg Gadamer, and of Heidegger before him, that for ink on a page to be more than an interruption in an expanse of white, for vocalizations to be more than "sound and fury, signifying nothing" and that for a work of art to be more than so much matter distributed in some physically describable way, crucial meaning-determining context is required as well as interpretative commitment on the part of a reader or interlocutor. Just so for our human lives. From the standpoint of disinterested physical science we are nothing but ephemeral biologically driven organizations of matter—local, temporary counter-entropic eddies in a vast indifferent universal flow to cold, homogenous darkness.

Our lives derive meaning, just as do our inscriptions, not from their intrinsic physical or biological properties, nor from any properties reducible to these, but from their context; not as solitary embodied texts but as moments in living traditions; and finally, not in virtue of anything available to the disinterested gaze, but only through the engagement made possible by interpretive commitment. The meaningfulness of any human life is hence always the collective achievement of the community in which that life is lived and of the tradition by which that community understands itself and by which its members can understand themselves and each other. In this context we must remind ourselves that the relevant interpretative commitment—the willingness and determination to find meaning and to take that meaning as important—includes the commitment to take one's own life seriously as well as the reciprocal commitment to take others' seriously. *Dasein* is only possible in the context of *Mitsein*.

For many cultures, including both the cultures descending from classical Greece and those descending from classical India and China, central to the traditions constituting the interpretive background against which their participants' lives gain meaning are textual traditions: extended sequences of written texts; written and oral replies to and commentaries on those texts; identifications of part of those traditions as canonical; and characterizations of what is excluded. More specifically, in all of these cultures, specific textual traditions take as their explicit problematic sorting out the canons of interpretation, accounts of the good, and so forth in their respective cultures, and hence working out the meaning of life. Among these textual traditions are those identified as religious and philosophical traditions.

It is important to remember that philosophy and religion as pretheoretically individuated share this hermeneutical role if we are to understand the curious ambivalence toward religion and religious traditions in contemporary Western philosophy. The antipathy that allows the use of "religious" as a dismissive epithet (again, bracketing for now its descriptive adequacy) for Asian philosophy is not in the first instance the antagonism toward that which is alien, but more an instance of the special vitriol reserved for members of the family or that erupts in civil war, but in this case accidentally directed outward. The most significant difficulty with the dismissal of Asian philosophy as religion is not the fact that in the relevant sense that charge is false, but that in that very sense, as well as in the deeper sense at which I am driving at here, Western philosophy is also profoundly religious.

3 Philosophy and Religion after the Enlightenment

Contemporary Western philosophy, despite having roots as old as classical Greece, derives much of its contemporary problematic and professional profile from the European enlightenment. Even the most contemporary postmodern philosophical developments can

Jay L. Garfield

only be understood as reactions to and *sequelae* of the upheavals of early modernity. European philosophy's professional self-understanding as, inter alia, an opposition to religion and its identification of its own canon and organon in contrast to those of religion also originates at that moment.[1] It is easy to make too much of individual figures or events salient in retrospect, and it is not good history to do so. But so long as we are careful not to take ourselves to be doing intellectual history but rather collective professional phenomenology, sketching the outlines of the self-understanding common to our tradition, it is not too much of a distortion to say that the Galileo affair forced philosophy to make a choice: science had at that moment thrown down the gauntlet at the church door, and there was never again to be a genuine coincidence or reconciliation between Western science and Semitic religion, as opposed to an uneasy and forced coexistence, abetted either by platitude or lame apology. Philosophy had to choose sides, and philosophy, of course, backed science.

The choice was indeed forced, and philosophy made the right decision. But the forced character of the choice and the correctness of the decision derives crucially from the specific character of the Semitic religions (principally, of course, Christianity) against which science was rebelling. First and foremost, these are revealed religions whose central tenets require that kind of faith Mark Twain aptly characterized as "believing what you know ain't so." Second, they are theistic religions, and hence religions that propose an account of reality according to which there is a terminus to explanation, and hence according to which there is a final horizon to all self-understanding. Given its own epistemic commitments, and given the success these commitments demonstrated and promised, science could never accommodate itself methodologically to revelation. And given the endless frontier of discovery it anticipated, a creator would be not only superfluous but also obstructive.

The progressive, empirical character of science, with its emphasis on the autonomy of reason and the consequent power to transform the natural world, gave rise to its image in a progressive humanism envisioning the possibility of endless reconceptualisation of what it is to be human, progressively deeper self-understanding, and through this autonomous, empirical and rational practice, the transformation and improvement of humanity itself. Modernity, so conceived, was a very good idea indeed, especially when contrasted with the available alternative. Academic philosophy could not but choose the side of science, and the great philosophical texts of that period, prominently including Descartes's *Meditations,* Kant's *Critique of Pure Reason* as well as his essays "What Is Called Enlightenment" and "Conflict of the Faculties," document and confirm this choice.

In choosing to side with science, philosophy was hence emphatically choosing against religion and in doing so it was defining itself explicitly in contrast to religion. This emerges most clearly, of course, in Kant's critical philosophy in which the domains of reason and faith are so carefully circumscribed. In defining itself against religion, though, academic Western philosophy was also defining religion as its antithesis: philosophy is rational; religion dogmatic; philosophy progressive and humanistic; religion static and transcendental in its epistemic authority; philosophy atheistic, at least methodologically; religion theistic, particularly epistemologically.

Philosophy and religion so conceived are indeed as different as night and day. But the conception is misleading. We have to face squarely the fact that academic philosophy in the West never fully repudiates its Semitic religious background. The respects in which this is true are too numerous for complete enumeration, but here are some examples: Descartes finds it necessary to prove the existence of God, and Kant can't get by without at least the idea of God; divine commands remain the model of morality in deontological ethics; liberal democratic theory happily adopts a conception of human beings self-evidently "endowed by their Creator with certain inalienable rights . . ."; the professional specialization "philosophy of religion" invariably means "philosophical discussion of Christianity." I emphasize that these are only examples. For a more extended treatment, I advise reading Schopenhauer and Nietzsche, each eloquent on this point.[2]

So the divorce was never complete, and the religious roots of Western philosophy ensure that even its most recent fruits are Christian in character however determined the effort to occlude that fact. That this is so is partly to be explained by the deeper respect in

Jay L. Garfield

which Western philosophy is religious: its purpose has been from its classical period (and though this was more explicitly articulated by Aristotle, the skeptics and Stoics than by modern and postmodern successors, it remains at the heart of the enterprise) the articulation of the context in which we can give meaning to our lives. "Articulation" is here used in both senses of that term: through philosophy, as through religious thought, we both constitute and come to understand the ground of that meaning, and we do so through a hermeneutically self-conscious textual tradition. Paraphrasing Clausewitz, we can say that philosophy is the continuation of religion by other means, just so we also realize that those means are only ever so slightly "other."

4 Philosophy and Religion on the Path to Enlightenment

The history of philosophy and its relation to religion is of course not uniform in the world's cultures. A comparison with Buddhist culture is instructive here (though it is important to bear in mind that we cannot simply generalize from the Buddhist context any other Asian, let alone African or other non-Western context). The European enlightenment has no historical counterpart in India or China. There was never a cataclysmic rift between religion and science, and so philosophy never had to take sides. Buddhism is atheistic, rejects revelation as epistemically authoritative, and is committed to infinite human perfectibility through empirical inquiry and rational analysis, culminating in full awakening, or buddha-hood. And most Buddhists follow Siddhartha Gautama in regarding this perfectibility as the individual responsibility of each person. Buddhism as a religion, of course, has the trappings and social functions we expect to find in a religion: prayer, spiritual practices, rituals, temples, festivals, and so forth. Their efficacy or propriety can be questioned, and there could be good reason to reject any part or all of Buddhist religion as a rational or efficacious practice, just as there could be with respect to Christian religious practices.

Buddhist philosophy, like Western philosophy, aims to understand the fundamental nature of reality, the nature of human life, and so provides a hermeneutical context in which those in Buddhist cultures constitute and understand the meaning of their lives. Buddhist religious practice, like Christian religious practice, aims at similar goals. But in the Buddhist context religious and philosophical practice have never been prised apart as distinct and independent cultural practices, as opposed to connected parts of a seamless cultural artifact. And this is not simply because Western science was late to come to the Buddhist world or because when it did it had little impact. Its impact has indeed been marked. It is because the particular features of Semitic religions just adumbrated that generate the rift between philosophical and religious traditions in the West are simply not present in Buddhism.

This is, of course, neither a brief for Buddhism as a religion nor a brief for Buddhist philosophy as in any sense superior to Western philosophy. Rather it is an argument for the cultural specificity of the truth of the claim—even to the limited degree that it is true—that the categories of religious and philosophical discourse determine a dichotomy. The dichotomy in question is determined not by the respective characters of religious thought and philosophical thought, per se but rather by the particular methodological and substantive commitments of specific religious and philosophical traditions at particular historical junctures. Seen from the standpoint of their role in the project of human self-understanding the continuity between religious and philosophical discourse—and indeed between them both and literary and historical discourse—is more dramatic than any differences.

Let us now return to the facile dismissal of Buddhist or other Asian philosophy as "just religion." In doing so we can reconstruct a slightly more plausible, but still fallacious argument, and can thereby diagnose the deeper errors committed by those who would be so dismissive: philosophy and religion represent distinct and incompatible hermeneutical and epistemic enterprises. Buddhism is manifestly a religion. Therefore any thought bound up with it is not properly philosophical. We can now see that it is the first premise that must go—falsified not only by the very case under consideration but also by the Western tradition itself that is supposed to provide the best evidence. Our vision of philosophy as handmaiden to the sciences must be replaced with a vision of philosophy as a synoptic discipline providing the interpretive context for the full range of epistemic, artistic and moral activities. Understanding philosophy in this way forces us to see that it also has a central role in constituting the narrative in the context of which we become persons and not mere physical objects. Then it joins a host of other allied hermeneutical activities in that position, and it cannot help but be interpenetrated by them.

Philosophy must hence be seen as intimately bound to other humanistic, hermeneutic activities such as religion and history. The fact that in some Asian cultures philosophical and specifically religious practice remain more closely bound than they are in contemporary Western culture can in no way stand as a reason for disparaging the philosophical character or merit of those traditions.

5   Hermeneutic Practice, Humanism, and Human Life

I said at the outset that this is an essay about the meaning of life. That, of course, does not mean that it is an attempt to articulate that meaning. (Philosophers, after all, notoriously retreat from real, first-order questions to the safer ground of meta-theory!) Instead, I am concerned with the sense in which life can be found meaningful and the intellectual activity through which that meaning can be discovered. The crucial insight is provided by Gadamer's hermeneutical theories: the discovery of meaning is always a circular movement embracing the reciprocal relation between parts of texts and the whole that comprises them at the level of text and the larger image of this reciprocity in the relation between texts and the traditions that comprise them. Only the horizon of a text can determine the meaning of any part thereof; only the totality of the meanings of the parts can constitute the semantic horizon that text provides. Only the horizon of a tradition can determine the interpretation of any text; only the totality of texts comprised by a tradition can constitute that larger semantic horizon.

We can conjoin this first insight with a second—that human beings, qua persons constitutively, though not of course exhaustively, are both bearers of meaning and creative participants in the set of meaning-bearing and meaning-determining practices that constitute the cultures and traditions in the context of which they live their lives. These cultures hence constitute the rich semantic horizon against which our lives come into relief as significant, and through that significance construct that very horizon. No sequence of words, however intelligently constructed and carefully printed and bound, absent a tradition in which it can be read and understood, can be interpreted as an eminent text, and rise to real cultural significance. For exactly the same reasons, absent the hermeneutic context provided by a culture, no human life, whatever its internal structure, can be more than a "walking shadow . . . full of sound and fury and signifying nothing." Every bit as much as our literary and philosophical works depend for their meaning on their intertextuality, our lives each depend for their meaning on our interdependence with our fellows.

The hermeneutical counterpart of the collapse of the duality between conceptual scheme and empirical content is the collapse of anything pretending to be a duality of truth and method. Every tradition carries within it not only a set of texts demanding interpretation but a canon of interpretive practices that are themselves textually encoded and subject to interpretation. We encounter here yet another significant hermeneutic circle. This interweaving of object and method of interpretation is also, of course present in the relation between human life and human culture. Our cultures do not only comprise sequences of interdependent lives calling for understanding but also sets of practices encoded in those lives themselves through which lives are understood and in which meaning is assigned and constituted. The variety of the interpretive practices involved in the assigning of meaning to lives in their cultural contexts is every bit as great as the variety of practices used in the assigning of meanings to texts in their traditional contexts. This variety is neither surprising nor is it any insurmountable bar to cross-cultural understanding. In fact, such difference facilitates the kind of cross-cultural dialogue that ultimately leads to greater self-understanding. We recognize an initially alien form of interpretation not by finding it to be in all respects like our own (after all, it would then not be alien), but in virtue of recognizing a homology of function. It does for its users what ours does for us. This homology of function can then provide a fulcrum for understanding difference, for dialogue, and eventually, perhaps, for the fusion of horizons that can permit genuine collegiality and the appreciation of those features of our own life invisible to us precisely because of their proximity.

In the modern and postmodern West, as in the textually articulated Hindu, Buddhist, T'aoist, and Confucian cultures of Asia, the practices centrally concerned with the interpretation of life are those of the humanities, including at least in the West philosophical practice, religious, historical, and text-critical practice. Again, any claim to universality of these precise disciplines, or especially the distinctions marked between them in twenty-first-century European, American, and Australasian universities and those patterned on them would have to be tempered by the reflections above. We look for homologies of function, not mirror reflections of our own practices and commitments. But the homologies are real and reflect a common purpose. Humanism, here understood as a commitment to that purpose common to these disciplines, is unavoidable. It is unavoidable because human beings, qua persons, are committed to self-understanding; because all understanding presupposes meaning-constituting practices; because self-understanding requires practices constituting lives as meaningful; because only cultures comprising sets of interpretive practices taking as their object human life can do that. Rejection of the hermeneutic imperative is thus rejection of one's own humanity.

Now seen from this perspective, it is clear that this commitment—this humanism—binds philosophical and religious practice more tightly than any culturally contingent rift such as that caused by the particular interpretative practices espoused by the Christian church on the one hand, and the nascent natural sciences on the other, in the sixteenth and seventeenth centuries.[3] This is not to deny the real difference between the modes of interpretation encoded by Semitic religious traditions and the Western project of modernity and its aftermath in which Western academic philosophy is appropriately involved. It is instead to urge both that that distinction is in a larger context not so deep after all, and more importantly that to expect that distinction to appear universally both would be ill-motivated and a serious barrier to intercultural understanding, particularly in encounters with cultures in which no such distinction can be drawn. At its worst it permits us to ignore deep and important philosophical traditions, an ignorance which in the present postcolonial historical context has significant moral and political implications as well as posing more obvious intellectual problems.

Ignoring the philosophical traditions of other cultures is in fact a continuation of the colonial project of the subordination of those cultures to our own. That project was "justified" by the white man's burden of bringing civilization to the benighted heathen, a burden of which we can only make sense if we deny their manifestly existent intellectual traditions the epistemic status we grant ours. Giving the Western philosophical tradition pride of place as "philosophy" while marginalising in our departments or in our individual life all other traditions, if the arguments I have offered are cogent, hence implicates us directly in institutional racism. Recognizing that we are so implicated and refraining from changing our individual practice and from working to change our institutional practice hence constitutes, however passive it may be, individual racism. It also constitutes a profound epistemic vice—that of willfully ignoring sources of knowledge we know to be relevant to our own activities. It is a measure of the importance of Gadamer's hermeneutic theory that it allows us to come to see these failings in ourselves and to see our way to remedying them.

Finally, I note that a fixation on this rather superficial distinction also can lead to a mis-taking of the role of philosophical activity itself, a mislocation of philosophy in the *Naturwissenschaften* and a failure to appreciate the essentially soteriological character of philosophical activity. For philosophy always begins in *aporia*, always aims always at *nous*, and always for the sake of *eudaimonia*. Or to put it another way, philosophy always begins in *avidya* and *samsara*, always aims at *prajñā*, and always for the sake of *nirvana*. This quest turns out to be built into Dasein itself.

Acknowledgments

I thank Tricia Perry, Susan Levin, and the Ven. Geshe Ngawang Samten for comments on earlier drafts of this essay.

Jay L. Garfield

Notes

1. This is not precisely true. There is a complex relationship between philosophy and religion in ancient Greece, with philosophical thought sometimes deriving content and problematic from explicitly religious ideas (Xenophanes) and philosophy sometimes taking religion to task (Plato). But that history is not directly relevant to the issues with which we are concerned here, since they are historically quite discontinuous with the present relationship between philosophy and religion in the West, and certainly not relevant to the relationship between Asian and Western philosophy.

2. There are two distinct levels at which I here note the affinity between specifically philosophical and specifically religious thought: On the one hand we often detect *residues* of religious ideas preserved unwittingly, or prereflectively in philosophical discourse (the categorical imperative). This is, to be sure, significant in demonstrating the pervasive impact of Semitic religious thought on "secular" philosophy. But more important for our purposes is the fact that philosophy and religion, as will be argued below, share important hermeneutic roles, even in the postenlightenment West (and this is explicitly acknowledged, for instance in Kant's understanding of the mission of the first *Critique* as circumscribing reason in order to make room for faith.

3. And here we see that second, deeper level of affinity at work.

7

Understanding Perspectivism: Nietzsche's Dialogue with His Contemporaries

Robert C. Holub

I

In the debate between Jacques Derrida and Hans-George Gadamer, which did not quite take place, the French deconstructionist concluded his remarks by sketching two questions about Friedrich Nietzsche.[1] The initial query Derrida formulates as one concerning the name "Nietzsche," but it actually entails issues of Nietzsche's identity. More precisely Derrida takes up here matters he had pursued in earlier texts: to what extent can we conceive of Nietzsche as an integral, unified subjectivity controlling all his texts, endowing them with a consistency and coherence of thought? Does the signature "Nietzsche" possess the status of a guarantee for the reader? Or do perhaps the biographical facts that stand behind the name and the life of the person named Friedrich Nietzsche provide some assurance of cohesion?[2] This question is particularly interesting for Nietzsche, since he insisted quite often on masks and disguises in his writing. In his various works he often appears as someone other than "Nietzsche," as Prince Free-as-a-Bird (*Prinz Vogelfrei*), or Zarathustra, or simply as an interlocutor whose remarks contradict or question claims made in a previous section of a given text. There are other thorny issues of identity about Nietzsche's writing as well: for example, those pertaining to the status of his literary remains and whether they contain his authentic philosophy or, rather, are simply thoughts and formulations that were rejected by the genuine

Nietzsche; the status of Nietzsche's letters and conversations, in which he occasionally expresses views that may not be consonant with his published texts; and finally the myriad Nietzsches that have appeared after his death, the result of interpreters exhibiting good and bad will in recruiting Nietzsche for various and sometimes nefarious causes. In short, the question of the name Nietzsche is sufficiently complex that it admits no easy answer.

The second question, to which Derrida devotes only a few pages, is closely related to the first and perhaps implied by it. It involves the notion of totality and asks whether we can conceive of Nietzsche's writings as coherent, as having a center or defining goal. If Nietzsche's name is conceived as a unity or a source, then there exists a locus from which the totality emanates. Conversely, if there is a grand concept informing Nietzsche's entire oeuvre, then we have reason to suspect an origin of this concept in a uniform and constant intention or subjectivity. Like the question of name, the question of totality is particularly urgent for Nietzsche's writings. Most of his major works consist of aphorisms, which give the impression of dispersion, rather than unity of purpose. Often even consecutive aphorisms treat apparently different topics; occasionally aphorisms are grouped together thematically, but even in these cases the reader has the impression that each aphorism could be read, interpreted, and understood on its own terms without the consideration of context or textual logic. The writings that are nonaphoristic are only loosely essayistic (*On the Genealogy of Morals*) or consist of parables and maxims (*Thus Spoke Zarathustra*). And again Nietzsche's reception supplies prima facie evidence for a nontotalized conception of his project: many commentators have sought a key to Nietzsche's writings, a term that unlocks the mystery of his sometimes elusive texts, and in the century or so since exegetes have busied themselves with his works, there have been numerous endeavors to construct a total Nietzsche from the disperse moments of his thought.

Derrida's questions about Nietzsche are posed by means of Heidegger, who was for a time Gadamer's teacher and from whom Gadamer drew a great deal for his ontologically based hermeneutics. With regard to the name Nietzsche, Derrida outlines two alternatives: one can regard this issue from the perspective of the different masks and simulacra employed by Nietzsche, rejecting traditional notions of identity, while affirming the nonidentical, always deferred "name" that constitutes itself beyond any empirical life in "the future of the world."[3] Here Derrida comes closest to Gadamer, his putative adversary in debate, since he suggests that "Nietzsche" acquires a meaning and unity in a sort of effective history, and that this history is a never completed process of which one is only one moment in a long chain or series of interpretations. Heidegger, however, chooses "the other way," defining the essence of the name "Nietzsche" from his thought. At the same time, Heidegger abjures everything biographical as inessential and peripheral. The biographical writings of Nietzsche's sister, Heidegger informs us, are helpful only for a position rejected as "life philosophy"; indeed, even Nietzsche's quirky autobiography, *Ecce Homo,* is characterized not as a part of Nietzsche's life history, but as a moment in the development of Western philosophy: "In truth, it is a matter of a 'destiny,' the destiny not of an individual but of the history of the era of modern times, of the end of the West."[4] What concerns Heidegger about the name "Nietzsche" is solely "the *trace* that that thought-path toward the will to power made into the history of Being."[5] With regard to the question of wholeness or totality, Heidegger tries to reconcile two Nietzschean principles, the will to power and eternal recurrence, making them both the totality of being (*die Ganzheit des Seienden*). According to this notorious interpretation, elaborated in the essays and lectures Heidegger wrote during the 1930s and 1940s, Nietzsche is the last metaphysician, the final philosophical voice, albeit one of the most interesting, in a lengthy tradition that neglected the question of the Being of beings.

What has Heidegger's influential, but rather eccentric view of Nietzsche to do with Gadamer's hermeneutics? How does Derrida's parting contribution, entitled "Guter Wille zur Macht (II)" (Good Will to Power II), engage his interlocutor and bring the "debate" between the two forward? At most it is an oblique response to Gadamer's more direct rejoinder, "Macht des guten Willens" (Power of Good Will).[6] Derrida had originally enlisted Heidegger's support in his initial, critical comments, as part of his objections to Gadamer's proposition of "good will."[7] The definition of the Being

of beings as will or as willing subjectivity, Derrida wrote in a Heideggerian vein, appears to belong to a former epoch characterized by
a metaphysics of the will. Derrida continues in his first contribution
by questioning Gadamer's reference to psychoanalysis, which calls
into question the simple, direct, and unified notion of good will to
which Gadamer has recourse.

In his second contribution Derrida adopts a different strategy: in
criticizing Heidegger's interpretation of Nietzsche, he is apparently
intent on conflating Heidegger and Gadamer, questioning the former's views, while implicating implicitly the latter. In order to understand Nietzsche, Heidegger insists on a unified subjectivity standing
behind his thought. Like Gadamer, therefore, whose hermeneutical
procedures similarly depend on an autonomous subject exhibiting
good will, Heidegger ignores the masks and simulacra that Derrida
considers the preferred path for exploring the name "Nietzsche."
The unified name "Nietzsche" produces a unity of thought, in which
the parts join in harmony, just as in a Gadamerian interpretation
the dialogical partners assume that question and response emanate
from discreet and unified sources. In Derrida's reading, Heidegger
and Gadamer are thus cast in the role of metaphysicians, while Derrida, antihermeneutical exegete par excellence, joins with Nietzsche
in celebrating postmetaphysical dissemination of will, beyond good
and evil intent.

The debate between Derrida and Gadamer demonstrates two
paths of interpretation that are apparently irreconcilable. One bases
the hermeneutical enterprise on encounters between sovereign subjects and assume that both parties seek to reach an understanding
in good faith. The presuppositions of this perspective are thus at
least a tentative fixation of meaning, although Gadamer emphasizes
repeatedly that understanding is a process, that meaning transforms
and is transformed, and that there is no single determinate sense to
any utterance. Derrida's path focuses on the qualifications and cave-
ats, which become the center of his interpretive undertaking. Proceeding from the questioning of a center from which meaning
emanates and the impossibility of stabilizing meaning, he affirms
play, dissemination, and undecidability. Yet he would concede, it
appears, that good will and understanding are an essential ethical

demand for any linguistic community, and that it would be absurd to deny that understanding between persons acting in good faith with one another does not occur. Thus the two models of interpretation, although different in their philosophical presuppositions, are mirror images in their results: Gadamer's center is Derrida's periphery, and vice versa. With regard to Nietzsche, Derrida emphasizes the nonunified status of his thought, while Gadamer would presumably postulate a "fusion of horizons," whereby we enter into a dialogic process with Nietzsche via his texts.

Does either of these two exegetical paths do justice to Nietzsche? Which procedure allows us to reach an authentic understanding of Nietzsche? In the following brief reading of "perspectivism," I would like to consider Nietzsche in a slightly different fashion from the alternatives Derrida sketches, viewing him as the result, not the origin of dissemination, and as a synchronic rather than a diachronic dialectician. This consideration may then suggest that the debate that did not really occur was too narrow to comprehend both Nietzsche's name and the totality over which that name presides.

II

In its most accessible form, perspectivism suggests simply a relativism about observations and evaluations of the phenomena in the external world, and this understanding of the term that has made it popular in the liberal interpretations of Nietzsche, especially those who cast Nietzsche in the role of champion of individual values against the hegemony of scientific objectivism. The actual term "perspectivism" occurs relatively infrequently in Nietzsche's writings, although related adjectival and substantive forms such as "perspectival" and "perspective" are somewhat more common. In passages in which "perspectivism" occurs, it is usually paired with or opposed to some other term. Perhaps the most suggestive citation for the liberal relativistic understanding of perspectivism comes from notes written during the 1880s where Nietzsche contrasts positivism with perspectivism. The former term, which had for Nietzsche an association with the empirical sciences in the nineteenth century, is criticized for its claim that there are only facts. Nietzsche counters with the assertion: "No, it is precisely facts that do not exist; what exists are interpretations. We can determine no fact 'in itself': perhaps it is senseless to even want to."[8] The conclusion that has frequently been drawn from this passage and others resembling it is that Nietzsche is claiming that in the absence of facts, each individual's view or "interpretation" is equally valid. Since perspectivism and natural science are antithetical, and since the latter propounds objective knowledge free from subjective distortions as its ideal, a reader can easily be deceived into believing that perspectivism entails "subjectivism," and that each perspective on the external world is legitimate.

Although there is no doubt that Nietzsche disputes the ability of human beings to grasp the world objectively, and that he therefore undercuts some presumptions of a simplistically conceived scientific method, his actual notion of perspectivism is more complex and, in fact, has a good deal to do with his understanding of the natural world. Indeed, to anticipate the subjectivist error, he explicitly criticizes the facile understanding of perspectivism as a subjective comprehension of the world: "'Everything is subjective,' you say: but even that is an interpretation. The 'subject' is nothing given, rather something added on, something that hides behind.—Is it not ultimately necessary to place the interpreter behind the interpretation? Even that is fiction, hypothesis."[9]

Since these are notes, it is not always easy to separate Nietzsche's voice from that of his hypothetical interlocutor. What seems obvious from this passage, however, is that Nietzsche does not believe in the relativism that is often attributed to him in simplistic interpretations. His particular criticism here is aimed at the notion of an already constituted subject perceiving from a fixed position. If we go along with Nietzsche and consider the subject itself as something that is a result of interpretation, just as the different views of the world are interpretations, then we cannot subscribe so easily to a relativistic hypothesis predicated on individual sovereignty and equality. The question concerning the necessity for positing an interpreter, a subject, a source, a cause for an interpretation would then come from the interlocutor, and Nietzsche's answer would be that there is no necessity for this supposition either. The central point here is that the nonexistence of facts or an objective standard does not imply an equality of interpretations or subject positions.

Indeed, the remainder of this passage demonstrates that Nietzsche employs perspectivism to criticize not only the philosophical presuppositions of natural science but also a long tradition in epistemology. Throughout his later work one of Nietzsche's main concerns is to question the most commonly held theories about how we know the world. Time and again he stresses what we find in this discussion of perspectivism: there is no eternal sense or meaning behind the world of perceptions. Nietzsche is openly antagonistic to Kantian epistemology: the division of the world into a realm of noumena and a realm of phenomena is consistently and repeatedly criticized as a deception. As Nietzsche writes in *Twilight of the Idols,* "The 'apparent' world is the only one: the 'real' world has only been *lyingly added. . . .*"[10] But Nietzsche is also rejecting the long tradition of Western thought which postulates something real or something more real than what we perceive. Plato's realm of ideas, which Nietzsche considers to be the first in a long line of epistemological errors, is exemplary for a tradition that propagates a split between appearance and reality. For Nietzsche, this split is the fundamental principle of all metaphysical thought, and his opposition to it is consistently maintained in his writings of the 1880s. About perspectivism, Nietzsche writes: "To the extent that the word 'knowledge' has any meaning at all, the world is knowable: but it is interpretable in different ways; it does not have any meaning behind it, rather countless meanings 'Perspectivism.' "[11] These are not the views of a subjective idealist; Nietzsche is not making the existence of the world dependent on the existence of a knowing subject. Rather, he is stating that knowledge is a human way of interacting with the world, and that for this reason there is no sense or meaning hidden from us. The interpretations or perspectives that we have are all that there is.

Most more recent and perceptive commentaries recognize that perspectivism is not an affirmation of relativism, and that it relates to Nietzsche's epistemological concerns in his late works. Alexander Nehemas, for example, contends that while perspectivism claims "that there is no view of the world that is binding on everyone"[12] and while it amounts to "a refusal to grade people and views along a single scale,"[13] the notion does not commit us to "the relativism that holds that one's view is as good as any other."[14] In his individual-istic interpretation of Nietzsche's notion, Nehemas contends that perspectivism posits that "one's own views are the best for oneself without implying that they need be good for anyone else."[15] Tracy Strong similarly disclaims a relativist interpretation of perspectivism when he writes that it "cannot mean that everything is in the eye of the beholder, nor that all is 'subjective.' "[16] But Strong, in contrast to Nehemas, does not incline to a radical affirmation of individuality, but rather to a dissolution of the individual. For him the perspectival world is one without an author,[17] and the perspectives of an "I" are themselves a multiplicity, irreducible to a single point or source. With perspectivism we do not have a pluralism of views and opinions of individual subjects, but rather the incorporation of multiple views into the individual subject. Perspectivism asserts, Strong contends, "that 'I' am a number of different ways of knowing and that there is no such entity as a permanent or privileged self."[18] Thus Nehemas and Strong represent two extremes of perspectivism: the radical af-firmation of the individual and its radical dissolution.

Neither of these views on perspectivism captures fully what Nietzsche invested in the term, since they both underestimate the degree to which Nietzsche's epistemological concerns were bol-stered by his understanding of natural science. Nietzsche's general outlook, especially in the 1880s, is anthropological and biological, and his "philosophical" positions are consistently informed by his somewhat unusual view of the physiology of the human being. Critics have long recognized that Nietzsche questions the existence of a unified subject, but his antisubjectivism, expressed clearly in the cita-tion above from the notebooks, is more often viewed in the context of Nietzsche's philosophy of language, when actually it relates more closely to his theory of instincts. Nietzsche is not content with the claim that everything is an interpretation; he asks further, as he does so often, what function does interpretation have in the larger scheme of life. His answer is that the very fact that we interpret the world in interacting with it reveals that interpretation is a human need. His reasoning is that the human being, in contrast to other creatures on earth, is the only species that exhibits the quirk of trying to understand the world during its confrontations with it. That there is no necessity to have knowledge, to interact with the world as a knowing being, seems to him proven by the observation of other animal species. For him it is not a subject located somewhere inside the brain or a spirit somewhere outside the body that enters into cognition, but rather a part of the material being.

Our cognition is therefore part of the necessity that comes with our humanity: it is "our needs" that interpret the world. But Nietzsche also believes there is no single position from which we interact with the world; rather, there may exist several competing positions from which we may receive conflicting interpretations. This proposition would follow from the fact that we have various competing needs and not one unified need about external phenomena. It is "our drives and their pro and con" that determine our interpretation and cognition: "Every drive is a type of thirst for power; every one has its perspective, which it wants to force on the other drives as a norm."[19] The human being is comprised of warring factions, not of unanimity. Our knowledge of the world is a product of conflicts and victories that go on within us and without our knowledge. Perspectivism, far from describing a notion of liberal tolerance for all viewpoints, is actually closer to a theory of drives and of the way in which internal struggles are fought out in the process we conceive as cognition.

The single mention of perspectivism in Nietzsche's published works bears out this view. It occurs in *The Gay Science* in one of the lengthiest aphorisms (354), which bears the title "On the genius of the species."[20] The largest part of the discussion revolves around consciousness, its origins, its functions, and its ramifications for the human being. Not surprisingly Nietzsche alludes from the outset to two realms of knowledge that have helped to provide the explanations he finds most useful: physiology and evolution ("the history of the animals"). Physiology and its adjectival forms appear with increasing frequency in Nietzsche's works of the 1880s and designate types of explanations that are tied to vital life forces. Often physiology is placed in juxtaposition to metaphysics, theology, ethics, politics, and economics as a mode of clarifying real interactions rather than their reflexes in the mind. Evolutionary biology was a constant source of

Robert C. Holub

reference for Nietzsche, as it was for all Nietzsche's contemporaries, when formulating judgments on human development,[21] and to exclude Nietzsche's dependence on the biological sciences, as Heidegger does,[22] can only lead us away from Nietzsche's own, most vital concerns.

Nietzsche's reading of the scientific theories of his times leads him to believe that consciousness is a secondary organ. All of the functions that are necessary for life can be carried out well—perhaps even better—without recourse to consciousness, which consists of a mirror of these actions in the mind. "We could think, feel, will, and remember, and we could also 'act' in every sense of that word, and yet none of all this would have to 'enter our consciousness' (as one says metaphorically)." Indeed, for most of what we do, consciousness is superfluous or, as Nietzsche will contend when he dissects moral values, pernicious. "Even now, for that matter, by far the greatest portion of our life actually takes place without this mirror effect; and this is true even of our thinking, feeling, and willing life, however offensive this may sound to older philosophers."[23] On the basis of his natural scientific knowledge Nietzsche is thus claiming that consciousness is a late-developing feature of the species and something that is wholly unnecessary to life. Although it is lauded as the "genius of the species," in reality it is extra baggage, something that has no value for those actions that we usually consider most important in our lives.

This reevaluation of the role of consciousness is perhaps the most original and provocative dimension of Nietzsche's philosophy. It is posited in radical opposition to most previous philosophical thought, in particular to German idealism from Kant through Hegel and their epigones, in whose writings consciousness was conceived as the pinnacle of development and as the most commonly cited feature distinguishing the human being from the animal world. Nietzsche had inverted expectations regarding the human-animal distinction as early as the second *Untimely Meditation*, where he makes human beings envious of creaturely happiness. In his later works he critiques his idealist predecessors as well as traditional opinion by repeatedly deprecating consciousness, intellect, reason, and the realm of ideas. While most philosophers have considered consciousness a source of perfection, Nietzsche feels it is a symptom of immaturity; while previous thinkers count on consciousness to rectify mistakes and to bridle the wayward passions, Nietzsche believes it is the source of errors; and while common wisdom places thought above drives in their contribution to human behavior, Nietzsche overturns this hierarchy:

> Consciousness is the last and latest development of the organic and hence what is most unfinished and unstrong. Consciousness gives rise to countless errors that lead an animal or man to perish sooner than necessary, "exceeding destiny," as Homer puts it. If the conserving association of the instincts were not so very much more powerful, and if it did not serve on the whole as a regulator, humanity would have to perish of its misjudgments and its fantasies with open eyes, of its lack of thoroughness and its credulity—in short, of its consciousness; rather, without the former, humanity would long have disappeared.[24]

In this passage Nietzsche, as always, conceives of the development of consciousness in terms of the paradigm of evolutionary biology and physiology. For him consciousness is one way—and not a very efficient way at that[25]—in which the human being mediates drives and desires with the external world.

Two problems arise from this view of consciousness. The first has to do with the reason that most previous thinkers and traditional wisdom assigns such a priority to thought. If the situation is as Nietzsche describes it, then why have we been deceived for so long about the real role of consciousness in our interactions with the world? For Nietzsche the answer to this question is that the hegemony of consciousness—not over our actions, but over our belief concerning what guides our actions—is itself a long process in the evolution of humankind. Nietzsche clarifies this process with regard to reason in one of his notebooks. If the human being had acted according to reason, he maintains, the species would have died out long ago. Reason, like consciousness, is a faculty that itself has a history inside the human economy: "Reason is a slowly developing auxiliary organ that for an extremely long time fortunately had no power to determine human beings; it worked in the service of the organic drives and emancipated itself slowly to equality with them . . . and later, much later to predominance."[26]

Because of this development to predominance, we usually misconstrue not only the role of consciousness and reason, but the true sequence in any given action. Nietzsche repeatedly uses our confusion of cause and effect to demonstrate his point. He does not mean that cause and effect do not exist in nature, that one billiard ball striking another does not produce motion in the second. Rather, he is referring to our predilection to attribute a priority to our own thoughts, ideas, or intentions when we ourselves perform an action. The confusion here is that, according to Nietzsche, the consciousness of the thought, the idea, or the intention, is actually itself one of the effects of something more primary—the satisfaction of some instinct or drive, for example—and it is only our customary way of thinking about our own consciousness and will as sovereign that leads us to believe that somehow a nonmaterial force is a controlling power. Our high regard for consciousness, reason, intellect, ideas, thoughts, and autonomous will are products of a long evolution, but they are simultaneously obfuscations of the genuine hierarchy that is operative in the preservation of the human species.

The second problem that Nietzsche's explanation of consciousness raises is why it came into being in the first place. If reason and intellect are so inefficient in dealing with the world, if we are better off relying on our instincts, then why did the species need to develop an organ that reflects on knowledge? Nietzsche's answer to this is that the development of consciousness was ultimately driven by our need to communicate with one another. At first this need arose only between human beings, in particular between human beings in the hierarchical relationship of master and slave. But Nietzsche also suggests that human beings, as vulnerable creatures, needed communication in order to protect themselves from the dangers of the external world. Gradually the human species therefore had to receive some kind of understanding of its actions, thoughts, feelings, and movements, and the entrance of these "reflections" into consciousness occurs in order to facilitate communication with others. Consciousness develops, in short, so that the human being will "know" him- or herself and can pass this "knowledge" along to others members of the species. Nietzsche is explaining something that is quite unusual here, and it requires a dual use of the notions of knowing and thinking. He is often compelled to qualify these words or put them in quotation marks because the knowledge and thinking that reach consciousness are only a small portion of the knowledge and thinking that a human being possesses: "Man, like every living being, thinks continually without knowing it; the thinking that rises to consciousness is only the smallest part of all this—the most superficial and worst part—for only this conscious thinking takes the form of words, which is to say signs of communication, and this fact uncovers the origin of consciousness."[27]

We can see that Nietzsche is not completely consistent in facing this problem. If consciousness, intellect, and reason are truly superfluous, or even "in the main superfluous,"[28] then they could presumably be eliminated without any adverse effect on the species. Yet Nietzsche suggests that these capacities and organs do respond to human needs and may even be beneficial to human survival. Nietzsche's main achievement, however, does not lie in his providing a reason for the appearance of consciousness but rather in his reduction of consciousness to an auxiliary role in our physiological existence.

Interesting in the passage just cited is the role Nietzsche ascribes to language. In contrast to twentieth-century theorists who place language at the center of the human universe, linguistic ability represents for Nietzsche a secondary characteristic that is on the same level as consciousness. Language, of course, is not representation in Nietzsche's scheme; it does not simply reflect the external world. But it is a mirror, however distorted this mirror may be, of internal sensations. Nietzsche's position on language as a response to inner stimuli is consistently maintained from the 1870s, when he turned to this theme in connection with reflections on rhetoric, until the 1880s, when his hypotheses received a more physiological underpinning. In his notes for a lecture course on ancient rhetoric, Nietzsche had already provided a brief sketch of linguistic utterance based on a neurological model:

The human being creating language does not capture things or events, but stimuli: he does not reproduce sensations, but rather reproductions of sensations. The sensation, through which a nerve stimulus is called forth, does not capture the thing itself: this sensation is represented externally by an image . . . . It is not things that enter our consciousness, but the way in which we relate to these things: the πιθανόν [the persuasiveness]. The complete essence of things is never captured. Our tonal utterances in no way wait until our perception and experience has helped us to a many-sided, somehow respectable cognition of things: they occur immediately when the stimulus has been felt.[29]

In 1888 the explanation is similar in its scientific assumptions. Nietzsche believes that internal experience enters consciousness after it finds a language that the individual understands, but the entire process is precipitated by the stimulation of nerves: "The whole notion of 'inner experience' rests on the fact that one seeks and imagines a cause for the excitation of nerve centers."[30] The secret to language, whose development goes "hand in hand"[31] with the appearance of consciousness, is that it is reaction to neurological stimuli.

One of the consequences Nietzsche draws from this "scientifically" informed view of language and consciousness is that both are inaccurate registers of individual sensations. By the time that nerve stimuli have been translated into consciousness and are expressed in language, they have been reduced to a common denominator and robbed of their uniqueness. The social nature of language and consciousness is part of our "herd mentality" and has to be carefully distinguished from one's individuality, which is leveled in the process of translation. This is the essence of perspectivism for Nietzsche, a word that he uses synonymously with phenomenalism. It refers not to the equal validity of all viewpoints, but rather to the necessary inaccuracy of all contents of consciousness and all expressions of these contents in language.

Owing to the nature of animal consciousness, the world of which we can become conscious is only a surface- and sign-world, a world that is made common and meaner; whatever becomes conscious becomes by the same token shallow, thin, relatively stupid, general, sign, herd signal; all becoming conscious involves a great and thorough corruption, falsification, reduction to superficialities, and generalization.[32]

References to perspectivism in Nietzsche's work are therefore usually accompanied by disparaging remarks. For example, in an extensive note written during the spring of 1884, Nietzsche observes that in making the "mechanical world order" conscious, we need a "perspective-apparatus" that makes possible "(1) a certain standing still [*ein gewisses Stillstehen*], (2) simplification, (3) selection and elimination."[33] This apparatus creates the impression of stable being instead of allowing us to perceive eternal becoming, and it permits us only a limited and therefore inaccurate perspective on the world. For this reason Nietzsche claims: "This perspectival world, this world for the eye, feeling, and ear is very false, compared even with a much finer sensory apparatus."[34] Nietzsche holds out the possibility that we can achieve more sensitive and accurate views of the world as our consciousness develops. He emphasizes that in evolutionary terms consciousness is a recently acquired capability that has perhaps not reached its fullest potential in the species. But for the time being, consciousness, language, reason, and intellect—those features of the human species that have usually been valued most highly—condemn us to a false and limited perspectivism.

III

How did Nietzsche acquire his views on perspectivism? What were the dominant influences on his thinking about the way in which human beings take in and process phenomena in the world? In a general fashion the answer to these questions has already been given: Nietzsche's perspectivism is an outgrowth not only of his philosophical readings and in particular of his rejection of the idealism so prevalent in official academic circles after German unification but also, and more importantly, of his intensive occupation with natural science in the last half of the nineteenth century. Most interpreters of Nietzsche—and to a large degree Derrida, Heidegger, and Gadamer could be included in this group—have downplayed Nietzsche's connections to discourses in his own era. To some extent Nietzsche contributed to the view that he was distant from his contemporaries. From almost the beginning of his writings he cultivated the image of the untimely mediator whose thoughts conflicted with his epoch, and who was largely unrecognized by a philistine and insipid intellectual milieu. When his books during his lifetime did not receive the recognition Nietzsche thought they deserved, he was privately disappointed and bitter, but he concealed his dismay

Robert C. Holub

behind a facade of untimeliness, thus separating himself even further from those with whom he was really in closest intellectual contact.

Nietzsche also adopted a style that tended to obscure his contemporary interlocutors: he seldom engages directly the books and authors he was reading, and when he does include proper names, they are usually those of more venerable authorities, rather than contemporaries. Thus his allusions, especially in his published works, give a distorted view of his actual reading as reflected in his personal library or his borrowings from numerous public or university libraries. Many of the works that influenced him most are rarely cited directly, and although he borrowed from others his views on important philosophers, he prefers to write about the known thinkers rather than about his actual sources. This writing practice has led or misled most commentators into thinking that Nietzsche was simply one "giant" communicating with others "across the bleak intervals of ages," an image he himself employed in *On the Advantage and Disadvantage of History for Life.*[35] Only more careful research has demonstrated that Nietzsche paid considerable attention to discourses of nineteenth-century Europe, and that he was much more in touch with his contemporaries, albeit often in a critical fashion, than one suspects from his writings.

One need not search far for Nietzsche's dialogical partners with regard to his views on perspectivism. Friedrich Albert Lange, whose *History of Materialism* was perhaps the dominant source of Nietzsche's knowledge of the natural sciences, evinces a dependence on species-centered sense-experience that closely parallels Nietzsche's views. Like Nietzsche, Lange occasionally pushes his thoughts on perspectivism to extremes, including in his speculations the possibility that even our sense of three-dimensional space may be perspectival. At one point he asks us to imagine a being who can only perceive in two dimensions; certain mathematical and geometrical knowledge would be possible for such a being, although it would never be able to fathom any of our notions about three-dimensional spaces and figures. It would remain trapped in its perspective, deceived into believing that the phenomenal world is somehow true, and not merely an interpretation.

Lange also takes us in the other direction and speculates about the possibility of beings who can perceive a fourth dimension unknown to us. In this case we can see that our view of the world would be a partial one, and that once these perceptions are further processed by a consciousness that flattens out individual difference, we are dealing with a superficial and falsified reality, even if it is the only one to which we have conceptual access. Lange's point has to do ultimately with our inability to fathom the thing-in-itself, while Nietzsche eventually will want to eliminate the thing-in-itself as a illegitimate philosophical projection. But it is nonetheless evident that Nietzsche's anthropologically tinged notions of perspectivism are developed in conjunction with previous discourses on materialism and the natural sciences.[36]

Lange does not introduce the word "perspectivism" to deal with our sense-experience and our ability to comprehend only a phenomenal reality. Gustav Teichmüller, however, employs this notion in a fashion that is very similar to Nietzsche's. When Nietzsche arrived in Basel in 1869, Teichmüller was one of the two philosophy professors at the Swiss university. The chair he occupied had been established only in 1867; its first occupant was Wilhelm Dilthey, who left after a year. Teichmüller did not last much longer: in 1871 he accepted a position at Dorpat (Tartu), and Nietzsche applied unsuccessfully to become his successor, probably because he was simply lacking credentials in philosophy.[37] Nietzsche does not appear to have developed any particular friendship with Teichmüller during their short overlapping tenure at Basel. In the 1880s, however, although his name never appears in a published volume, Nietzsche's notebooks contain a dozen direct references to Teichmüller and multiple allusions to his thought.

At issue for "perspectivism" is the monograph *Die wirkliche und die scheinbare Welt* (*The real and the apparent world*), which was published in 1882. Nietzsche evidently solicited a copy of this book from his friend and former colleague at Basel, Franz Overbeck, after he had been impressed with Teichmüller's three-volume work *Neue Studien zur Geschichte der Begriffe* (*New Studies on the History of Concepts*, 1876–79). His feeling of intellectual proximity to Teichmüller is indicated by his comment that he is "grist to my mill."[38] Nietzsche's relationship

Robert C. Holub

to Teichmüller is typical for his relationship to contemporaries: those who he valued may receive favorable mention in letters, and their writings may be cited or even excerpted in notebooks, but Nietzsche rarely divulges to his readership the people with whom he was in closest intellectual contact.

Teichmüller associates perspectivism with our ability to perceive and process phenomena of the world. "The perspectival image that we gain" is "appearance" (*Schein*); the world as it appears to our eyes is "perspectivally ordered," and neither a telescope nor a microscope, which enhance our visual powers, can reveal the "real" structure of the world.[39] Teichmüller thus differs from the mature Nietzsche and agrees with Kant about the dualistic structure of things: as phenomena for us and as essences about which we can no nothing. But Teichmüller comes closer to Nietzsche when he interprets this dualism in a pragmatic fashion: since we can never know the essence of things, we have to accept the phenomenal world as the only reality we have and act accordingly. God may be able to gain an overview of "reality," but human beings are limited and have to work with the restricted means at our disposal. "The only thing that remains for us to do is to take the multiplicity of sensations themselves as the object and declare their congruence in the subject for the perspectival image."[40] Teichmüller's recourse here to a subject that escapes the perspectival is something to which Nietzsche would object in his later works; for Nietzsche the subject remains a projection that is ultimately a result of our inevitably restricted perspective as well.

Despite their differences, however, it is evident that Teichmüller and Nietzsche share a common perspective on perspectivism. Indeed, the former Basel professor of philosophy supplied not only the term itself, but also some of the inspiration for its radical appropriation in Nietzsche's writings. At one point Teichmüller notes that temporal order is regulated by a thinking subject. There is no reason that we cannot think in reverse, just as we can conceive of b + a as easily as a + b. "In fact," he concludes, "we can go through temporal sequence forward or backward as we wish in our thoughts."[41] In the fifth book of *The Gay Science,* Nietzsche comments as follows: "We cannot look around our own corner: it is a hopeless curiosity that wants to know what other kinds of intellects and perspectives there *might* be; for example, whether some beings might be able to experience time backward, or alternately forward and backward (which would involve another direction of life and another concept of cause and effect)."[42] Here Nietzsche takes Teichmüller's notion of the perspectival nature of time and of the reversibility of temporal sequence in thought and converts it into a radical statement about temporal perspectivism in all human perception. Nietzsche and Teichmüller do not think alike about every philosophical issue; Nietzsche is more radical and daring, and less tied to the Kantian tradition. But both philosophers share the fundamental belief that our perception of the world is perspectival: human beings are biologically equipped for specific and limited interactions with the world, so that our knowledge, even the knowledge gained from the natural sciences, is only, ultimately, *our* knowledge.

The relationship between Nietzsche and Teichmüller has hardly been a secret to Nietzsche scholarship. As early as 1913 Hermann Nohl pointed to *Die wirkliche und die scheinbare Welt* as a source for Nietzsche's perspectivism,[43] and since that time others have reiterated the structure of influence.[44] In the tradition of historical studies on Nietzsche there have been sporadic efforts made to discover other influences, and a catalogue of writers whose thought has affected Nietzsche could be easily compiled. Customarily when we discover a similarity in terminology or thought between Nietzsche and someone whose work predates his, we regard Nietzsche as the recipient, and the older author as a source or inspiration, just as we consider Nietzsche the source for someone's thought who comes after him. But the matter of influence can be viewed somewhat differently.

It is perhaps misleading to consider Nietzsche, or any significant thinker, to be the product or result of the books he read, just as it is inaccurate to regard him as simply genial and creative, and cast his followers as pure epigones. Nietzsche is not an end point, nor can he be viewed purely as a beginning or origin, but rather he, like any pivotal figure in intellectual history, serves as a transmission point, a junction where thoughts cross and become intensified in a particularly concentrated fashion. As a participant in a conversation, or in various conversations that occurred in the second half of the nineteenth century, he is formed by the thoughts of others in a dialogic relationship, and he, in turn, becomes for those who read him an interlocutor in further discourses. Nietzsche does not take from Teichmüller or Lange as much as he enters into an ongoing discussion of which they are a part. He may have various impacts on particular discussions: through him a given discourse may be popularized, concluded, shunted into dead ends, productively continued, or prematurely abrogated. But it is important, if we are going to understand his contributions, to establish what the discussion was about, as well as how, where, and why he engages in the conversation.

Derrida's response to Gadamer took up the questions of Nietzsche's name and his totality. The foregoing remarks show that these two questions can be conceived differently from the way they were posed by Derrida himself, by Derrida's foil Heidegger, or, implicitly, by his adversary Gadamer. Nietzsche's name is not only the place of a subject, whether unified or dispersed, autonomous or heteronomous, but also, and perhaps more importantly, the site at which discourses meet, become transformed, and emerge for his future interlocutors. Identity from this perspective does not adhere to a subjectivity as a point of emerging thought, but to the intersections where we encounter contributions to a series of varied conversations. Similarly, the totality of Nietzsche's work does not entail a center or original point from which his philosophy unfolds, but a bundle of nexuses through which discourses pass. Within this framework the unity of his thought is perhaps less interesting than the continuity and trajectory of the discourses with which he interacts.

Ultimately the question is one of hermeneutics: how do we understand Nietzsche and his writings? Derrida suggests that there are multiple Nietzsches and even more possible understandings of him, and that seeking a determinate meaning for him and his texts is not only illegitimate philosophically but also against the Nietzschean spirit. Gadamer, by contrast, considers understanding solely from the perspective of the dialogue into which we enter with Nietzsche's works. But if we are to be consistent with Gadamer's hermeneutics and at the same time give credence to Derrida's insights, then we will want to consider as well the multiplicity of discussions that Nietzsche himself conducted, since a neglect of such considerations deprives his writing of its most important context and attenuates his meaning. Viewing Nietzsche outside of his nineteenth-century context, an all-too-frequent occurrence especially in "philosophical" commentary, leads to a facile and quite often distorted misconstrual of his *oeuvre;* by understanding what he understood, however, we have a better opportunity of engaging in a meaningful dialogue with his multivalent thought.

Notes

1. The texts in this debate are contained in *Text und Interpretation,* edited by Philippe Forget (Munich: Fink, 1984), 24–77.

2. See Jacques Derrida, "Octobiographies: The Teaching of Nietzsche and the Politics of the Proper Name," translated by Aviatal Ronell, in *The Ear of the Other: Octobiography, Transference, Translation* (New York: Schocken, 1982), 1–38.

3. Jacques Derrida, *"Guter Wille zur Macht* (II)," in *Text und Interpretation,* edited by Forget, 66.

4. Martin Heidegger, "Nietzsche as the Thinker of the Consummation of Metaphysics," *Nietzsche,* vols. 3 and 4 (bound together), translated by Joan Stambaugh et al. (San Francisco: Harper & Row, 1991), 3.

5. Heidegger, "Nietzsche as Thinker," 4.

6. Hans-Georg Gadamer, "Und dennoch: Macht des Guten Willens," in *Text und Interpretation,* edited by Forget, 59–61.

7. Jacques Derrida, "Guter Wille zur Macht (I)," *Text und Interpretation,* edited by Forget, 56–58.

8. Friedrich Nietzsche, *Sämtliche Werke, Kritische Studienausgabe,* 12, edited by Giorgio Colli and Mazzino Montinari (Munich and Berlin: dtv & de Gruyter, 1967–77), 315. Translations from the German texts are my own.

9. Nietzsche, *Sämtliche Werke,* 12, 315.

10. Friedrich Nietzsche, *Twilight of the Idols, in Twilight of the Idols/The Antichrist,* translated by R. J. Hollingdale (London: Penguin, 1968), 46.

11. Nietzsche, *Sämtliche Werke,* 315.

12. Alexander Nehemas, *Nietzsche: Life as Literature* (Cambridge: Harvard University Press, 1985), 67.

13. Ibid., 68.

14. Ibid., 72.

15. Ibid.

16. Tracy B. Strong, *Friedrich Nietzsche and the Politics of Transfiguration* (Berkeley: University of California Press, 1988), 299.

17. Ibid., 305.

18. Ibid., 308.

19. Nietzsche, *Sämtliche Werke*, 12, 315.

20. The first four books of *The Gay Science* were published in 1882, but the fifth book, which contains aphorisms 343–383, was appended to the work in 1887. Nietzsche's views on perspectivism in *The Gay Science* thus occur at about the same time he wrote the notes cited above from volume 12 of his *Sämtliche Werke* (*Complete Works*).

21. See Andrea Orsucci, *Orient-Okzident: Nietzsches Versuch einer Loslösung vom europäischen Weltbild* (Berlin: Walter de Gruyter, 1996): "Nietzsche hat, wie es scheint, die Entwicklung der Biologie zwischen den 60er und 80er Jahren genau verfolgt. . . . Die verschiedenen Problemstellungen und Forschungsrichtungen, die in der Biologie jener Jahre nacheinander ins Zentrum des Interesses rücken, finden in Nietzsches Aufzeichnungen und Veröffentlichungen nachweisbaren Niederschlag" (56–57).

22. See Heidegger, "Nietzsche's Alleged Biologism," *Nietzsche*, 3 and 4, edited by David Farrell Krell, 39–47.

23. Friedrich Nietzsche, *The Gay Science*, translated by Walter Kaufmann (New York: Vintage Books, 1974), 297 (§354).

24. Ibid., 84–85 (§11).

25. In a later aphorism in *The Gay Science* (§257–§327) he calls intellect "a clumsy, glooming, creaky machine that is difficult to start."

26. Nietzsche, *Sämtliche Werke*, 9, 533.

27. Nietzsche, *The Gay Science*, 298–299 (§354).

28. Ibid., 297 (§354).

29. Friedrich Nietzsche, *Werke. Kritische Gesamtausgabe*, 2, ed. Giorgio Colli and Mazzino Montinari (Berlin: De Gruyter, 1967), 426.

30. Nietzsche, *Sämtliche Werke* 13, 459.

31. Nietzsche, *The Gay Science*, 299 (§354).

32. Ibid., 300 (§354).

33. Nietzsche, *Sämtliche Werke* 11, 99.

34. Ibid., 146.

35. Friedrich Nietzsche, *On the Advantage and Disadvantage of History for Life*, translated by Peter Preuss (Indianapolis: Hackett, 1980), 53.

36. Friedrich Albert Lange, *Geschichte des Materialismus und Kritik seiner Bedeutung in der Gegenwart*, vol. 2 (Leipzig: J. Baedeker, 1908), 429–430.

37. See Curt Paul Janz, *Friedrich Nietzsche: Biographie in drei Bänden*, 1 (Munich: Carl Hanser, 1993, 2nd rev. ed.), 398–400.

38. Friedrich Nietzsche, *Sämtliche Briefe*, 6 (Berlin: De Gruyter, 1975–1984), 449.

39. Gustav Teichmüller, *Die wirkliche und die scheinbare Welt* (Breslau: Wilhelm Koebner, 1882), 183.

40. Ibid., 185.

41. Ibid., 203.

42. Nietzsche, *The Gay Science*, 336 (§374).

43. Hermann Nohl, "Eine historische Quelle zu Nietzsches Perspektivismus: G. Teichmüller, die wirkliche und die scheinbare Welt," *Zeitschrift für Philosophie und philosophische Kritik* 149 (1913), 106–115.

44. Karl-Heinz Dickopp, "Zum Wandel von Nietzsches Selbstverständnis—Afrikan Spir und Gustav Teichmüller," *Zeitschrift für philosophische Forschung* 24 (1970), 50–71; Janz, *Friedrich Nietzsche: Biographie in drei Bänden*, vol. 2, 399; Klaus Spiekermann, *Naturwissenschaft als subjektlose Macht? Nietzsches Kritik physikalischer Grundkonzepte* (Berlin, De Gruyter, 1991), 135.

8

"We Understand Differently, If We Understand at All": Gadamer's Ontology of Language Reconsidered

Jens Kertscher

I

The view that linguistic meaning is not simply present to us in the same way as are natural objects has become increasingly prevalent within modern philosophy of language and is today widely accepted. On this point, Gadamer's hermeneutics is in agreement with other contemporary approaches to language—whether they be Wittgenstein's later philosophy, Davidson's theory of radical interpretation, or even the theories of communication of Habermas and Apel.[1] Considering that what we actually understand when we understand a language is indeed not an object of our experience, either natural or artificial, the truth of the view at issue here might seem quite self-evident. Yet despite this, it nevertheless represents something of a philosophical challenge to common sense: if linguistic meaning does not exist in the same way as something that can be represented in an objective manner, then what is the character of its particular existence in the world—assuming that it does exist at all?

On the one hand, language might be considered as a presupposition of our relationship to the world through which objective being is disclosed. In this case, language may appear as a limitation of my world, and so as something that cannot be objectified within my world, in much the sense that is set out in Ludwig Wittgenstein's *Tractatus*.[2] Wittgenstein's method of drawing a limit from within language is directed against the metaphysical attempt to describe the relationship *between* world and language on the model of what exists or happens *in* the world and can therefore be given linguistic representation or description. Similar accounts also appear in the work of Heidegger and Gadamer.

On the other hand, one might conceive linguistic meaning as objective, as something existing independently of a concrete natural language and its speakers. Meaning could then be viewed as either an ideal object, as constituted through a subjective speaker intention or as based in objective designation conventions. Theories of linguistic meaning that conceive meaning as something merely expressed or designated by linguistic signs, thus referring to an object given in an internal experience, have been called *objectivistic*.[3] According to objectivistic theories of meaning, the function of linguistic signs is to designate, make explicit, or communicate what is given as an ideal object. Hence the main problem is to explain how ideal objects can guarantee determination of linguistic meaning in the constantly changing and varied situations of their application by speakers.

The aim of this essay is to outline the extent to which Hans-Georg Gadamer's hermeneutical ontology of language can indeed be interpreted as exemplifying an antiobjectivistic conception of language and understanding. First, I will explain in more detail what is meant by an objectivistic conception of meaning and how it can be criticized. I will do so by discussing Edmund Husserl's theory of meaning, which can be considered a paradigm of the objectivistic view of language. Second, I will characterize in detail Gadamer's position. One of the most important insights of his philosophy is that historicity and the conditions of finitude, which are manifested in the "horizontality" of all understanding, are a limit as well as a condition of the possibility of understanding. A radical consequence of accepting this insight is the disappearance of the objective foundations of both meaning and understanding. If linguistic meaning can no longer be analyzed adequately as an object that exists in an ideal manner in the world, it follows then that understanding cannot be conceived as the identification or correct grasping of an ideal entity intended or designated by a linguistic expression or sign. Gadamer concluded from this that the difference between understanding correctly and understanding differently fails, and should therefore be abandoned.

This claim has been the subject of much controversy. Critics of Gadamer have disputed his ideas of both the finitude and situation relativity of understanding by outlining the importance of the ideals of truth, or at least of validity, that guide attempts to understand linguistic expressions.[4] This criticism is partially justified if one takes into consideration Gadamer's reliance on Heideggerian concepts as traditionally understood. The last part of this essay, however, outlines an antiobjectivist conception of understanding that avoids Gadamer's conservative presuppositions by emphasizing the practical aspect that is implied in the processes of language use and understanding.

II

At the beginning, I referred to objectivism in the philosophy of language as a view that conceives meaning as an ideal entity existing independently of concrete natural languages and individual speech acts and patterns. What this means can be exemplified by an examination of Husserl's theory of meaning in the *Logical Investigations*. This examination will be relatively brief, but its aim will be merely to provide a general characterization of objectivistic semantics rather than a detailed discussion of the particular problems connected with Husserl's theory of meaning. Husserl is an obvious starting point, in the present context, since he is, along with Frege, one of the most prominent representatives of semantic objectivism. Moreover, as Gadamer explicitly points out in an essay from 1963, entitled *Die phänomenologische Bewegung* (*The Phenomenological Movement*), it is also clear that Husserl neglects language as a philosophical problem in its own right. Indeed, it is Gadamer's claim that this limitation in Husserl's views on language is what inspired Heidegger's own philosophy of language as well as Gadamer's attempt to complete and to surpass the phenomenological method by hermeneutical reflection on language and its roots in everyday life, or in more general terms, in the forms of life of particular cultures.[5]

The theory of linguistic propositions that was developed in the *Logical Investigations* is based upon certain presuppositions that can no longer be considered self-evident. According to Husserl, linguistic propositions are expressions (*Ausdrücke*), that is, external, sign-mediated representations of an internal thought process. In this light, the meaning of linguistic signs is the result of the subjective fulfillment of so-called *intentional experiences,* which relate the sign with the intended object of reference, the object of the expression. These are the basic presuppositions of Husserl's phenomenological theory of meaning that are also responsible for the difficulties to which it is exposed.

In the first *Logical Investigation,* entitled "Expression and Meaning" (*Ausdruck und Bedeutung*),[6] Husserl's characteristic combination of objectivism and intentionalism (his reduction of linguistic expressions to ideal or mental representations and, consequently, their reduction to linguistically expressed meaning-intentions) becomes particularly clear. Husserl leaves no doubt that, according to him, the decisive function of language does not lie in the communicative exchange of information but in the monologue of a solitary speaker who expresses and discloses, by means of linguistic signs, the contents of his consciousness.[7] The ascription of the determination of sense to the solitary speaking subject is based upon the conviction that linguistic signs are the material side of ideal meaning which, for its part, represents the pure essence of linguistic expression. As Husserl maintains, meanings "are an ideally closed set of general objects, to which being thought or being expressed are alike contingent."[8] The contingency of expression mentioned by Husserl, extends not only to what Frege has called the grasping (*Fassen*) of a thought, but also to the *form* of expression. In Husserl's view, it is of no importance whether ideal meanings are expressed in a poetic, rhetoric, or in the fact-stating manner of scientific speech. His thesis, which he shares with all objectivistic semantics, is that meaning is an independent linguistic function, in the sense of an ideal object that has to be phenomenologically separated from individual speech acts.

The strict separation of meaning and expression follows not only from the fact that one specific meaning can obviously be formulated in different ways, but that different sentences can be understood as sentences with the same sense. Husserl therefore asserts consistently: "If we or others repeat the same sentence with like intention, each of us has his own *phaenomena,* his own words and his own nuances of understanding. Over against this unbounded multiplicity of individual experiences, is the selfsame element expressed in them all, 'selfsame' in the very strictest sense."[9] Husserl would never have questioned this assumption; on the contrary, he claimed that it was evident from a phenomenological standpoint, and therefore he conceived the relationship between identity of meaning and difference of expression against the background of what we might, along with Derrida, call the philosophy of "presence."[10] In this light, the meaning of a linguistic expression is that which a speaker intends by the use of linguistic signs and it is that intention that must be grasped by the hearer when he perceives those signs. Consequently, the hearer can only approach the intended sense to a greater or lesser degree of precision. Hence the problem of the relationship between identity of meaning and difference of expression does not only touch the relationship between the identical meaning and the variety of linguistic signs but also that of its relationship to the variety of individual acts of understanding which are always extended in time.

One must then ask how to describe this relationship between the individual act of understanding and the meaning understood and what is the result of this kind of understanding. Husserl has explained this relationship between identical, absolutely determined meaning and temporally individuated acts of understanding by introducing what he calls a "meaning intention" (*Bedeutungsintention*).[11] Its function is to connect linguistic signs with meaning in order to conceive signs as representatives of the object of reference rather than of the meaning itself. According to Husserl's own explanation, a meaning intention is "an understanding, a peculiar act-experience relating to the expression, [which] is present . . . shines through the expression . . . lends it meaning and thereby a relation to objects."[12] Understanding is a mental process, which consists in grasping what is being spoken about, or, in Husserl's terms, what intentional object the speaker is referring to when he speaks.

Meaning thus has the structure of identity in difference.[13] In the *Logical Investigations,* Husserl interprets the identity of meaning as an identity of species. It is a generic class that is individuated in particular acts of meaning "just as Redness *in specie* is to the slips of paper which lie here, and which all 'have' the same redness."[14] This permits Husserl to characterize the identity of meaning as repeatable, communicable, and translatable. Meaning is repeatable because it is beyond time;[15] it can be fulfilled by subjective, temporally variable meaning-intentions as an ideal and fully determined identity. It is communicable because meaning, as a logical thought, can be grasped identically by different reasonable subjects. Finally, it is translatable because the content of meaning is not exclusively and necessarily linked to its materialization in a specific phonetic or graphic system.

The aim of a correct translation is to render the sense of the sentences of one language through illustration by means of analogous sentences in the other language. What is said in a sentence—its sense—corresponds to what persists in all correct translations. Variations may appear where contingent factors come into play, for instance, connotations that throw into bold relief the content of what has been said in a certain manner. By doing so, however, such connotations and colorations of thought bring into light a dimension of language that varies not only from language to language but also from speaker to speaker, and therefore cannot be classed with the logical essence of what has been said. In short, objectivistic theories of meaning conceive understanding as the correct grasping of the meaning expressed or intended by linguistic signs—a meaning that is already present and needs only then to be identified, grasped, expressed, or translated by a speaker or hearer. The ideal meaning is therefore also a measure for the correctness of understanding since it can be grasped either correctly or incorrectly.

The inconsistencies and deficiencies in Husserl's theory have often been noted and criticized—sometimes with devastating results.[16] In addition to putting forward objections concerning the immanent inconsistencies in Husserl's position, however, it is also possible to dispute its theoretical starting point as such. This was precisely Gadamer's strategy when he opposed Husserl and cited the universal importance of language for any phenomenological investigation. If one takes into consideration the fact that philosophical thought is dependent on its expression in language it is, as Gadamer explains,

astonishing "in wie geringem Grade das Problem der Sprache in der
Phänomenologie, bei Husserl wie bei Scheler, überhaupt bedacht
wird" ("how little importance is generally given to the problem of
language in the phenomenology of Husserl and Scheler").[17] Gadamer proceeds by referring explicitly to the *Logical Investigations:*
"Erst im Vollzug des Sprechens, im Weitersprechen, im Aufbau eines
sprachlichen Kontextes, fixieren sich die bedeutungstragenden Mo-
mente der Rede, indem sie sich gleichsam gegenseitig zurecht-
rücken" ("Only in the act of speaking, in continuing to speak, in
working out a linguistic context, are the meaningful elements of
speech determined and located in mutual relation").[18] One could
consider this statement as expressing the basic principle of Gadamer's antiobjectivist conception of meaning and understanding.[19] It will be the task of the next sections to explain, in detail, how
to interpret that statement. In doing so, it will also become clear to
what extent Gadamer remains in agreement with the phenomenological tradition and, in particular, with Heidegger.

III

Outlining his concept of understanding as a fusion of horizons
allows Gadamer the opportunity to use and further evaluate the Husserlian position, including the idea that the object of reference is
constituted in a way that is dependent on the activity of speaking.
This is evident as soon as one considers the fact that Husserl identifies the object intended by a speaker with the object of reference of
his utterance.[20] If this is right, then the object of reference of an
expression cannot be determined independently of the achievement
of meaningful speech acts. In other words, the objects, properties,
facts, and logical inferences that constitute the sense of an expression are formed in the horizon of different, correlative speech acts.
Husserl would not have gone so far as to state that these objects are
only or just constituted in the activity of speaking. But the structure
of the object of reference is, according to his theory, at least dependent on the pragmatic aspect of the activity of speaking.[21] This connection between the pragmatic side of language and the ideal
character of pure meaning, which is evident in Husserl's account,

Jens Kertscher

is dissolved in a significant fashion in that of Gadamer, as the above-mentioned quotation clearly shows.

The starting point of Gadamer's criticism of Husserl is the every-day situation of communication and dialogue. Sentences are given in a practical context, and it is possible to demonstrate that their meaning can only be understood correctly from the performative perspective of those who are involved in the dialogical process of communication. In this respect, a major contribution of Gadamer-ian hermeneutics has been its development of an account of the understanding-process that starts from an analysis of the dialectic of question and answer.

Gadamer's main thesis in relation to meaning, understanding, and language, as expressed in *Truth and Method,* is that language, or to use Gadamer's own terms, verbal experience, determines the object as well as the achievement of understanding. Language is therefore not a mere instrument of communication, but a dimension that is indepen-dent and constitutes the space of understanding.[22] The fact that Ga-damer does not clearly distinguish between the achievement and the object of understanding may appear problematic inasmuch as the so-called object can be articulated and understood only through lan-guage. Gadamer avoids this difficulty by comparing the act of under-standing with that of translating: to understand an utterance is a matter of being able to translate its sense in one's own words.[23] Ac-cording to Gadamer, this is only possible if the speaker succeeds in embedding the utterance to be understood within a dialogical context.

Such a "dialogical" context should also be conceived as a *practical* context. An interpretation that points out the practical dimension of the dialogical context permits one to take into account a prag-matic side of language that is hidden by Gadamer's speculative on-tology of language. This practical side consists in the fact that it is usually the reaction of the hearer of an utterance that shows if he has understood or not. This reaction should, of course, not be con-fused with what follows from an order or an instruction. It concerns rather the role that a speaker assigns to an expression in the actions that follow the expression's utterance. It is no doubt also possible in such cases to give a paraphrase of the sentence and to make it known to the interlocutor. The paraphrase does not prescribe the use that is to be made of the sentence, however, given that it can be applied variously. This fact is often forgotten in everyday situations of communication not only as the paraphrase is usually enough to satisfy us, but also as we tend to focus on just one application.

The fundamental and final criterion as to whether someone has understood an expression lies in the application and the use that the speaker makes of it. This point has been set forth by Wittgenstein.[24] It can be summarized by stating that we understand a language when we are able both to make use of the sentences in certain situations and to react adequately when hearing them. Understanding sentences and having the capacity to make correct utterances are correlative. Gadamer has expressed a similar idea by establishing in a more general way that mastering a common language is an unquestionable presupposition of understanding.[25] Even misunderstanding would remain inconceivable without this background of blind understanding, which is manifested in the mastering of one's own language. Language is therefore the paradigm of a fundamental horizon while simultaneously being an indispensable medium of understanding. The famous and often quoted principle of Gadamer's ontology of language (*"Being that can be understood is language"*)[26] can be interpreted in just that sense.

Blind understanding, however, is only one example of understanding, although a very prevalent one. It is also possible to respond to an utterance in ways that correspond to a variety of other speech acts.[27] For instance, one may make a comment on the utterance that is being directed to one, one may also raise a question, argue, or suggest an explanation. Often such responses arise when one is unsure if one has really understood an expression, and it is just such cases that raise hermeneutical problems in a stricter sense and require an adequate embedding of the sentences at issue in a dialogical context. Such embedding itself implies the existence of already acknowledged common orientations, whether they consist in generally accepted practical norms or rules or fixed meanings that are mediated by tradition.

The dialogical contextualization permits the speakers to bring their understanding into play and to observe their misunderstandings at work so that they can correct them and come to agreement about them. If we set aside the trivial examples of blind or automatic understanding, then it may seem that Gadamer's thesis implies that linguistic meaning is fixed only in the concrete activity of speaking and in building up a dialogical context. In that case it is not sufficient simply to utter a sentence to be understood. On the contrary, understanding is possible only if speaker and interlocutor succeed in establishing an appropriate context of utterance. Otherwise, the utterance remains both incomprehensible and obscure. As has been pointed out, it is important to recognize that the dialogical contextualization of an utterance should also be conceived as a *practical* contextualization. This is because any such contextualization presupposes the inclusion of practical elements in the dialogical environment of the sentence as well as the reaction of the hearer and the use to which the sentence is then put.

In the light of Gadamer's account, it is obvious that understanding must not be seen to consist either in the grasping of an ideal meaning or a mental event, nor in the grasping of the speaker's intention. Gadamer takes a step even further when he states that both the meaning *and* the understanding of what is said has to be considered as the result of the dialogical process between speech partners in which understanding as such emerges.

In common speech situations, we are inclined to accept the speaker's own explanation of what he has said as adequate to provide an account of the meaning of the sentence in question. We thus concede that the speaker has what is known as "first-person authority" on the assumption that the author of an utterance will best know what he has said. According to Gadamer, however, we have to give up this view: the sense of a sentence is not something that is simply present and needs only to be discovered. That this is so is evident when one asks how the intention of the speaker is present in cases of misunderstanding. The answer is that the intention is only accessible on the basis of information acquired from the speaker—we can ask him what he has meant by using certain words or how he uses certain expressions. Having done so, we can suggest another formulation for his utterances, add comments, explanations, or interpretations. In doing so, we determine the sense of what is said on the basis of a dialogue that encompasses both ourselves and our interlocutor and in which the interlocutor's own initial understanding is not only drawn upon, but may also end up being progressively altered.

The role of intention here loses its importance, since the initial utterance can always be expanded or substituted. The speaker-intention must thus be considered as something that is itself formed in the common process of understanding.[28] As a result, the determinations of meaning that result from the dialogical process at issue here may also be surprising to the speaker. If it is right that the use that we may make of a sentence in a particular case is not given in an objective manner before it has been applied successfully, then it follows that what arises out of the dialogical process between speaker and interlocutor is decisive for the determination of the meaning of an expression in a given context to which it has to be related. According to Gadamer, as speakers, we are in the same situation as when we are hearers, since we only come to understand what we have said through our interpretative engagement with others in which the meanings of our own utterances as well as theirs are questioned, responded to, and worked out. What we mean is articulated and exhibited through our utterances and responses, that is, through linguistic and practical activities in which utterances are embedded. On this basis Gadamer is not only able to avoid objectivistic views of meaning and understanding but also to establish the productive dimension of understanding.

From this Gadamer concludes that a speaker will never be able to anticipate all possible hermeneutical questions. There is no single linguistic expression that can be considered as a complete manifestation of what might have been said in order to obtain an integral understanding. A complete determination of a sentence for all hermeneutical questions is impossible, as it is impossible to anticipate all the questions that may have to be answered in various contexts. It is also impossible to anticipate our explanation of that which has been said if our utterances fail to sufficiently orient others. Hence we can never say all that we would like to say.[29] To presuppose the intelligibility and full transparence of an expression would therefore presuppose that its meaning is simply communicable. As has been shown, Gadamer's antiobjectivist conception of meaning and understanding is incompatible with this view. The theory that our linguistic

Jens Kertscher

intentions are transparent and fully determinate, and that our utterances at best articulate them in an imperfect manner, has therefore to be abandoned. The same holds for the idea that possible misunderstandings are a problem of the medium of expression rather than of the content.

What must now be investigated is how Gadamer deals with objections concerning the possible relativistic consequences of his position. Gadamer's response comprises a number of often ambiguous lines of argument. On the one hand, he explicitly rejects the ideal of correct understanding, while on the other he simultaneously refuses an unlimited relativism.[30] To address this issue, Gadamer claims that the meaning of the *interpretandum* is subject to historical change, while its identity as a text endures throughout time: "to understand a text always means to apply it to ourselves and to know that, even if it must always be understood in different ways, it is still the same text presenting itself to us in these different ways."[31] To understand why Gadamer emphasizes the importance of application in understanding, one has to take into account his use of the concepts of truth and validity in understanding.

IV

Gadamer clearly has not failed to observe the difficulties related to his position and so he does not abandon the normative aspects of understanding or the idea of truth. The question that now arises is whether, by defending this normative conception, Gadamer is forced to refer to presuppositions that undermine his antiobjectivist intentions.

If Gadamer is right in his assumption that the idea of progress in understanding does not make sense as well as in his claim that it is impossible to provide clear and objective criteria to distinguish between true and false interpretations, then it has to be asked what could substitute, in Gadamer's conception, for the objectivistic idea of transparent, fully determined, and objective meanings? Gadamer's response is that it is the reference to truth—which unites every speaker and hearer beyond all particular horizons— that replaces the idea of objective linguistic meaning.

According to Gadamer, the centrality of truth is evident in the
fact that the point of reference to which all meaning and understanding must be related consists, in every case, in the need to arrive
at an agreement on a subject matter that is placed before the dialogue partners.[32] The famous concept of the fusion of horizons
should be understood in this sense. Interpretation is guided by reference to truth and to a subject matter that relates the interpreter to
the interpreted text or likewise to the partners in a conversation. If
one takes the conversation seriously, then according to Gadamer,
one is involved in the language, and in the specific subject matter
of the conversation, in a way that highlights the horizon of both
one's own language and of one's own previous understanding. In
the light of the idea of understanding as a fusion of horizons, understanding is conceived as a matter of interpreting the claim to truth
of an utterance from the speaker's own present horizon. Therefore,
from the speaker's perspective, understanding is also a reinsertion
of meaning from within the speaker's own present horizon.

Gadamer emphasizes that both the speaker's and the interpreter's
present horizons stand as limits as well as conditions of the possibility
of understanding. If this is right, then it is also clear that the idea
of an objective meaning that belongs to the *interpretanda*—whether
they be texts or linguistic utterances that are part of a conversation—
is inconceivable since it would presuppose the idea of a neutral
standpoint beyond all horizons. The same point also holds for the
idea of progress in understanding inasmuch as this presupposes the
possibility of arriving at a form of language that would be fully transparent and with which no interpretation would be needed. In such
a case linguistic communication would have overcome its own finitude, and truth would have been made transparently present to all
speakers of the language.

What has been said above also concerns the everyday situation of
communication in which a speaker has to interpret the utterances
of his interlocutor. In relation to this the interpreter not only operates by anticipating the intelligibility of what has been said but also
by presuming its rationality. Gadamer calls this a "fore-conception
of completeness" (*Vorgriff der Vollkommenheit*).[33] By this he means not
only that it is necessary to presuppose the sense of that which has

to be interpreted if one wants to understand it, but in addition that it is necessary to embed understanding in a communicative process that itself involves concepts of the truth, the correctness and the appropriateness of utterances. To understand why this is so, we have to take into account the fact that we understand an utterance only in the manner in which it could have been meant in a specific situation. We have to presuppose, therefore, that it is appropriate to this situation. We are only able to do this, however, if what we say involves the making (or the denying) of claims to validity, so that understanding always stands in relation to the making of judgments.[34] Judgments, on their part, always presuppose the intelligibility of what is said. We can finally propose, therefore, that the anticipation of the appropriateness of an utterance to a situation implies an anticipation of its intelligibility. This means that we can view every utterance as being placed in a space of truth, correctness, and appropriateness. That which stands outside of such a space must be viewed, at least in everyday conversation, as being both incomprehensible and inaccessible to understanding.

From the perspective of the understanding that is relative to both context and situation, the reference to a subject matter and to its validity is implied in a twofold sense: first, inasmuch as understanding includes an anticipation of the meaning that is immanent to the situation; second, inasmuch as the aim of linguistic communication is, according to Gadamer, to arrive at an understanding in the sense of an agreement upon the subject matter of the conversation. On this reading of Gadamer's dialogical conception of understanding, however, there remains a problem with the gap between historicity and truth. On the one hand, Gadamer emphasizes the historical aspect of understanding. The varieties of languages, and meaning shifts within those languages, clearly demonstrate that the conditions that make understanding possible must themselves be conceived of in process-terms.

On the other hand, Gadamer does not give up the idea of truth. This is because he is convinced that the universal understanding achieved in and through language already implies the acceptance and recognition of traditional orientations and fore-understandings. This becomes particularly clear if one takes into consideration his attitude toward juridical and theological hermeneutics.[35] The texts at issue here reveal a truth that has only to be actualized, adopted, or applied to specific situations—although adapted in different ways in different situations, it is nevertheless a single truth that is at stake. The same is true in relation to juridical hermeneutics in which the task is one of applying legal codes to new and ever-changing situations. The fact that Gadamer uses juridical and theological hermeneutics as models for his own conception of understanding explains why the aspect of *application* in understanding is so much more important here than that of *criticism*. The mediation of truth through the authority of the text and the mediation of meaning in language are the nonrelativistic moments in Gadamer's conception of understanding. Truth and meaning as worked out in relation to the history of effects (*Wirkungsgeschichte*) is, of course, only intelligible from the standpoint of one's own horizon. The process of interpretation is therefore never finished. Truth is conceived by Gadamer, however, as an event that has already occurred, one that can therefore only be adapted to a specific situation but not submitted to criticism,[36] whereas linguistic meaning already implies a standard of correct understanding inasmuch as understanding is itself viewed as truth-disclosing.

One of the consequences of Gadamer's unsatisfactory solution is a conception of truth—in terms of its mediation through linguistic utterances and texts—that views it in Heideggerian terms as both world-disclosive and as always having gone before. On this basis, interpretation not only becomes the application of a truth that is always prior to any particular instance of understanding, but it is also reduced to a moment of disclosure as that occurs in particular texts or linguistic utterances. Rather than a matter of grasping an objective meaning, understanding becomes, therefore, a matter of the taking up of a meaning that has already been revealed.[37]

The consequences, in relation to the question of language and understanding, of this aspect of the Gadamerian position must now be investigated. Moreover, the last section, outlines a position that shares Gadamer's antiobjectivistic intentions without accepting the Heideggerian presuppositions that are inherent in his ontology of language.

V

Obviously, if one were to accept Gadamer's basic presuppositions about the ontology of language, then one would arrive at a different reading from that advanced here. Nevertheless, the focus on the actual use to which language is put when reconsidering Gadamer's dialogical model of meaning and understanding was not at all arbitrary. Indeed, it can be seen to be consistent with the emphasis on the practical aspect of language that is already implicitly present in Gadamer's conception. Moreover, it also provides a way of avoiding some of the problematic consequences of his Heideggerian conception of truth, while preparing the way for a more satisfactory anti-objectivist account of meaning along lines to be set out below.

The criticism of Gadamer's position developed in the discussion so far began by outlining the discrepancy between the obvious anti-objectivistic motives that underlie that position and Gadamer's own reiteration of views that emphasize the centrality of tradition to the process of understanding. If the importance of the practical aspect that is implied by the dialogical model of understanding is accepted, along with the idea of the context-relativity of understanding, then it will be possible to arrive at a conception of understanding that views it in a way that is inseparable from the careful description or redescription of the use of words and sentences within contexts in the sense associated with Wittgenstein's later philosophy.

The well-known principle of context in its strictest form was introduced into the philosophy of language by Frege when he stated in the *Grundlagen der Arithmetik* (*Foundations of Arithmetics*) that the meaning of words should be explained in the context of the sentences in which they occur.[38] This principle has since been further developed in holistic fashion by philosophers of language influenced by Frege.[39] Despite Gadamer's not belonging to the analytic tradition in modern philosophy of language, one can find in his work ideas that are similar to the holistically interpreted principle of context derivable from Frege—thus, from *Truth and Method:* "As the single word belongs in the total context of the sentence, so the single text belongs in the total context of a writer's work, and the latter in the whole of the literary genre or of literature."[40] As has already been shown, the understanding as well as the meaning of an utterance is constituted in both a dialogical and practical speech context.

This idea can now be further developed by stating that such a meaning-constituting context could be viewed in the last and most general instance as a "world-picture" (*Weltbild*)—what Gadamer would refer to as a horizon. A world-picture in this sense is a system of conceptions and beliefs that have been handed down to us and against the background of which, not only are words and sentences capable of having meaning, but the difference between truth and falsity arises as a possibility.[41] Consequently, as Wittgenstein has pointed out, the possibility of understanding arises only on the basis of a form of life and its associated practices, the correct mastery of which is the only criterion for the understanding of linguistic utterances. There are, moreover, no theoretical, that is, practice-independent criteria that can distinguish correct from false rule-following or understanding.[42]

We are only able to understand what we have found words for, and thus we understand through being able to describe not only the use of words but also actions, artworks, persons, literary works, and so on. At the same time, we will only understand correctly when we abide by the rules that such description must follow. Those rules are, on their part, entrenched in actual linguistic practice as it is constitutive of the contexts of understanding. Those rules may be applied, followed or even themselves described. It is, nevertheless, impossible to view them, even in their entirety, as simply constitutive of understanding as such. More pointedly: the whole world-picture on which those rules are based cannot be understood from any external standpoint or in an objectifying fashion—it is not possible to make general assertions that would pretend to grasp such a world-picture as a whole or to grasp it "objectively"—since it constitutes the very presupposition of understanding and as such cannot be made the direct focus of reflection.

If one accepts this interpretation of the generalized principle of context, then obviously, that which is regarded as right or wrong, true or false in the context of a world-picture cannot be founded on an external point of view and neither can the rules that underlie the use of language be so founded. As Wittgenstein says, "This is simply what I do,"[43] and similarly one should therefore say: "This is simply what I understand." The understanding of language is, in this respect, limited to being able to describe linguistic practice. Moreover, any such description must itself be seen as arising within a particular language game and as directed at a practice that is similarly bound within such a game. Language and understanding thus cannot be derived from some metaphysical concept, such as reason or a tradition-mediated and world-disclosing truth.

This general view of understanding, in opposition to Gadamer's own conception, must also be related and limited to a specific language game—understanding is, after all, simply a word with various and describable forms of use in language.[44] How should we then conceive of the understanding of language? After all that has been said so far, it would seem clear that the answer can appeal neither to the Husserlian notion of grasping an ideal meaning nor to the Gadamerian idea of the concretization of something that has already occurred. In opposition to both these views, the account outlined here is antiobjectivist inasmuch as it affirms that the mastery of a language is, above all else, a *practical* ability. This does not exclude reflection on or explanation of it, but in the last analysis, a linguistic understanding of language has to reveal itself as a capacity that cannot be reduced to what can be said about it in theoretical terms.

At this point, it is useful to appeal more directly to Wittgenstein to further clarify the difference between Gadamer's hermeneutical conception of understanding and the sort of antiobjectivistic and practice-oriented conception of meaning and understanding advanced here. Undoubtedly both positions look to the way in which understanding is constituted within a linguistically structured and dialogical-articulated horizon. This horizon may also be conceived as a world-picture. On this basis, understanding is seen as, in every instance, an *immanent* process, since there can be no horizon-independent criterion of correct understanding. The correctness of understanding is therefore not only always relative to the description of a specific linguistic practice, but it is also above all relative to these practices themselves. The integration of understanding in the framework of an ever-changing world-picture, however, should not be confounded with the sort of truth-mediating and disclosing process that Gadamer sets out. This becomes clearer when we consider the way in which the embedding of understanding in a dialogical and practical context—in the context of a linguistic practice that is capable of description—sets a limit to understanding. This limit can only be drawn from within a language game by those speakers involved that game. At the same time, this limit, inasmuch as it constitutes the presupposition of understanding, also establishes the difference between that which we *can* and that which we *cannot* understand. It also makes possible our capability of distinguishing between correct and incorrect understanding without falling into arbitrariness. The need for such a distinction cannot be satisfied by reference to the meaning-mediating event of understanding that, according to Gadamer, occurs in language, but only by the delimitation of understanding through the delimitation of the contexts that determine linguistic usage. Gadamer's idea of an experience of being that is mediated by language does not achieve this, since it relies on a purely metaphysical presupposition, namely, that the event of understanding is a rational and meaningful process that is constitutive of the framework of understanding, and thereby not only discloses and mediates truth, but also gives a foundation to our relationship with the world as a whole.

What we can learn in the present context from Wittgenstein's philosophy of language is that there is no theoretical solution to the problem of linguistic meaning, but only a practical one found in the use of language and the forms of life intertwined with that use. This practice has to be described in different and ever-new ways in order to clarify and make explicit the difference between that which only appears to have been understood and that which really has been understood. Clearly this involves considerations of a hermeneutical nature as well as questions of truth and validity. In the last instance, however, it is the practice of language, of describing and embedding utterances in their specific context, that sets a limit to understanding and, in doing so, makes understanding possible. It is the task of the speakers to discover this limit if they do not want to content themselves merely with understanding in different ways.

Translated by Michael Isenberg

Jens Kertscher

Notes

1. See Albrecht Wellmer, "Zur Kritik der hermeneutischen Vernunft," in *Vernunft und Lebenspraxis. Philosophische Studien zu den Bedingungen einer rationalen Kultur,* edited by Christoph Demmerling, Gottfried Gabriel, and Thomas Rentsch (Frankfurt am Main: Suhrkamp, 1995), 123–156, esp. 123–126.

2. Ludwig Wittgenstein, *Tractatus Logico-Philosophicus* (London: Routledge & Kegan Paul, 1963), author's preface, 3.

3. See Ruth Sonderegger, "A Critique of Pure Meaning: Wittgenstein and Derrida," *European Journal of Philosophy* 5 (1997), 183–209, esp. 183–186. The following characterization of semantic objectivism owes much to the results of Sonderegger's essay.

4. See Karl-Otto Apel, "Regulative Ideas or Truth Happening? An Attempt to Answer the Question of the Conditions of the Possibility of Valid Understanding," in *The Philosophy of Hans-Georg Gadamer,* edited by Lewis Edwin Hahn (La Salle: Open Court, 1997), 67–94.

5. Hans-Georg Gadamer, *Gesammelte Werke,* 3 (Tübingen: J. C. B. Mohr [Paul Siebeck], 1987), 141–142. See also Gadamer's comments on Husserl in *Gesammelte Werke,* 2 (Tübingen: J. C. B. Mohr [Paul Siebeck], 1986), 361.

6. Edmund Husserl, *Husserliana, XIX / 1: Logische Untersuchungen, Zweiter Band, Zweiter Teil* (The Hague: Martinus Nijhoff, 1984). English translation: *Logical Investigations,* 1, translated by J. N. Findlay (London: Routledge and Kegan Paul, 1970).

7. *Logical Investigations,* p. 279.

8. Ibid., 333.

9. Ibid., 329.

10. Ibid., and see also Jacques Derrida, *De la Grammatologie* (Paris: Éditions de Minuit, 1967), for instance, 17 and 23.

11. *Logical Investigations,* 330.

12. Ibid., 302.

13. See Rudolf Bernet, *Bedeutung und intentionales Bewußtsein, Husserls Begriff des Bedeutungsphänomens,* in *Studien zur Sprachphänomenologie, Phänomenologische Forschungen,* 8, edited by Ernst Wolfgang Orth (Freiburg: Alber, 1979), 31–64, esp. 55.

14. *Logical Investigations,* 330.

15. Husserl explicitly speaks of the "timeless 'being' of the ideal" (*Logical Investigations*), 352.

16. See for instance John E. Atwell, "Husserl on Signification and Object," *American Philosophical Quarterly* 6 (1969), 312–317; and Jacques Derrida, *La voix et le phénomène. Introduction au problème du signe dans la phénoménologie de Husserl* (Paris: Presses Universitaires de France, 1967).

17. *Gesammelte Werke*, vol. 3, 141. By neglecting language, Husserl belongs, as Gadamer has pointed out in *Truth and Method*, translated by Joel Weinsheimer and Donald Marshall (New York: Continuum, 2nd rev. ed. 1989), 418 (*Wahrheit und Methode* [Tübingen: J. C. B. Mohr, 5th ed. 1986], 422), to a tradition of forgetfulness of language (*Sprachvergessenheit*) that was initiated by Plato.

18. *Gesammelte Werke*, 2, 197.

19. Another example of Gadamer's criticism of objectivistic or, as he calls it, instrumental, conceptions of language, can be found in *Truth and Method*, 413–414: "this consequence results from the negative discussion of the *Cratylus* and is sealed by knowledge being banished to the intelligible sphere. Thus, in all discussion of language ever since, the concept of the image (*eikon*) has been replaced by that of the sign (*semeion* or *semainon*)" (*Wahrheit und Methode*), 418.

20. *Logical Investigations*, 330.

21. See Rudolf Bernet, Iso Kern, Eduard Marbach, *Edmund Husserl. Darstellung seines Denkens* (Hamburg: Meiner, 1996), 163.

22. *Truth and Method*, 450, where Gadamer comments on the prevalence of language as follows: "in language the world itself presents itself. Verbal experience of the world is 'absolute.' . . . Our verbal experience of the world is prior to everything that is recognized and addressed as existing. *That language and world are related in a fundamental way does not mean, then, that world becomes the object of language.* Rather, the object of knowledge and statements is always already enclosed within the world horizon of language" (*Wahrheit und Methode*, 453–454). See also *Truth and Method*, 389: "*language is the universal medium in which understanding occurs. Understanding occurs in interpreting*" (*Wahrheit und Methode*, 392).

23. *Truth and Method*, 383–385 (*Wahrheit und Methode*, 387–389).

24. Ludwig Wittgenstein, *Philosophical Investigations*, translated by G. E. M. Anscombe (Oxford: Basil Blackwell, 1976), §146.

25. *Truth and Method*, 385: "Mastering the language is a necessary precondition for coming to an understanding in a conversation" (*Wahrheit und Methode*, 388).

26. *Truth and Method*, 474 (*Wahrheit und Methode*, 478). See also *Truth and Method*, 404: "What is true of understanding is just as true of language. Neither is to be grasped simply as a fact that can be empirically investigated. Neither is ever simply an object but instead comprehends everything that can ever be an object" (*Wahrheit und Methode*, 408).

27. See Friedrich Kambartel, "Versuch über das Verstehen," in *Der Löwe spricht . . . und wir können ihn nicht verstehen. Ein Symposion an der Universität Frankfurt anläßlich des Hundertsten Geburtstags von Ludwig Wittgenstein* (Frankfurt am Main: Suhrkamp, 1991), 121–137, esp. 123–124.

28. Ibid., 126.

29. *Truth and Method*, 469: "To say what one means . . . to make oneself understood—means to hold what is said together with an infinity of what is not said in one unified meaning and to ensure that it is understood in this way" (*Wahrheit und Methode*, 473). See also *Truth and Method*, 458: "Thus every word, as the event of a moment, carries with it

Jens Kertscher

the unsaid, to which it is related by responding and summoning" (*Wahrheit und Methode,* 462). See also Gadamer's essay from 1993, entitled "Europa und die Oikoumene," in *Gesammelte Werke* 10 (Tübingen: J. C. B. Mohr [Paul Siebeck], 1995), 267–284, esp. 274.

30. *Truth and Method,* 397: "And interpretation that was correct in itself would be a foolish ideal that mistook the nature of tradition. . . . Being bound by a situation does not mean that the claim to correctness that every interpretation must take is dissolved into the subjective and occasional" (*Wahrheit und Methode,* 401).

31. *Truth and Method,* 398 (*Wahrheit und Methode,* 401).

32. *Truth and Method,* 378 (*Wahrheit und Methode,* 384).

33. *Truth and Method,* 294 (*Wahrheit und Methode,* 299). The various forms of the "fore-conception of completeness" in both contemporary hermeneutics and philosophy of language have been investigated in detail by Oliver R. Scholz, *Verstehen und Rationalität. Untersuchungen zu den Grundlagen von Hermeneutik und Sprachphilosophie* (Frankfurt: Vittorio Klostermann, 1999). Referring to Gadamer's conception see esp. 134–141.

34. See *Philosophical Investigations,* §242, and Albrecht Wellmer, "Zur Kritik der hermeneutischen Vernunft," 131.

35. This as well as the following points have been laid out in more detail by Albrecht Wellmer, "Zur Kritik der hermeneutischen Vernunft," 142–143.

36. Karl-Otto Apel is certainly right in his assumption that no text and no utterance can be excluded from critical examination. See Karl-Otto Apel, "Regulative Ideas or Truth Happening? An Attempt to Answer the Question of the Conditions of the Possibility of Valid Understanding," 81.

37. See Hans Albert, *Kritik der reinen Hermeneutik. Der Antirealismus und das Problem des Verstehens* (Tübingen: J. C. B. Mohr, 1994), 73, who criticizes this Gadamerian view as a "revelation model of knowledge."

38. Gottlob Frege, *Die Grundlagen der Arithmetik. Eine logisch-mathematische Untersuchung über den Begriff der Zahl* (Hildesheim: Olms, 1961), xxii.

39. See for instance Wittgenstein's famous holistic formulation of the context-principle: "It is only in a language that something is a proposition. To understand a proposition is to understand a language" (Wittgenstein, *Philosophical Grammar* [Oxford: Blackwell, 1974], 131). See also *Philosophical Investigations,* §199.

40. *Truth and Method,* 291 (*Wahrheit und Methode,* 296).

41. Ludwig Wittgenstein, *On Certainty* (Oxford: Blackwell, 1969), §§94–105.

42. *Philosophical Investigations,* §241.

43. Ibid., §217.

44. *Philosophical Grammar,* 49 and 74–76.

9

On Not Having the Last Word: Thoughts on Our Debts to Gadamer

Alasdair MacIntyre

My question in this essay is: what have I learned and perhaps could only have learned from Gadamer? Gadamer himself, on reading it, may well reply "not enough." And indeed there are crucial differences between my philosophical positions and his. Yet I am keenly aware that, even in disagreement, I have reason to be extraordinarily grateful to him. Gadamer is the author of two books that will be accounted among the classics of twentieth-century philosophy: *Wahrheit und Methode* and *Die Idee des Guten zwischen Plato und Aristoteles*. To accord a text the status of a classic is to say that it is a text with which it is necessary to come to terms, that failure to reckon with it will seriously harm our enquiries. Yet there are sometimes obstacles to be overcome, before we can learn what such a text has to teach us.

In my own case one obstacle is that the tradition within which I have worked for almost twenty years is one that Gadamer had rejected dismissively from the outset, finding no merit in what he took to be "the dogmatic overlay superimposed on Aristotle by . . . neo-Thomism."[1] Although Gadamer has discussed particular theses of Aquinas with his characteristic sympathy and accuracy, he has never entered into dialogue with a distinctively Thomistic Aristotelianism. This is not surprising, and not only because of Gadamer's own preconceptions.

For modern Thomism only exhibited an awareness of the importance of the historical turn and the hermeneutic turn in philosophy relatively late in its history. And Thomistic Aristotelians have still perhaps not taken adequate measure of the implications of these turns. So part of the importance of Gadamer's work lies in the help that it can afford in understanding the bearing of hermeneutics on the Aristotelian tradition. It has often been thought by Thomists, for example, that to acknowledge the historically conditioned character of philosophical—or for that matter of scientific or historical—inquiry is to make a certain kind of relativism inescapable. And it was one of the several achievements of *Wahrheit und Methode* to have shown that this is not so. But it is worth inquiring a little further just why it is not so and I begin that inquiry by posing questions about one of Gadamer's key theses that I take to be unquestionably true: to have become aware of the historically conditioned character of our philosophical enquiries and interpretations is not to have escaped from it. There is no standpoint outside history to which we can move, no way in which we can adopt some presuppositionless stance, exempt from the historical situatedness of all thinking. "The standpoint beyond any standpoint . . . is pure illusion."[2] It is not incompatible, however, with a recognition of this truth to argue that a great deal turns on the nature of our awareness of the contingencies of our historical situatedness and that a certain kind of awareness, while not providing a standpoint outside history, can transform our relationship to that history.

I shall argue that, when we have understood our relationship to some past philosophical texts that belong to different historical contexts from our own and to that about which those texts speak to us, we will find that we have reached conclusions that presuppose an appeal to standards of rationality and truth that do in some measure transcend the limitations of historically bounded contexts. It is not that we have been after all able to escape from our particular historical situation into some extrahistorical realm of timeless judgment, but rather that we come to recognize that our historical situation is itself partly constituted by the possibility of appealing beyond and even against that situation.

I

Consider the kind of case in which we are reading a text that provides answers to questions that we ourselves, given our present situation, are no longer able to pose. "Only in an inauthentic sense can we talk about understanding questions that one does not pose one-self—e.g. Questions that are outdated or empty," writes Gadamer.[3] We understand them only by understanding the presuppositions that once gave point to asking them, but since we no longer share those presuppositions, the questions are no longer relevant, and Ga-damer cites, as an example of this irrelevance, questions that presup-pose that the possibility of a defensible conception of perpetual motion is open.

Notice that in this case the questions posed within the text are no longer posed by the text, because of what we have come to believe about that of which the text speaks. But notice too that our dialogue with the text is not necessarily at an end, just because we have identi-fied certain presuppositions that we no longer share with its author. And here Gadamer's example of perpetual motion may be mis-leading. For the possibility of perpetual motion is excluded by con-cepts and theses so fundamental to our present physics and to the history of its development that we have not been left with the barest idea of what it would be for such a possibility to be considered a live possibility once again. But not all the questions "that we regard as out of date and pointless" are of this kind.

Imagine a philosopher who, either because he has hitherto worked within a neopositivist tradition or because his philosophical education has been at the hands of a certain kind of follower of Heidegger, regards some of the questions posed within traditional metaphysics, within what Heideggerians have learned to call "onto-theology," as out-of-date, pointless, or even meaningless. Among those might well be questions posed by Descartes in his pursuit of an incontestably certain foundation for the sciences, questions that presuppose the possibility of constructing a sound version of the ontological argument for the existence of God. The key concepts of Cartesianism, so this imagined philosopher firmly believes, have as little prospect of vindication as the concept of perpetual motion. And our imagined philosopher is not after all imaginary. There have been a number of philosophical milieus in the past decades in which it has been taken for granted that Cartesianism consists of bad an-swers to worse questions, questions that we now know better than to ask. But when our imagined philosopher recognizes that his or her presuppositions preclude the posing of Cartesian questions, does this recognition simply rule out these questions as a similar recognition did in the case of perpetual motion? The answer must be: not at all.

For our imagined philosopher now has to choose between two alternative ways of proceeding. Given that his or her present presuppositions preclude the posing of Cartesian questions, then either the posing of Cartesian questions must be treated as something that is indeed out-of-date and pointless or instead the philosopher's presuppositions must themselves now be questioned. And a philosopher may well find grounds for adopting the latter rather than the former alternative. That is, he or she may, for example, find grounds for reopening the questions posed by Descartes, by considering whether Descartes may not have been to some significant degree misinterpreted by those who had argued for an unqualified rejection of the Cartesian project. Perhaps our imagined philosopher reads Jean-Luc Marion's *Questions cartesiennes: Méthode et metaphysique*[4] and by so doing achieves not only a new reading of key texts, but also a recognition that it is possible for someone whose philosophical idiom and mode of inquiry is deeply indebted to Heidegger to take Descartes's project seriously.

In this way philosophical issues that had previously seemed to be closed and settled may always be reopened. What had appeared to be conclusive arguments against some position turn out not to be conclusive after all, perhaps because the position against which they were directed has been reinterpreted, perhaps because the arguments have been reevaluated. About the possibility of reinterpretation, Gadamer has written that it always confronts the reader of a text: "The line of meaning that the text manifests to him as he reads it always and necessarily breaks off in an open indeterminacy. He can, indeed he must, accept the fact that future generations will understand differently what he has read in the text."[5] But the possibility of such a change in understanding is not only a matter of the perspective of some future generation. A single reader's perspective changes over time; what was at one time at or near the horizon may always become part of the foreground. And so it is always possible that my future reading of some passage within a text or some text or some body of texts will not be the same as my present reading.

This in itself should be sufficient to teach us that we are never entitled to confidence that we have finally come to terms with some text or set of positions in the history of philosophy. Finality in our dealings with Plato or Aristotle or Aquinas or Descartes or Kant— or indeed with Gadamer—is always denied us. Neither they nor we have ever said the last word. Yet at any given time of course we are nonetheless entitled to conclusions that derive from the best arguments available so far, on the basis of the best interpretations available so far. We are entitled to treat certain arguments as conclusive, until and unless, as happened with our imagined philosopher, we find reason to think otherwise. And indeed in understanding the kind of change of mind that happened to our imagined philosopher, some conception of the difference between a conclusive and an inconclusive argument is indispensable. The rejection of finality requires that we recognize that in treating more argument as conclusive we may always be mistaken. It does not at all preclude judging that in this or that particular case we have no reason to believe that we are mistaken and every reason to believe that we are not.

The concept of conclusive argument is ineliminable from interpretations of philosophical texts. About the contentions advanced by the author of any philosophical text we cannot avoid asking three questions: are the arguments presented for this or that conclusion presented as conclusive? If so, was the author, given the premises of and the presuppositions underlying those arguments, right to treat them as conclusive? And should we now, given our presuppositions and beliefs about the truth or falsity of those premises, treat them as conclusive? If so, then there are questions, concepts, and standards that are to some significant degree shared by philosophers at work in very different historical contexts with very different beliefs and presuppositions, namely those questions, concepts, and standards that are involved in asking and answering questions about whether this or that argument is or is not conclusive.

That there are such standards of argument, standards whose authority no philosopher, whatever her or his historical situation, can reject without detriment, is something that we learn and can only learn from the history of philosophy. This is not a conclusion reached by some transcendental argument whose key premise is that only respect for such standards renders inquiry possible. It is rather a matter of how meager our resources for argumentative inquiry become, how impoverished our philosophy is, when we do not give such standards their due. So philosophy becomes at a certain point—and in Western philosophy decisively with Socrates—an activity constituted in part by respect for such standards and after Socrates to defect from them is to defect from philosophy.

Such standards are therefore not mine rather than yours or yours rather than mine, they do not belong to this period rather than that, but to anyone at any subsequent time who aspires to carry the history of philosophy one stage further beyond her or his predecessors. And by accepting their authority we constitute ourselves members of a community able to engage with others in dialectical inquiry. For it is crucial to dialectical inquiry that in posing questions, whether to our contemporaries or to texts out of the philosophical past, we invite a type of answer that is open to evaluation in respect of the quality of the arguments that would have to be advanced in order to sustain it. The sequence of questions and answers in any adequate version of what Collingwood called the logic of question and answer proceeds fruitfully only insofar as we are able to distinguish good from bad answers by appeal to, among other things, standards of argument, including those that enable us to distinguish conclusive from inconclusive arguments.

A shared respect for the authority of such standards is of course compatible with extensive disagreement in philosophical conclusions. But it is only because and insofar as, explicitly or implicitly, we treat the utterances of others as open to evaluation by appeal to those standards that we are able to interpret and to understand what they say as a contribution to the conversations of philosophy. This is something that, although only sometimes made explicit in Gadamer's account of hermeneutic inquiry, is always implicit.

II

Consider now another way in which, even if we acknowledge that all philosophical inquiry is from some particular historically conditional standpoint with its own perspective, we are not only able to judge but compelled to judge that some standpoints and some perspectives are rationally superior to others. The examples of philosophical work that provoke this reflection are drawn from the history of Platonic interpretation and I begin with one of Gadamer's own interpretations in which he explicitly appeals to just those standards of argument that have been discussed here.

Gadamer has argued that we should initially understand Plato's notion of *eidos* with reference to its introduction into the argument of the Phaedo "for the stated purpose of putting a stop to the antilogical acts of inducing confusion."[6] Plato instructs us that we are not in our arguments to appeal to the characteristics of particulars, except insofar as they exemplify some *eidos*. Otherwise we will be liable to move illicitly from treating some particular as having one set of properties to treating it as having another incompatible set, so entangling ourselves and others in contradiction and confusion. "All logical confusion has its origin in not keeping the *eidos* separate from what only participates in it."[7] And to avoid this confusion is crucial for Gadamer, just because whether or not we have grasped an *eidos* makes a difference to practice and not only to theoretical understanding.

Gadamer's illuminating interpretation of the relationship of *eidos* to particulars is important not only for its contribution to the interpretation of particular Platonic texts but also for the part that it plays in his account of the relationship of Plato to Aristotle and more especially of the relationship of Plato's conception of the good to Aristotle's. It is not necessary to find Gadamer's arguments for his overall interpretation of that relationship conclusive—and I do not—to recognize that he has opened up a way of understanding Aristotle's debt to Plato that in some times and places in the earlier part of this century would not or rather could not have been seriously entertained. Why not?

Paul Natorp's brilliant and original *Platos Ideenlehre*[8] throws light not only on Plato and on those possibilities for understanding Plato that had emerged from within neo-Kantianism but also on the corresponding limitations that a neo-Kantian perspective had imposed on interpretation. To read Plato from within a neo-Kantian perspective was to read Plato with a severely restricted view of how we might make sense of some of his central theses, including those that concern the relationship of *eidos* to particulars, theses that were assimilated by the neo-Kantians to their own claims about the relationship of the forms of experience and of the laws governing experience a priori to particulars as experienced. As Gadamer's English translator, P. Christopher Smith, has pointed out, the Platonic *eidos* was thereby misconceived as the solution to an epistemological problem, although in neo-Kantian eyes Plato so understood had been paid the high compliment of being transformed in this respect at least into a forerunner of Kant.[9]

To say this is not to denigrate Natorp, whose book still repays reading for its many incidental insights. And it seems very doubtful that from within a neo-Kantian perspective in the history of philosophy, a more compelling interpretation of Plato could have been provided. If this is true, then there must be something gravely defective in any neo-Kantian perspective as a starting point for interpretation. It is not that Natorp was any more guilty than other interpreters of Plato in allowing his own philosophical position partly to dictate his interpretative conclusions. Just because any worthwhile interpretation will be governed by a principle of charity, requiring us to read a text, as far as possible, so as to impute significance rather than lack of meaning, plausibility rather than implausibility, truth rather than falsity, an interpreter's own view of where and how the line is to be drawn between the significant, the plausible, and the true on the one hand and the meaningless, the implausible, and false on the other is bound to inform his or her mode of interpretation. Just because this is so, we can compare the different degrees to which and the different ways in which different philosophical starting points influence the outcome of interpretative enquiries. If we discover, as we do in the case of neo-Kantianism, that some particular set of philosophical commitments disables those whose commitments they are, by making it impossible for them to understand or even to perceive key aspects of what is said in some of the texts that they are confronting, then that in itself is a reason for rejecting their standpoint. If neo-Kantianism disables us in our reading of Plato, we have good reason not to be neo-Kantians.

Against this it will be said: this argument is question-begging. It appeals to how the Platonic text is read from one interpretative standpoint—Gadamer's—in order to conclude to the superiority of that same standpoint over its rivals. It allows the adherents of that standpoint both to act as a contending party in the dispute between the rival standpoints and to act as judge in deciding between their competing claims. And this is in a way true, but it is less damaging than might at first appear. For the contrast is between an interpretative standpoint—Gadamer's—that allows Plato's text to speak for itself without constraint, even if it speaks in answer to Gadamer's questions, and a rival interpretative standpoint—Natorp's—that straitjackets the text, compelling it, at least on certain issues, to speak as the interpreter requires it to speak. There is then an appeal to a standard for judging between the claims of rival standpoints that is itself independent of the commitments of this or that particular standpoint, namely that supplied by asking how far any particular standpoint allows texts that are subjected to interpretation from that standpoint to put the interpreter's questions in question, to talk back and to do so in its own terms rather than in those of the interpreter.

We only learn how to make this distinction between different types of interpretative practice by engaging systematically in such practice ourselves and by engaging in conversation with interpreters who are addressing the same texts as we are, but whose starting point is significantly different from our own. Once we are able to make it, we can identify those starting points that are apparently inescapably disabling, something that has escaped the notice of those critics of Gadamer's hermeneutics who have supposed that, on his view, one is always and necessarily imprisoned with one's own starting point, whatever it may be. And there are indeed some starting points that do imprison those who are committed to them. But there are others, and they are of very different kinds, that do not imprison just because they allow those whose starting point they are to learn from the texts that they address in such a way that they are able to correct their own initial errors and shortcomings.

To this it may be said: the argument so far is formulated as though being open to what a particular text has to say to one were an all or nothing matter, as though either a particular interpreter's mind was wholly open to what a text has to say or else that interpreter's mind was unrestrained in imposing the preconceptions of its own starting point upon the text. Not only is such openness a matter of degree, but some interpreters are open to some texts or to some aspects of some texts, but not to others. When we have noticed the nature and degree of the shortcomings of, say, neo-Kantians, such as Natorp, in respect of their reading of Plato, we have still left open the question of how their interpretations of other very different texts and indeed of other aspects of Plato's texts are to be evaluated. So my thesis must be modified: to the degree in which and by reason of the ways in which a particular philosophical starting point disables us as interpreters of some text or texts, that philosophical stance is discredited. Insofar as some set of philosophical commitments prevents those whose commitments they are from entering into dialogue with some text or body of texts, they are protected from the negative effects of hearing what that text or texts have to say and so from entertaining thoughts that might give them good reason to modify or to abandon their commitments. Their rationality has thereby been diminished.

III

The first part of this essay argued that the historically conditional character of our philosophical inquiries, including our hermeneutic inquiries, does not rule out appeal to standards of argument that are shared with others whose historical situation may be different from our own, standards that turn out to be indispensable for any philosophical inquiry that is not to be sterile. The second part argued that the claims of some philosophical standpoints to our allegiance can be significantly discredited, if they turn out to impose disabling constraints upon our ability to enter into dialogue with and to learn from texts of some other different point of view. In both cases we learn to identify standards, independent of any particular historical perspective, that are indispensable to philosophical inquiry. And this we could only have learned from the history of philosophy. But in so learning it seems undeniable that we have made philosophical progress, the same kind of progress that is both recorded and extended in Gadamer's narrative in *Wahrheit und Methode* of the development of hermeneutics from Schleiermacher through

Droysen, Dilthey and Heidegger, up to his own work, work that embodies the insights of earlier approaches but avoids their errors and overcomes some of their limitations. I am therefore puzzled when I find Gadamer expressing his "conviction that philosophy is a human experience that remains the same and that characterizes the human being as such, and that there is no progress in it, but only participation."[10] Progress in philosophy is of course different in key respects from progress in the natural sciences and nowhere more so than in this, that in order to advance from our present condition we may always and often have to make detours into and through past texts, theses and arguments that we may have mistakenly believed that we had long ago put behind us.

This, I believe, is the true moral to be drawn from Gadamer's achievements in his Platonic studies. It is not that progress in philosophy should be denied, but that it should be reconceived. And, if we reconceive it, we will recognize at once that Gadamer's own work exhibits the progress of philosophical inquiry, for example when he moves beyond his hermeneutic predecessors by characterizing hermeneutic practice in terms drawn from Aristotle's account of practice, by reformulating Aristotle's distinctions between *phronesis* and *episteme* and between *techne* and *phronesis*.

Gadamer employs these reworked distinctions in order to make two separate points, although he himself does not always clearly distinguish them. The first is that, in approaching particular texts, we do indeed bring to bear upon them general interpretative principles, but our grasp of those principles consists in our knowledge of how to bring them to bear upon this or that particular text or passage. It is a practical, not a theoretical comprehension that the interpreter exhibits. And it seems that Gadamer correspondingly denies that any purely theoretical comprehension of those principles will be of any assistance at all to interpreters. Second, Gadamer argues that in asking what some particular text has to say to us in our particular condition, we exhibit our interpretative understanding of that text in finding application for it to ourselves. And Gadamer seems correspondingly to deny that there is any such thing as the understanding of a text that is prior to and independent of its applications. In using Aristotle's concept of *phronesis* to make these points,

Gadamer makes significant progress in resolving philosophical issues that had been inadequately dealt with by earlier hermeneutic theorists. But more than that, by making these points in this Aristotelian way, Gadamer opens up still further critical questions, questions that arise from his interpretation of *phronesis.*

What Gadamer affirms about hermeneutics on the basis of his understanding of Aristotle's concepts I take to be clearly right. But the denials that seem to accompany those affirmations are much more dubious. For Aristotle's conception of the *phronemos* is not only that of someone who is practically directed through habituation into the virtues and thereby toward the human good but also of someone who may be able on occasion, by reflection upon his own and others' activity, to arrive at some degree of theoretical understanding of the virtues, including *phronesis,* and their relation to human good. And the *phronemos* may then be able to bring this theoretical knowledge of practical concepts to bear upon his practice, as Aristotle points out at the beginning of the *Nicomachean Ethics* (1094a23) with his observation that a theoretical knowledge of the good will be of use in a way analogous to that in which knowledge of the target is useful to an archer: it gives him something to aim at.

Gadamer has of course discussed this passage[11] and he rightly lays stress on the fact that the possession of this kind of knowledge is never sufficient for an archer, but he never asks whether it may not sometimes be necessary. He therefore never confronts the question of whether the exercise of *phronesis* may not stand in some more complex relationship to a theoretical knowledge of the human good than his own discussion has suggested, as I should want to argue. Practice, in Aristotle's view, as I understand it, always presupposes theoretical truths. The exercise by the *phronemos* of his capacity for making true practical judgments presupposes something close to Aristotle's theoretical account of the human good and of the virtues, for to be a *phronemos* is to be directed toward that good by one's virtues. It is to know how to bring to bear on the particularities of one's situation a conception of the good that it is the task of the theoretical understanding to articulate, and to which in their practice *phronemoi* may need to appeal, for example, when doing the work of legislators. So practice involves theoretical commitments and insofar as hermeneutic practice is, as Gadamer claims, Aristotelian, it involves Aristotelian theoretical commitments. The concept of *phronesis* cannot after all be detached from the theoretical framework of which it is an integral part, as Gadamer detaches it, and put to uses that do not presuppose some of Aristotle's theoretical and indeed metaphysical commitments.

To take this argument further would require a more extended characterization of interpretation as a type of activity that, if it is to achieve its aims, must exemplify the virtues of the *phronemos* and avoid those vices that allow inadequate interpreters to distort and obscure texts, often by projecting themselves on to and into those texts. We all of course, virtuous and vicious interpreters alike, as Gadamer has emphasized, bring to our readings of texts the prejudices, the prejudgments, that we have inherited. But those prejudices can vary in the extent to which they leave us open to confront the texts that we read more or less fruitfully and our own individual relationships to our prejudices also varies. It is in this latter respect that the virtues or vices of the interpreter play a crucial part. Hermeneutics so viewed is a subdiscipline of ethics and the suggestion that I have been making is that, just as an Aristotelian ethics presupposes an Aristotelian metaphysics, so a hermeneutics informed by Aristotelian concepts will have very much the same presuppositions. But if that is so, the philosophical commitments of hermeneutic inquiry extend beyond hermeneutics into metaphysics.

IV

The direction of Gadamer's thought has of course been very different. Where I have tried to suggest that hermeneutic inquiry remains incomplete until it has recognized its metaphysical presuppositions, Gadamer has stressed the incompleteness and therefore the one-sidedness of even what he takes to be the best work in any metaphysical mode. And this is nowhere more evident than in his writing on Hegel's dialectic, Hegel being the philosopher who has insisted most vehemently on having both the first and last word, on the inescapability both of his starting point and of his concluding stance, and on how every thought that is apparently at odds with his account of the dialectic turns out to be itself a moment or an aspect of a moment in the self-development of the Concept.

Gadamer has rejected Hegel's conception of the dialectic as in this way self-sufficient, but nonetheless he has given us a deeply sympathetic reading of Hegel, while insisting that "Hegel's logic indirectly points beyond itself."[12] It does so because "the logical" always needs further explication, explication which takes us beyond speculative statements and the level of the logical to natural language, for "language is an 'element' in which we live in a very different sense than reflection is."[13] Gadamer had earlier remarked that "concepts are only what they are in their functioning and this functioning always rests on the natural logic of language."[14] So both the elaboration and the analysis of concepts always have to refer us back to natural language. And it is, because this is so, that dialectics cannot claim the last word. "The more radically objectifying thought reflects upon itself and unfolds the experience of dialectic, the more clearly it points to what it is not. Dialectic must retrieve itself in hermeneutics."[15]

This hermeneutic retrieval is what Gadamer has accomplished in his essays on Hegel. Yet it is not, on Gadamer's view, that hermeneutics, rather than dialectics, has the last word. The resources of hermeneutics are the resources of language and it is to language and only to language that Gadamer ascribes a condition that is beyond critique and beyond prescription. "Words themselves prescribe the only ways in which we can put them to use. One refers to that as proper 'usage'—something which does not depend on us, but rather we on it, since we are not allowed to violate it."[16] Language itself, on this Heideggerian view, is given, or rather cannot but utter, the last word. Here is not just one more topic for disagreement, but perhaps the matter about which Gadamer and I are most profoundly at odds. Our differences about the relationship in which metaphysical, including dialectical, modes of thought stand to hermeneutics turn out to be partly rooted in differences about the relationship between the language of metaphysics and the natural languages.

The natural languages, on the view that I am taking, may not in their earlier stages be adequate to, but can become adequate to the tasks of metaphysical inquiry, and both poets and philosophers have played key and complementary parts in making them into what they originally were not. And it is sometimes dangerous to be too respectful toward what is taken to be proper usage. At any given stage in the history of a natural language, the rules of usage that are accorded respect by contemporary users of that language may turn out to be obstacles to further inquiry, metaphysical, scientific or moral, and poets and philosophers may therefore have to move beyond them—to violate them—in order to express questioning thoughts that it would not previously have been possible to express. The natural languages are not in origin, but later become in part at least works of art, made what they are by, among others, poets and philosophers.

This conflict with both Gadamer and Heidegger is one that I cannot pursue further here. It is one in which, as with my other disagreements with Gadamer, my own arguments and theses cannot claim and certainly will not have the last word. There are answers to them on Gadamer's behalf that are not too difficult to anticipate. Even as I take notice of the range of our disagreements, however, I become all the more aware of how often I have been better able to articulate my own thought by reflecting upon Gadamer's arguments and insights. This is because he has for so long exemplified both in his person and in his writings the moral dimensions of the hermeneutic project. He has been for much of our time the *phronemos* of hermeneutics, the exemplary practitioner of the hermeneutic virtues, both intellectual and moral. It may be that in the future others will be able to advance the hermeneutic enterprise further, but, if so, it will only be because they have first been able to learn what Gadamer has taught.

Notes

1. *The Idea of the Good in Platonic-Aristotelian Philosophy,* translated by Christopher Smith (New Haven: Yale University Press, 1986), 2.

2. *Truth and Method,* translated by Joel Weinsheimer and Donald Marshall (New York: Continuum, 2nd rev. ed., 1989), 376.

3. Ibid., 374.

Alasdair MacIntyre

4. Translated as *Cartesian Questions: Method and Metaphysics* (Chicago: University of Chicago Press, 1999).

5. *Truth and Method,* 340.

6. Gadamer, *The Idea of the Good,* 101.

7. Ibid. See also Gadamer, "The Proofs of Immortality in Plato's Phaedo" in *Dialogue and Dialectic: Eight Hermeneutical Studies on Plato,* translated by Christopher Smith (New Haven: Yale University, 1980), 33.

8. Leipzig: Felix Meiner, 1902.

9. See especially *Platos Ideenlehre* V, D, 146–159.

10. *The Idea of the Good,* 6.

11. Ibid., 163–164.

12. Gadamer, *Hegel's Dialectic: Five Hermeneutical Studies,* translated by Christopher Smith (New Haven: Yale University Press, 1976), 95.

13. Ibid., 97.

14. Ibid., 93.

15. Ibid., 99.

16. Ibid., 93.

10

Gadamer and Davidson on Understanding and Relativism

John McDowell

I

That I might pay a small tribute to Hans-Georg Gadamer by considering the comparison indicated in my title was suggested by some remarks of Michael Friedman.[1]

In *Mind and World*[2] I wrote of a conceptually mediated openness to reality, partly constituted by inheritance of a tradition. My invocation of tradition was inspired by Gadamer. The idea of inheriting a tradition helps us to understand what is involved in possessing conceptual capacities, in a certain demanding sense: capacities of freedom, capacities whose paradigmatic actualization is in cognitive activity that is under its subject's control, centrally judgment. I urged that conceptual capacities can also be drawn into actualization in operations of sensibility outside the subject's control. My aim was to allow us to see perceptual experiences as events in which, in operations of their sensibility, subjects take in facts—elements of the world, in the sense determined by the opening remark of Wittgenstein's *Tractatus:* the world as everything that is the case.[3] With this conception, we can hold that operations of our sensibility exert a rational influence on our formation of belief, impinging on our capacities for judgment from within the conceptual sphere. And since in experience—at any rate when they are not misled—perceivers take in elements of the world, experiences allow the world itself to figure in the rational background of the fixation of belief.

I contrasted this with Davidson's picture, in which the operations of sensibility make only a brutely causal impact on belief formation, from outside the conceptual sphere.

Friedman thinks this contrast places me close, at least, to "the traditional idealist doctrine that the world to which our thought relates is a creature of our own conceptualization."[4] And he thinks Davidson is immune to any such charge, just because of the difference between his picture and mine. The occasion for this essay is that Friedman thinks he can reinforce this accusation by exploiting my Gadamerian invocation of tradition. About the accusation in general, I am inclined to echo Gadamer's remark: "It is a sheer misunderstanding if one appeals against idealism—whether transcendental idealism or 'idealistic' philosophy of language—to the being-in-itself of the world. This is to miss the methodological significance of idealism, the metaphysical form of which can be regarded, since Kant, as outmoded."[5] We shall see how this misunderstanding shapes Friedman's critique.

As Friedman notes, Davidson exploits the so-called principle of charity to avoid any threat of linguistic or conceptual relativism. On the ground that I follow Gadamer in insisting that any understanding consciousness is situated in tradition, Friedman suggests I cannot share Davidson's invulnerability to relativism. After citing my Gadamerian claim that "languages and traditions can figure not as '*tertia*' that would threaten to make our grip on the world philosophically problematic, but as constitutive of our unproblematic openness to the world,"[6] he goes on: "One might wonder, accordingly, how McDowell himself would respond to the threat of cultural or linguistic relativism. Are we not faced, in particular, with the threat that there is not one space of reasons but many different ones—each adapted to its own cultural tradition and each constituting its own 'world'?"[7] The implication is that where Davidson is protected against relativism, Gadamer's thinking positively exacerbates the threat. And the further implication is that Gadamer thereby slides toward the "traditional idealist" picture of the world as a creature of our conceptual activity. This is implied in Friedman's characterizing his comparison between Davidson and Gadamer on relativism as "further elucidat[ing] the sense in which McDowell's own position is actually more idealistic than Davidson's."[8] The sense he means, as he has already made clear, is the sense in which idealism depicts the world as a creature of our mental activity.

In section II, I explain why I think this is wrong. In the respects in which it follows Gadamer's, my own thinking is no doubt more idealistic than Davidson's, but not in a sense that has anything to do with representing the world as a product or reflection of our intellectual activity. I am sorry to have drawn Friedman's fire in Gadamer's direction, and I shall try to deflect the attack, in order to begin a renewed expression of the admiration for Gadamer's work that I meant to signal in my book. In section III I consider the contrast between Davidson and Gadamer over the philosophical significance of tradition in its own right, without the supposed connection with idealism in that sense.

II

Davidson averts the threat of relativism by justifying a refusal to make sense of a certain supposed idea, the idea of a repertoire that is meaning-involving, and so intelligible, but not intelligible to us.[9] As he remarks, "it is tempting to take a very short line indeed"[10] with that supposed idea—blankly rejecting it. The principle of charity is central to a less blunt treatment, which displays the rejection as warranted. The argument undermines a conception of a language, or a conceptual scheme, as something that enables a certain sort of confrontation with the world conceived as "something neutral and common that lies outside all schemes."[11] Against this, Davidson insists that when we make play with a conception of languages as confronting the world, we can conceive the world only as the world that we understand our own practice to engage with. Accordingly he writes: "In giving up the dualism of [conceptual] scheme and world [this is the world conceived as "something neutral and common that lies outside all schemes]," we do not give up the world, but reestablish unmediated contact with the familiar objects whose antics make our sentences and opinions true or false."[12] This is perfectly in line with Gadamer's thinking.

Davidson argues that we are entitled to refuse to make sense of the idea of a case of intelligibility that is radically inaccessible to us. What matches this in Gadamer is his contention that "each [worldview] potentially contains every other one within it—i.e., each worldview can be extended into every other."[13] The "horizon" constituted by a specific situatedness in tradition is not closed. On the contrary, it is always open to "fusion" with the horizon constituted by a different specific situatedness.[14] Friedman registers Gadamer's appeal to the possibility of fusion of horizons, but he does not properly acknowledge its force.

Again, the target of Davidson's argument is a conception of the world as "something neutral and common that lies outside all schemes." What matches this in Gadamer is his contention that the openness of every view of the world to every other "makes the expression 'world in itself' problematical."[15] Gadamer writes: "Those views of the world are not relative in the sense that one could oppose them to the 'world in itself,' as if the right view from some possible position outside the human, linguistic world could discover it in its being-in-itself."[16] There is no relativism in saying we cannot draw a distinction between the world itself and the topic of our worldview. As Gadamer writes: "In every worldview, the existence of the world-in-itself is intended."[17] And the world-in-itself, as it figures in this thought, is not Davidson's target but the topic of our worldview—the familiar world with which Davidson says we reestablish unmediated contact when we give up the dualism of scheme and something outside all concepts.[18] Our worldview, precisely because it is, qua worldview, open to every other, has as its topic the world itself, not some supposed item constituted by just what we think. (Such an item would be, at least in part, no better than notional, since we are certainly wrong about some things, and would differ from the corresponding item associated with a different worldview.) Our worldview includes its own receptiveness to the possibility of correction, not only by efforts at improvement that are internal to our practices of inquiry but also through coming to appreciate insights of other worldviews in the course of coming to understand them.

As I said, on the conception of perceptual experience that I recommend, experience lets the world itself figure in the rational background of our fixation of belief. In experience worldly states of affairs themselves exert a rational influence on belief formation, working within the conceptual sphere. I expressed this in *Mind and World* by saying we should not picture the world as lying outside an outer boundary that encloses the conceptual sphere.[19] This image, which is avowedly idealistic in one sense, is part of what prompts Friedman to accuse me of embracing idealism in the sense of representing the world as a creature of our conceptual activity. He writes: "In Davidson's picture the world that our beliefs and judgments are about is, at least in principle, characterizable wholly independently of the conceptual-psychological domain of human intentionality. Indeed, the causal (as opposed to rational) relations between our thinking and the world must ultimately be supported by the entirely nonintentional characterization of the world as the domain of physical natural fact. In this sense, experience relates thought to an independent objective reality across an outer boundary; and it is precisely such a boundary that McDowell himself is most concerned to erase."[20] But this is a travesty of my image. The boundary Friedman insists on is not the one I am concerned to erase.

Of course the facts that constitute the world (apart from facts about human intentionality) are characterizable "independently of the conceptual-psychological domain of human intentionality." It would be crazy to hold that characterizing an object as cubic (for instance) requires concepts of intentionality—in the sense, not of concepts employed in thought, but of concepts whose satisfiers are thinkers or acts of thinking. As Gadamer writes: "No one doubts that the world can exist without man and perhaps will do so. This is part of the meaning in which every human, linguistically constituted view of the world lives."[21] No one doubts that the world exists for the most part outside a boundary that can be drawn around the domain of intentionality. (For the most part only, because of course there are facts to the effect that, for instance, someone thinks such-and-such a thought.) But consistently with its being true, as it obviously is, that facts typically do not concern thought, we can understand the world's impacts on belief formation as being already within the conceptual sphere, not impingements from outside it. The world's impacts on belief formation are the actualizations of conceptual capacities that constitute experiences.

John McDowell

In sustaining the mere sanity of refusing to picture the world as a creature of our conceptual activity, it certainly helps that we can see our thinking as causally influenced by the world we think about. Friedman is wrong to imply that this is unavailable to me, as if the rational relation I discern between operations of sensibility and belief formation—enabling a rational relation between the world itself and our thinking—excluded a causal connection. My objection to Davidson's picture is not that it takes the impact of sensibility on our thinking, and thereby the impact of the world on our thinking, to be causal, but that it takes the impact to be *brutely* causal—causal to the exclusion of being rational. That a relation's being rational can cohere with its being causal—that not all causal relatedness is brutely causal—is of course a doctrine of Davidson's own.[22]

The thought that causal relations "must ultimately be supported by a characterization of the world as the domain of physical natural fact," which Friedman suggests is essential to the way Davidson sustains the world's independence from our intellectual activity, is in fact superfluous to the possibility I am exploiting, the possibility of pointing to a causal connection between thinking and the world in order to disclaim an idealism that depicts the world as a creature of our conceptualizations. This physicalism about causal relations reflects a scientistic hijacking of the concept of causality, according to which the concept is taken to have its primary role in articulating the partial worldview that is characteristic of the physical sciences, so that all other causal thinking needs to be based on causal relations characterizable in physical terms. This might be warranted if there were a reason to credit physical science with a proprietary capacity to penetrate to the real connectedness of things. But I follow Gadamer in holding that there is no such reason.[23] And I think this is Davidson's view too, though he slips from it in his conception of causal relations. The thought that causal relations between mental activity and the extra-mental world require an ultimate anchorage in physical nature, so far from being necessary for Davidson's common-sense realism as Friedman suggests, is out of line with Davidson's best thinking.

Friedman concedes that for Gadamer the possibility of a fusion of horizons is supposed to save us from relativism.[24] But he juxtaposes this concession with saying that for Gadamer, unlike Davidson, the "cultural and linguistic traditions" that account for the initial positions of horizons "can certainly be conceptually divergent from one another."[25] I think this contrast is a misreading of Gadamer. When Davidson attacks the very idea of conceptual divergence between languages, his target is the thought that there might be a way of thinking, a conceptual scheme, constituted as such by the fact that its exercises are suitably directed at the world, with this relation to the world conceived as independent of whether the exercises are intelligible to us: "The idea is . . . that something is a language, and associated with a conceptual scheme, whether we can translate it or not, if it stands in a certain relation (predicting, organizing, facing, or fitting) to experience (nature, reality, sensory promptings)."[26] Rejecting this conception, or supposed conception, is perfectly compatible with acknowledging, as Davidson of course does,[27] that different languages can express different, even strikingly different, ways of thinking. When Gadamer writes of different "worlds" corresponding to different horizons,[28] his point—precisely because this talk of different "worlds" comes in a context in which Gadamer insists that "the multiplicity of these worldviews does not involve any relativization of the 'world' "[29]—cannot be more than what Davidson thus acknowledges. This talk of different "worlds" is only vivid imagery for the undisputed idea of striking differences between mutually accessible views of the one and only world. There is not the contrast that Friedman draws.

This matters for Friedman's suggestion that my aligning myself with Gadamer leaves me without a response to a relativistic challenge. With this suggestion Friedman implies that Gadamer's appeal to the possibility of fusing horizons cannot, as Gadamer supposes, genuinely protect him from problems of relativism. About coming to understand an initially alien thinker, I wrote in terms that were intended to recall Davidson's conception of the standpoint of a radical interpreter, who takes note of how the alien subject's expressions of thought relate to the world the subject lives in.[30] I sounded a Gadamerian note by urging that what the radical interpreter aims at is coming to share a horizon with the other. About this, Friedman writes:

John McDowell

In what sense, however, is the world *with which the alien thinker is engaged* open to our view? For Davidson . . . the principle of charity guarantees that there is only one such world. . . . For McDowell, by contrast, the realm of the conceptual is absolutely unbounded . . . . If the conceptual contents of an alien thinker's engagements with the world are not yet available to us, therefore, how can the world corresponding to these conceptual contents be so? Are we not faced— *before* a fusion of horizons—simply with two different conceptual systems together with two different "worlds" constituted by these systems?[31]

This passage reflects Friedman's misreading of my image of the unboundedness of the conceptual, and his misreading of Gadamer's talk of different "worlds," as if these bits of imagery made unavailable the common-sense point that there is only one world. The world with which the alien thinker is engaged, in a way that is open to our view, is simply the world, which—this is a point that Davidson and Gadamer share—we cannot distinguish from the topic of our worldview. What we are faced with before a fusion of horizons is the world, together with a candidate for being understood as another way of conceiving it, and we have a guarantee—if what confronts us really is another thinking subject—that it will be possible to understand the other's engagements with the world as expressive of another view of the world we had in view all along. (Here we see how the idea that horizons can be fused can be expressed in what amounts to a formulation of the principle of charity.) When we come to understand the other subject, that can involve a change in how we view the world. When the horizons fuse, the horizon within which we view the world is no longer in the same position. But what is in view, now that the horizon is in its new position, is still the world, everything that is the case, not some supposed item constituted by this particular new positioning of the horizon—everything that seems to be the case from within a horizon so positioned. There is no devaluing of reality's independence from thinking here.[32]

III

My main point so far has been that Davidson's exploitation of the principle of charity (at least in this connection) matches Gadamer's exploitation of the possibility of fusion of horizons. Friedman is wrong to suggest that the divergence between them—about whether or not there must be something shared, language or tradition, in the background of the very idea of an understanding consciousness—reveals a difference in respect of vulnerability to a threat of relativism, and thereby to a threat of being unable to pay sufficient respect to the independence of reality. A way to bring this out is to note that Davidson's argument against relativism, in his paper "On the Very Idea of a Conceptual Scheme," predates his even raising (at least in print) the question whether idiolects or shared languages should be primary in our reflection about the meaning of linguistic expressions, let alone settling it in favor of idiolects.[33] Davidson's argument against relativism turns on the thought that—to put it in a way that emphasizes the correspondence with Gadamer—any linguistic practice is intelligible from the standpoint of any other. Put like that, the thought is neutral on what the primary context for the intelligibility of linguistic items is: a community's language or the linguistic practice of an individual. The former might have seemed to cohere with Davidson's early papers on meaning and understanding.[34] In more recent papers he has urged the latter. The argument against relativism works equally well either way; the divergence Friedman tries to exploit is simply not relevant to the argument's success.

But the divergence is surely worth discussing in its own right. I do not believe Davidson has addressed considerations of the sort he would need to address if he were to engage with Gadamer on the significance of shared languages and traditions. And if that is right, there is at least an incompleteness in Davidson's defense of his attribution of priority to the practice of individuals. In fact I believe Davidson's disparagement of sharing deprives him of a wealth of insight that we can find in Gadamer, though I shall not be able to substantiate that properly here.

Davidson plays down the significance of shared languages in the course of reacting against a certain conception of linguistic competence. According to this conception, mastery of a language is "the ability to operate in accord with a precise and specifiable set of syntactic and semantic rules," and "verbal communication depends on speaker and hearer sharing such an ability, and it requires no more than this."[35] Malapropisms (see especially "A Nice Derangement of

Epitaphs") provide clear counterexamples—cases where understanding is not disrupted by mismatches between speaker and hearer
in respect of anything we might see as rules to which they conform
their linguistic behavior. In what he himself describes as "a leap,"[36]
Davidson moves to the thesis that there is "no reason, in theory at
least, why speakers who understand each other ever need to speak,
or to have spoken, as anyone else speaks, much less as each other
speaks."[37] Of course he does not deny that we have a use for the
idea of languages spoken by several people. But he suggests that this
familiar idea can be reconstructed in terms of speakers tending "to
use the same words to mean the same thing," and that the defini-
tional transition from individual practice to shared language is "a
short, uninteresting step."[38] Mutual understanding is massively easier
if one shares ways of using words and constructions with one's interlocutors. This merely practical utility is the only importance Davidson is willing to concede to shared linguistic practice. Because
sharing makes mutual understanding easier to arrive at, people who
live together are in practice brought up into conformity with one
another in their linguistic behavior, but Davidson suggests that in
principle there need not be any such sharing.

By Gadamer's lights, Davidson is surely right to deny that a shared
ability to produce linguistic behavior in conformity to specifiable
rules could suffice for mutual intelligibility. Even restricted to people who, as we would ordinarily say, speak the same language, this
is unacceptable. Looking back over his inquiry into what sharing a
language might amount to, Davidson writes: "We have discovered
no learnable common core of consistent behaviour, no shared grammar or rules, no portable interpreting machine set to grind out the
meaning of an arbitrary utterance."[39] And this chimes well with
Gadamer. Nothing could be further from the spirit of Gadamer's
reflections about hermeneutics than to suppose there could in principle be a method, in a narrow sense, for arriving at an understanding of another person's linguistic productions—something that
could be followed mechanically, or, in Davidson's image, a "portable
interpreting machine."

Davidson is also surely right that people who understand each
other need not share a language with each other in the ordinary

sense. Suppose after a disaster two monoglot survivors from widely divergent linguistic communities encountered each other. Surely they could in principle, given sufficient imagination and good will, come to understand each other's linguistic performances. We could concoct an extraordinary sense in which, in making sense of each other, they would share a language, one defined by specifying what counts as speaking in the same way in terms of the translation scheme they use for each other's utterances.[40] But as Davidson says, "this is not what anyone would call sharing a language, nor what anyone has meant by a common practice or a shared set of rules or conventions."[41]

In this thought experiment, we envisage mutual understanding between people who do not share a language with each other. But Davidson's "leap" goes further, to the claim that understanding does not require anyone ever to *have spoken* as anyone else speaks. Now we could make "speaking as someone else speaks" imply the conception of a sharing that suffices by itself for understanding, and then it would be simply a way of putting Davidson's main point to say that no one needs ever to have spoken as anyone else speaks in that sense. I have suggested that this coincides with a fundamental thought of Gadamer's. Mutual intelligibility is never a matter of the parties having internalized an interpreting machine, and that holds in particular for previous abilities of the parties in our thought experiment to come to an understanding with fellow speakers of their divergent mother tongues. But this just emphasizes that on a more ordinary interpretation of "speaking as someone else speaks," our thought experiment as it stands involves people who previously spoke as others did—say, one speaks German and the other speaks Xhosa, and before the disaster they spoke these languages in interacting with others who spoke them too. If Davidson is to sustain his doctrine that shared practice is of no philosophical interest beyond what derives from its utility in facilitating communication, he must suppose this feature of the thought experiment is inessential. Davidson's claims commit him to denying that one needs to learn to speak as others do, in the ordinary sense, in order to become a human subject, a potential party to an encounter with another that leads to mutual understanding, at all.

Gadamer says: "man's being-in-the-world is primordially linguistic."[42] A follower of Davidson might want to appropriate these words, glossing "linguistic" in terms suitable to Davidson's devaluing of shared languages. But Gadamer is discussing Humboldt's reflections on the differences between languages—languages in the ordinary sense, in which they are shared by their speakers and have histories; languages in the sense that Davidson claims has only practical importance and is devoid of philosophical interest. Gadamer's wording is meant to capture the real significance of Humboldt's doctrine that "languages are worldviews."[43] The thought is that the being-in-the-world of any human subject is shaped by one or another language in the ordinary sense.

I do not believe Davidson ever considers the thought that shared languages might matter for the constitution of subjects of understanding. His target is always the conception of a sharing that would suffice of itself for communication. His implied denial that shared languages might matter in another way is ungrounded by argument. Perhaps it is unintentional, and it may seem harsh to hold him to it. But the fact remains that, focusing exclusively on what is required for communication, he draws a conclusion that is generally disparaging to shared practice. He proceeds as if shared practice could be philosophically interesting only if it were true that it suffices, of itself, for mutual understanding between parties to it. This looks like a blind spot for an alternative possibility.

Davidson writes: "It . . . seems to me important to emphasize that much successful communing goes on that does not depend on previously learned common practices, for recognizing this helps us appreciate the extent to which understanding, even of the literal meaning of a speaker's utterances, depends on shared general information and familiarity with non-linguistic institutions (a 'way of life')."[44] This seems well placed against his standard target, the idea that shared linguistic practice might suffice for mutual understanding. But in pointing in the other directions it points in, the remark opens the question whether shared languages might be philosophically significant in a different way. A worldview, with the same world in view as one's interlocutor has in view ("shared general information"), and familiarity with a human way of life are surely not just aids to arriving at understanding, but conditions for being potential subjects of understanding at all. And can we make sense of subjects meeting these conditions without having been initiated into languages in the ordinary sense, shared linguistic practices?

A human way of life is pervasively shaped by language, not just on occasions of verbal behavior but also in its "non-linguistic institutions." ("Man's being-in-the-world is primordially linguistic.") A "language-game" cannot be confined to bursts of speech. It is a whole in which verbal behavior is integrated into a form of life, including practices that if considered on their own would have to be counted as nonlinguistic.[45] In one sense, there are no nonlinguistic human institutions. Does it make sense to suppose there could be this pervasive shaping of life by language if everyone's verbal behavior was completely idiosyncratic? Surely the understanding baulks if we are asked to envisage initiation into and maintenance of a distinctively human way of life in a context in which there is no such thing as simply hearing the meaning in another's words—in which all communicative interactions require the parties to work at interpreting one another, as they would have to if the ordinary idea of a shared language had no application.

Humboldt considered the differences between human languages in terms of different forms of a universal faculty. Conceding that such an approach yields insights, Gadamer writes: "Nevertheless this concept of language constitutes an abstraction that has to be reversed for our purposes. *Verbal form and traditionary content cannot be separated in the hermeneutic experience.* If every language is a view of the world, it is so not primarily because it is a particular type of language (in the way that linguists view language) but because of what is said or handed down in this language."[46] Humboldt already had a thought that Gadamer puts like this: "language maintains a kind of independent life vis-à-vis the individual member of a linguistic community; and as he grows into it, it introduces him into a particular orientation and relationship to the world as well."[47] But Humboldt understood this thought in terms of "the formalism of a faculty,"[48] whereas Gadamer, reversing that abstraction, understands it in terms of "the unity between language and tradition."[49]

Here the very idea of having the world in view is made intelligible in terms of having grown into a tradition, which is part of what it is to have learned to speak a language in the ordinary sense. In learning to speak a language in the ordinary sense, one does not just acquire propensities to respond verbally to aspects of the passing show. One learns what to say, which in the first instance coincides with what we say, about general features of the world, including, importantly, the past—though it can become clear to one that this is what one is learning only when one is already some distance into the development. Can we keep an application for this idea of growing into a tradition while we try to suppose that no two individuals share a way of speaking? (What becomes of, for instance, listening to the stories of the elders, or more sophisticated counterparts to that?) Or can we dispense with the idea of having grown into a tradition and still make sense of possessing a worldview? Does it make sense to suppose an individual might acquire a worldview by his own efforts of concept-formation and investigation? It cannot help to bring in the efforts of others, if one must already have a worldview in order to be able to interpret their attempts to tell one what they have found out.

Davidson accepts that the very idea of speaking meaningfully presupposes "the distinction between using words correctly and merely thinking one is using them correctly."[50] He argues against the thesis that the required use of "correctly" involves norms of a shared practice. Instead he urges that the relevant norm is determined by a speaker's intention to be understood in a certain way. A speaker uses words correctly, in the only sense that matters, if he uses them in such a way as to be understood as he intends. Depending on one's audience, this may involve using words incorrectly by the lights of grammarians of languages in the familiar sense.

Davidson is right in this resistance to elitism in our reflections about meaning. But without claiming that one can make oneself understood only if one uses some common language in ways that would be approved by a certain sort of authority, we can wonder if the conceptual apparatus that Davidson here helps himself to would be available if there were no such thing as a shared language. The ability to intend some performance to be understood in one way or another has to be learned, like the ability to intend to trump one's right-hand opponent's ace. Such an intention is not a purpose that might

Gadamer and Davidson on Understanding and Relativism

simply start to animate a creature's activity in the course of its animal life, as the purpose of grooming itself can start to govern the behavior of a cat. Is it only a superficial fact, a reflection of mere practicalities, that as things are we acquire the ability to have such intentions at all by learning to speak a language in the ordinary sense—by acquiring a repertoire of potential actions that belong to such a practice, much as trumping one's opponent's ace belongs to the practice of certain games? Does it make sense to suppose that the repertoire of actions whose acquisition enables the formation of such intentions in the first place might be specific to an individual? This is not to suggest that in uttering a string of words one can mean, and be understood to mean, only what the words mean in some shared language. But it is one thing to agree with Davidson that that is not so, and quite another to abandon the thought that the primary form of the ability to mean something by verbal behavior is the ability to mean what one's words mean, independently of the particularity of one's communicative situation—that is, what they mean in the language, in the ordinary sense, that one is learning to speak.

Davidson holds that "verbal behaviour is necessarily social."[51] And, since he takes language and thought (in a certain sense) to be interdependent, this necessary sociality embraces thought as well: "there must be an interacting group for meaning—even propositional thought, I would say—to emerge."[52] Unsurprisingly, given how he disparages the significance of shared practice, the sociality he has in mind is minimal: there must be at least a pair of subjects who interpret each other, and there is no necessary role for shared practices. When there are more than two parties to linguistic interaction, each encounter is in principle similarly confined to its participants, with no need for communal practices in the background. This is to depict the sociality of language as *I-thou* sociality, in contrast with *I-we* sociality—to use terminology introduced by Robert Brandom.[53] Davidson only sketches an *I-thou* conception of the sociality of language, but Brandom undertakes a detailed *I-thou* picture, culminating in provision for making objective purport explicit, that hinges on the idea that the participants in the language-game keep score of one another's deontic statuses, their commitments and entitlements.

It would be impossible to do justice in a few sentences to Brandom's mammoth enterprise, which includes far more than just elaborating this Davidsonian inspiration. But without going into detail, we can see that the scepticism I have expressed, starting from Gadamerian considerations, about Davidson's conception carries over to Brandom's, in the shape of the question whether an *I* and a *thou* can be intelligibly in place without a shared language—something that belongs to a *we*—to enter into constituting them. It is mysterious how the appeal to scorekeeping can help here. How can a pair of items neither of which is on its own intelligible as a perspective on the world—this is why the construction is supposedly necessary—somehow become perspectives on the world by means of the inclusion, in what they are not on their own intelligible as perspectives on, of stretches of each other's behavior?

There is no such difficulty about the Gadamerian *I-we* picture. Here familiarity with a natural language, in which verbal form and traditionary content are inseparable, constitutes an individual stance that is perfectly intelligibly all on its own an orientation toward reality. As Gadamer puts it: "In language the reality beyond every individual consciousness becomes visible."[54] All on its own: not, of course, that a permanently solitary individual could intelligibly have such an orientation toward reality—the language that makes the orientation possible is essentially the possession of a *we;* but there is no reason to accept that the way sociality underlies the possibility of objective purport is by way of multiple individuals keeping tabs on one another.

Brandom suggests that *I-we* pictures are bound to be objectionable. A picture of a linguistic practice has to incorporate subjection to norms, and Brandom suggests that *I-we* pictures, if they undertake this burden, speak of "the community" as acting in norm-involving ways in which only persons can intelligibly act, such as assessing the performances of speakers. Thereby such approaches unacceptably treat "the community" as a superlative individual.[55]

We should not be misled here by a verbal divergence between Brandom and Davidson. The norms involved in this argument of Brandom's are not the expediencies that figure in Davidson's gloss on "correctly," when Davidson undertakes to provide for the distinction between merely thinking one is using words correctly and using them correctly. What Brandom has in mind is, ultimately, norms embodied in the very idea of objective purport. ("Ultimately": he has an idiosyncratic conception, which I am bypassing for these purposes, of norms whose formulation does not involve talk of objective purport, in terms of which he thinks the possibility of objective purport is to be understood.) For instance: that "red" on my lips means what it does involves its being *correct* for me to use the word in saying how a thing is only if the thing is *red*. The normativity this exemplifies makes contact with Davidson's thinking at the point at which he undertakes to provide for objective purport, a separate point from that at which he acknowledges "norms" put in place by a speaker's intention of being understood. Davidson considers the need to distinguish merely thinking one is using words correctly from using them correctly only in connection with being mistaken about what uses of words will get one's meaning across, but the need for a distinction that we can formulate in those terms arises equally in connection with saying how things merely appear to be, as opposed to how they are. I think it does not indicate any substantive divergence from Brandom that Davidson talks of correctness in the use of words only in connection with successfully expressing one's mind and not in connection with whether the mind one expresses is in line with how things are.[56]

Brandom's argument against *I-we* conceptions certainly tells against some philosophical appeals to "the community." But there is no super-person in the picture I have been recommending. I have not credited the *we* who share a language with a super-personal counterpart to the deontic attitudinizing by individuals that is central to Brandom's picture. It might seem that the point of invoking a *we* must be to ensure that there is someone—if not other individuals then a super-individual—to hold speakers to the norms (in Brandom's rather than Davidson's sense) of their linguistic practice. But this reflects a metaphysical scruple about the very idea of subjection to norms, a scruple that finds comfort in seeing norms as instituted by personal activity—if not on the part of ordinary persons then, in a version of the picture that would certainly be confused, on the part of a super-person. And I think the scruple is baseless.[57] If that is right, there is no ground for Brandom's suggestion that anyone who refuses to reduce the necessary sociality of language to inter-actions between individuals must make a super-person out of a *we*. Languages are among what Gadamer calls "the suprasubjective powers that dominate history."[58] They give a normative shape to our life-world, in a way that is not to be reduced to the activities of subjects, but saying that is not crediting personal performances to super-persons.

I have barely scratched the surface of Gadamer's thinking about language. My purpose in this section has been no more than to urge that its basic orientation stands up well in comparison with the *I-thou* orientation of Davidson and Brandom. Thereby I hope to have removed one obstacle that might blind philosophers of "analytic" formation to the riches of the third part of *Truth and Method*.

Notes

1. "Exorcising the Philosophical Tradition: Comments on John McDowell's *Mind and World*," *The Philosophical Review* 105 (1996), 427–467; see esp. 464–467.

2. Harvard University Press, Cambridge, Mass., 1994; reprinted with a new introduction, 1996.

3. Ludwig Wittgenstein, *Tractatus Logico-Philosophicus*, translated by D. F. Pears and B. F. McGuinness (Routledge and Kegan Paul, London, 1961), §1.

4. "Exorcising the Philosophical Tradition," 464.

5. *Truth and Method*, translated by Joel Weinsheimer and Donald Marshall (New York: Continuum, 2nd rev. ed., 1989), 448, n. 84.

6. *Mind and World*, 155.

7. "Exorcising the Philosophical Tradition," 465.

8. Ibid., 464.

9. See "On the Very Idea of a Conceptual Scheme," in Davidson, *Inquiries into Truth and Interpretation* (Oxford: Clarendon Press, 1984), 183–198.

10. Ibid., 185.

11. Ibid., 190.

12. Ibid., 198. This paragraph gives a compressed summary of salient points in a rich and complex article. The only substantial divergence from Davidson's text is that I have re-

placed Davidson's specification of his target, as the idea of languages untranslatable into ours, with a specification in terms of languages unintelligible from our standpoint. This does no harm to the argument, and it is a better fit with Davidson's usual focus on interpretation, rather than translation, as a focus for reflection on understanding. In a limiting case, we simply adopt into our own linguistic repertoire our subjects' means of giving expression to thoughts we have contrived to understand, in order to say what it is that we have come to understand them as saying; this is hardly translation.

13. *Truth and Method*, 448.

14. On the fusion of horizons, see *Truth and Method*, 300–307. This passage is concerned in particular with historical understanding, directed at our own cultural precursors, and in this context Gadamer can use the image of a single horizon that shifts with the passing of time. But the idea of horizons being fused easily transposes to any case where the occurrence of understanding involves overcoming an initial alienness.

15. *Truth and Method*, 447.

16. Ibid.

17. Ibid.

18. That the contact is unmediated, in the sense Davidson intends, is perfectly consistent with what I mean by talking of conceptually mediated openness. Davidson's point is to rule out mediation by epistemic intermediaries, on the lines of sense-data as often conceived, objects of a direct awareness that yields indirect awareness of things in the environment. In the picture of perceptual awareness I recommend, nothing intervenes like that between us and things in the environment. Part of the point of the conceptual mediation I talk of is precisely that it allows us a picture of experience in which it is environmental things themselves, not stand-ins for them, that are "given to the senses."

19. *Mind and World*, 26.

20. "Exorcising the Philosophical Tradition," 462.

21. *Truth and Method*, 447.

22. See "Actions, Reasons, and Causes," in Davidson, *Essays on Actions and Events* (Oxford: Clarendon Press, 1980), 3–19. Davidson there discusses reasons for action, but his considerations apply equally well to reasons for belief.

23. See, for example, *Truth and Method*, 449: "the truth that science states is itself relative to a particular world orientation and cannot at all claim to be the whole." See also the elaboration of this thought at 450–453.

24. "Exorcising the Philosophical Tradition," 464.

25. Ibid.

26. "On the Very Idea of a Conceptual Scheme," 191.

27. Ibid., 183–184.

28. For example in *Truth and Method,* 447, in a passage Friedman quotes.

29. Ibid.

30. *Mind and World,* 34–36.

31. "Exorcising the Philosophical Tradition," 466.

32. Friedman in effect refuses to allow Gadamer and me to distinguish a change in our view of the world from a change in the world. See "Exorcising the Philosophical Tradition," 466, n. 50, where, besides his misreading of Gadamer's talk of "different 'worlds,'" he also tries to justify this conflation—from which he concludes that "the possibility of fusion does nothing to diffuse the threat of idealism"—by citing from me a remark to the effect that when we are not misled in perception, there is no difference between how we perceive things and how they are. But that is a truism. It cannot dislodge me (or Gadamer) from the thought that every worldview has the world in view as everything that is the case, not as everything that it takes to be the case.

33. For this latter doctrine of Davidson's, see, among other papers, "A Nice Derangement of Epitaphs," in *Truth and Interpretation: Perspectives on the Philosophy of Donald Davidson,* edited by Ernest LePore (Blackwell, Oxford, 1986), 433–446; and "The Social Aspect of Language," in *The Philosophy of Michael Dummett,* edited by B. McGuinness and G. Oliveri (Dordrecht: Kluwer, 1994), 1–16. It may not be quite accurate to describe Davidson's position as giving priority to idiolects; see Michael Dummett, "A Nice Derangement of Epitaphs: Some Comments on Davidson and Hacking," in *Truth and Interpretation,* 459–476, at 469. But Davidson does not dissent from this characterization, and it is a convenient way to bring out the flavor of his thinking.

34. See, for example, "Truth and Meaning," in *Inquiries into Truth and Interpretation,* 17–36.

35. "The Social Aspect of Language," 2.

36. Ibid., 7.

37. Ibid.

38. Ibid., 3.

39. "A Nice Derangement of Epitaphs," 445.

40. See "The Social Aspect of Language," 7.

41. "The Social Aspect of Language," 7.

42. *Truth and Method,* 443.

43. Ibid.

44. "The Social Aspect of Language," 10.

45. This is one of the ways in which Wittgenstein uses the expression "language-game"; see *Philosophical Investigations,* translated by G. E. M. Anscombe (Oxford: Blackwell, 1953),

§7: "I shall also call the whole, consisting of language and the actions into which it is woven, the 'language-game'" See also §19: "to imagine a language means to imagine a form of life." Davidson must mean to sound this Wittgensteinian note with his use of "way of life." *Truth and Method* antedates Gadamer's encounter with Wittgenstein, but its conception of the linguistic character of human life resonates with Wittgenstein's later work.

46. *Truth and Method*, 441, Gadamer's emphasis.

47. Ibid., 443.

48. Ibid., 440, 442.

49. Ibid., 441.

50. "The Social Aspect of Language," 10.

51. Ibid., 5.

52. Ibid., 15.

53. *Making It Explicit: Reasoning, Representing, and Discursive Commitment* (Cambridge, Mass.: Harvard University Press, 1994); see the index, under "*I-thou/ I-we* sociality." See in particular 659, n. 50, for an approving citation of Davidson as taking the sociality of "linguistic practice and therefore intentionality" to be of the *I-thou* variety.

54. *Truth and Method*, 449.

55. See *Making It Explicit*, 38–39.

56. See "The Social Aspect of Language," 10–14, for "normativity" as communicative expediency, and 14–15 for objectivity, which Davidson treats in a way that does not involve acknowledging a role for an idea of correctness.

57. In *Making it Explicit*, 661, n. 64, Brandom mentions without comment (citing Heidegger) the kind of considerations that show the scruple to be baseless. But this does not deter him from letting its effects control his own thinking about normativity. Consider the implication, at xiii–xiv, that normativity is "mysterious" unless seen as instituted by activities on the part of those who are subject to the relevant norms.

58. *Truth and Method*, 460.

11

Gadamer, Davidson, and the Ground of Understanding

Jeff Malpas

In his contribution to Gadamer's volume in the *Library of Living Philosophers,* Donald Davidson makes an explicit attempt, taking Plato's *Philebus* as his focus, to connect his own thinking with that of Gadamer in a way that, while it does not ignore possible points of difference, is also suggestive of important continuities in their approaches.[1] In the same volume David Hoy argues that "the hermeneutic theory of interpretation can enter into a dialogue with the Davidsonian account" and attempts to "draw on some of Davidson's arguments to defend Gadamer's hermeneutic theory against its critics."[2] Elsewhere Simon Evnine has suggested that Davidson belongs more in the company of two of Gadamer's own philosophical heroes—Plato and Hegel—"than in the company of the Vienna Circle and Quine, with their austere, anti-metaphysical scientism."[3] In my own work I have advanced a reading of Davidson that brings him into proximity, not only with Gadamer, but also with Gadamer's teacher, Martin Heidegger.[4]

The very idea of drawing comparisons between thinkers from such different philosophical backgrounds is sometimes viewed as of dubious value—perhaps one can find some ideas in Davidson that also appear in Gadamer, but why should the mere fact of such similarity be regarded as of anything more than curiosity value? The worth of any such comparison, however, is not to be found in the mere observation of philosophical convergence but rather in the new light that can be shed through such a "fusion of horizons" on the ideas that are themselves at issue. Such comparison can, moreover, itself be seen as a way of advancing a particular philosophical position. To bring Davidson into proximity with Gadamer, for instance, is already to suggest a view of Davidson that goes against any narrowly "analytic" account of his thinking (given the widespread misreadings of Davidson within the English-speaking analytic literature this might well be an important corrective in itself). More generally, of course, the cross-fertilization that occurs through contact between different approaches and styles is an especially significant factor— this is so in every discipline and not just philosophy—in driving new intellectual developments. In this respect, comparative work across traditions, and between philosophical styles, can be seen as an antidote to the insularity and parochialism that otherwise provides a sure recipe for intellectual stagnation.

Yet while one might acknowledge the value in trying to bring different thinkers into some sort of "conversation" with one another, the work of Davidson and Gadamer might be thought to derive from such completely opposed philosophical traditions and styles that any similarity between them could be only superficial. Davidson, for instance, might well be thought, in spite of claims to the contrary, to be committed to a naturalism, an extensionalism, even perhaps, a scientism, quite antithetical to the humanistic tradition to which Gadamer belongs.

Indeed, Gadamer himself, for all that he seems to feel a proximity between his own position and that of Davidson, has also voiced some uncertainty on the matter. In replying to the aforementioned essay by David Hoy, Gadamer writes: "I have certain reservations concerning a further elaboration of the investigation of the relations between Davidson's efforts and my own," and he goes on, "The problem lies . . . in the fact that it still sounds as if conversation, and the structure of conversation in all areas dealing with understanding, primarily only referred to the attainment of correct knowledge. But what is fundamentally at issue is not primarily science and epistemology but . . . the 'ontology' of life communicating itself through language. Even the model proposition that Davidson employs—'snow is white'—seems strange to me from this viewpoint. Who uttered this, even if it is true? I am only interested in asking about the precondition of human communication: namely, that one really tries to understand what the other thinks about something."[5] Gadamer's concerns here are reflected in some of Rüdiger Bubner's comments on the relation between Davidson's thought and that of Gadamer and Heidegger. Bubner argues that Davidson's approach stands within a largely pragmatist frame that, in contrast to the Heideggerian-Gadamerian approach, simply assumes the relation of language to the world, thereby cutting short any real concern with the ground of understanding, referring us instead to the simple fact of pragmatic success.[6] As Bubner reads Davidson, it seems there is no question of grounding understanding because the fact of understanding is already given.

The question raised by Bubner's and Gadamer's comments is significant inasmuch as it indicates that any attempt at an exploration of possible convergence between the work of thinkers such as Gadamer and Davidson, who come from otherwise divergent traditions, must address some quite basic questions concerning the general character of the philosphical projects in which they are engaged. What is raised here is thus not a matter of whether or not certain Gadamerian theses can be found to have analogues in Davidson, or vice versa,[7] but, more pointedly, whether there is any sense in which these two thinkers might, in spite of their differences in background, be said to share a similar philosophical *orientation* or overall approach. The possibility of such shared orientation is what I intend to explore in the discussion that follows through an investigation of the extent to which Davidson and Gadamer might both be seen to be similarly engaged in an inquiry into what Bubner calls "the ground of understanding" or, in Gadamer, the "precondition of communication." Any investigation of this matter, however, cannot be pursued independently of the broader question as to the very nature of the inquiry into "ground" or "precondition" as it arises in the work of both Gadamer and also Heidegger. It is with this broader question that I will begin.

It is notable that Bubner's own discussion of Davidson is fairly peripheral to the essay in which it appears. The main focus of that essay is not the Davidsonian position but rather certain basic differences, as Bubner sees it, in the way in which Heidegger and Gadamer each respond to the question of ground. It is Bubner's contention that Heidegger's treatment of Dasein as "always already called understanding,"[8] grounds understanding in the ontological structure of Dasein (in the "Interpretation of Existence") in such a way that "the question about the ground is made superfluous"[9]—as soon as Dasein is, so is understanding. Things are no better in this respect, according to Bubner, in relation to Heidegger's later thought, except that Being itself (understood in terms of *Ereignis*) now plays the role earlier given to Dasein. It is against this reading of Heidegger that Bubner argues for the distinctiveness of the Gadamerian approach to the problem of ground—an approach that Bubner presents as oriented toward the historical rather than the ontological. Yet in spite of the important differences that he argues are to be found between the Heideggerian and Gadamerian approaches, Bubner nevertheless presents both Heidegger and Gadamer as concerned with uncovering "the ground of understanding." Since his concern is with the particular way in which the ground of understanding is articulated in Heidegger and Gadamer, however, rather than with the way in which any such grounding, or indeed the inquiry into ground, is itself structured, so he gives relatively little attention to the question of what might be involved in the inquiry into ground that is at issue here.

Still, Bubner does provide some indication of his views on this matter, and at one point he talks of "making precise once again the question regarding the ground of understanding."[10] With reference to the possibility of understanding as it arises in ordinary experience, Bubner comments that "when we want to know why we possess this possibility, then we have to clarify the source of this universal capability, which is bound to no region of objects or field of science. Philosophical hermeneutics stands or falls with this question."[11] Elsewhere Bubner talks of "naming" the ground of understanding, arguing that the ground is not "our own nature" (the answer supposedly given by early Heidegger), not an "anonymous life-process" (Dilthey), not "a quasi-mythical Being" (later Heidegger), not an "all-encompassing world spirit" (Hegel). Instead the ground is to be found in "the history of effect" (*Wirkungsgeschichte*), which is to say, in history as it involves us in tradition, and this is the answer that Bubner finds in Gadamer.

Gadamer, Davidson, and the Ground of Understanding

The way in which Bubner presents matters here—in terms of clarifying the "source" of understanding and of "naming" its ground— is suggestive of a view according to which the ground or "source" to be identified is actually something that stands apart and is distinct from the understanding that it grounds. Yet if one attends to the actual character of the inquiry into ground as Bubner describes it, then it seems that it is not a matter of locating a single distinct source to which understanding is somehow related, but rather of identifying a larger frame or "horizon" within which the possibility of particular acts of understanding, and understanding as a whole, can be located and so given justification. Moreover, the frame or horizon at issue here is not some single structure that stands behind understanding or in which understanding is simply instantiated, but a structure with which understanding is already thoroughly entangled. Gadamer's grounding of understanding in history is thus a matter of our being always already given over to history and to the historical as itself arising only through the dialogical process of understanding.[12]

As Bubner writes of the Gadamerian position: "If we must have recourse to history as the ground for the activity of understanding, we have recourse to something which we have always already implicated in our understanding. There is no independence of the ground irrespective of our effort of justification . . . . the ground of understanding lies in history itself, but this ground is not to be sought independently of that which is grounded through it."[13] Described in this fashion, the relation between ground and what is grounded is not a relation between two independent elements or structures.[14] Understanding is grounded in history, but history is itself worked out only in relation to understanding. Indeed, one might say that there is only the one structure here that is both the structure of understanding and the structure of the historical, and that is worked out in ongoing dialogue.

Notwithstanding the contrast that Bubner draws between the Gadamerian and Heideggerian positions, the "circularity" or reciprocity that is evident in the grounding of understanding as it appears in Gadamer also seems to have a correlate in Heidegger. As Bubner emphasises, understanding is grounded in Dasein's mode of being, and yet Dasein's mode of being is itself worked out only in relation to Dasein's understanding—Dasein is "in" the world (that is to say, Dasein "exists") in and through Dasein's capacity to understand.[15] The reciprocity that is evident here can be stated "ontologically"— that is in terms of the reciprocal relation between the ground and what is to be grounded—as well as methodologically. Stated in methodological terms, such reciprocity or circularity amounts to the idea that the inquiry into ground must implicitly presuppose what it nevertheless aims to question. If understanding is grounded, as in Gadamer, by reference to history, and as history itself refers us back to the process of understanding, then so it would seem that exactly what is in question, namely the possibility of understanding, must already have been presupposed.

As is well known, such circularity is explicitly acknowledged by Heidegger in his discussion of the nature of the question of being near to the beginning of *Being and Time*—there the inquiry into being is seen already to presuppose a prior grasp of what is to be inquired into.[16] Heidegger argues, however, that the circularity at issue here is not damaging to the inquiry being pursued—it is not, for instance, a version of the fallacy of *petitio principii*. He writes that "It is quite impossible for there to be any 'circular argument' in formulating the question about the meaning of Being for in answering this question, the issue is not one of grounding something by such a derivation; it is rather one of laying bare the grounds for it and exhibiting them."[17]

Although the details are not spelled out, it seems that here Heidegger is really distinguishing between two ways of conceiving of the project of grounding. The first involves the grounding of one thing in another by means of some derivation or demonstration. One might take as a paradigm here the way in which a theorem is "grounded" through being derived from some set of axioms and rules of inference within a formal system. In such a case, the grounding relation can be construed as a matter of the formal relating of one thing to another—as theorem is related to axioms by means of rules of inference. But such a "derivation" or "demonstration" need not always take on such a formal character. Indeed, Bubner's talk of "source" and "name" might be taken as tending toward such a view of what it is to ground precisely inasmuch as it tends to view the ground as to some extent distinct from what it grounds. The second way does not involve a process of "derivation" of one thing from another—indeed it is not a process that could ever be properly formalized in terms of a sequence of logical inferences from the more to the less basic—but is instead a matter of grounding an entire "region" by uncovering the very structure of that region as such. To the extent that the project of *Being and Time* can be understood, in Bubner's terms, as a matter of establishing a certain ground of understanding, so it is not directed at the derivation of some *instance* of understanding from something more basic, but rather of "laying out" and "exhibiting" the structure of understanding *in its entirety*. Within the framework of *Being and Time*, that means exhibiting the structure of "existence"—the structure of Dasein's being—as a whole.

Laying bare the structure of existence in this way involves exhibiting its underlying unity in a way that nevertheless maintains the multiplicity of elements that make it up—of locating these elements within a single framework or horizon. The being of Dasein must thus be exhibited in terms of a "multiplicity of characteristics" that are constitutive of it and that are also, writes Heidegger, "equiprimordial."[18] Heidegger contrasts this approach with what he regards as a common tendency in ontology "to derive everything and anything from some simple primal ground."[19] The preservation of a multiplicity of elements—and so the insistence on a ground that is itself complex but unitary—is thus an essential feature of the grounding project as it appears in Heidegger, and this is reflected in Heidegger's comment elsewhere that "our investigation does not then become a 'deep' [tiefsinnig] one nor does it puzzle out what stands behind Being."[20] This is clearly also an important element in Gadamer. Indeed, the Gadamerian emphasis on dialogue, and on the immersion of understanding in history or tradition, along with the working out of history itself in relation to the play of understanding, is exemplary of the kind of structure that is at issue here. The ground of understanding is thus uncovered, not through the derivation of understanding from some more basic underlying structure or principle, but rather through exhibiting or "laying out" the structure of understanding itself. Such a "laying out" will often be a matter of exhibiting the broader horizon within which understanding is itself located—as in Gadamer, it will mean locating the understanding in relation to history and to tradition, or else, as in Heidegger, in relation to the structure of existence.

It should already be obvious that the way in which the inquiry into ground proceeds, and the reciprocity that evidently obtains between ground and what is grounded, mirrors the structure that hermeneutic theory has often taken to be characteristic of the movement of understanding as such and that it often refers to in terms of "hermeneutic circularity" or the "circle of understanding." Heidegger is himself quite explicit in treating his own inquiry into the question of being as hermeneutic in character—"only as phenomenology," he writes, "is ontology possible"[21]—while he also argues that the phenomenological method he deploys must itself be construed hermeneutically—"the meaning of phenomenological description as a method lies in interpretation."[22] The idea that the inquiry into the ground of understanding is itself an interpretative inquiry is one way of giving expression to the idea of such an inquiry as properly a "laying out" and exhibiting of reciprocal interconnections rather than a "derivation" or "demonstration." It also draws attention to the way in which the grounding *of* understanding is something that can be undertaken only by reference *to* the understanding. The uncovering of a ground for understanding is not to be achieved independently of the actual operation of the understanding and as such the inquiry into ground turns out to be self-referential in that it uncovers the ground of its own possibility.[23]

The hermeneutic dimension of the inquiry into ground, and the structure that it brings with it, can usefully be illustrated by reference to a more mundane example. When confronted with a text whose meaning we wish to uncover—say a dramatic or poetic work—understanding the meaning is not a matter merely of coming to understand what each word or sentence in the text means independently of the whole. Indeed, one may be able to read the whole of the text and yet still not understand anything of what the text "means." Here the understanding of each word or sentence is dependent on our understanding of the larger structure of which they are a part and within which they "show up" in a particular way (of, course there is a sense

in which for them to "show up" as meaningful at all is already for
them to be located within that larger whole which is the language).
Any such understanding of the text, however, is not itself independent of the understanding of the component words and sentences.
We might characterize this in terms of the familiar "circularity" of
understanding, but in fact it really amounts to the point that understanding in this case is something that must always be worked out by
reference to the text itself.[24] Interpretation is thus a matter of achieving a certain sort of integration or unification (though a complex
unification) of the elements of which the text is composed. The
meaning of any particular element of the text, and so also the meaningfulness of the text as a whole, is itself justified or "grounded" by
reference, not to anything independent of the text, but to the text
itself and the integrity or unity that can be found within it.

The circularity or reciprocity that can be discerned in ordinary
textual interpretation as well as in the philosophical "interpretations" undertaken by Heidegger and Gadamer, refers us to the character of interpretative inquiry—and also, in Heideggerian terms, of
ontology or phenomenological description—as always a matter of
exhibiting the interconnectedness of the elements that make up a
certain region or domain (once one arrives at the appropriate level
of description) rather than through their reduction or derivation,
which can only be carried out "internally" to that region.[25] Strictly
speaking, this does not mean that the region in question is itself
possessed of some "circular" structure. Instead, any such circularity
arises as a result of the fact that the only way the integrity or unity
of some domain can be articulated is through a process that involves
working through the elements of which that domain is composed,
and such working through will indeed give an appearance of circularity. Thus the prior assumptions and expectations on the basis of
which one's current interpretation is based are constantly tested out
against the actual interpretative situation, and often revised in the
light of that situation, as one seeks to arrive at an overall interpretation that optimizes the integrity or unity of the domain in question.

Thus in reading a text, one is constantly involved in playing off
one's overall understanding against one's understanding of particular parts and sections and vice versa. Put in terms of the inquiry into

ground, the establishing of such a ground is not a matter of relating that which is grounded to something that stands apart from it; instead it is a matter of providing an interpretation that will exhibit the integrity or unity of the domain or region in question, and that will thereby bring to light the conditions that make possible what stands within that region, while also exhibiting the region's own interconnected structure. This broadly "interpretative" approach to the question of the ground is clearly tied, in the work of both Heidegger and Gadamer, to a phenomenological-hermeneutic framework, but there is no reason to suppose that it has to be so tied. Indeed, just such an "interpretative" approach also seems to be evident in Davidson's work, albeit couched in the language of analytic epistemology and philosophy of language.

Davidson's early essays, in which the focus on the problem of developing a formal theory of truth—the famous "snow is white" being the archetypal example in this connection—was very much to the fore, may well give the impression of a narrowly technical concern with language in which issues of understanding and communication are subordinated, as in Quine, to questions of scientific epistemology, and in which any question concerning the ground of understanding or the preconditions of communication is completely removed from view. Yet one has only to read Davidson's work more broadly, especially his more recent writings over the last fifteen years or so,[26] to see how mistaken such an impression would be. The question as to how an interpreter can come to understand the words of another has long been a central concern in Davidson's work, but as his thinking on that question has developed, so too has the scope of the question become much broader and its real significance much more explicit. It is not just a matter of how one understands another, but of how one understands oneself as well as the world;[27] not just a matter of understanding the exemplary sentences of Tarski, but also the literary exuberance of Joyce;[28] not just a matter of understanding the character of interpretation given the fact of its pragmatic success, but of uncovering the conceptual linkages that make any such interpretation possible.

The idea of "radical interpretation" provides the original focus for much of Davidson's thinking about understanding. The situation of radical interpretation is one in which an interpreter is faced with a completely unknown language. How, in such a situation, can the interpreter come to understand the language in question? Davidson claims that it is possible only through the interpreter's ability to interact both with the speaker and with the objects and events that make up the speaker's environment and with which the speaker also interacts. An interpreter can thus look to the objects and events in a speaker's environment—objects and events that are also part of the interpreter's surroundings—in order to identify the attitudes and interpret the utterances of the speaker. Indeed, Davidson claims that the mutual interaction between interpreter and speaker in relation to a common set of objects and events is the indispensable foundation for all communication and linguistic understanding.

The importance for the possibility of understanding of a common set of objects and events with which both interpreter and speaker are causally and intentionally related was originally expressed by Davidson in terms of the centrality of the "principle of charity."[29] More recently, however, Davidson has tended to drop talk of "charity," along with reference to "radical interpretation," and he has instead emphasized the way in which understanding, communication and knowledge all depend on a tripartite relationship between interpreter, speaker, and world that can be expressed in a number of different ways: in terms of the way in which the interpreter is able to access the meanings and attitudes of another through their differing positions in relation to some common object; in terms of the interdependence between different forms of knowledge (knowledge of self, knowledge of others, and knowledge of the world); and in terms of the dialogical interplay between speaker and interpreter in the face of some common subject matter. Davidson's approach has thus been essentially to provide an account of the possibility of understanding in a holistic structure that encompasses individual, society, and environment. The delineation of the structure of understanding is a matter of articulating a set of complex and dynamic relationships—a matter of "laying out" a structure that is already present in our actual interpretative-communicative practice. This appears to be a structure that is closely analogous to that which can also be found in Heidegger and Gadamer—one that "grounds" understanding

through exhibiting its interconnected structure—while the Davidsonian approach in general exhibits the same hermeneutic "circularity" as that which is so charcateristic of the Heideggerian and
Gadamerian accounts.

Of course, Davidson's way of presenting this inquiry into ground
is, as I noted above, rather different from the way in which it is presented in Heidegger or Gadamer. For the most part, Davidson's inquiries into "the ground of understanding" take the form, at least
as Davidson presents them, neither of an "ontology" nor a "history."
Instead, the approach has been more oriented toward a variety of
conceptual analysis: exploring the preconditions necessary for interpretation and understanding through a careful mapping out of the
linkages between certain fundamental notions—notions such as
meaning, belief, truth, and knowledge—and of the interelations between the participants in the interpretive-communicative process.
Davidson is quite explicit about the nonreductive character of this
style of analysis as well as its indispensability. Thus he writes:

> . . . however feeble or faulty our attempts to relate these various basic concepts
> to each other, these attempts fare better, and teach us more, than our efforts
> to produce correct and revealing definitions of basic concepts in terms of clearer
> or even more fundamental concepts. . . . For the most part, the concepts philoso-
> phers single out for attention, like truth, knowledge, belief, action, cause, the
> good and the right, are the most elementary concepts we have, without which
> (I am inclined to say) we would have no concepts at all. Why then should we
> expect to be able to reduce these concepts definitionally to other concepts that
> are simpler, clearer, and more basic?[30]

Here Davidson is not only making a claim about philosophical
method but also about the character of the concepts themselves.
In this respect his comments can be seen as mirroring Heidegger's
insistence on ontological inquiry as a matter of the uncovering of
an interconnected structure rather than of reducing it to something
simpler that somehow lies "behind" or "beneath."

Yet any similarity between the Davidsonian and Heideggerian-
Gadamerian approaches may well be thought to arise merely from
the employment of too general a level of analysis, and that Davidson
never moves beyond an inquiry into the immediate "structural suppo-
sitions" (the phrase is Bubner's)[31] of our everyday interpretative prac-

tice—a practice whose possibility is taken as already given rather than inquired into. As Bubner writes: "[In Davidson] the relation of language to the world is assumed and reflexively thematized, and is not substantially grounded in sources other than the correct understanding of language. . . . Davidson has integrated into his theory of interpretation the old argument of pragmatism that, on the whole our systems of orientation do their work, because an eccentric relationship to the world would constantly threaten our basic actions with failure."[32] Just as Gadamer worries that Davidson's concerns remain within the frame of "science and epistemology," so, on this reading, Davidson may be seen merely as providing an account of the presuppositions that must be made in the practice of interpretation—as explicating how interpretation works—rather than providing any account of that on which the possibility of understanding rests. As a consequence, neither "human Dasein" nor "a meaningful history" is seen as playing any grounding role in the Davidsonian account, since there is "no theoretical impetus" to uncover such a ground.[33]

It is certainly true that Davidson does not "name" the ground of understanding in the way that Bubner claims Heidegger and Gadamer do. Yet this does not mean either that the "historical" or the "existential-ontological" have no role to play in his account. The triangular structure that encompasses interpreter, speaker, and thing is a structure that already contains within it a historical dimension inasmuch as it gives expression to the idea that all understanding and interpretation takes place only within the realm of our ongoing socio-linguistic engagement with others[34]—an engagement that is always based in what has gone before. Moreover, the structure that Davidson describes here is not required only as a "structural supposition" of interpretative practice or its explication. Rather, it is a necessary precondition for there to be anything to interpret or to communicate, for there to be a speaker capable of being interpreted or being understood, for there to be an interpreter to interpret or to understand. Indeed, although Davidson often makes use of the language of epistemology, his account ought to be viewed as properly ontological in much the same sense that the term is used by Heidegger and Gadamer. Thus, when Davidson argues that knowledge of self, of other, and of world form a "tripod" in which "if any leg were lost, no part would stand,"[35] he is not making a claim merely about how it is we *know* anything, but rather about what it is for such knowledge *to be*.

Davidson undoubtedly gives a certain priority to our actual communicative-interpretative practice as the touchstone for the inquiry into the nature of understanding. Rather like Wittgenstein, Davidson views understanding not as some occult "inner" process but rather as a matter of our ongoing capacity to "get along" in the world—to "get along" with the objects and events around us and to "get along," both conversationally and behaviorally, with the other persons with whom we share the world. Yet to view understanding and communication in this way does not, by itself, imply a commitment to any significant form of "pragmatism." Instead it represents a commitment, first, to a particular view of what understanding and communication should be seen to consist in—both involve capacities for ongoing *activity*—and, second, to a particular conception of the proper place from which any inquiry into the ground of understanding and communication must begin and back to which it must always be referred. In these respects, however, it may be better to view Davidson in terms that suggest less of a contrast and more a continuity with the Heideggerian and Gadamerian positions.

Rather than as prioritizing the pragmatic, then, the Davidsonian approach can be viewed as giving recognition to what appears in Heidegger and Gadamer as the priority of "the factical"—our being already given over to the world and our activity within it. In being already given over to interpretative-communicative activity—in being "always already called understanding"—we are already given over to the interplay between what appears in Davidson as the triangular dynamic of self, other, and world. And it is in just this interplay that the "precondition of communication" or the "ground of understanding" is to be found—in the working out of the unitary connections that bind together the various elements within the interpretative domain and that therefore give a certain dynamic unity to the triadic field that comprises interpreter, speaker, and thing.

In Davidson's case, this emphasis on the interplay of elements as that in which understanding is properly grounded is also closely tied to a rejection of any approach that would treat understanding or interpretation as a matter of the mastery of a set of rules or conventions.[36] Significantly, it is in relation to just this matter of the role of rules or conventions that Davidson takes issue with Gadamer. In his paper in the *Library of Living Philosophers* volume, Davidson quotes a lengthy passage from Gadamer that includes the comment that "Every conversation presupposes a common language, or, it creates a common language."[37] Davidson notes his agreement with Gadamer on almost all points but then adds:

> Where I differ (and this may merely show I have not fully understood Gadamer) is that I would not say a conversation presupposes a common language, nor even that it requires one. Understanding, to my mind, is always a matter not only of interpretation but of translation, since we can never assume we mean the same thing by our words that our partners in discussion mean. What is created in dialogue is not a common language but understanding: each partner comes to understand the other.[38]

Elsewhere Davidson argues independently that while a shared language may well facilitate linguistic understanding, such sharing is not essential for understanding to be possible. Indeed, for the most part, communication and understanding proceed in spite of differences in linguistic practice and any agreement in such practice that is arrived at is always open to fluctuation.[39] Yet Davidson does allow that he may have misunderstood Gadamer on this point, and, indeed, it seems that Gadamer no less than Davidson is committed to a similarly dynamic conception of the interpretative-communication process. This should be obvious enough from Gadamer's own emphasis on the dialogic or "conversational" character of understanding, but it is also evident in Gadamer's well-known rejection of method as adequate to guarantee truth. Neither for Gadamer nor for Davidson can understanding be reduced to a set of rules, conventions, or principles.

It may be that, for Davidson, the basic concordance between his own and Gadamer's position on this point is obscured by Gadamer's particular emphasis on language as the medium in which understanding always takes place. As Gadamer writes in the essay "What is Truth?": "I believe that it is language that achieves a constant synthesis between the horizon of the past and the horizon of the present. We understand each other inasmuch as we speak with one another, inasmuch as we constantly talk past each other and in the end we are brought, nevertheless, through the use of words, before the things that are said with words."[40] That it is indeed by means of language that understanding is made possible is something with which Davidson would himself agree.[41] What he rejects is that it is possible only on the basis or through the establishing of a *single* language. It is, however, just such an idea that Davidson apparently takes as suggested by the passage he quotes from Gadamer. And while that passage can certainly be read in the way Davidson reads it, what is really at issue there is not to do with the need for a single, shared language prior to any interpretative encounter as the basis on which that encounter is possible, but rather with the role of language as that in which understanding is articulated and expressed. In this respect, the comment need not be taken to commit Gadamer to any strong claim concerning the necessity of a common language for the possibility of understanding. Indeed, as Gadamer explicitly notes in lines that follow the passage from "What is Truth?" quoted above:

> It is the case that language has its own historicity. Everyone of us has his own language. Two people who share their lives with each other have their language. There is no problem at all of one language for all, rather there is only the miracle that although we all have a different language we can nevertheless understand beyond the limits of individuals, peoples, and times. . . . What we grasp with great difficulty is that we cannot speak the truth without the commonality of a hard won agreement. But most astonishing about the essence of language and conversation is that I myself am not restricted by what I believe when I speak with others about something, that no one of us embraces the whole truth within his beliefs but that the whole truth can however, embrace us both in our individual beliefs. A hermeneutics that was adequate to our historical existence would take as its task the development of this meaningful relation between language and conversation that carries us away in its play.[42]

Understanding is possible, then, in spite of differences in language. And this is because understanding is based not in the agreement that consists in a single shared way of speaking but rather in our being already given over to the play of language and conversation.

Just as understanding cannot itself be reduced to a set of rules, conventions, or methods, neither can understanding be *grounded* in any similar fashion. It cannot be reduced to something more basic than it nor derived from anything that stands apart from it. The project of grounding understanding is thus a matter of exhibiting the complex and dynamic structure that is understanding itself and in which all understanding, from the everyday to the existential, from the general to the particular, finds its ground. Of course, just how that structure is set out depends on the particular interpretative approach that is adopted, and clearly Heidegger, Gadamer, and Davidson all offer different analyses of the dynamic structure that is at issue here. Inasmuch as Heidegger takes the structure of understanding to be given in the existential-ontological structure of Dasein, so it is through the interplay among the elements that are constitutive of Dasein's own being, particularly as worked out in relation to care and temporality, that is the real ground for understanding; in Gadamer's hermeneutics, it is the interplay that is encompassed by our relation to history and tradition; and in Davidson it is the interplay that arises through our linguistic engagement in relation to a common object or objects. Yet these differences should not be allowed to obscure the very similar grounding strategy that is evident in all three approaches—a grounding strategy that is essentially hermeneutical and interpretative.

As Bubner presents matters, however, the similarity at issue here does indeed seem to be obscured, in part, through Bubner's focus on the question as to exactly *what* it is that is taken to be the ground of understanding in each case—whether that be ontology, history, or, in Davidson's case, nothing at all. But this way of approaching matters is already problematic in that it takes as its focus not the dynamic relation between elements but rather, as we saw above, the "naming" of one such element *as* a ground or "source"—in so doing, it also tends toward the problematic assumption that the ground of understanding must be seen as something that, at least notionally, stands apart from understanding.[43] Perhaps this is what underlies Bubner's criticism of the Davidsonian position as well as his claim that the Heideggerian approach renders the question about the ground of understanding "superfluous."[44] In Davidson there is nothing beyond understanding to which appeal can be made to ground understanding, while in Heidegger understanding is simply collapsed into that which is supposed to be its ground.

Jeff Malpas

In spite of the obvious differences between them, both Davidson and Heidegger—as well as Gadamer—ground understanding, not through identifying one element as its "source," nor through relating understanding to something apart from it, but precisely through exhibiting its own interconnected and dynamic structure. Strictly speaking, then, the ground of understanding is not Dasein, nor Spirit, not Life, nor even History. It is rather to be found in the complex, dialogical interplay between speakers, and between speakers and their world, that always takes place in relation to language and tradition, and yet is never held captive by them. Something of this idea is surely captured in the lines from Rilke that stand at the head of Gadamer's magnum opus:

Catch only what you've thrown yourself, all is
Mere skill and little gain;
But when you're the catcher of a ball
Thrown by an eternal partner
With accurate and measured swing
Towards you, to your centre, in an arch
From the great bridgebuilding of God:
Why catching then becomes a power—
Not yours, a world's.[45]

Acknowledgments

This essay was begun during a period as a Humboldt Research Fellow at the University of Heidelberg and I gratefully acknowledge the support of the Alexander von Humboldt Foundation as well as the *Philosophisches Seminar* of the University of Heidelberg.

Notes

1. "Gadamer and Plato's *Philebus*," in *The Philosophy of Hans-Georg Gadamer*, edited by Lewis Edwin Hahn (LaSalle: Open Court, 1997), 421–432. The points of disagreement noted by Davidson do indeed seem to be, as Davidson admits is possible, more a product of misunderstanding than real difference.

2. "Post-Cartesian Interpretation: Hans-Georg Gadamer and Donald Davidson," in *The Philosophy of Hans-Georg Gadamer,* edited by Hahn, 110–128.

3. Simon Evnine, *Donald Davidson* (Cambridge: Polity Press, 1991), 154.

4. See *Donald Davidson and the Mirror of Meaning* (Cambridge: Cambridge University Press, 1992).

5. Hans-Georg Gadamer, "Reply to Hoy," in *The Philosophy of Hans-Georg Gadamer,* edited by Hahn, 129–130.

6. Rudiger Bubner, "On the Ground of Understanding," in *Hermeneutics and Truth,* edited by Brice Wachterhauser (Evanston, Ill.: Northwestern University Press, 1994), 81.

7. Bubner himself refers to "the convergence of hermeneutics with Davidson's semantics" noting that "It is astonishing that this essential relationship has received so little attention" ("On the Ground of Understanding," 80).

8. Ibid., 76.

9. Ibid., 78.

10. Ibid.

11. Ibid., 78.

12. Ibid., 74ff.

13. Ibid., 79–80.

14. Ibid.

15. See Heidegger, *Being and Time,* translated by John Macquarrie and Edward Robinson (New York: Harper & Row, 1962), esp. H143ff.

16. See Heidegger, *Being and Time,* H7–H8; see also H150–H153.

17. Ibid., H7–H8; see also H153.

18. Ibid., H131.

19. Ibid.

20. Ibid., H152.

21. Ibid., H35.

22. Ibid, H37.

23. Such self-referentiality is itself something to which Bubner himself draws attention in his well-known discussion of the structure of transcendental argument. Bubner claims that it is characteristic of such arguments and he illustrates the point with reference to Kant as well as to Quine, Strawson, and Wittgenstein. See Bubner, "Kant, Transcendental Arguments, and the Problem of Deduction," *Review of Metaphysics* 28 (1975), 453–467.

24. Even extra-textual considerations are only relevant inasmuch as they are brought to bear on the text and enable us to configure the text in a certain way. In this respect

Jeff Malpas

such considerations really do no more than provide clues as to how the text should be understood.

25. The general structure, and accompanying method, that is outlined here is one that I have elsewhere termed "topological." See Malpas, *Place and Experience* (Cambridge: Cambridge University Press, 1999), 39–41.

26. It is notable that Davidson has written more in the period since the publication of the two Oxford volumes (*Essays on Actions and Events,* Clarendon Press, 1980 and *Inquiries into Truth and Interpretation,* Clarendon Press, 1984), than in the period preceding it and yet for many philosophers—no matter what their background—their only real acquaintance with Davidson's work will be with the essays in those two volumes. It is hoped that the republication of the more recent essays—collected together in three volumes scheduled to appear with Harvard University Press—will go a long way toward rectifying this situation.

27. See especially "Three Varieties of Knowledge," in *A. J. Ayer: Memorial Essays,* edited by A. Phillips Griffiths (Cambridge: Cambridge University Press, 1991), 153–166.

28. See Davidson, "James Joyce and Humpty Dumpty," in *Midwest Studies in Philosophy* 16, edited by P. A. French, T. E. Uehling, and H. K. Wettstein (Minneapolis: University of Minnesota Press, 1991), 1–12.

29. See, for instance, "Radical Interpretation" in *Inquiries into Truth and Interpretation,* 125–140.

30. "The Structure and Content of Truth," *Journal of Philosophy* 87 (1990), 264.

31. See "On the Ground of Understanding," 82.

32. Ibid., 81.

33. Ibid., 82.

34. Some might argue that the structure Davidson sets out here, a structure that seems to minimally involve only two persons is hardly sufficient to sustain any real sense of the social let alone of the historical. It is quite clear, however, that Davidson intends the structure to be a schematic one that captures something of the same structural relation that appears in Gadamer as dialogue or conversation and that might also be taken, minimally and schematically, to involve just two partners, but more properly will always be worked out in ongoing fashion within a linguistic, and hence necessarily also sociohistorical, dimension.

35. "Three Varieties of Knowledge," 166.

36. On this point see: "Communication and Convention," in *Inquiries into Truth and Interpretation,* 265–280; "A Nice Derangement of Epitaphs," in *Truth and Interpretation: Perspectives on the Philosophy of Donald Davidson,* edited by Ernest LePore (Oxford: Blackwell, 1986), 433–446; and also "The Social Aspect of Language," in *The Philosophy of Michael Dummett,* edited by B. McGuinness and G. Oliveri (Dordrecht: Kluwer, 1994), 1–16.

37. Quoted in "Gadamer and Plato's Philebus," 431; the passage is from Gadamer, *Truth and Method,* 341.

Gadamer, Davidson, and the Ground of Understanding

38. Davidson, "Gadamer and Plato's *Philebus*," 431–432.

39. See, for instance, "A Nice Derangement of Epitaphs."

40. Gadamer, "What Is Truth?" in *Hermeneutics and Truth*, edited by Wachterhauser, 45.

41. See, for instance, "Thought and Talk," in Davidson, *Inquiries into Truth and Interpretation*, 155–170, and "Seeing through Language," in *Thought and Language*, edited by John Preston (Cambridge: Cambridge University Press, 1997), 15–27.

42. Ibid, 45–46. It is interesting to note that in a section of this passage not quoted here, Gadamer emphasizes that the things about which we speak are themselves only brought to appearance as common through our speaking about them. This may be thought to mark a different point of disagreement with Davidson, but it is only so if one neglects the way in which, in Davidson too, the common object stands at one apex of a triangle the base line of which—namely the engagement between speaker and interpreter—is itself constituted through linguistic interaction.

43. If either "ontology" or "history" are to be taken as providing a ground for understanding, then it is because they themselves refer us to the interplay of elements that is properly at issue here.

44. Ibid., 78.

45. *Truth and Method*, translated by Joel Weinsheimer and Donald Marshall (New York: Continuum, 2nd rev. ed., 1989), v.

12

Gadamer's Hegel

Robert B. Pippin

So mußte vor allem Hegels Denkweg erneut befragt werden. (Above all else, the path of Hegel's thought must be interrogated anew.)
—*Hans-Georg Gadamer*[1]

I

Gadamer's philosophical hermeneutics is as much a reaction as an initiation: a reaction against a relativistic historicism that "locked" speakers and actors "inside" worldviews; a reaction against the overwhelming prestige of the natural sciences and the insistence on methodology inspired by that success; and a reaction against the "bloodless academic philosophizing"[2] of neo-Kantian philosophy and its perennialist "great problems" approach to the history of philosophy. But in several of his autobiographical remarks, Gadamer singles out an opponent that seems to loom oddly large in his reminiscences about provocations. "Using Heidegger's analysis, my starting point was a critique of German Idealism and its Romantic traditions,"[3] he writes in one such recollection. And in the same essay, he writes of trying to avoid or to "forfeit" (*einbüßen*) "the *fundamentum inconcussum* of philosophy on the basis of which Hegel had written his story of philosophy and the Neo-Kantians their history of problems—namely, self-consciousness."[4] And later, "So I sought in my hermeneutics to overcome the primacy of self-consciousness, and especially the prejudices of an idealism rooted in consciousness. . . ."[5] I want to explore here what Gadamer might mean by giving to hermeneutics the task of "overcoming the primacy of self-consciousness," and to ask whether he has Hegel in his sights as he attempts to do so.

II

Let me first address the conflicting strands of deep solidarity with Hegel, coupled with just as deep a rejection. With respect to the former strand there is much to cite. Indeed, the selection of Hegel as such a principal opponent is somewhat odd because there are so many passages throughout Gadamer's writings that warmly embrace Hegel as a comrade-in-arms. While the major influences on Gadamer's development of a philosophical hermeneutics are unquestionably Plato, Aristotle, and Heidegger, Hegel is not far behind, as the opening epigraph indicates. This is so for a number of reasons.

In the first place, one would expect from Gadamer a sympathetic embrace of Hegel's own reaction against Kantian formalism, an embrace of Hegel's denial of transcendental subjectivity and pure practical reason, an embrace of Hegel's attack on philosophies of transcendence or "the beyond" (*Jenseitsphilosophie*), and so Hegel's attempt to situate or embed the human subject in time, and an embrace of Hegel's attack on all attempts to understand concepts, or language as means employed by a subject, or as rules applied by a subject. The Heideggerean and Gadamerean "dialectic" between "being in a world" (and being always already subject to a particular life-world) and "having a world" (being a potentially critical, reflective subject of such a world) was already clearly explored by Hegel.[6] And Gadamer sees that thereby Hegel had already anticipated a great deal of the dialectic of later European philosophy. Hegel had understood that we would need a way of achieving this rejection of formalism and this sociohistorical "embedding" without ending up with a kind of sociological, empirical, descriptive, nonphilosophical enterprise, and with a diverse plurality of incommensurable language games (an option already on the horizon in Herder). And all this must be accomplished without, by rejecting this empiricism and relativism, reanimating a new hope for some decisive meta-language or transcendental philosophy of necessary conditions for the possibility of sense-making, experience, practical life, and so on; a hope for temporally and methodologically stable conditions, "scientifically" arrived at by a proper "control," or methodology (what turned out to be the neo-Kantian temptation).

It is thus no surprise that, in the exciting calls for a new "life" philosophy swirling throughout Germany in Gadamer's early adulthood, he would recall and astutely take his bearings from such a passage as the following from the preface to *Hegel's Phenomenology of Spirit*:

The form of study in ancient times differs from that of the modern period in that study then was a thorough process of education appropriate for a natural consciousness. In specific probing of each aspect of its existence and in philosophizing about all that occurs, it generated for itself a universality actively engaged in the whole of its life. In the modern period on the other hand, the individual finds that the universal [*die abstrakte Form*] is already prepared for him. It would therefore be better to say that in his effort to grasp it and to make it his own he directly forces the inner essence into the open without the mediatory experience of the natural consciousness. Thus the generation of the universal here is cut off from the manifold of existence—the universal does not emerge out of that manifold. The task now is not so much to purify the individual of his immediate dependency on his senses and to raise him to the substance which thinks and is thought, as it is the reverse, namely, to actualize the universal and to infuse it with spirit by dissolving the fixed determinations of thought.[7]

Hegel's attempt to "infuse" the traditional categories of the understanding "with spirit" (*sich begeistern*),[8] and in his *Phenomenology* his attempt to understand the determinacy and authority of such discriminations by understanding the actual roles they play in a social community, and in their systematic interrelatedness across many different activities of such a community, looks like an attempt to construe norms and principles as having a "life" of their own that in principle is quite close in spirit to Gadamer's two-pronged hermeneutical attack on transcendentalism and relativism.

Moreover, any claim that we have lost something "vital" that was a taken-for-granted aspect of ancient Greek life would be welcome to Gadamer (whose great disagreement with Heidegger stems from

Robert B. Pippin

Gadamer's resolute refusal to see his beloved Plato as "the origin of Western nihilism"), and Gadamer indeed sometimes writes in almost a tone of gratitude for Hegel's philosophical rehabilitation of Greek thinkers as philosophers. He even goes so far as to refer to the Greeks "and their latest and greatest follower, Hegel."[9] As seen below, Gadamer will disagree with Hegel's appropriation of the ancient art of dialectic, with Hegel's account of the deficiencies in the Greek theory of subjectivity, and with Hegel's readings of key passages, but he still credits Hegel, alone among the Titans of modern philosophy—Descartes, Spinoza, Leibniz, Locke, Hume, and Kant—with an appreciation of the "speculative" moment in Greek thought, an appreciation that remained unique in the history of modern philosophy until Heidegger.[10]

Indeed, only Hegel and Heidegger (and, one should now of course also say Gadamer) have shown how philosophy itself should be understood not merely to have a history, but to be its history, that the work of philosophy itself is a speculative recollection of its history, and since it is so speculative and philosophical, it so "reconceptualizes" (*aufhebt,* cancels, preserves, and raises up) historical "thinking and knowing" that the objects of study should no longer count as merely historical texts. ("The first person who wrote a history of philosophy, that was really such, was also the last to do so—Hegel.")[11] As will be shown, there are various ways of comprehending philosophical recollection as a living conversation, ranging from Heidegger's "destruction" of the still living, still ontologically pernicious Western metaphysical tradition, to Hegel's developmental account of how "they" were trying, incompletely, to accomplish what "we" are still trying, more completely, to accomplish, to Gadamer's own account of the eternally inexhaustible residue of meaning in past texts and events, but the denial of any separation between philosophy and its history, and so the refusal to see past philosophers and writers as failed versions of us certainly unites them. At the end of the first part of *Truth and Method,* Gadamer writes, "Hegel states a definite truth, inasmuch as the essential nature of the historical spirit consists not in the restoration of the past but in *thoughtful mediation with contemporary life.*"[12]

Finally, Gadamer makes clear that he understands the radicality of Hegel's enterprise, especially how decisively Hegel broke with "the metaphysical tradition" so constantly under attack by Heidegger and his followers. Whatever Hegel is up to in his account of "spirit's experience of itself" in his *Phenomenology*, and in his treatment of "thought's self-determinations" in his *Science of Logic*, it cannot be understood as a continuation of the "substance metaphysics of the Western tradition."[13] Gadamer realizes that Hegelian spirit, *Geist*, refers just as little to an immaterial substance as Dasein refers to human nature.[14] He notes that in pursuing his own life-long goal of attacking traditional, substance metaphysics, "I do not stand alone in all this; Hegel also held such a view."[15] He even goes so far as to write some things that stand in some considerable tension with what he also says about the need to overcome Hegel's absolutization of the principle of self-consciousness: "In particular, Hegel's powerful speculative leap beyond the subjectivity of the subjective Spirit established this possibility and offered a way of shattering the predominance of subjectivism. . . . Was it not Hegel's intention, also [i.e., together with Heidegger after the latter's 'turn'], to surpass the orientation to self-consciousness and the subject-object schema of a philosophy of consciousness?"[16]

III

That question is somewhat rhetorical, of course, and Gadamer's final answer is that whatever Hegel may have intended, his philosophy did *not* completely break free of "subjectivism," and for all his sympathy with the speculative, historical, "Greek," and antimetaphysical, antisubjectivist elements in Hegel, he cannot finally travel all that far down Hegel's *Denkweg*, the path of his thought.

For one thing, Gadamer is clearly a post-Heideggerean philosopher of finitude, in several different respects. He judges, "Kant's critique of the antinomies of pure reason to be correct and not superceded by Hegel. Totality is never an object, but rather a world-horizon which encloses us and within which we live our lives."[17]

Robert B. Pippin

He might have also added his frequent objections to the idea of such a totality as a *completion*, since any claim for an inner teleology and the completion of a development would have to be made from some position external to historical forms of life, arrived at by some reflective methodology, and it would have to suggest that understanding the past is less a matter of an unformalizable "conversation" and an eventual "fusion" of opposed horizons of meaning (*Horizontverschmelzung*), than it is a result of the application of some independent theory, with epochs as instances of moments in that theory.[18] Gadamer is forever returning to examples from art as paradigmatic problems of understanding, insisting in such passages that it would be ridiculous for someone to claim that Shakespeare could be considered "superior" to Sophocles because farther along in such a putative development.[19] Even more important, such an ideal of a final, absolute self-consciousness, even as a regulative ideal, runs counter to what Gadamer regards as Heidegger's successful demonstration of the unending, unresolveable interplay of "revealing" and "concealing" in claims for truth. "Truth is not the total unconcealment whose ideal fulfillment would in the end remain the presence of absolute spirit to itself. Rather Heidegger taught us to think truth as an unconcealing and a concealing at the same time."[20]

By contrast, Gadamer somewhat ironically embraces what Hegel called the "*bad* infinite" when he claims that the "soul's dialogue with itself" has no teleological end point, no inner direction, and so is inexhaustible. As Gadamer is wont to put it, the "otherness" of the "the other" in, say a conversation or attempt at a textual or historico-cultural meaning, the opacity that originally called for interpretation, is never overcome, can only be partially "revealed" by another sort of "concealing," contrary to Hegel's claim that in modernity especially (in *some* sense brought to its full realization by Hegel) human beings finally recognize themselves, make their own, what had originally seemed, and is now no longer, other.[21]

Gadamer thus takes sides with the enormously influential (for all later modern "Continental" philosophy) Schellingean and Kierkegaardean insistence on finitude against Hegel, and, on this score, is particularly critical of an aspect of Hegel's project that he otherwise praises—Hegel's attempted revivification of ancient dialectic. On the one hand, in Gadamer's view, Hegel appreciated that the kind of Eleatic dialectic on view in the *Parmenides* and in Zeno helps one understand the "interweaving" of and "fluidity" among ideas, especially the way in which statements about certain categorial distinctions undermine the very distinctions themselves (the same must be the same as itself, but also other than "other" and so forth) and so seem to prompt a way of thinking about determinate meaning very different from that possible in standard assertoric judgments. And of course what Gadamer calls the "hermeneutic priority of the question" would lead him to be quite sympathetic to the dialogic, statement and counterstatement, question and answer model or origin for the Hegelian dialectic.[22] On the other hand Hegel, for Gadamer, greatly exaggerated the possibility that some positive doctrine could actually result (for Plato, especially) from such contradictions, and so misinterpreted crucial passages, like Plato's *Sophist*, 259b.[23] (According to Gadamer, Plato is there, in his famous parricide of Parmenides, attempting to *dissolve* the appearance of unavoidable contradiction with his distinction between "otherness" and "not being," not at all to embrace the results as the beginning of a new speculative doctrine.)[24] Gadamer agrees that the undecideability, *aporia* and confusion that result from the Socratic *elenchus* in the *Dialogues,* point to a positive result, but not a positive doctrine, or anything that can be stated as such. The real speculative moment in the *Dialogues* is the dialogue drama itself which, for Gadamer, captures the unsayability but yet the presence of what cannot be said. Hegel, on the other hand, according to Gadamer, in passages that represent the extreme end of his criticism of Hegel, tried to present dialectic as a philosophical method, and in so doing fundamentally compromised his own insights about the limitations of language, the limitations arising from the historical embeddedness of Dasein, and the inherent limitations of natural consciousness itself. Hegel's dialectic is a "splendid monologue," and "relies far more upon the principles of Cartesian method, on the learning of the Catechism, and on the Bible."[25] Or: "In his [Hegel's] dialectical method I see a dubious compromise with the scientific thinking of modernity."[26]

Finally, the most comprehensive criticism of Hegel is intimated by Gadamer's report that one of the earliest influences on his work

Robert B. Pippin

in ancient philosophy was Julius Stenzel, who observed in Greek philosophy what Stenzel had called "the restraining of subjectivity,"
what Gadamer refers to as the Greek "superiority . . . in which out
of self-forgetful surrender they abandoned themselves in boundless
innocence to the passion of thinking."[27] It is hard to imagine more
un-Hegelian phrases than "self-forgetful surrender" and "boundless
innocence," unless it is "the passion of thinking." What Gadamer is
referring to here goes by the general term, "the problem of reflection," (or, said from the Hegelian side, the "impossibility of innocence") and for Gadamer and Heidegger, Hegel's account of the
priority and status of reflection drastically qualifies his achievement
in otherwise opening up ways of considering the "life" of human
spirit without rendering that life an "object" of methodological
study.

IV

And the problem is not an easy one to summarize, especially since
Hegel considered himself a fierce critic of what he termed "finite"
versions of "reflective" philosophies. We need first to note that the
question opened up by Gadamer's restrictions on methodological
access to the lived meanings of texts and utterances concerns the
possibility of the intelligibility of experience itself. The issue is not
a formal account of the interpretive human sciences; the issue is
"ontological" or concerns human being itself. Our very mode of being is interpretive; we exist "understandingly," in an always already
"understood" world. There is no way of conceiving a subject "before"
any act of interpretation, and so no way of understanding the interpretations as accomplished by such a subject. The question Gadamer
is posing about the role of reflection in this large context concerns
then the right way to understand the "understandingly mediated,"
or, said in the German Idealist language, the self-conscious character
of all experience, an issue given great weight by Kant, but already a
key element in modern philosophy as such.

Locke had called reflection "that notice which the mind takes of
its own operations,"[28] a view that typified the "theatre of the mind"
approach of early modern philosophy, wherein what we were con-

scious of in ordinary consciousness could not be said to be spatiotemporal external objects in any immediate sense, but sensory effects, "ideas," "impressions," "representations," and so forth, such that the work of the understanding left us either, for the empiricists, "fainter" and, because more generalized, vaguer "ideas," or, for the rationalists, "clearer and distincter" versions of what were only imperfectly and deceptively apprehended immediately. But for both camps, *consciousness itself was reflective.* (There wasn't first consciousness of objects in the sense of some direct "awakeness" as in the premodern tradition, and then, as a subsequent act, reflective attention to our own modes of apprehending. Being aware was being aware already of one's own mental items, *re*presentings, which then had somehow to be reconnected to their real source or origin.)

This situation (and its resulting skepticism) was unbearable for Kant and in the course of rethinking it, he came to deny a touchstone for both earlier modern traditions: the possibility of some immediacy and givenness in experience at all, whether of the world or of the self. The mind was, Kant argued instead, active in *any* determinate experience and could not be said ever to apprehend directly a given content, even an idea or impression. This meant that the reflective nature of consciousness had to be put another way. In being aware of objects, say external objects, of "outer sense," the mind could still be said to be also "aware of itself," but this not because of awareness of inner content or of "a self." We are manifestly not aware of ideas or impressions of chairs when we are aware of chairs. We are aware of chairs, but we are also *taking* ourselves to be perceiving chairs, not imagining or remembering them, not perceiving stools or tables, and we are ourselves "holding" the elements of such thinkings together in time, all according to various rules that could not be otherwise if such contents are to held together in one time (or so Kant argued). We are conscious, in a way, self-consciously— are adverbially self-conscious. In any act of intending, I am taking myself to be just thus and so intending, and there are elements of that "apperception" that cannot ever be said to be due to our contact with the world, but must be subjectively contributed.[29]

This adverbial self-consciousness meant that there was an element of self-determination (a required active element that could not be

Robert B. Pippin

attributed to the deliverances of the senses) in how I took myself to be engaging the world, and through Fichte and then Hegel, this acquired an almost mythic status as a "divine" sort of freedom. And this element, to come to the decisive point for hermeneutical theory, means that one cannot ever be said simply to be "in" a state of consciousness without also at the same time *not* being wholly "in" such a state, not being wholly absorbed in the intended object, except as an occasionally contingent and always recoverable self-forgetting. As Gadamer puts it in *Truth and Method,* speaking of a subject, understood as in Idealism as a reflective consciousness, "what is essential to it as consciousness is that it can *rise above* that of which it is conscious"[30] (emphasis added). One cannot likewise just be "carrying on," at some level unavailable to reflective consciousness, the practices and rules of a community life. In Hegel's account, *there is no such level unavailable to reflective life or the activity could not count as an activity belonging to us.* Therein lies the deepest disagreement between Gadamer and Hegel.

This approach ultimately meant that for the post-Kantians, especially Fichte and Hegel, the central act of consciousness was not a representing, or picturing, or grasping, or simply being in a state, but an activity, a construing thus and such, a judging, in *some* sense a making. (Hegel, for all the speculative qualifications, does not abandon this revolutionary Kantian insight, and that is partly what Gadamer means by saying that Hegel remains a philosopher of subjectivity.)[31] The position also required that the mind's relation to itself in such consciousness could not be accounted for in any standard bipolar (subject-object) model of intending. In judging, even in judging about ourselves, we are always judging self-consciously, and so reflectively, even while not judging *that* we are judging. (The judgment does not occur unless we judge, and still hold open the possibility of judging rightly or not, and we cannot *do* that without taking ourselves to be doing *that.*)

At some appropriately defined level, the proper explanation of why we organize our experience the way we do, and hold each other to account the way we do, is that we, the subjects of experience, and not the contents resulting from our contact with the world, are "responsible" for such elements. When one begins (with Fichte) to insist that we cannot discover such rules "lying ready made in the mind,"[32] but must be understood to have instituted or founded or "posited" such rules, we have begun to move away from any finite reflective model and have begun to attempt an absolute reflection, an understanding of the process itself of such self-regulation and its necessary moments. The ineliminability of the reflexive character of experience is supposed to provide us with the supreme condition by appeal to which our own determinate requirements for experience can be nonempirically developed. And we have thus arrived at the beginning of Hegel's historical and "logical" account of how and why we hold each other to the norms we do.

This is the background behind many of the things Gadamer says about Hegel, reflection, and self-consciousness, and about this attempt, as he puts it, to develop "the entire content of knowledge as the complete whole of self-consciousness."[33] For example, he writes: "That, according to Hegel, is the essence of dialectical speculation— thinking nothing other than this selfhood, thinking the being of self itself, in which the ego of self-consciousness has always already recognized itself. . . . It (pure, speculative reflection) thus discovers in itself the origin of all further determination."[34]

However the particular transitions in Hegel's *Logic* are argued for, and however much Hegel attempts to avoid the traditional paradoxes in the subject's attempt to know itself absolutely, the whole idea of being able to make anything like the logical structure of intelligibility "for itself," or explicit, is a nonstarter for Gadamer. There is, in the first place, no way, he claims, to extract such normative dimensions from the "lived" language spoken in a community at a time.[35] If that is conceded, we can then appreciate the full force of Gadamer's Heideggerean objections. We are now (with any concession about the unformalizability or rendering explicit of the logical forms of language) prepared to say something like: "We do not speak such a language. It speaks us."[36] "Language completely surrounds us like the voice of home which prior to our every thought of it breathes a familiarity from time out of mind."[37]

Demonstrating this point about the limits of reflection, with all its presuppositions, is what Gadamer meant by claiming that his task was the "overcoming of the primacy of self-consciousness." Such a result would involve acknowledging that the expression "the subject of thought and language" involves both a subjective as well as an objective genitive. The much cited summation of his position is from *Truth and Method*: "Understanding is to be thought of less as a subjective act than as participating in an event of tradition [*Einrücken in ein Überlieferungsgeschehen*], a process of transmission in which past and present are constantly mediated. This is what must be expressed in hermeneutical theory. . . ."[38]

Gadamer, in other words, would have us reverse the canonical relation between Hegel's *Phenomenology* and *Science of Logic*. It is in experiencing the insufficiencies of a disembodied account of our categorial requirements that we would *then* learn the necessity of returning to the lived experience of the "house of being," language. Were a more linguistically oriented *Phenomenology* to be the culmination of this antisystem, one small step would have been taken toward Gadamer's ultimate suggestion: "Dialectic must retrieve itself (*sich zurücknehmen*) in hermeneutics."[39]

V

Before venturing a brief reaction to Gadamer's invocation of and separation from Hegel, I want to endorse enthusiastically the basic principle of his approach to all hermeneutics. There is no essential historical Hegel whose personal intentions we can retrieve, or whose historical world we can objectively reconstruct as the central necessary condition in understanding what his texts meant or mean, and there is no essential or core meaning-in-itself in Hegel's texts, eternally waiting to be unearthed. Gadamer is right: we can only look back at Hegel from where we are now, from within our own "horizon." As Gadamer has shown in a wealth of valuable detail, that does not mean that we cannot be confronted by an "alien" strange Hegel from whom we might learn something, or that the necessity of this "prejudiced" understanding prohibits a challenge to and development of our "fore-understandings." But, in my view, this means we ought, at the very least, to be much less confident that we simply long ago correctly boxed up and shelved "the Hegelian option" and can periodically drag it out and invoke his claims about "thought's self-determination," "development," "progress," "totality," or "Absolute Knowledge," as if straightforward candidates to be either accepted, rejected and modified. We ought, at any rate, to be less confident about these matters than, it seems to me, Gadamer is.

Consider Gadamer's laudatory characterization of Hegel as hermeneut, cited earlier: "Hegel states a definite truth, inasmuch as the essential nature of the historical spirit consists not in the restoration of the past but in thoughtful mediation with contemporary life [*in der denkenden Vermittlung mit dem gegenwärtigen Leben*]."[40] The question of the modesty just mentioned is obviously most at issue in what one might mean by "thoughtful" (here the objections to Hegel's "dialectical methodology," and his developmental, progressive understanding of spirit, and notion of "totality" are relevant), "mediation" (the issue of *reflective* mediation and so the status of the *Logic*), and especially "contemporary life." There are several aspects of the last issue that raise the first questions for Gadamer's approach.

The "horizon" within which Hegel's philosophy reemerged as of possible philosophical relevance for Gadamer and his contemporaries was first of all the systematic question of the human sciences, the *Geisteswissenschaften*. And so Hegel's sensitivity to all the unique, nonreducible elements in such an understanding, to a "conversational logic" in interrogating the past, his insistence on a self-correcting process of historical change, his stress on taking everywhere account of what Gadamer calls the "history of effect" (*Wirkungsgeschichte*) in understanding our own situation, his entire systematic attempt to show that understanding other human beings and their cultural and political achievements could never happen were they to be understood as "objects," attracted a great deal of attention, if also qualification.[41]

But we might look at this as in a way only a first step in clearing a space for understanding the human-qua-human in the modern world. It is understandable that such an initial strategy would so heavily stress what cannot be comprehended by an objective methodology and that we would be occasionally tempted to argue for such a claim by arguing for a *fundamental* inaccessibility. But we stand now in some sense on the other side of the early debates with relativists and positivists and neo-Kantian, "scientistic" naturalists about the very legitimacy of the category of meaning and the relation between understanding (*Verstehen*) and explanation (*Erklären*). Our own "contemporary life situation" thus helps us to see other possibilities in Hegel than those of importance in Gadamer's appropriation and transformation of Hegel. The debate about what we now call "folk psychology" still goes on of course, and the notions of "person" or Geist or Dasein, not to mention belief, desire, intention, and so forth, must, apparently still contend with their naturalist opponents. But the original debate which so decisively influenced Heidegger's early work in phenomenology and therewith Gadamer's project was the psychologism controversy, and Husserl's response in his *Logical Investigations*. That debate made it appear that the alternatives were a psychologistic naturalism, versus some sort of realism about meaning, often a quasi-Platonic realism about meanings, commitment to intentional inexistence, ideal entities like "values" in Scheler's "material ethics," and so forth. Much of Heidegger's animus against idealism and philosophies of subjectivity, and his own insistence on the question of being, draw their inspiration from such realist reactions.

The effects of that early controversy can certainly be seen in Gadamer and in the various claims about what must be independent of, or what must precede and remain unreachable by, the constructions of subjectivity.[42] But the situation looks different now. For one thing, there are not many such Husserlean or Fregean realists around anymore. For another the epistemological problems and the dogmatic implications of such a realism now appear impossible to overcome. For another, the linguistic turn, the success of various attacks on the dogmas of conventional empiricism and analytic philosophy, the influence of Quine's holism, Kuhn's attack on positivist history of science, and a great revival of philosophical Kant scholarship in the spirit of such a postanalytic turn, have all created a different way of understanding Kantian idealism and so a different way of understanding the post-Kantian idealist tradition. So what has drawn attention to Hegel in the last twenty-five years or so are two issues somewhat different from those that connect Gadamer to Hegel.

In the first place, Gadamer was so concerned to limit the pretensions of a "reflective philosophy" and so to insist on a kind of embeddedness and inheritance not redeemable "reflectively," in either

Hegelian or left-Hegelian (practical) or Habermasean terms, that the curious, uniquely modern phenomenon first noticed with such brilliance by Rousseau is difficult to discuss in his terms. One can, to speak somewhat simplistically, come to understand and especially to experience virtually all of one's inheritance, tradition, life-world, and so forth, as coherent and intelligible but *not* "one's own," and so as, root and branch, *alien.* I can even, in some sense that requires much more qualification, become alienated "from myself," from my own life; indeed, paradoxically, can be the agent of such alienation. Or, said another way, all the formal conditions insisted on by modern democratic life as necessary for institutions to count as just (that is as somehow products of my will) can *all* be satisfied without any "identification" with such products; as if I made them, but do not see or experience that making as mine.[43] If there is such a phenomenon and if the language of identity and alienation is as indispensable as the language of rights or the language of finitude in understanding the modern social and political world, then the Hegelian language of subjectivity, reflection, and Geist's "reconciliation with *itself*" will also be ultimately indispensable.[44] And in the last twenty-five years or so, Hegel's approach has come to be more and more in evidence, especially in so-called identity or recognition politics.[45]

The second point can be made by reference to one of Gadamer's favorite images. When he wants to stress the unformalizable and largely unreflective character of everyday human experience of meaning, our mode of understanding, responding to, correcting, ignoring, and so forth meaningful utterances and deeds, Gadamer invokes the image of a game and the activity of play. And it is true that in "understanding" how to play the game and in actually playing it, I cannot rightly be said to be consulting the rules of play and/ or reflectively "applying" them in practice. The founding argument of Heidegger in *Being and Time* about "being in the world" remains for much of the post-Heideggerean Continental tradition decisive on those points.[46] But this also means that such games (to be games) are normatively structured; there is a right and a wrong way to "go on," and the *active adherence* to such rules on the part of (what can only be described as) subjects doing the adhering makes the appeal to some sort of "entering a transmission event," rather than my sustaining a commitment, hard to understand. Such "game-playing" may not be rightly described as "guided" by individual subjects who make episodic, mental decisions, but game-playing is nevertheless certainly "minded" and normatively *guided* in some sense, and one of the topics of recent interest in discussions of Hegel has been attention to how he raises and discusses such questions, especially at the institutional level. (I don't mean to suggest that Gadamer denies this aspect of the problem, but I am not sure that his dialogic model of interrogation and "agreement" is adequate to account for it.)

Subjectivity in Hegel, even the collective kind that he is interested in, can then, on such a view of mindedness, be understood itself as a kind of collective human achievement (in no sense, as Gadamer would agree, a traditional substance), that achievement being the establishment of normatively successful, mutually bound communities. As Nietzsche also noted, we have *made* ourselves into creatures with the right to make promises (we are not "by nature" such creatures), and thus, by holding ourselves and each other to normative constraints, have made ourselves subjects and remain subjects only by finding ways to sustain such results.[47] *Geist,* Hegel regularly says in one of his most puzzling and paradoxical formulations "is a result of itself,"[48] or nothing but the achievement of such rule-following, reflectively rule-assessing communities, and that process must somehow be understood (at its most basic level) as a kind of continual negotiation about normative authority.[49]

Gadamer would be fine with the self-correcting, negotiating, aiming at agreement parts of all this, but without Hegel's argument for the relevance of criteria of genuine *success* in such attempts (ultimately the so-called Absolute viewpoint), we will end up with simply a narrative of what had been taken, as a matter of historical fact, to be failure, success, reformulation, and so forth (in so far as we, by our lights, could understand them now). And there is no reason in principle why such a narrative must be so radically distinct as a mode of knowledge; it seems compatible with a certain kind of cognitive, hermeneutically reflective, historical anthropology (which is what philosophical hermeneutics, without this normative animus, becomes).[50]

The idea of meaning or intelligibility in general as a *result* of normatively constrained or rule bound human practices, or the legacy of Kant's theory of judgment in Hegel (and paradigmatically in Fichte)[51] is, I am claiming, the source of the deepest disagreement between the Idealist and the Heidegger-influenced hermeneutical project, inspired as the latter is by a very different notion of the understanding of meaning and ultimately of truth as "disclosedness" or "unconcealment," and so of understanding as "itself a kind of happening."[52] On this Hegelian view, understanding cannot just happen (*geschehen*); it does not "occur" as we try to "occupy" or seize (*einrücken*) a place in a "transmission-event."

For reasons again having to do essentially with Kant (this time his theory of the unity of reason and the tasks of reflective judgment), this project assumes also a semantic holism, or understands any instance of a meaningful assertion to involve a variety of other implications and commitments without which such an assertion could not be properly made. And this raises the question of how to present an account of the form any such relation of implication, presupposition, inappropriateness, and so forth would have to take were such interconceptual relations really to make possible meaningful assertions. Without attention to this sort of normative dimension and this sort of holism, the project of *Hegel's Logic* would have to look, as it so often has, like a kind of neo-Platonic theory of "concept emanation."

Gadamer's disagreement with this view is why he argues in *Truth and Method,* in a remarkable section on "The limitations of reflective philosophy," against all claims that nothing "pre-reflective" can determine or condition actions or utterances without our really having reflectively incorporated such a pre-reflective level, arguments based on the claim that otherwise such instances could not count as actions or utterances. He insists that these always rests on a kind of rhetorical trick of sorts, that though the argument is successful after its fashion, we know the claim is not true.[53] It is clearer, I think, with respect to the way the "ineliminability of reflection" thesis descends from Kant through Fichte to Hegel, and with respect to these issues of normative reflection, why one would want to say that the game we are playing with norms always involves a possible interrogation about reasons for holding such norms, and that *only* such reasons can "determine"

Robert B. Pippin

our *commitment* to norms (or only beliefs can determine other beliefs). From "where we stand now" the distinctiveness of the "human sciences," following this Hegelian lead, stems from the distinctiveness of human experience in being "fraught with ought" in Sellars's phrase, from the distinctive human capacity we might call our responsiveness to reasons, "oughts." Viewed this way, we can understand why "this is traditional," "this is the way we go on," and so forth could never ultimately count as such reasons, however much time it takes us to learn that.[54]

Acknowledgment

Another version of this essay will appear in the forthcoming *Cambridge Companion to Gadamer,* edited by Robert Dostal.

Notes

1. *Gesammelte Werke,* 2 (Tübingen: J. C. B. Mohr [Paul Siebeck], 1986), 505.

2. Hans-Georg Gadamer, "Reflections on My Philosophical Journey," in *The Philosophy of Hans-Georg Gadamer,* edited by Lewis Edwin Hahn (LaSalle: Open Court, 1997), 9.

3. Ibid., 27.

4. Ibid., 7.

5. Ibid., 27.

6. Ibid., 36.

7. This is a difficult sentence to translate: "die Anstrengung, sie zu ergreifen und sich zu eigen zu machen, ist mehr das unvermittelte Hervortreiben des Innern und abgeschnittene Erzeugen des Allgemeinen als ein Hervorgehen desselben aus dem Konkreten und der Mannigfaltigkeit des Daseins," G. W. F. Hegel, *Die Phänomenologie des Geistes* (Felix Meiner: Hamburg, 1952), 30. Gadamer quotes it in "Hegel and the Dialectic of the Ancient Philosphers," in *Hegel's Dialectic: Five Hermeneutical Studies,* translated by Christopher Smith (New Haven: Yale University Press, 1976), 8.

8. *Hegel's Dialectic,* 16.

9. "Reflections on My Philosophical Journey," 15. Gadamer means to echo here Heidegger's early remark, that Hegel is the most radical of the Greeks. See "Hegel and Heidegger," in *Hegel's Dialectic,* 107.

10. A well-informed study of the Hegel/Heidegger/Gadamer theme, with a focus especially on the common theme of Greek philosophy, is Riccardo Dottori's *Die Reflexion des*

Wirklichen: Zwischen Hegels absoluter Dialektik und der Philosophie der Endlichkeit von M. Heidegger und H. G. Gadamer (Heidelberg: Carl Winter, 1984). See esp. chapter four, "Hegel und Gadamer," 240–299.

11. "Reflections on My Philosophical Journey," 35. See also *Hegel's Dialectic*, 104.

12. *Truth and Method*, translated by Joel Weinsheimer and Donald Marshall (New York: Continuum, 2nd rev. ed., 1989), 168–169.

13. "Reflections on My Philosophical Journey," 34.

14. Going beyond Gadamer and anticipating what will be discussed below, *Geist* refers instead to the collective achievement, in various "developing" ways, of a human community, communities more and more successfully self-authorizing and self-regulating over time. This would require a book-length gloss for it to become clear. For some indications, see my "Naturalness and Mindedness: Hegel's Compatibilism," *The European Journal of Philosophy* 7 (1999), 194–212; also "Hegel, Freedom, the Will: *The Philosophy of Right*, no. 1–33," in *Hegel: Grundlinien der Philosophie des Rechts*, edited by Ludwig Siep (Berlin: Akademie Verlag, 1997), 31–53; and also "What Is the Question for Which Hegel's 'Theory of Recognition' is the Answer?" in *The European Journal of Philosophy* 8 (2000), 155–172.

15. "Reflections on My Philosophical Journey," 34. These claims are also somewhat confusing because Gadamer also attributes to Hegel the intention of reviving "the logos-nous metaphysics of the Platonic-Aristotelian" tradition, but in a way "founded upon Descartes' idea of method" and undertaken "within the framework of transcendental philosophy" (*Hegel's Dialectic*, 78–79). This seems to me an impossible, internally inconsistent characterization.

16. "Reflections on My Philosophical Journey," 37. See also "Hegel and Heidegger." It is Hegel who explicitly carried the dialectic of mind or spirit beyond the forms of subjective spirit, beyond consciousness and self-consciousness. *Hegel's Dialectic*, 104.

17. *Hegel's Dialectic*, 104. See the discussion of Aeschylus on "learning by suffering" in *Truth and Method*, and Gadamer's claim that "Real experience is that in which man becomes aware of his finiteness," 320, and the explicit contrast there with Hegel. See also the helpful discussion by Paul Redding in *Hegel's Hermeneutics* (Ithaca: Cornell University Press, 1996), 35–49.

18. The status of Gadamer's own proposals for a nonmethodological hermeneutics and his somewhat transcendental "theory of the possibility of meaning," and the examples cited to confirm it (not to mention the status of his model, Heidegger's *Daseinanalytik*), in the light of this critique of totality and theory, is another, complicated matter. See his discussion in *Truth and Method*, 306ff and his discussion in "The Scope of Hermeneutical Reflection," in *Philosophical Hermeneutics*, translated by David Linge (Berkeley: University of California Press, 1976), 18–43. Gadamer himself has had to face charges of defending some form of linguistic idealism (from Habermas) and an implicit teleology in his concept of a fusion of horizons (by Wolfhart Pannenberg), and he denies both ascriptions in this essay.

19. Note that the issue depends on what one means by "superior." With respect to the realization of art as such, Hegel goes so far as to defend the superiority of Greek art *as art* over modern. There is, though, another sense in which he claims that the ethical life

Robert B. Pippin

behind Shakespeare's presentation and the kind of self-awareness visible in Hamlet, say, does represent an advance or moment of progress.

20. "Reflections on My Philosophical Journey," 35; see also *Truth and Method*, 269: "To be historically means that knowledge of oneself can never be complete."

21. As is often, indeed endlessly repeated, this hope for a kind of superceded difference and totality, especially when it reappears in Marx's theory of labor, is held to be responsible for "totalitarian thinking" of all sorts (see Gadamer, *Hegel's Dialectic*, 98, on Hegel as forerunner of Marx and positivism!), notwithstanding Hegel's repeated insistence that the state of freedom in question, "being one's self in an another," still requires the self-other relation be preserved. See Jürgen Habermas, *The Philosophical Discourse of Modernity*, translated by Frederick Lawrence (Cambridge: MIT Press, 1987), 36, 42, 84; Theodor Adorno, *Negative Dialectics*, translated by E. B. Ashton (London: Routledge and Regan Paul, 1973), 22–23; and my "Hegel, Modernity, and Habermas," in *Idealism as Modernism*, 157–184.

22. See *Truth and Method*, 362–379.

23. *Hegel's Dialectic*, 22.

24. On this score, about this particular passage, I think Gadamer is quite right. See my "Negation and Not-Being in Wittgenstein's *Tractatus* and Plato's *Sophist*," *Kant-Studien* 70 (1979).

25. *Hegel's Dialectic*, 7.

26. "Reflections on My Philosophical Journey," 45. See also *Hegel's Dialectic*, 79 and *Truth and Method*, 332–333: "Hegel's dialectic is a monologue of thinking that seeks to carry out in advance what matures little by little in every genuine conversation." From Hegel's point of view, in the terms he used early on to discuss such issues of finitude, what Gadamer is defending is a form of "faith" (*Glauben*) not philosophy or knowledge (*Wissen*).

27. "Reflections on My Philosophical Journey," 9.

28. John Locke, *An Essay Concerning Human Understanding*, edited by A. S. Pringle-Pattison (Oxford: The Clarendon Press, 1967), I, 44.

29. I introduce and defend this "taking" and "adverbial" language in my *Kant's Theory of Form* (New Haven: Yale University Press, 1981) and in chapter two of *Hegel's Idealism: The Satisfactions of Self-Consciousness* (Cambridge: Cambridge University Press, 1989).

30. *Truth and Method*, 341.

31. It is also why Hegel's phenomenology is ultimately so different from Husserl's attempt to return to a kind of realism in his phenomenology. For a defense of this claim about the continuities in the Kant-Hegel relationship, see my *Hegel's Idealism*.

32. Contra Heidegger, for the same sorts of reasons, we cannot be said to "find" such formal constraints in the world into which we have been "thrown."

33. *Hegel's Dialectic*, 77.

34. Ibid., 19.

35. Ibid., 95.

36. See "To What Extent Does Language Perform Thought," supplement II to *Truth and Method*, 491–498.

37. *Hegel's Dialectic*, 97.

38. *Truth and Method*, 290. The passage is italicized in the original, *Wahrheit und Methode, Gesammelte Werke* 1 (Tübingen: J. C. B. Mohr [Paul Siebeck], 1986); 274–275.

39. *Hegel's Dialectic*, 99.

40. *Truth and Method*, 168; *Wahrheit und Methode*, 161.

41. A *locus classicus:* the discussion of "observing reason" in the *Phenomenology of Spirit*, translated by A. V. Miller (Oxford: Oxford University Press, 1977), 139–210.

42. I argue that this sort of Heideggerean critique of subjectivity confuses a compelling anti-Cartesianism with a much less persuasive antisubjectivism, in "On Being Anti-Cartesian: Hegel, Heidegger, Subjectivity, and Sociality," in my *Idealism as Modernism* (Cambridge: Cambridge University Press, 1997), 375–394.

43. Gadamer has his own notion of a kind of emancipatory effect of hermeneutical reflection, the results of which assure that ". . . I am no longer unfree over against myself but rather can deem freely what in my preunderstanding (prejudice, *Vorurteil*) may be justified and what unjustified" ("On the Scope and Function of Hermeneutical Reflection," 38). From a Hegelian (or critical theory) perspective, the question of justification raised here, and its historical as well as logical presuppositions, looks like a welcome return to traditional notion of reflection, but in the next paragraph, Gadamer makes clear that he considers this reflective justification to be only a "transformation" of some preunderstanding into another, or the "forming of a new preunderstanding." This seems to me to take back with one hand what was given by another, and is responsible for such Gadamerean claims as that every historian "is one of the 'nation's' historians; he belongs to the nation," and so, whether he acknowledges it or not is "engaged in contributing to the growth and development of the national state" ("On the Scope and Function of Hermeneutical Reflection," 28). See Dottori, *Die Reflexion des Wirklichen*, 289–299.

44. I do not here mean the kind of experience Heidegger discusses in *Being and Time*, when "anxiety" detaches me in some way from my involvement in a world and I experience the ground of my being as a "nullity." The phenomenon of alienation in modernity is, for want of a better word, considerably more dialectical. It is also not captured by Gadamer's invocation of Schiller's notion of disharmony and aesthetic harmony, cited as an isse of alienation in Gadamer's "Hegel and Heidegger" essay in *Hegel's Dialectic*, 106. Schiller, in the seventeenth letter on *On the Aesthetic Education of Man*, translated by Reginald Snell (New York: Fredrik Unger, 1965), 85, locates the origin of our unfreedom in "external circumstances," and "a fortuitous exercise of his freedom." The puzzling issue in Hegel involves self-alienation and is not fortuitous.

45. An important event in this development was the publication of Charles Taylor's influential *Hegel* (Cambridge: Cambridge University Press, 1975).

46. In "On the Scope and Function of Hermeneutical Reflection," he makes two other important points about this game analogy. No one is "it," or has a privileged position ("On

Robert B. Pippin

the Scope and Function of Hermeneutical Reflection," 32) and someone who keeps trying to question or undermine the motives of another player himself falls out of the game, becomes a "spoil sport" ("On the Scope and Function of Hermeneutical Reflection," 41). Both claims lead to Gadamer's objections to Habermas's use of the psychoanalytic model of liberation. One easy summation of Gadamer's Hegel criticism is that Gadamer is accusing Hegel in effect of being such a "spoil sport."

47. Friedrich Nietzsche, *On the Genealogy of Morals,* translated by Walter Kaufmann (New York: Vintage, 1969), 57ff.

48. *Hegel's Philosophy of Subjective Spirit,* translated by M. Petry (Dordrecht: Riedel, 1978), 7.

49. For more discussion and defense of such an interpretation, see "Naturalism and Mindedness: Hegel's Compatibilism."

50. The direction suggested by this claim no doubt brings to mind Habermas's exchanges with Gadamer. See *Hermeneutik und Ideologiekritik* (Frankfurt: Suhrkamp, 1971), and "On the Scope and Function of Hermeneutical Reflection," 26–43. For the differences between the position that I am attributing to Hegel and Habermas's position, see my "Hegel, Modernity, Habermas."

51. See chapter three of *Hegel's Idealism,* "Fichte's Contribution," and "Fichte's Alleged Subjective, Psychological, One-Sided Idealism," in *The Reception of Kant's Critical Philosophy: Fichte, Schelling, and Hegel,* edited by Sally Sedgwick (Cambridge: Cambridge University Press, 2000), 147–170.

52. "On the Scope and Function of Hermeneutical Reflection," 29.

53. *Truth and Method,* 341–346. See Gadamer's formulation of Heidegger's (and his) position in his "Hegel and Heidegger" essay. In discussing "fate" (*Geschick*) and "our being fated" (*Geschicklichkeit*), he writes, ". . . it is a matter of what is allotted [*zugeschickt*] to man and by which he is so very much determined [*bestimmt*] that all self-determination and self-consciousness remains subordinate" (*Hegel's Dialectic,* 109).

54. This of course still leaves a good deal unresolved about how any sort of "universal history" could be possible on such an interpretation, what the Hegelian account of totality would look like, how to understand the relation between thought and language in Hegel, and so forth. All that can be said here is that the direction sketched above does not, I think, lead to what Gadamer calls "the total unconcealment whose ideal fulfillment would in the end remain the presence of absolute spirit to itself" (in "Reflections on My Philosophical Journey," 35). There is no metaphysics of presence in one of Hegel's most sweeping and helpful characterizations of the task of the *Logic,* that this "truth of actuality" must never be represented as a "dead repose," and that ". . . by virtue of the freedom which the Concept attains in the Idea, the idea possesses within itself also the most stubborn opposition; its repose consists in the security and certainty with which it eternally creates and eternally overcomes that opposition, in it meeting with itself" (*Hegel's Science of Logic,* translated by A. V. Miller [London: George Allen & Unwin, 1969], 759).

13

Temporal Distance and Death in History

Paul Ricœur

This essay originates in a rereading of Gadamer's remarks on the "hermeneutic significance of temporal distance" in *Truth and Method*.[1] By way of introduction, the author recalls that all hermeneutic activity is ultimately triggered by a "hermeneutic condition" described as our "belonging to a tradition."[2] This, he goes on, raises the question of the polarity of familiarity and strangeness in our connection with the transmitted past. When strangeness results from distance in time—temporal distance—the question gains in precision. Gadamer claims that "time is no longer primarily a gulf to be bridged, because it separates, but it is actually the supportive ground of process in which the present is rooted."[3] The reason for the fecundity of temporal distance is the persistence of the effects of the events themselves in spite of and across that distance, a persistence that Gadamer refers to by means of the phrase *history of effect* (*Wirkungsgeschichte*). The history of effect turns the transmission itself into an effective action.

I would like to extend the discussion here by introducing the question of death as a paradigm of distance. For the historian, who will be our preferred interlocutor, temporal distance assumes the form of the absence of the past from discourse on it. This absence is itself dramatized by the physical disappearance, the effective death, of past persons. The split between the dead and the still-alive is among the criteria used to differentiate between the historic past and the recent past where living persons—"survivors"—as well as the dead take to the stage, and where the live words of the former blend with the mute words of archival documents. Gadamer does not ponder this difficulty concerning the belonging of persons and institutions to the historic past, or rather he does not consider that aspect of it that might be called their "Being dead already." He does point out, however, that the "permanent significance of something can first be known objectively only . . . when it is dead enough to have only historical interest,"[4] and he refers also to the "mortification of our interest in the object" as a meaning readily assumed by temporal distance.[5] The question, then, is this: how do we deal with death as an extreme form of temporal distance? If the past has as its fundamental meaning that of having-been, then we are indeed separated from that earlier time by the not-being-anymore of all those who, in the words of Michel de Certeau, are the "absentees of history" (*les absents de l'histoire*). In history, the not-being-anymore is not only a general feature of the pastness of all past but also a specific feature of the disappearance of the very actors of history. History is that particular science for which those who have produced or undergone past events are already dead.

One could hope to find some solace in Heidegger's analytic of Dasein. After all, Heidegger defined death as "Dasein's *ownmost* possibility."[6] "Being toward death," as a fundamental ontological structure, belongs according to the author to the most originary and authentic level of our ownmost potentiality-for-Being. As such, it specifies the deepest meaning of originary temporality. But the existential understanding that we are able to have of this primordial structure has no effect on our critical inquiries into the human sciences (*sciences de l'esprit*) in general and history in particular. There are several reasons for this. First, the authentic relationship with death, according to Heidegger, is too personal, too private, too ineffable to be echoed in the relationship with the historic past which appears to have to be relegated to the anonymous level of "one dies" (*man stirbt*). On the other hand, historiography in *Being and Time* only surfaces at a derived level of temporality, namely that of "historicality," which retains of ordinary experience only the phenomenon of "extension" between birth and death, and not mortality as such. As a matter of fact, the only concept discussed at this level is Dilthey's notion of the "connectedness of life,"[7] criticized on account of its lack of ontological depth. Moreover, the authentic meaning of this phenomenon appears to be too much affected by scientific objectification to retain the slightest echo of the original anxiety about death. Finally, and ultimately, historiography is too much marked by a backward looking view on the past to retain in its circle of understanding the pure relationship to the future implied by "Being toward death." For all these reasons, nothing is to be gained for a better understanding of death in history from the presumed originary and authentic understanding of "Being toward death." Not only that: death in history remains without a counterpart in the existential phenomenology of authentic dying.

In an attempt to build a bridge between the way in which the phenomenon of death appears within history as a human science, on the one hand, and Gadamer's reflections on death as one of the paradigms of temporal distance on the other, I shall first explore an alternative to Heidegger's approach to our relationship with death. I shall then elaborate a response, from the historiographical perspective, that could be made to this alternative approach. Finally, I shall try to link up again with the brief remarks in *Truth and Method,* where the concept of temporal distance is absorbed in that of *Wirkungsgeschichte:* at that point, the dead of the historic past will be recalled to life and named as the living of the past.

1   Toward a New Interpretation of Our Relationship with Death

I would like to contrast the idea of death as an intimate possibility of our own most potentiality-for-Being with an alternative reading centering on our potentiality-for-Dying. I shall replace the kind of short circuit instituted by Heidegger between potentiality-for-Being and mortality with a long detour, the details of which follow. It appears to me as though one particular theme is missing from the Heideggerian analysis of care, namely, that of the relationship with our very bodies, our flesh. Thanks to this relationship, our potentiality-for-Being assumes the form of desire, in the broadest meaning of the term that includes Spinoza's *conatus,* Leibniz's appetition, Freud's *libido,* and Jean Nabert's desire-to-be and effort-to-exist. How can death be inscribed into this relationship with the flesh? This is where the long detour starts. First, one learns of death as an unavoidable fate for the body-as-object (*"corps-objet"*). One learns of it through biology, confirmed by daily experience: biology tells one that mortality constitutes the second half of a pair, the first half of which is sexual reproduction. Should this knowledge be judged unworthy of inclusion in the ontology because of its factualness, of its empirical character? Should it be cast into the spheres of *Vorhandenheit* or of *Zuhandenheit*—among the things that are either present-at-hand or ready-to-hand? The answer is no: the flesh confounds this separation of the various modes of being. A separation could only prevail if this objective and objectifying knowledge of death were not internalized, appropriated, impregnated in the flesh of the living beings, the beings of desire that we are. But it is internalized, appropriated, impregnated—and once separation or distantiation has been *overcome* by appropriation, death can be inscribed into one's self-understanding as death proper, as mortal condition. But at what cost?

All that biology offers is a generic statement of the type "one has to"; because we are that sort of living being, we have to die, there is a "to die" in store for us. Internalized, appropriated though it may be, however, this knowledge remains distinct from our desire to live, our will to live, this most primitive of all desires, of our "potentiality-for-Being-a-whole." We have to work on ourselves for a long time before the entirely factual necessity of death can be converted, and when it is, it will not be in a potentiality-for-Dying, but in a mere acceptance of having-to-die. The ultimate constraint of an imperfect conversion turns death into an unavoidable and at the same time haphazard interruption of our originary potentiality-for-Being. To eliminate the gap through acceptance remains one of the tasks to which all of us are subjected, and to which all of us face up with more or less good fortune. A rereading of chapter 20 in book I of Michel de Montaigne's *Essays* ("To philosophize is to learn how to die") will be beneficial in this regard.[8] Such is the enemy that we cannot get away from: "we must learn to stand firm and to fight it. To begin depriving death of its greatest advantage over us, let us adopt a way clean contrary to that common one; let us deprive death of its strangeness; let us frequent it, let us get used to it; let us have nothing more often in mind than death. At every instant let us evoke it in our imagination under all its aspects."[9] And again: "A man who has learned how to die has unlearned how to be a slave. Knowing how to die gives us freedom from subjection and constraint."[10] Still, even though we may have accepted it, death remains frightening, and fills us with fear, precisely because of its nature which is radically distinct from our desire and from the cost involved in its forced acceptance.

On the way toward the internalization of the potentiality-for-Dying, understood as a having-to-die, a mediating role is played by the death of close relatives, whose passing figures prominently among all other deaths, which in turn include those that belong to the historic past. The ingenuity that we apply in order to elude the moment of truth that is the confrontation with our own deaths can also, of course, be used to pretend that the experience of someone else's death, where that someone else is close to us, will not arise. Of far greater use than such meaningless ingenuity, however, are the resources of veracity contained in the experience of the loss of a beloved person, especially when they are viewed in the light of the difficult task of appropriating knowledge of death. In addition to the loss itself, which implies severed communication, there is the task of mourning, which involves internalisation of the irredeemable object of our love as well as the attempted reconciliation with the loss itself. Could we then not anticipate, at the horizon of our mourning for someone else, the mourning that would follow the anticipated loss of our own lives? On the road toward doubled internalization, an anticipation of the mourning for our disappearance which our close relatives will have to engage in can help us accept our future passing as a loss we try to come to terms with beforehand. In the conditions created by the task of mourning, however, the relationship with death never becomes a "Being toward death" (*un être-pour-la-mort*), but remains a "Being against death" (*un être-contre-la-mort*).

Should we take one more step in the direction of death in history and, in doing so, gather a message of authenticity from the death of all those others who are not our close relatives? We would move too fast, I believe, if we were to transfer on the "one" in "one dies" the sum total of inauthentic relationships that we may have with those others. Their deaths hold a lesson that we could not possibly draw either from the relationship of self to self, or from the relationship of self to close relatives. That lesson is of a generally accepted banality: it says simply that "one dies." Could this banality not regain a modicum of ontological significance? It could if we were able to contemplate the threat of an interruption to our desire as an equitable equalization: like everyone else before and after me, I must die. With death, the time of privileges comes to an end. Montaigne was acutely aware of this piece of wisdom. He spoke a moment ago about death as the enemy to whom we must grow accustomed. We must also hear him pay justice to death: "The first part of equity is equality. Who can complain of being included when all are included?"[11] The same message is conveyed by the somber account of the death of the Kings of Israel ("He rested with his fathers")[12] Not to mention the book of *Genesis,* in which we read, first with reference to Isaac, then to Jacob, that in death they were "gathered to [their] people."[13]

2   Death in History

The question that has now opened up is whether *history* has a privileged relationship with this dying of others who are neither self nor close relatives. I, for one, feel that the historian is not condemned to remain without a voice against the reputedly solitary discourse of the philosopher talking about death. The new life breathed into this theme as a result of the alternative reading suggested for the Heideggerian conception of "Being toward death" offers an opportunity for a conversation between philosopher and historian. The conversation opens at the point where what I have called the generally accepted banality of "one dies" is dramatized and magnified by the act of the historian who welcomes all of the past's dead into the space of distance to the past covered by the eye cast on the historic past.

Before moving on, let us remind ourselves once more of the simple fact that in history our dealings are not just with the dead of the past. The history of the present time is a partial exception, since it builds on the testimony of the living, even though only as witnesses who have survived events that are quietly slipping away into bygone absence. So inadmissible to the ordinary understanding of their contemporaries appear the extraordinary events on which they report, and which therefore look even more "bygone" than any and all abolished past, that the voices of these witnesses are often inaudible— sometimes they die of the incomprehension they encounter.

An objection to the emphasis on death in history could be that it is only relevant in a history of events where nothing counts but the decisions and also the passions of a few remarkable personalities. Additionally, the coupling of events and structures would lead to anonymization of the features of mortality associated with individuals considered one by one. It must be borne in mind, however, that, even in forms of history in which structures prevail over events, historical narrative does attribute features of mortality to entities treated like quasi-persons: the death of the Mediterranean, depicted in Fernand Braudel's *The Mediterranean and the Mediterranean World in the Age of Philip II*[14] as a collective hero in sixteenth-century political history, assumes a grandeur in keeping with that of the quasi person it is made out to be. Furthermore, the anonymous death of all those individuals who discreetly cross the stage of history silently raises for the meditating mind the question of the very meaning of this anonymity. The question of "one dies," whose ontological density we were actively restoring a moment ago by referring to the cruelty of violent death and the equity of death as an equalizer of destinies, is as it were being hurled onto the stage of history. It is that death in particular that history is involved with.

The question is how and in what terms.

The first of two possible answers is to visualize the relationship with death as one of those representations-as-objects ("*représentations-objets*") of which modern history has been keen to take account. There is indeed a history of death—in the Western world as well as elsewhere—which is among the most recent achievements of the history of mentalities and representations. Although this "new object" is arguably unworthy of the philosopher's attention, the same cannot be said about death as a player in the unfolding of history. Death then becomes involved in representation as a historiographical operation. In some ways, it signifies absence from history, absence from historiographical discourse. At first sight, if the past is represented as the kingdom of the dead, history seems set to be condemned to offering the reader no more than a shadow theater agitated by survivors waiting for their turn to be put to death. There is a way out, however, namely, to view the historiographical operation as the scriptural equivalent of the social rite of confinement to the grave or in other words of burial.

Burials are confined in space: they typically occur in places at a certain distance from our cities, places called graveyards, where we leave the remains of the living who return to dust. They are not confined in time, however; far from being punctual events that end once the interment is completed, burials are deeds that remain. They remain because the act of interment remains. They coincide in time with the ongoing process of mourning that turns the physical absence of the lost object into an internal presence. Confined in (material) space, burials thus become durable symbols of mourning, memoranda of burial acts.

Historiography transforms these burial acts into writing. The most eloquent spokesperson of this transfiguration of anonymous death by means of the historian's burial act has to be Michel de Certeau. The evolution of de Certeau's thought deserves closer scrutiny.

In *L'absent de l'histoire*,[15] the dead are those who are missing from historical discourse, as a harsh consequence of the generalized usage of the category of interval in historiography. The other, in this type of discourse, is carved out of the self, but it is itself only a trace of what has been. History is therefore a form of discourse organized around a "missing present."[16] That being the case, can the voices of the living be heard? The answer is no: "Writing is manufactured out of permanently mute traces; what has passed does not come back and the voices are lost forever; death imposes silence on the trace."[17] This bold advance in thinking about absence was required to lend the theme of burial its full force. Burial seems indeed to exhaust its effect in the act which "makes present in language the social act of existence today and provides it with a cultural reference point."[18] Only the self-position of the social present appears to compensate the act that refers the past to its absence. Absence is then no longer a state, but the result of the action of history, whose machinery is a genuine producer of intervals, a genuine originator of heterology, or *logos* of the other. The image of a cemetery reserved for the disappeared then comes quite naturally.

In this moment of suspense, Michelet's discourse seems to be that of "the literary hallucination (the return, the 'resurrection') of death."[19] The fact remains, however, that the traces are silent and that the only "continuing discourse" is the historical narrative: "it can talk about the meaning made possible by absence when there is no other place left but discourse."[20] The graveyard theme continues on from the theme of absence: "historical writing makes room for lack and hides it; it creates the sort of narrations of the past that are the equivalent of the graveyards in our cities, it exorcises and owns up to a presence of death amongst the living."[21]

In a later development of de Certeau's thought, admirably expressed in an essay on the historiographical operation published as the second chapter of *The Writing of History*,[22] death is pictured in a less negative light. The symbolic meaning of the burial has been turned on its head and is now quite different from the entirely negative image of the graveyard. More specifically, the turnaround has occurred at the very heart of the burial theme: a few magnificent pages on "the place of the dead and the place of the reader"[23] elaborate the equation between writing (in history) and burial.[24] According to de Certeau, they each constitute an act of exorcism and they each construct a place for the dead. First of all, "writing plays the role of a burial rite. . . . [I]t exorcises death by inserting it into discourse."[25] Like the seventeenth-century "galleries of history" or collections of historical portraits, which excel at it, "writing places a population of the dead on stage—characters, mentalities, or prizes";[26] both appear to confirm the phantasy of the *danse macabre*. On the other hand, writing "possesses a symbolizing function" that "allows a society to situate itself by giving itself a past through language."[27] Writing "marks" a past, and, says de Certeau, "'to mark' a past is to make a place for the dead";[28] in short, "writing constructs a *tombeau* for the dead."[29] On the opposite side of this place in discourse is the place of the (living) reader, the addressee of the writing of history. A dynamic relationship is thus established between the two, the place of the dead and the place of the reader.

"Language exorcises death and arranges it in the narrative that pedagogically replaces it with something that the reader must believe and do."[30] In addition, "'To mark' a past" is not just to make a place for the dead, but also "to determine negatively what *must be done,* and consequently to use the narrativity that buries the dead as a way of establishing a place for the living."[31] We are dealing here with a form of "scriptural conversion"[32] that goes way beyond simple narrativity, in order to play a performative role; performativity assigns to the reader a place, a place to be filled, a "task to be undertaken."[33]

3   Today's Dead Were the Living of the Past

The last word of the historian talking about death in history has not yet been said. The full meaning potential of the concept of a literary burial goes way beyond the act of consigning the dead to their place: the tomb remains symmetrically positioned against the place of the reader in the text (de Certeau). The act of interment can only be truly detached from the purely sepulchral meaning imposed on it by the comparison with the graveyards in our cities if today's dead are not only represented as the absentees of history-being-written, but also as the living of the past at the heart of history-in-the-making. What is at stake here is the elevation of the burial act to some sort of an act of devotion pledged by the historian to the main players of bygone history.

What is it that, in our most lively experience of time, makes possible this act of devotion? Which concrete steps are required for its integration into the historiographical operation? Three pivotal concepts stand along the road of the fundamental experience of temporality leading toward the historical experience articulated by the historiographical operation.

The first of these relates to the very meaning of the pastness of the past. Linguistic usage is a good guide here. Indo-European languages have two sorts of expressions to refer to the past: on the one hand, there are adverbs of time of the form "no longer" joined to verbs in the present tense: "no longer is," "he/she is no longer here"; on the other hand, there are verbal tenses: "this once was," "he/she has been here." The former turn of phrase is negative and can be appropriately used to express the relationship between the present and the bygone past, that is, the historic past which is absent from history-being-written. The latter construction is positive and expresses the Being in the past itself. We are inevitably reminded here of Heidegger's strong distinction between *Vergangenheit*—bygone past—and *Gewesenheit*—having-been. The requalification of the past as having-been is raised in *Being and Time* in connection with the primacy of the futural in the constitution of fundamental temporality: the "anticipatory resoluteness," which carries us forward toward our deaths, is said to have as its counterpart on the ontological level the having-been that conjugates the being "that we are" in the past, whereas *Vergangenheit* is said to express only the nonavailability of the past as an object on which we might wish to exert control. Such a wish, bearing on the past, would be fraught with inauthenticity, or at least with significantly reduced authenticity. This ontological declassification of *Vergangenheit* is remarkably different from real-life experience and its expression in ordinary language, which attaches equal weight to the "no longer" and to the "having-been." From this point of view, historical experience is an excellent guide: it suggests that the best way to proceed is from the "no longer" to the "having-been," from the no-longer of the absentees of history to the having-been of the living of the past.

On the road that leads us back to the past from the future stands a second concept, equally well formulated by Heidegger, namely, the concept of "being indebted" (*Schuld*). Once delivered of its moral sting of culpability[34] and brought back to its pure ontological effectiveness, debt expresses our pure dependence on the past in the positive sense of a transmitted and inescapable heritage. The notion of debt involves more than the notion of trace. Traces extend an invitation to a source or an origin: they signify the cause that has given rise to them. In other words, a trace is an effect-as-sign (*"effet-signe"*) of its cause; crucially, though, it merely signifies without issuing an obligation. Debt, on the other hand, does oblige. But it is not to be construed as some sort of a charge, a weight, or a burden. The obligation is issued by nothing else but the own most potentiality-for-Being. Debt links the human being affected by the past to the potentiality-for-Being hidden in that past and in quest of the futural in the form of promise.

The positive side of debt is in turn underscored by the third concept of linkage—that of "repetition." Heidegger interprets "repetition," which can be traced back to Kierkegaard, in association with the concept of anticipatory resoluteness (in which it is existentially grounded): repetition is repetition "of a possibility of existence that has come down to us."[35] It does not imply a subsequent reconstruction of the past, or a reenactment, but an actualization over again.[36] It expresses "the 'force' of the possible."[37] And there is more. Foreshadowing Gadamer's idea of the transmission of traditions, Heidegger talks about the crossing of the "history of transmission," by which he means the depth of the interpretative processes interpolated between the present representation of the past and the having-been of the "repeated" past.

This brings us to the threshold of Gadamer's notion of the transmission of tradition. In *Truth and Method,* this notion expresses at the same time the efficiency of the mediations that turn temporal distance from an empty space into a field of energy. Gadamer uses the superb phrase *Wirkungsgeschichte,* or the history of effect, which adds a positive aspect to what would otherwise be a simple crossing of temporal distance. In the end, it is all about reopening the past onto the future, more precisely onto the future of that past. Repetition *qua* reopening allows for the completion and the enrichment of the preceding meditation on death in history. The latter has led us to the burial act by means of which the historian, all at once, *gives* a place to the dead and *makes* a place for the living. A meditation on the concept of repetition allows us to take one step more, and that is to say that the living of the past were once alive and that history, in a certain way, reduces the distance to their having-been-alive. Today's dead are yesterday's living, complete with their actions and sufferings.

Historians specialize in retrospection. How are they to go about this additional step beyond the confinement to the grave?

To try to answer this question, we shall call upon two authorities, namely, the French historian Jules Michelet and the British historian R. G. Collingwood.

Michelet will forever remain the visionary who, having discerned France, set out to give it a history. He proclaimed (in the 1869 preface of his *Histoire de France*) that he saw France's history as that of an active and living human being:

> Before me, no one had yet embraced her, looked at her in the living unity of the natural and geographic elements that have constituted her. I was the first to see her as one soul and person. . . . Historical life can only be recovered through a patient pursuit of all its ways, all its forms, all its elements. But what is needed as well is an even greater passion, to reconstruct and restore the interplay of all of these, the reciprocal action of these living forces in a powerful dynamic that thus comes back to life again.

And here surfaces the theme of resurrection: "Even more complicated and more frightening was the historical problem of resurrecting life in its integrality, not just in its superficiality, but in its inner and deepest organisms. No wise person would have ever dreamt of such an undertaking. Just as well I wasn't one myself."

Half a century later, R. G. Collingwood echoes Michelet in more moderate terms; his theme is that of the past's reenactment in the present.[38] The historiographical operation involves the removal of distantiation—identification with what once was. This requires extraction, however, out of each physical event described, of its "internal" face, its "inside," which "can only be described in terms of thought."[39] Having reached a reconstruction that calls upon historical imagination, the historian's thinking may be considered a way of rethinking what has been thought before. In a sense, Collingwood announces Heidegger: "The past, in a natural process, is a past superseded and dead."[40] Whereas, in nature, instants die and are replaced with others, a past event, "so far as it is historically known, survives in the present."[41] Its survival coincides with its reenactment in thought. What is obviously missing from this conception based on identity is the moment of alterity included in the idea of "repetition"; reenactment is more radical inasmuch as it rests on dissociation of occurrence and meaning at the level of the historical event. "Repetition," on the other hand, seizes and respects this joint belonging.

It is possible to do justice to the romantic conception of "resurrection" and the idealist conception of "reenactment" by placing the reiterated horizon of the expectation of past persons under the heading of the idea of repetition. It is important to realize that the retrospective nature of history should not imply a surrender to full determination. Such an implication would result if one were of the view that the past cannot be changed anymore and therefore appears to be entirely determined. According to this view, only the future can be considered uncertain, open and thereby nondetermined. Even though what has been done cannot be undone, and even though what has happened cannot be made not to have happened, the import of what has happened is not determined once and for all; moreover, past events can be narrated and interpreted in different ways, and the moral burden associated with the relationship of debt to the past can be increased or alleviated.

This is the basis on which talk about a backlash of the future in respect of the past within the retrospective viewpoint of history becomes a possibility. Historians have the ability to use their imagination to relive a moment in the past as one that once belonged to the present, and therefore as having been lived by past persons as the present of their past and the present of their future, to use the words of Augustine. Like us, past persons were subjects mounting initiatives, looking back and looking forward. The epistemological ramifications of this insight are immense. The knowledge that people of the past formulated expectations, previsions, desires, fears, and projects leads to a fracturing of historical determinism through a retrospective reinsertion of contingency in history.

An insistent theme of Raymond Aron's *Introduction to the Philosophy of History*[42] is encountered here, namely, the fight against the "retrospective illusion of fatality."[43] Aron intended his remarks in support of the historian's appeal to unreal constructions, echoing Weber's notion of the "causal imputation of individual phenomena." But he also broadened that theme by reflecting on the link between contingency and necessity in historical causality: "We understand here by contingency both the possibility of conceiving the other event and the impossibility of deducing the event from the totality of the previous situation."[44] This general reflection on historical causality invites us to link the reaction against the retrospective illusion of fatality with a global conception of history defined by "the effort to resurrect, or more exactly the effort to put oneself back at the moment of the action in order to become the actor's contemporary."[45]

Hence the history of historians is not condemned to the inauthentic historicality that Heidegger declares to be "blind for possibilities."[46] This would be the fate reserved for any form of historiography confined to a museographic attitude. Historiography, too, can understand the past as a "return" of hidden possibilities.

At the end of this philosophical journey, let us briefly return to the dialectic between the "no longer" of the bygone past and the "having-been" of the living past. I have shown that the dialectic relationship between the absentee from now-told history and the living person of history as it evolved makes a place for the death of the other on the other side of the reader's place in the text. But if death in history preserves the negative side of Gadamer's idea of "temporal distance" as separation, interval, and loss, the resurrection of the past and its living magnifies the positive side of the idea of *Wirkungsgeschichte*. Temporal distance understood in this particular way becomes a condition for the "history of effect" of the past. "Historical interest," writes Gadamer, "is directed not only toward the historical phenomenon and the traditionary work but also, secondarily, toward their effect in history (which also includes the history of research)."[47]

Translated by Bert Peeters

Notes

1. Hans-Georg Gadamer, *Wahrheit und Methode* (Tübingen: J. C. B. Mohr, 6th ed. 1990), 258ff; *Truth and Method*, translated by Joel Weinsheimer and Donald Marshall (New York: Continuum, 2nd rev. ed., 1989), 291ff.

2. *Truth and Method*, 290.

3. Ibid., 297.

4. Ibid., 298.

5. [The English translation of *Truth and Method* talks about *extinction* (298) instead of *mortification*. The latter is used here as a translation of the German term *Abtötung*. Both the French and German terms are related to the idea of death (*mort* in French, *Tod* in German). The French translation of *Wahrheit und Methode* used by Ricœur (*Verité et Méthode* [Paris: Seuil, 1996]) refers to "la mort de l'intérêt personnel pour l'objet," which appears

Paul Ricœur

to be closer to Gadamer's original phrase ("Abtötung des eigenen Interesses am Gegen-
stand").—Tr.]

6. Martin Heidegger, *Sein und Zeit* (Tübingen: Niemeyer, 17th ed., 1993). English transla-
tion: *Being and Time,* translated by John Macquarrie and Edward Robinson (San Fransisco:
Harper, 1962), 307; alternative English translation by Joan Stambaugh (Albany: SUNY
Press, 1996). The translation employed here is that of Macquarrie and Robinson.

7. *Being and Time,* 425.

8. Michel de Montaigne, *Les Essais,* edited by Pierre Villey (Paris: Presses Universitaires
de France, 1992). English translation: *The Complete Essays of Michel de Montaigne* (Harmondsworth: Penguin, 1991).

9. *Essays,* 96.

10. Ibid.

11. Ibid., 104.

12. 1 *Kings* 11:43, and dozens of other similar phrases in 1 *Kings* and 2 *Chronicles.*

13. *Genesis* 35:29; 49:33.

14. Fernand Braudel, *La Méditerranée et le monde méditerranéen à l'époque de Philippe II,* 2 vols.
(Paris: Colin, 6th ed. 1985); English translation: *The Mediterranean and the Mediterranean
World in the Age of Philip II* (New York: Harper & Row, 1972–1973).

15. Michel de Certeau, *L'absent de l'histoire* (Paris: Mame, 1973). This work has not been
translated into English.

16. *L'absent de l'histoire,* 19.

17. Ibid., 11.

18. Ibid., 159.

19. Ibid., 179.

20. Ibid., 170.

21. Ibid., 103.

22. Michel de Certeau, *L'écriture de l'histoire* (Paris: Gallimard, 1975); English translation:
The Writing of History (New York: Columbia University Press, 1988).

23. *The Writing of History,* 99–102.

24. [To get Ricœur's summary of de Certeau's section on the place of the dead and the
place of the reader across without the need for an excessive number of translator's notes,
I have, from here until the end of this paragraph, parahrased Ricœur rather than directly
translated him.—Tr.]

25. *The Writing of History,* 100.

26. Ibid., 99.

27. Ibid.

28. Ibid.

29. Ibid. [In the published English translation, the word *tombeau* ("tomb") is written in French. It is not to be understood in its literal meaning: n. 116 (*The Writing of History*, 113) explains that the word is used to refer to a genre to which also the historiographical narrative belongs, namely a "literary and musical commemorative genre dating to the seventeenth century." More recent examples include the *Tombeau d'Edgar Poe* and the *Tombeau de Charles Baudelaire*, both by the French nineteenth-century poet Stéphane Mallarmé, and also Ravel's *Tombeau de Couperin*.—Tr.]

30. *The Writing of History*, 101.

31. Ibid., 100.

32. Ibid.

33. Ibid., 102.

34. [The German concept of *Schuld* corresponds not only to debt but also to guilt.—Tr.]

35. *Being and Time*, H437.

36. Ibid.

37. Ibid., H447.

38. R. G. Collingwood's *The Idea of History* (Oxford: Clarendon, 1946; reprint 1994) is a posthumous work published by T. M. Knox, on the basis of lectures written in Oxford in 1936, after Collingwood's appointment to the chair of philosophy and metaphysics. The lectures were partially revised by the author until 1940.

39. *The Idea of History*, 213.

40. Ibid., 225.

41. Ibid.

42. Raymond Aron, *Introduction à la philosophie de l'histoire. Essai sur les limites de l'objectivité historique* (Paris: Gallimard, originally published 1938, rev. ed. 1997); English translation: *Introduction to the Philosophy of History. An Essay on the Limits of Historical Objectivity* (London, Weidenfeld and Nicolson, 1961).

43. Aron, *Introduction to the Philosophy of History*, 183.

44. Ibid., 222.

45. Ibid., 232.

46. *Being and Time*, H443.

47. *Truth and Method*, 300 (*Vérité et méthode*, 322).

14

Are We Such Stuff as Dreams Are Made On?
Against Reductionism

Stanley Rosen

This essay is dedicated to the celebration of the hundredth birthday of Hans-Georg Gadamer. His work has been of importance to me since I first met him in Heidelberg in 1961 through the mediation of my teacher, Leo Strauss. Gadamer is a representative of the imposing philosophical generation of Europe and in particular, Germany, between the two great wars, a generation that combined erudition and theoretical reflection in a way that we seldom if ever find today. This generation, and Gadamer in particular, serves as a paradigm for those of us who try to preserve the tradition of *philosophia perennis,* not in a spirit of antiquarianism but as the very soul of western history, and hence as the inner voice of what is most genuinely contemporary.

As one who came to philosophy from poetry, I have been especially assisted by what I shall call Gadamer's hermeneutical reconciliation of the disputants in the quarrel between philosophy and poetry. The present essay is an effort to respond to themes that Gadamer has represented throughout his long and unusually productive life. I hope that he will regard it as a sign that I have not failed to appreciate his attempt to combine the spirit of Plato with a recognition of human historicity.

A preliminary remark about the subtitle of my paper is in order. I do not oppose all forms of reduction but only those that falsify or obscure the original phenomena. There are obviously many instances in which we need to explain a complex structure by reducing it to its generating elements. But life is not a structure, or at least certainly not one that is understood when it is reduced to its constituent elements. Dreaming is a function or power of life; the reduction of life to a dream amounts to the equation of wakefulness or genuine life with death. Unfortunately, the view of life as a dream recurs throughout our tradition and may even be said to constitute an essential ingredient in our psychological makeup. If this is so, then the tendency to effect this reduction cannot be extirpated, and life assumes the form of a nightmare in which we attempt to persuade ourselves that we do not exist.

From the times of Solomon and Sophocles, the great poets of our tradition have emphasized the vanity, transience, and dreamlike nature of human existence. At the same time, of course, one finds in the poetic tradition a celebration of the vividness of particular moments of existence such as love or sorrow. An example of this second tendency can be found in book eleven of the *Odyssey,* where the ghost of Achilles asks the living Odysseus during his journey to Hades, "how could you endure to come down here to Hades' place, where the senseless dead men dwell, mere images of perished mortals?"[1] Achilles goes on to assure his visitor that he would rather be a bondsman on the surface of the earth than the king of the dead.[2]

One may suggest that for Achilles, as perhaps for Hamlet, it is not life but death that is a dream; his words certainly support the inference that he does not doubt the substantiality of human existence, however brief its duration. By referring to the dead as "images of perished mortals" (*broton eidola kamonton*) Achilles indicates that life is the original of which death is a pale copy. Achilles, however, is a warrior, whereas Prospero is a magician and philosopher-king. The poet as metaphysician laments the dreamlike insubstantiality of life, whereas the poet as warrior celebrates the vividness of its joys and sorrows. Actions speak louder than words; it is not activity but reflective meditations that convince us of the dreamlike nature of life. The attempt to discover the meaning and value of life, whether through poetry, philosophy, or science, detaches us from life and reduces it to a phantom image.

When the followers of Prospero tell us that life is a dream, what do they understand by wakefulness? We can distinguish very generally two kinds of response, the religious and the nonreligious, but there is a further division within the category of the religious. The words of Achilles illustrate the pagan view that life is wakefulness whereas death is a dream.[3] The testimony in the Hebrew Scripture is nuanced, but it contains no doctrine of personal immortality. If life is the vanity of vanities, the dead person lives on in the corporate existence of the people of Israel as obedient to the word of God. And this seems to entail the striking thesis that life becomes real, not when we are awake, but when we are asleep in the bosom of the Lord, or as a deconstructionist might put it, when we are incarnated discursively in the divine text.

If this is at all right, then one would expect Christian poetry to exemplify the contrast between heavenly and earthly existence as one between wakefulness and dreaming. I leave the examination of this hypothesis for another occasion. Let me suggest only that Jews and Christians stand together in contrast to the followers of Achilles by relegating secular life, but not of course a life transformed by faith or grace, to the domain of dreams. Note that I do not make the stronger claim that all pagan poets are followers of Achilles. It is true, however, that the perception of the brevity of human life is for a pagan compatible with an acceptance of its wakefulness. To say that life is fragile is not the same as to say that it is a dream. In what follows, I shall not try to develop the type of response to my question that religion offers. Suffice it to say that religious faith, or even the quasi-secular version of faith that we call hope, is not so easy to distinguish from a dream.

The intention here is to emphasize the problematic side of the thesis that life in this world is a dream. More precisely, I shall be primarily concerned with the two main types of philosophical thinking that I call, for convenience, the mathematical and the poetical. I am especially interested in what happens when these two dimensions of philosophy separate and assume independent and hyperbolical forms. My thesis, broadly stated, is that there is a reductivist tendency in both these modes of thought, stemming from a common perception of the transience of life. The poetic mode culminates in a celebration of transience, thereby reducing structure to the modalities of transience itself, whereas the mathematical mode attempts to bypass transience by explaining it as an epiphenomenon of structure. Note these modes are considered here in their paradigmatic forms. The tendencies I have just identified do not constitute the entirety of poetry or mathematics, but express something fundamental to them. Modern science, it seems to me, suffers from an inverted schizophrenia that manifests itself as the attempt to combine the mathematical and the poetic paradigms; on the one hand, life is reduced to structure; on the other, structure is transformed into an artifact. I will consider modern science as it presents itself rhetorically: at first as the fulfillment of mathematical philosophy, and finally, in our own time, even though as mathematical, nevertheless as a species of poetry. I will argue that in both these rhetorical stances, modern science leads directly to the view that life is a dream. I shall finally suggest that this view can be avoided, or at least mitigated, only by restricting the excessive activities of an emancipated poetry or mathematics by philosophy, which is reducible neither to the one nor to the other, but which emerges from and remains faithful to the unity and totality of human existence.

To begin with, I want to cite an important and usually neglected passage in Plato's *Republic*.[4] The passage is especially important because it provides a crucial modification to the central role assigned by Socrates to mathematics in the education of potential philosophers. Mathematics, to be sure, points in the direction of the Ideas or genuine natures of things, but mathematicians, Socrates says, "dream about being" whereas dialecticians perceive the beings as they genuinely are and reason directly about them without the use of hypotheses or axioms on the one hand or images on the other. Mathematics stands to dialectic or wisdom as does dreaming to wakefulness. This is a specification of an earlier passage in which Socrates says that in dreaming we take a likeness to be not a likeness but the thing it is like.[5] Unfortunately, all talk of dialectic is apparently dreaming as well, like talk of perfect justice, since human beings, as Socrates says in the *Symposium* and *Phaedrus*, are incapable of wisdom but must rest content in the best case with philosophy, that is, with loving or desiring wisdom.[6] That the city described in the *Republic,* together with its wise rulers is "not altogether a daydream," as Socrates asks us to believe, is hard to accept if to be wise is to know that one does not know.[7]

According to the Platonic Socrates, mathematicians believe that geometrical figures and pure numbers are the genuine or original beings of which their spatiotemporal counterparts are images and reflections. But human life is an epiphenomenon of those counterparts, an epiphenomenon that corresponds to nothing in the original or genuine figures and numbers. More precisely, life is not an image of a triangle or of the Pythagorean theorem. Our everyday experience, including our experience of ourselves as mathematicians, corresponds to no mathematical originals. We are thus faced with a choice of interpretations. Either human life is a simulacrum, something less than an image and barely to be characterized as a dream, or else it constitutes a distinct type of originality, other than the mathematical forms and irreducible to them. One would expect the philosopher, and in particular the philosopher who is concerned to know himself, to choose the second alternative. But this is not the conclusion at which Socrates explicitly arrives.

He cannot do so because philosophical dialectic in its purest form duplicates the mathematical reduction of life to formal structure. The dialecticians, assuming that there are any, are said to be awake in the sense that they are reasoning about the pure forms rather than about mathematical entities. And here is the problem. Dialectical reasoning has no more to say about human life, or about the human significance of philosophizing, than does the mathematician. Most important, it cannot tell us how to live the good life that Socrates asserts to be his major concern. It would seem that living the good life is equivalent to personal extinction in the pure contemplation of formal structure. What we normally refer to as life is then something like a dream of wakefulness. Otherwise stated, when Socrates turns from everyday experience to reflection upon the soul and its earthly life, he turns away from dialectic to myth.

The problem, then, is that human existence is not a copy of Platonic Ideas. It seems therefore to be not merely formless but entirely insubstantial. In the *Phaedrus*,[8] where Timaeus speaks of the construction of the world-soul *eis mian idean*. Nothing is said here of the individual soul because the life has to be lived; it cannnot be constructed in advance since there is nothing out of which to produce activities other than the process of activity itself, which is precisely the process by which we construct our lives as we live them, and not as a copy of something else. Socrates says that it is not possible for mortals to describe the Idea of soul but only to tell what it is like. Socrates is referring here not to the soul of the cosmos, the principle of change (*arche kineseos*), but to the soul of the individual person. This is obvious because, in order to tell what the soul is like, he narrates the myth of the winged charioteer and the noble and base horses, or in other words, the intellect and the two opposite forms of erotic spiritedness.

In somewhat more expansive terms, Ideas correspond to natural kinds and abstractions like the properties and relations of things, or to moral qualities, but not to actions or integrated sequences of actions, and certainly not to what we now call self-consciousness. Even if there were an Idea of the soul, then, it would tell us nothing about life. There is no genuine domain of waking existence in some place beyond the heavens that is the original of which our dreamlike existence is the image. In Socrates' myth, he tells how the bodiless divine souls rise to the roof of the cosmos and there view the pure Ideas. But our souls are not copies or instances of these divine beings; we are held back by our bodies and see only reflections of the Ideas, as though through a glass darkly. To see the Ideas themselves, we must be dead.

In the *Symposium*, the priestess Diotima tells the young Socrates that Eros is continuously changing its shape, that is, continuously dying and returning to life.[9] Accordingly, there is no Idea of Eros, but only a myth of the erotic ascent to the Ideas by the human soul. One could infer from the mythical status of the doctrine of Eros that the ascent to the Ideas is a dream. No one could suppose that the winged charioteer and his two steeds are the genuine reality of the human soul. The soul is patently not the dream-image of an actual charioteer and his horses. It would be more correct, but still unsatisfactory, to refer to the image of the charioteer as a dream-image of the soul. In this case, the original condition of wakefulness is that of unsatisfied Eros. And since Eros is defined by the object of desire, we are once more left with no conceptual access to the intrinsic nature of consciousness.[10]

In sum, a quasi-mathematical rationalism not only cannot explain the phenomenon of human existence but serves to empty it of independent substance and significance. If we try to reconcile Plato's myths of the soul with his doctrine of Ideas, the myths look like subterfuges, or philanthropic attempts to conceal the bitter truth under a salutary veil of rhetoric. They look like noble lies. This is why those who repudiate myth or for whom reason is equivalent to calculation and formal analysis arrive sooner or later at the surrender to, or celebration of irrationalism. Whether they affirm or deny reason is irrelevant; the crucial point is that both affirmers and deniers exclude life from the sphere of the rational. At the very least, mythical thinking must play a decisive role in supplementing the thin gruel of traditional rationalism when it comes to understanding ourselves.

On my view, then, the soul is itself an original; it is not an image like the one constructed by Socrates. There is no Platonic Idea of the soul to which the living soul stands as itself an image or dream-creature. If there is an answer in the Platonic dialogues to the question "what is the soul?" that answer is not a rational account of determinate structure but rather the dialogues themselves, as we come to understand them through the exercise of recreating them in our discursive imagination. If we pursue this analysis, we seem to arrive at the following result. The answer to the question "what is the soul?" cannot be a scientific explanation or logically clarified empirical description. Images, metaphors, or models assist us in understanding the soul, and it is plausible to say that understanding is to ignorance as wakefulness is to dreaming. But images, metaphors, and models are artifacts of the activity of the soul. Whatever structure they possess is not the same as the structure of the soul because in fact the soul has no structure. Structure defines and delimits; it is closer to death than to life. The cognitive soul produces structures which, when we succumb to the temptation to apply them to ourselves, destroy us.

If this is right, then we need a sense of "theory" that is neither the pure intuition of formal structure nor the modern constructivist interpretation that results in technical artifacts standing between us and what we wish to understand. We cannot "see" or theorize our-selves in a state of unconsciousness induced by the intuition of pure forms. But neither can we see ourselves if the direct effect of self-inspection is to generate a private perspective that blocks us from public view. It is words selfdefeating to define reason as incapable of understanding human life; but it is also contrary to our everyday experience, an experience about which, it must candidly be admit-ted, art in general and poetry in particular are much more illuminat-ing than the baroque rationalist constructions of the philosophers. And this is why the mathematical dimension of Platonism, once its initial impetus of liberation is spent, begins its steady decline into poetic ideology. If life is a dream and its explanation a myth, then reason, as the instrument of explanation, must explain itself as a myth. The typical modern formulation of that myth, which is stated as an act of both daring and despair, is the assertion that we know only what we make.

Platonism explains the soul as the mythical bearer of the powers of the unstructured intuition of pure form and discursive reflection. Modern philosophy is characterized decisively by the separation of these two elements into mathematical epistemology on the one hand and doctrines of self-consciousness or subjectivity on the other. The mathematical epistemologists fluctuate uneasily between doctrines of pure formal intuition, which has no inner structure, and linguisti-cally oriented philosophies of mind, which attempt to extract the structure of thinking from the structure of language. If theoretical discourse is the identification of structure, one can only be silent about intuition. On the other hand, the search for cognitive struc-ture in the structure of language leads inevitably to conventionalism or historicism. This is because languages are themselves historical artifacts. And this is also the fate of doctrines of subjectivity, which culminate in solipsism, often under the alias of intersubjectivity. The attempt to develop a scientific or theoretical account of subjectivity that is distinct from epistemology has the paradoxical consequence of the reinstitution of a comprehensive myth, as is so obvious in late-modern or postmodern thought. The dissolution of Platonism, in short, gives rise to two separate and warring dybbuks, each a simula-crum of one-half of the original.

For Plato, the correct medium for the philosophical discussion of human life is myth or more specifically dramatic poetry: in particular, the poetry of the Platonic dialogues. In particular, but not exclusively; in the *Republic,* even while exalting mathematics and sharply criticizing the poets, paramount among them Homer, Socrates continues throughout to quote the poets, paramount among them Homer, in order to illustrate human life as it is actually lived. This is of crucial importance. Homer, as we are told in the *Theaetetus,* is the general of what one could call Socrates' ontological enemies, namely, those who assert that everything is change.[11] All appearances to the contrary, however, he is Socrates' ally and even paradigm in the attempt to understand the living soul. Socrates could hardly have quoted the mathematicians in this attempt, or for that matter the pre-Socratic thinkers like Parmenides and Heracleitus.

In sum, philosophers must employ poetry not only to explain life but to praise philosophy and so too dialectic. Thus employing poetry, however, they are not themselves poets but philosophers, namely, persons who are awake and who attempt to awaken the rest of us by altering the structure and content of our dreams. To restrict oneself to myth or poetry to explain life is self-defeating. Myths are too successful; in their openness to every explanation, they encourage the view that life is a dream. The key to the riddle of the Platonic dialogue is thus how to understand human life without reducing it to a bogus mathematical entity on the one hand or a myth on the other.

I am now at a transitional moment in my argument. Let me therefore summarize my remarks to this point. There is a powerful tendency in human reflection to think of life as a dream. This is encouraged by philosophy to the extent that formal structures are presented as paradigms, models, or essences of which spatiotemporal particulars are only copies. Since there is no eternal paradigm of human life, we are tempted in two different but finally related ways, either to construct a formal model of life or to transform human being into a myth. Philosophy falls apart into mathematics and poetry. I want now to show that although one might think that mathematics is the initial victor in the struggle for the human soul, it is actually poetry that triumphs. As separate from poetry, mathematics,

Stanley Rosen

the ostensibly purest form of reason, becomes radically nonrational. It can neither explain nor justify itself, and so must have recourse to poetry or myth in order to repair its inability. In so doing, mathematics becomes a myth.

By way of transition between the two parts of my essay, allow me one more remark about Plato. The most curious characteristic of the Platonic dialogues is that they are poems apparently devoted to the celebration of mathematics and the denigration of poetry. I offer here only a brief explanation for this feature. Plato knew that poetry has more power than mathematics over the soul. He therefore attempted to inoculate us against the former and in favor of the latter. It would have been absurd to write a mathematical celebration of mathematics; not merely absurd, but impossible. This is one way to understand why Plato wrote dialogues. Unfortunately, human beings have a difficult time in reconciling two diverse intellectual modalities. Hence the disappearance or dissolution of the dialogues into the history of philosophy, or into what one could call the pseudo-Platonic dialectic of poetry and mathematics.

Otherwise put, Plato attempted to unify philosophy, mathematics, and poetry within philosophical *episteme*. But his attempt was too subtle to withstand the necessary brutality of the hermeneutical diversity his dialogues invoke. Plato, whose comprehensive artistry is in keeping with the aristocratic nature of the founder and president of the first university, was attacked almost immediately by his greatest student, Aristotle, a bourgeois professor who is celebrated as the founder of the division of intellectual labor into the separate sciences. The history of philosophy actually begins with Aristotle, who transformed Plato's poetic language into professional terminology, thereby eliciting the observation from Immanuel Kant that whereas Plato's philosophy is *Schwärmerei*, "die Philosophie des Aristoteles ist dagegen Arbeit" ("The philosophy of Aristotle is on the other hand work").[12] Let us now look briefly at the process by which *Schwärmerei* was transformed into work in the modern epoch and then back again at the end of modernity into *Schwärmerei*.

Modern philosophy begins substantially with the birth of experimental and mathematical science, which carries with it the distinction between primary and secondary attributes. Primary attributes, of which genuine knowledge is said to be possible, are number, geometrical figure, magnitude, and motion, to name the leading candidates. As primary, that is, as genuinely knowable, they are held to constitute genuine being, or what we see when we are genuinely awake. The secondary attributes include the full range of properties whose perception or apprehension depends upon our spatiotemporal existence within daily life and so too upon ourselves who see the primary attributes.

It is immediately obvious that modern philosophy, at least prior to the advent of Kant and German Idealism, could be called Platonism on two counts: first, it is rooted in the mathematical structure of genuine being; second, it implies when it does not explicitly state that human life is a dream, and a dream to which no waking stage corresponds, unless it be the Cartesian *lumen naturale*, that is, the radically nonsubjective cognition of pure forms by a special, nonreflexive power of subjectivity. This is the partial Platonism of the dybbuk of mathematicism, but it can be justified by the texts of the master, provided one forgets about the Platonic original and replaces it with an Aristotelian artifact.

The dream-status of human life is not emphasized, perhaps not even explicitly mentioned, by the founders of the modern epoch, with the massive exception of the Cartesian demon or malignant genius who, with his hypothetical power to deceive us on all particulars except consciousness of the deception, is one of the principal ancestors of contemporary modal metaphysics. And the role assigned to this demon by Descartes is to issue a wake-up call, to move us to extricate ourselves from the dreams of traditional philosophy. One could receive the impression, from studying the early modern period and the scientific Enlightenment, that science is pitted in a heroic struggle with poetry, alias traditional religion and philosophy, in order to awaken mankind from its dreamlike bondage to nature on the one hand and the religio-political establishment on the other. That modern science is itself a dream is gradually brought to consciousness by the evolution of the doctrine of subjectivity into that of historicism. Let me briefly clarify this observation.

The doctrine of the *lumen naturale,* as Descartes refers to the power of the intellect to apprehend mathematical form, is obviously a descendent of Platonic *noesis*. Descartes, however, unlike Plato, embeds the natural light in the *ego cogitans* or principle of subjectivity, which one could describe as the solipsistic revision of the communal or political character of Greek discursivity. Isolated from its fellow creatures by the paranoid fear of an evil genius who could be deceiving it into dreaming that it is awake, the ego, in seeking for security, awakens to the nightmare of late-modern historicism and perspectivism. It occurs to me that a Catholic might call this the natural consequence of the Protestant Reformation: the assertion of individuality dissolves into chaos. If so, then Descartes is not a Catholic but a Huguenot.

I use the term historicism to characterize the modern dissolution of the self-certifying Cartesian ego and so of the object as a project of the subject. The ego cannot explain itself on either of the two Cartesian models, since it is neither a geometrical and algebraic structure nor the intuitive apprehension of these structures. It is also deprived of recourse to myth or poetry, the second Platonic option, by the specious if compelling dream of scientific precision and the efficacious mastery of nature.

In order to explain itself, the ego must therefore have recourse to feelings and sensations, and this is the next historical step. These are treated in one of two ways: either psychologistically or transcendentally. In the first case, the result is empiricism or the impossibility of distinguishing between imagination and reality, that is, between wakefulness and dreaming, a distinction that is fatally assigned to the vividness of our impressions. In the second case, the result is the replacement of the activity of living by the ostensible conditions for the possibility of cognizing. When these conditions are seen to vary with the historical development of science, the transcendental ego is replaced at first by the historical ego and then by the historicist doctrine of the local linguistic horizon. The conviction gradually obtains, in a process culminating in Nietzsche, that the subject must itself be a project or object, that is, a construction of subjectivity, and even further, that there is no single subject but rather an infinite regression of multiple subjects, each opening a unique perspective, for each of which the others are arbitrary dreams of wakefulness.

The problem of the dreamlike nature of human life is thus an inheritance from our failure to have solved the riddle of the Platonic dialogue and haunts modern philosophy from Descartes to the present day. The evil genius postulated by Descartes as the possible cause of the illusory dream of human existence is the direct progenitor of the Martians whom contemporary modal metaphysicians warn may be saturating us with rays that cloak reality with a veil of illusion. As the progress of mathematical and experimental science accelerates, so too does the decay of subjectivity, the dissolution of the self, the disappearance of consciousness into the unconscious, and in short, of the *ego cogitans* into the dark jungle of neurophysiology. To say the same thing in a different way, philosophy moves inexorably toward assimilation into poetry, as one can see even in the philosophy of mathematics, with its talk of alternative axiom-sets, possible worlds, deviant logics, nonstandard integers, and at last the demotion of mathematics to a social activity of contingent historical beings. The world of ordinary experience is thus reduced to the status of an outmoded poem. As a single metaphor of the entire age, I note that the last book published by Nelson Goodman, the apostle of logical construction, is entitled *Ways of World-Making*. I myself prefer Marcel Proust.

As T. S. Eliot expresses the point in the idiom of our own time, "go, go, go, said the bird; human kind cannot bear very much reality." The detachment from experience that is ingredient to thinking, and by definition to abstract thinking, as for example in leaving the cave of political existence for the light of genuine being, renders the world insubstantial. Solipsistic meditation, whether of mathematical structures or the nature of God, soul, and immortality, is no more capable than Platonic *noesis* of validating the substantiality of our daily lives. We are no longer the triumphant eye that extends beyond the body of the cave but, in the beautiful words of Allen Tate, "we are the eyelids of defeated caves."

From this standpoint, one can understand Husserl's doctrine of the *Lebenswelt*, like Heidegger's existential analysis of Dasein, as twentieth-century attempts to revivify the philosophically unsatisfactory efforts of thinkers like Kierkegaard and Nietzsche in the nineteenth century to dismantle Absolute Idealism. Kierkegaard and Husserl start from the standpoint of the subject, Nietzsche and Heidegger from that of the abolition of the subject-object distinction. Kierkegaard turns away from philosophy toward revelation; Nietzsche dissolves philosophy into the chaos of modern scientific materialism and an amalgam of neurophysiology and psychology.

Husserl covers over the life-world with the categorial structures of phenomenology, even while bracketing out of consideration the engagement and values of actual existence; Heidegger contradicts himself by constructing existential categories out of historical contingencies and is forced to take refuge in the pure happenstance of Being as event.

So much for my account of how we have moved from universal subjectivity to particular history and beyond to sheer difference. Well, then, are we such stuff as dreams are made on? Was Prospero right after all? If to be awake is to live in the actual or genuine world, and if rationalism is right in defining the genuine world as consisting of formal structures, whether these be further defined as pure Being, Platonic Ideas, tables of categories, syntactical horizons, or DNA, then one could not even call one's life a dream, since to awaken is to disappear. If Nietzsche is right and formal structures are contingent projections of perspectival or historical thinking, then everyday life is surely a dream, and a noble lie or salutary respite from the nightmare of wakeful chaos.

I do not, however, infer from this summary and preliminary conclusion that Prospero is correct. To me the striking feature of the rationalist and existentialist accounts is that neither postulates a genuine form of existence that stands as wakefulness to the dream of life. On the contrary, life is identified as a dream precisely because, they say or imply, there is no condition of wakefulness, but only one version or another of chaos or nothingness. To awaken is to die, whether through an epiphany of pure forms, assimilation into the absolute, or dissolution into pure difference.

In short, whether we define it as the realm of Platonic Ideas, the syntax of a universal language, or an unknowable domain of things in themselves, not to say as chaos or difference, the heaven of traditional philosophy cannot be the original of which human life is an image. By the same token, it is simple nonsense to say that human beings are "actually" computers, or force fields, or slaves of their genes. If this is what human beings "actually" are, then there are actually no human beings. How then to explain the mass delusion known as historical existence, a delusion that is not merely defined by, but that includes the agents of, scientific, poetic, or philosophical reductivism?

I have suggested that the reason why we are tempted to think that human life is a dream is precisely because it cannot be reduced to anything else, whereas we are accustomed already in pretheoretical or prescientific experience to regard an explanation as a reduction of one set of phenomena into another. Everyone would grant the absurdity of saying that the beings or experiences reduced for explanatory purposes into some more general theoretical vocabulary have thereby ceased to exist. To take a famous example, the lectern on which my manuscript rests is no doubt correctly said to consist of atoms in the void. But this should not allow us to forget that my manuscript will not rest upon atoms in the void, nor can I lean on them, in any but a metaphorical sense.

The role of the lectern in the everyday world is not clarified by its reduction to atoms in the void; on the contrary, that role is rendered obscure and even empty, because the shift in discursive registers removes us entirely from the sphere of life. It is of course easy to think of circumstances in which knowledge of the atomic domain would be eminently useful or simply admirable to residents in the everyday world. But this requires the preservation of both domains, not the reduction of one to the other. It makes no sense to be told that the science of atomic physics, for example, is the noblest human possession, but that the humans who possess it are illusory residents of a dream world to which no wakeful state corresponds.

If there is an underlying unity of science and the humanities, its root is human life. I do not doubt that mathematics, philosophy, and poetry are the ramifications of that root, or to vary the metaphor, the passages by which we emerge from fragility, transience, and ambiguity into a more substantial domain. In so emerging, however, we become what we are; we do not cease to be what we were. Life is not a dream in the sense that there exists a state of wakefulness external to it. The only condition external to life is death. The only transcendence to eternity that possesses a human meaning is one that preserves our humanity.

I began this essay by isolating the mathematical dimension of the Platonic dialogues on the one hand and the general testimony of the western poetic tradition on the other. I want now to prepare my conclusion by returning to the poetical dimension of Platonism, and in that way to the general question of the poetical dimension of the philosophical response to life. A mathematical or purely formal Platonism condemns human existence to the domain of dreams because there is no Idea of the living soul. As I have contended, the absence of such an Idea, very far from constituting a deficiency, is essential to the extraordinary fecundity of human existence. We are free to create our lives; on this point the poetic champions of contingency are right. But this freedom deteriorates into anarchy and chaos if it is emancipated from mathematics and formal structure. One does not rectify the mistake of attempting to mathematicize human existence by poeticizing mathematics and formal structure.

It follows from this that poetry is by itself incapable of protecting us from the vitiating interpretation of wakefulness as dreaming. Art must be reinforced by religion or philosophy in order to overcome the dreamlike status it assigns to life as it is lived, in contrast to life as portrayed or celebrated. The work of art stands to the daily events of life as do Platonic Ideas to their spatiotemporal particulars. Even if art begins as the celebration of life, our attention is soon diverted from life to the work of art itself. For both artist and audience, the essential human being, the actuality or full wakefulness of which our own temporal existences seem to us to be dreamlike imitations, is the hero or antihero of the work of art itself. In an unheroic age, the situation deteriorates still further; life is reduced to the study of textuality.

At the same time, however, the formal or ideal function of the artwork is compromised by its own contingency: its uniqueness, its sensuousness, its historical context, the untranslatability of poetic diction, and so on. As one could put this, the artwork *qua* Idea is poisoned by the virus of the contingency of its own content or subject matter. The same thing happens in philosophy when subjectivity

deteriorates into subjectivism and the perception of historical progress evaporates into the random multiplicities of a decentered
perspectivism.

This essay has been devoted to the problem of the steady dissipa-
tion of our sense of reality. The very doctrines that are designed to
sustain a "robust sense of reality," in Bertrand Russell's phrase, are
turning us into phantoms, ghosts in the machine, the firing of syn-
apses, irrelevant rather than celebratory ornaments on the evolving
tree of life. The Nobel-prize winning physicist Steven Weinberg says
somewhere that the more we understand the nature of the universe,
the more pointless it seems.

I myself find more suggestive the following passage from a book
by the Italian physicist, Toraldo di Francia: "human beings are definitely contingent entities, very far from anything that is fixed and
constant in nature. We are either too large (e.g., our size and mass
as compared to those of elementary particles) or too small (e.g., the
speeds we can attain as compared with the speed of light). Is this
contingency, perhaps, an essential feature of our singular nature?"[13]

Toraldo is in part repeating a thought expressed first by Pascal,
namely, that human beings are caught between the two infinities of
the universe of the new science. Pascal sees this intermediateness as
a dilemma that will destroy our humanity unless we escape through
religious faith. Toraldo offers no development of his conjecture
about human nature, but it is fair to say that there is no trace of
religious faith or existential despair in his book. Whether he is entitled to the equanimity, one could even say the self-confidence deriving from modern science, is another question.

The reason I find his words so suggestive is that they open a space
within the same enterprise that leads Weinberg to suspect pointless-
ness. The space is certainly metaphorical or poetical rather than scientific, but that is precisely the point. Human life is not defined by
ontological or mathematical structures; it is not defined by laws or
rules but produces them. This is not to invalidate or even to relativize
the laws and rules but to restrict them to their proper domain. At
the same time, the singular or extralegal nature of human life does
not free us from obedience to those laws or rules because we define
ourselves by becoming citizens of their domain.

Stanley Rosen

In this last part of my essay, I want to say a few words about what I take to be the necessary next stage in the philosophical analysis of the problem of wakefulness. I anticipated myself previously by referring to the regulation of mathematics and poetry by a philosophical fidelity to the unity and totality of everyday life. As a first step in making this remark more substantial, let me say that what is required is a fundamental revision, or at least expansion, of Platonism. Still more precisely, I believe that, in the last analysis, the Platonic portrait of human existence on the one hand and the epistemic cognition of formal structure on the other, is not sustained within the dialogues by any line of argument, explicit or implicit. They are held together only dramatically, by the dialogue-form itself, which invites us to reenact in our own lives the twin paths of poetry and mathematics. But this is unfortunately unsatisfactory, since we are directed toward philosophy in order to discover not simply theoretical truth but even more urgently the good life. If the good life is available only as a dramatic enactment of dualism, then we are as it were dissolved by the very remedy for our internal disunion.

If I am not mistaken, this is why the young Hegel says in his *Differenzschrift* that philosophy begins in the division (*Entzweiung*) or "torn harmony" (*zerrissene Harmonie*) of the human spirit.[14] Whether or not this is what Hegel had in mind, I want to appropriate his words for my own purposes. It is in my view a fundamental error to conceive of the Platonic dialogues as the presentation of Plato's philosophical doctrines or system. The dialogues are instead a dramatic propaedeutic to philosophy, a representation of the problem of the disjunction of poetry from mathematics, and not at all a resolution of that problem. The silence of a dramatic representation has led to conflicting inferences on the part of Plato's readers. Some have taken him to indicate that there are no solutions to the fundamental philosophical problem; others believe that he concealed his solution out of aristocratic pride or perhaps philanthropy, whereas still others do not even notice the problem but busy themselves in the analysis of fragments of his enigmatic texts, on the tacit assumption that there is no enigma but only a random collection of technical puzzles.

Plato's silence, one could say, led to the history of philosophy as the development of the two distinct aspects of his dialogues. This development seems to have exhausted itself; hence the current obsession with postmodernism, the end of history, and most important, the end of philosophy. I suggest that instead of talking about the end of philosophy, we ought to see the present confused time as the opportunity for a new beginning. Unlike Heidegger, however, I do not mean by this a new epoch in the history of Being but rather a radical reinterpretation of the fragments of the old epoch. In a certain sense, this means business as usual, since the history of philosophy is by its nature a continuous beginning or retracing of old paths; if this were not true, there would be no such activity as philosophy, but only poetry.

Rather than advocating a startling new mode of thinking, I propose instead that we take the following three steps in order to initiate our own version of the perpetual philosophical beginning. First, we require a thorough reconsideration of how philosophy originates from ordinary experience. This reconsideration must not be defined by technical presuppositions about the nature of such experience, and in particular not by the scientific reductionism that leads to the conviction that life is a dream. Second, we have to take another careful look at dialectical thinking in the Hegelian sense, in order to acquire a deeper understanding of how to resolve the oppositions that are intrinsic to all forms of dualism, and in particular to static conceptions of form as opposed to the process of life. Third, the Kantian doctrine of the spontaneity of thinking must be reformulated in such a way as to free it from the problem that spontaneously produced laws, rules, or categories that infect the bloodstream of necessity with the virus of contingency. It is everyday life that is spontaneous, not the structure of intelligibility.

Underlying the formulation of these three steps is the following general conviction. Whereas philosophy is an extraordinary disruption of the ordinary, it is in response to the complexities of everyday life as we live it; hence its role is not to replace ordinary existence by some other mode of experience or intellectual activity but to explain how and why the problems or deficiencies of ordinary

Stanley Rosen

experience require extraordinary responses. But the responses cannot be extraordinary in the sense of substituting a technical artifact for ordinary experience. In particular, it makes no sense to speak of ordinary experience as a junk-heap of discarded scientific theories. Our lives need to be clarified and deepened, not transformed into computer software or random perturbations on the surface of chaos.

The view of life as a dream begins in reflection upon its transience and uncertainty; we accordingly attribute permanence and precision to the structures of wakefulness, thereby concealing from ourselves that if these structures were to define our own lives, we should cease to exist. The problem underlying the lament of Prospero is thus not how to wake up, but rather how to stay awake. Once more, I hope that I have not put the reader to sleep with this excerpt of my own insomnia. I close with yet another citation of a poet, Delmore Schwartz, who, no doubt while tossing one sleepless night "in the naked bed, in Plato's cave," came to understand that "in dreams begin responsibilities." But with responsibilities, wakefulness begins.

Acknowledgments

This essay was first presented as the author's inaugural lecture at Boston University in 1994.

Notes

1. *Odyssey,* XI. 474f, Lattimore translation modified.

2. Ibid., 489–491.

3. For discussion, see W. Burkert, *Greek Religion* (Cambridge, Mass.: Harvard University Press, 1983), 194–199.

4. *Republic,* 533b6f.

5. Ibid., V, 476c5–7.

6. *Symposium* 204a1ff, *Phaedrus* 278d3–6.

7. *Republic* VII. 540d1ff.

8. *Phaedrus* 246a1–6. The same situation obtains in the *Timaeus,* 35a1ff.

9. *Symposium* 202d11ff, 203d7f.

10. When objects come to be defined in the modern era as projects of consciousness, the indeterminate Eros becomes the will to power.

11. *Theaetetus* 152e2f.

12. "Von einem neuerdings erhobenen vornehmen Ton in der Philosophie," in *Kants Werke*, vol. 8 (Berlin and New York: Akademie Textausgabe, Walter de Gruyter, 1968), 392.

13. *The Investigation of the Physical World* (Cambridge: Cambridge University Press, 1981), 46.

14. In *Jenaer Kritische Schriften* (Hamburg: Felix Meiner Verlag, 1979), 10.

15

Understanding the Other: A Gadamerian View on Conceptual Schemes

Charles Taylor

The great challenge of this century, both for politics and for social science, is that of understanding the other. The days are long gone when Europeans and other Westerners could consider their experience and culture as the norm toward which the whole of humanity was headed, so that the other could be understood as an earlier stage on the same road that they had trodden. Now we sense the full presumption involved in the idea that we already possess the key to understanding other cultures and times.

But the recovery of the necessary modesty here seems always to threaten to veer into relativism, or a questioning of the very ideal of truth in human affairs. The very ideas of objectivity that underpinned Western social science seemed hard to combine with that of fundamental conceptual differences between cultures; so that real cultural openness appeared to threaten the very norms of validity on which social science rested.

What does not often occur to those working in these fields is the thought that their whole model of science is wrong and inappropriate. Here Gadamer has made a tremendous contribution to twentieth-century thought. He has in fact proposed a new and different model, which is much more fruitful, and shows promise of carrying us beyond the dilemma of ethnocentrism and relativism.

In *Wahrheit und Methode*, Gadamer shows how understanding a text or event that comes from our history has to be construed not on the model of the "scientific" grasp of an object but rather on that of speech partners who come to an understanding (*Verständigung*). Following Gadamer's argument here, we come to see that this is probably true of human science as such. It is not simply knowledge of our own past that needs to be understood on the "conversation" model, but knowledge of the other as such, including disciplines like anthropology, where student and studied often belong to quite different civilizations.

This view has come to be widely accepted today, and it is one of the great contributions that Gadamer has made to the philosophy of this and succeeding centuries. I would like to lay out here why this is so.

First, I want to contrast the two kinds of operation: knowing an object and coming to an understanding with an interlocutor. Some differences are obvious. The first is unilateral, the second bilateral. I know the rock, the solar system; I don't have to deal with its view of me or of my knowing activity. But beyond this, the goal is different. I conceive the goal of knowledge as attaining some finally adequate explanatory language, which can make sense of the object and will exclude all future surprises. However much this may elude us in practice, it is what we often seek in science: we look for the ultimate theory in microphysics, where we will finally have charted all the particles and forces, and we do not have to face future revisions.

Second, coming to an understanding can never have this finality. For one thing, we come to understandings with certain definite interlocutors. These will not necessarily serve when we come to deal with others. Understandings are party-dependent. And then, frequently more worrying, even our present partners may not remain the same. Their life situation or goals may change and the understanding may be put in question. True, we try to control for this by binding agreements and contracts, but this is precisely because we see that what constitutes perfect and unconstrained mutual understanding at one time may no longer hold good later.

Third, the unilateral nature of knowing emerges in the fact that my goal is to attain a full intellectual control over the object, such that it can no longer "talk back" and surprise me. Now this may require that I make some quite considerable changes in my outlook. My whole conceptual scheme may be inadequate when I begin my inquiry. I may have to undergo the destruction and remaking of my framework of understanding to attain the knowledge that I seek. But all this serves the aim of full intellectual control. What does not alter in this process is my goal. I define my aims throughout in the same way.

By contrast, coming to an understanding may require that I give some ground in my objectives. The end of the operation is not control, or else I am engaging in a sham designed to manipulate my partner while pretending to negotiate. The end is being able in some way to function together with the partner, and this means listening as well as talking, and hence may require that I redefine what I am aiming at.

So there are three features of understandings—they are bilateral, they are party-dependent, they involve revising goals—that do not fit our classical model of knowing an object. To which our "normal" philosophical reaction is: quite so. These are features unsuited to knowledge, real "science." The content of knowledge should not vary with the person who is seeking it; it can't be party-dependent. And the true seeker after knowledge never varies in her goal; there is no question of compromise here. Party-dependence and altered goals are appropriate to understandings precisely because they represent something quite different from knowledge; deal cutting and learning the truth are quite distinct enterprises, and one should never mix the two on pain of degrading the scientific enterprise.

How does Gadamer answer these "obvious" objections? His answer contains many rich and complex strands. I want to mention two here, leaving aside others that are equally, perhaps even more important (such as the whole issue of "linguisticality," which is another of Gadamer's crucial contributions to the thought of our time).

The first is a negative point. Gadamer does not believe that the kind of knowledge that yields complete intellectual control over the object is attainable, even in principle, in human affairs. It may make sense to dream of this in particle physics, even to set this as one's goal, but not when it comes to understanding human beings.

He expresses this, for instance, in his discussion of experience. Following Hegel, he sees experience, in the full sense of the term, as *"Erfahrung der Nichtigkeit"* (Experience of Negation).[1] Experience is that wherein our previous sense of reality is undone, refuted, and shows itself as needing to be reconstituted. It occurs precisely in those moments where the object "talks back." The aim of science, following the model above, is thus to take us beyond experience. This latter is merely the path to science, whose successful completion would take it beyond this vulnerability to further such refutation. "Denn Erfahrung selber kann nie Wissenschaft sein. Sie steht in einem unaufhebbaren Gegensatz zum Wissen und zu derjenigen Belehrung, die aus theoretischem oder technischem Allgemeinwissen fliesst" (". . . for experience itself can never be science. Experience stands in an ineluctable opposition to knowledge and to the kind of instruction that follows from general theoretical or technical knowledge").[2] Now Gadamer sees it as part of the finitude of the human condition that this kind of transcending of experience is in principle impossible in human affairs. To explain fully why would involve talking a great deal about linguisticality, which I have no space for here. But perhaps the main point can be made tersely in terms of the place of culture in human life. Whatever we might identify as a fundamental common human nature, the possible object of an ultimate experience-transcending science is always and everywhere mediated in human life through culture, self-understanding, and language. These not only show an extraordinary variety in human history, but they are clearly fields of potentially endless innovation.

Here we see a big watershed in our intellectual world. There are those who hope to anchor an account of human nature below the level of culture, so that cultural variation, where it is not trivial and negligible, can be explained from this more basic account. Various modes of sociobiology and accounts of human motivation based on the (conjectured) conditions in which human beings evolved share this ambition. They have the necessary consequence that most cultural variation is placed in the first category and seen as merely epiphenomenal, a surface play of appearances. And then there are those who find this account of human life unconvincing, who see it as an evasion of the most important *explananda* in human life, which are to be found at this level of cultural difference.

Gadamer is one of the major theorists in the second camp, and hence he sees the model of science that I opposed above to understanding as inapplicable to human affairs.

This may help explain why he refuses this model, but not the adoption of his alternative based on interpersonal understanding. How does he justify party-dependence, and what analogue can he find to revising goals?

The first can be explained partly from the fact of irreducible cultural variation. From this, we can see how the language we might devise to understand the people of one society and time would fail to carry over to another. Human science could never consist exclusively of species-wide laws. In that sense, it would always be at least in part "idiographic" as against "nomothetic." But for Gadamer party-dependence is more radical than that. The terms of our best account will vary not only with the people studied but also with the students. Our account of the decline of the Roman Empire will not and cannot be the same as that put forward in eighteenth-century England, or those that will be offered in twenty-fifth-century China, or twenty-second-century Brazil.

It is this bit of Gadamer's argument that often strikes philosophers and social scientists as scandalous and "relativist," abandoning all allegiance to truth. This interpretation is then supported by those among Gadamer's defenders who are in a "postmodern" frame of mind.

But this grievously misunderstands the argument. Gadamer is anything but a "relativist" in the usual sense of today's polemics. To see this, we have to bring out another way in which Gadamer breaks with the ordinary understanding of "science."

As we often have been led to understand it in the past, scientific explanation deploys a language that is entirely clear and explicit. It is grounded in no unthought-out presuppositions, which may make those who speak it incapable of framing certain questions and entertaining certain possibilities. This false view has been largely dispelled in our time by the work of such thinkers as Kuhn and Bachelard. We now understand that the practices of natural science have become universal in our world as the result of certain languages, with their associated practices and norms, having spread and being adopted by all societies in our time.

But what has been less remarked is that these languages became thus universally diffusable precisely because they were insulated from the languages of human understanding. The great achievement of the seventeenth-century scientific revolution was to develop a language for nature that was purged of human meanings. This was a revolution because the earlier scientific languages, largely influenced by Plato and Aristotle, were saturated with purpose and value terms. These could only have traveled along with a good part of the way of life of the civilizations that nourished them. But the new austere languages could be adopted elsewhere more easily.

We can see how different the situation is with the languages of "social science." These too have traveled, but very much as a result of the cultural influence of and cultural alignment of the "West." Moreover, they seem incapable of achieving the kind of universality we find with natural sciences. The study of human beings remains in a preparadigmatic condition, where a host of theories and approaches continue to compete, and there is no generally recognized "normal" science.

This difference in the fate of the two kinds of "science" is connected to the fact that the languages of human science always draw for their intelligibility on our ordinary understanding of what it is to be a human agent, live in society, have moral convictions, aspire to happiness, and so forth. No matter how much our ordinary everyday views on these issues may be questioned by a theory, we cannot but draw on certain basic features of our understanding of human life, those that seem so obvious and fundamental as not to need formulation. But it is precisely these that may make it difficult to understand people of another time or place.

Thus we can innocently speak of people in other ages holding opinions or subscribing to values without noticing that in our society there is a generalized understanding that everyone has, or ought to have, a personal opinion on certain subjects—say, politics or religion; or without being aware of how much the term "value" carries with it the sense of something chosen. But these background understandings may be completely absent in other societies. We stumble into ethnocentrism, not in virtue so much of the theses that we formulate, but of the whole context of understanding that we unwittingly carry over unchallenged.

Now this is not a danger that we can conjure once and for all by adopting a certain attitude. That is because the context that will give its sense to any theoretical account of human life we are entertaining will be the whole, tacit, background understanding of what it is to be a human being. But this is so wide and deep that there can be no question of simply suspending it and operating outside of it. To suspend it altogether would be to understand nothing about human beings at all. Here is where the striking contrast with the languages of natural science emerges. There it was possible to develop languages for the objects of science that bracketed out human meanings and still think effectively, indeed, more effectively, about the target domain. But bracketing out human meanings from human science means understanding nothing at all; it would mean betting on a science that bypassed understanding altogether and tried to grasp its domain in neutral terms, in the language of neurophysiology, for instance.

If our own tacit sense of the human condition can block our understanding of others, and yet we cannot neutralize it at the outset, then how can we come to know others? Are we utterly imprisoned in our own unreflecting outlook? Gadamer thinks not. The road to understanding others passes through the patient identification and undoing of those facets of our implicit understanding that distort the reality of the other.

At a certain point, we may come to see that "opinions" have a different place in our life-form than in theirs, and we will then be able to grasp the place of beliefs in their life; we will be ready to allow this to be in its difference, undistorted by the assimilation to "opinions."

This will happen when we allow ourselves to be challenged, interpellated by what is different in their lives, and this challenge will bring about two connected changes: we will see our peculiarity for the first time, as a formulated fact about us and not simply a taken-for-granted feature of the human condition as such; and at the same time, we will perceive the corresponding feature of their life-form undistorted. These two changes are indissolubly linked; you cannot have one without the other.

Our understanding of them will now be improved through this correction of a previous distortion, but it is unlikely to be perfect. The possible ways in which our background could enframe them distortively cannot be enumerated. We may still have a long way to go, but we will have made a step toward a true understanding; and further progress along this road will consist of such painfully achieved, particular steps. There is no leap to a disengaged standpoint which can spare us this long march.

"Wird ein Vorurteil fraglich . . . so heisst dies mithin nicht, dass es einfach beiseite gesetzt wird und der andere oder das Andere sich an seiner Stelle unmittlebar zur Geltung bringt. Das ist vielmehr die Naïvität des historischen Objektivismus, ein solches Absehen von sich selbst anzunehmen. In Wahrheit wird das eigene Vorurteil dadurch recht eigentlich ins Speil gebracht, dass es selber auf dem Spiele steht. Nur indem es sich ausspielt, vermag es den Wahrheitsanspruch des anderen überhaupt zu erfahren und ermöglicht ihm, das er sich auch ausspielen kann" ("If a prejudice becomes questionable . . . this does not mean that it is simply set aside and the text or other person accepted as valid in its place. Rather historical objectivism shows its naivete in accepting this disregarding of ourselves as what actually happens. In fact our own prejudice is properly brought into play by being put at risk. Only by being given full play is it able to experience the other's claim to truth and make it possible for him to have full play himself").[3]

We can now see how our grasp of the other, construed on the model of coming to an understanding, is doubly party-dependent, varying not only with the object studied but also with the student: with the object studied, because our grasp will have to be true to them in their particular culture, language, way of being. But it will also vary with the student, because the particular language we hammer out in order to achieve our understanding of them will reflect our own march toward this goal; it will reflect the various distortions that we have had to climb out of, the kinds of questions and challenges that they in their difference pose to us. It will not be the same language in which members of that culture understand themselves;

it will also be different from the way members of a distinct third culture will understand them, coming as they will to this goal through a quite different route, through the identification and overcoming of a rather different background understanding.

That is why the historiography of the Roman Empire, carried out in twenty-fifth-century China or twenty-second-century Brazil, is bound to be different from ours. They will have to overcome different blocks to understanding; they will find the people of that time puzzling in ways which we do not; they will need to make them comprehensible through a different set of terms.

The coming-to-an-understanding model fits here, with its corrolary of party dependence, because the language of an adequate science of the Ys for the Xs reflects both Xs and Ys. It is not, as with the knowledge-of-object model, a simple function of the object, the scientific theory that is perfectly adequate to this reality. It is a language that bridges those of both knower and known. That is why Gadamer speaks of it as a "fusion of horizons." The "horizons" here are at first distinct, they are the way that each has of understanding the human condition in their nonidentity. The "fusion" comes about when one (or both) undergo a shift; the horizon is extended so as to make room for the object that before did not fit within it.

For instance, we become aware that there are different ways of believing things, one of which is holding them as a "personal opinion." This was all that we allowed for before, but now we have space for other ways and can therefore accommodate the beliefs of a quite different culture. Our horizon is extended to take in this possibility, which was beyond its limit before.

But this is better seen as a fusion rather than just as an extension of horizons, because at the same time we are introducing a language to talk about their beliefs that represents an extension in relation to their language. Presumably, they had no idea of what we speak of a "personal opinions," at least in such areas as religion, for instance. They would have had to see these as rejection, rebellion, and heresy. So the new language used here, which places "opinions" alongside other modes of believing as possible alternative ways of holding things true, opens a broader horizon, extending beyond both the original ones and in a sense combining them.

Here we see the full force of the Gadamerian image of the "conversation." The kind of operation described here can be carried out unilaterally and must be when one is trying to write the history of the Roman Empire, for instance. But it borrows its force from comparison with another predicament, in which live interlocutors strive to come to an understanding, to overcome the obstacles to mutual comprehension, to find a language in which both can agree to talk undistortively of each. The hermeneutical understanding of tradition limps after this paradigm operation; we have to maintain a kind of openness to the text, allow ourselves to be interpellated by it, take seriously the way its formulations differ from ours; all things which a live interlocutor in a situation of equal power would force us to do.

Horizons are thus often initially distinct. They divide us, but they are not unmovable; they can be changed, extended. I want to discuss this notion of horizon next, but first I must say a word about why this picture of a language for science that varies with both knower and known is quite different from the common idea of "relativism" and has a clear place for the concepts of correctness and truth.

Relativism is usually the notion that affirmations can be judged valid not unconditionally but only from different points of view or perspectives. Proposition p could be true from perspective A, false from perspective B, indeterminate from C, and so forth; but there would be no such thing as its being true or false unconditionally.

It does not seem to me that Gadamer is into this position at all. If the historiography of the Roman Empire in twenty-fifth-century China is different from our own, this will not be because what we can identify as the same propositions will have different truth values. The difference will be rather that different questions will be asked, different issues raised, different features will stand out as remarkable, and so forth.

Moreover, within each of these enterprises of studying Rome from these different vantage points, there will be such a thing as better or worse historiography. Some accounts will be more ethnocentric and distortive than others, still others will be more superficial. Accounts can be ranked for accuracy, comprehensiveness, nondistortion, and so forth. Some will be more right than others, will approach closer to the truth.

But beyond this, we can also see a possible ranking between accounts from different starting points. Let us say that twenty-fifth-century Chinese historians take account of the work of Gibbon, Symes, Jones, Peter Brown, and so forth. They will be trying not just to fuse horizons with the Romans but also with us as we try to do the same thing. The fusion will not only be bipolar but triangular, or if we see Gibbon as a distinct standpoint, quadrangular.

We can see now that there is another virtue here of accounts. They can be more or less comprehensive in a new sense; not depending on how much detail and coverage they offer of the object studied, but rather on their taking in and making mutually comprehensible a wider band of perspectives. The more comprehensive account in this sense fuses more horizons.

The ideal of the most comprehensive account possible ought in a sense to take the place of the old goal of a point-of-view-less nomothetical science that grasps all humanity under one set of explanatory laws. Instead we substitute the ideal of languages that allow for the maximum mutual comprehension between different languages and cultures across history. Of course, this is a goal that can in the nature of things never be integrally realized. Even if, *per impossibile*, we might have achieved an understanding to which all cultures to date might sign on, this could not possibly preempt future cultural change, which would require the process of fusion to start over again.

But it is nevertheless an important ideal both epistemically and humanly: epistemically, because the more comprehensive account would tell more about human beings and their possibilities; humanly, because the language would allow more human beings to understand each other and to come to undistorted understandings.

For human affairs, the model of scientific theory that is adequate to an object is replaced by that of understanding, seen as a fusion of horizons. "Verstehen *ist* immer der Vorgang der Verschmelzung . . . vermeintlich für sich seiender Horizonte" ("understanding is always the fusion of these horizons supposedly existing by themselves").[4]

Charles Taylor

Gadamer's concept of "horizon" has an inner complexity that is essential to it. On one hand, horizons can be identified and distinguished; it is through such distinctions that we can come to grasp what is distorting understanding and impeding communication. But on the other hand, horizons evolve, change. There is no such thing as a fixed horizon. "Der Horizont ist vielmehr etwas, in das wir hineinwandern und das mit uns mitwandert. Dem Beweglichen verschieben sich die Horizonte" ("The horizon is, rather, something into which we move and that moves with us. Horizons change for a person who is moving").[5] A horizon with unchanging contours is an abstraction. Horizons identified by the agents whose worlds they circumscribe are always in movement. The horizons of A and B may thus be distinct at time t and their mutual understanding imperfect. But A and B by living together may come to have a single common horizon at $t + n$.

In this way "horizon" functions somewhat like "language." One can talk about the "language of modern liberalism," or the "language of nationalism," and point out the things they cannot comprehend. But these are abstractions, freeze frames of a continuing film. If we talk about the language of Americans or Frenchmen, we can no longer draw their limits a priori; for the language is identified by the agents who can evolve.

This way of understanding difference and its overcoming through the complex concept of a horizon is to be contrasted with two others. On one hand, we have the classic model that comes from the epistemological tradition, whereby our grasp of the world is mediated by the inner representations we make of it, or the conceptual grid through which we take it in. This way of construing knowledge easily generates the conjecture that there may be unbridgeable differences. What if our inner representations diverge, even as we stand before the same external objects? What if our conceptual grids are differently constructed, through which all the information we receive is filtered? How will we ever be able to convince each other, even understand each other? Any consideration that one may adduce in argument will already be represented or enframed by the other in a systematically different way. All reasoning stops at the borders of conceptual schemes, which pose insurmountable limits to our understanding.

In reaction to this, there is the attempt to establish the possibility of universal communication through an outright rejection of the idea of a conceptual scheme, as famously proposed by Donald Davidson.[6] Davidson means his argument to be taken as a repudiation of the whole representational epistemology. "In giving up the dualism of scheme and world, we do not give up the world, but re-establish unmediated touch with the familiar objects whose antics make our sentences and opinions true and false."[7]

As a rejection of the old epistemology (or at least attempted rejection; I am not sure that Davidson shakes off the shackles of the representational view), this is welcome. And Davidson's argument against the idea that we could be imprisoned in utterly incongruent schemes, invoking the "principle of charity," is obviously a powerful one. Davidson's principle of charity requires that I, the observer/theorist, must make sense of him, the subject studied, in the sense of finding most of what he does, thinks, and says intelligible; else I cannot be treating him as a rational agent and there is nothing to understand, in the relevant sense, at all.

What this argument shows is that total unintelligibility of another culture is not an option. To experience another group as unintelligible over some range of their practices, we have to find them quite understandable over other (very substantial) ranges. We have to be able to understand them as framing intentions, carrying out actions, trying to communicate orders, truths, and so forth. If we imagine even this away, then we no longer have the basis that allows us to recognize them as agents. But then there's nothing left to be puzzled about. Concerning nonagents, there is no question about what they are up to and hence no possibility of being baffled on this score.

The problem with this argument is that it is in a sense too powerful. It slays the terrifying mythical beast of total and irremediable incomprehensibility. But what we suffer from in our encounters between peoples are the jackals and vultures of partial and (we hope) surmountable noncommunication.

In this real-life situation, Davidson's theory is less useful. Mainly because it seems to discredit the idea of "conceptual schemes" altogether—this in spite of the fact that the argument only rules out our meeting a totally unintelligible one. But in dealing with the real, partial barriers to understanding, we need to be able to identify what is blocking us. And for this we need some way of picking out the systematic differences in construal between two different cultures, without either reifying them or branding them as ineradicable. This is what Gadamer does with his image of the horizon. Horizons can be different, but at the same time they can travel, change, extend— as you climb a mountain, for instance. It is what Davidson's position as yet lacks.

Without this, Davidson's principle of charity is vulnerable to being abused to ethnocentric ends. The principle tells me to make the best sense of the other's words and deeds as I can. In translating his words into my language, I should render him so that as much as possible he speaks the truth, makes valid inferences, and so forth. But the issue is to know what counts as "my language" here. It can mean the language I speak at the moment of encounter, or it can mean the extended language, the one that emerges from my attempts to understand him, to fuse horizons with him. If we take it in the first way, it is almost certain that I will ethnocentrically distort him.

The problem is that the standing ethnocentric temptation is to make too quick sense of the stranger, that is, sense in one's own terms. The lesser breeds are without the law because they have nothing we recognize as law. The step to branding them as lawless and outlaw is as easy as it is invalid and fateful. So the conquistadores had an easy way of understanding the strange and disturbing practices of the Aztecs, including human sacrifice. While we worship God, these people worship the Devil.

Of course, this totally violates Davidson's intent. But the problem is that we need to understand how we move from our language at the time of encounter, which can only distort those we encounter, to a richer language that has place for them, from making the "best sense" in our initial terms, which will usually be an alien imposition, to making the best sense within a fused horizon. I cannot see how we can conceive of or carry out this process without allowing into our ontology something like alternative horizons or conceptual schemes. This I think marks the superiority of Gadamer's view over Davidson's.

Davidson's argument is nonetheless very valuable in pointing out the dangers, even the paradoxes involved in using any such terms. We can see this when we ask the question, what does the concept "scheme" contrast with? The term "content" is certainly bad, as though there were stuff already lying there, to be framed in different schemes. There is certainly a deep problem here.

It belongs to the very idea of a scheme, in the sense one is tempted to use it in intercultural studies, that it indicate some systematic way in which people are interpreting or understanding their world. Different schemes are incombinable such ways of understanding the same things.

But what things? How can you point to the things in question? If you use the language of the target society to get at them, then all distinction between scheme and content disappears. But what else can you use? Well, let us say our language, that of the observer/scientists, about this target area. But then we still will not have got at the "content" we share in common, which would have to be somehow identifiable independently of both schemes.

The point is well taken and needs to be kept in mind in order to avoid certain easy pitfalls, such as thinking that one has a neutral, universal categorization of the structures or functions of all societies, for example, "political system," "family," "religion," and so forth, which provide the ultimately correct description for what all the different fumbling, cultural languages are aiming at, the noumena to their phenomenal tongues. But the notion of two schemes, one target area, remains valid and indeed indispensable.

Let's go back to the case of the conquistadores and the Aztecs. We might say that one thing the conquistadores had right was that they recognized that ripping out of hearts in some way corresponded in Spanish society to the Catholic Church and the Mass, and that sort of thing. That is, the right insight, yielding a good starting point for an eventual fusion of horizons, involves identifying what something in the puzzling life of an alien people can usefully be contrasted with in ours. In Gadamerian terms, what we are doing is identifying that facet of our lives which their strange customs interpellate, challenge, offer a notional alternative to.

An example will show what is at stake here. A few years ago a wildly reductivistic American social scientist produced a theory of Aztec sacrifice in which it was explained "materialistically" in terms of their need for protein. On this view the right point of comparison in Spanish society would be their slaughterhouses rather than their churches. Needless to say, from such a starting point, one gets nowhere.

The fruitful supposition is that what went on atop those pyramids reflected a very different construal of an X, which overlaps with what Christian faith and practice is a construal of in Spain. This is where thinking and inquiry can usefully start. It has one powerful—and in principle challengeable—presupposition: that we share the same humanness and that therefore we can ultimately find our feet in Aztec sacrifice, because it's a way of dealing with a human condition we share. Once this is accepted, then the notion of two schemes, same X becomes inescapable. Only we have to be careful what we put in the place of the "X."

In a general proposition, we might say that what we put in place of the X is dimension, or aspect of the human condition. In the particular case, it is much more dangerous to specify. "Religion" would be an obvious candidate word. But the danger is precisely that we happily take on board everything this word means in our world and slide back toward the ethnocentric reading of the conquistadores. So we perhaps retreat to something vaguer, like "numinous," but even this carries its dangers.

The point is to beware of labels here. This is the lesson to be learned from attacks on the scheme-content distinction. But that the Mass and Aztec sacrifice belong to rival construals of a dimension of the human condition for which we have no stable, culture-transcendent name, is a thought we cannot let go of, unless we want to relegate these people to the kind of unintelligibility that members of a different species would have for us. If rejecting the distinction means letting this go, it is hardly an innocent step.

The conception of horizons and their fusion shows how the "science" we have of other times and people is, like the understandings we come to, party-dependent. It will differ both with the object and the subject of knowledge.

But how about the analogue to the other property of understandings I mentioned above, that they may involve changing our goals? The analogous point here is that in coming to see the other correctly, we inescapably alter our understanding of ourselves. Taking in the other will involve an identity shift in us. That is why it is so often resisted and rejected. We have a deep identity investment in the distorted images we cherish of others.

That this change must occur falls out from the account of the fusion of horizons. To recur to our example: we come to see that attributing "opinions" to them is distortive. But we only ever did so originally, because it seemed to go without saying that this is what it meant to have beliefs in certain areas. To get over the distortion, we had to see that there were other possibilities, that our way of being isn't the only or "natural" one, but that it represents one among other possible forms. We can no longer relate to our way of doing or construing things "naively," as just too obvious to mention.

If understanding the other is to be construed as fusion of horizons and not as possessing a science of the object, then the slogan might be: no understanding the other without a changed understanding of self.

The kind of understanding that ruling groups have of the ruled, that conquerors have of the conquered—most notably in recent centuries in the far-flung European empires—has usually been based on a quiet confidence that the terms they need are already in their vocabulary. Much of the "social science" of the last century is in this sense just another avatar of an ancient human failing. And indeed, the satisfactions of ruling, beyond the booty, the unequal exchange, the exploitation of labor, very much includes the reaffirmation of one's identity that comes from being able to live this fiction without meeting brutal refutation. Real understanding always has an identity cost—something the ruled have often painfully experienced. It is a feature of tomorrow's world that this cost will now be less unequally distributed.

The cost appears as such from the standpoint of the antecedent identity, of course. It may be judged a gain once one has gone through the change. We are also enriched by knowing what other

Charles Taylor

human possibilities there are in our world. It cannot be denied, however, that the path to acknowledging this is frequently painful.

The crucial moment is the one where we allow ourselves to be interpellated by the other; where the difference escapes from its categorization as an error, a fault, or a lesser, undeveloped version of what we are, and challenges us to see it as a viable human alternative. This unavoidably calls our own self-understanding into question. This is the stance Gadamer calls "openness." As against the way I stand to what I see as an object of science, where I try "sich selber aus der Beziehung zum anderen herauszureflektieren und dadurch von ihm unerreichbar zu werden" ("reflecting [myself] out of [my] relation to the other and so becoming unreachable by him"),[8] "Offenheit für den anderen schliesst . . . die Anerkennung ein, dass ich in mir etwas gegen mich gelten lassen muss, auch wenn es keinen anderen gäbe, der es gegen mich geltend machte" ("Openness to the other . . . involves recognizing that I myself must accept some things that are against me, even though no one else forces me to do so").[9]

Gadamer's argument in *Wahrheit und Methode* deals with our understanding of our own tradition, the history of our civilization, and the texts and works which belong to this. This means that what we study will be in one way or another internal to our identity. Even where we define ourselves against certain features of the past, as the modern Enlightenment does against the "Middle Ages," this remains within our identity as the negative pole, that which we have overcome or escaped. We are part of the *Wirkungsgeschichte* of this past and as such it has a claim on us.

My point in this essay has been that Gadamer's account of the challenge of the other and the fusion of horizons applies also to our attempts to understand quite alien societies and epochs. The claim here comes not from their place within our identity, but precisely from their challenge to it. They present us different and often disconcerting ways of being human. The challenge is to be able to acknowledge the humanity of their way, while still being able to live ours. That this may be difficult to achieve, that it will almost certainly involve a change in our self-understanding and hence in our way, has emerged from the above discussion.

Understanding the Other

Meeting this challenge is becoming ever more urgent in our intensely intercommunicating world. At the turn of the millennium, it is a pleasure to salute Hans-Georg Gadamer, who has helped us so immensely to conceive this challenge clearly and steadily.

Notes

1. *Wahrheit und Methode, Gesammelte Werke* 1 (Tübingen: J. C. B. Mohr [Paul Siebeck], 1986), 360; *Truth and Method,* by Joel Weinsheimer and Donald Marshall (New York: Continuum, 2nd rev. ed., 1989), 354.

2. *Wahrheit und Methode,* 361; *Truth and Method,* 355.

3. *Wahrheit und Methode,* 304; *Truth and Method,* 299.

4. *Wahrheit und Methode,* 311; *Truth and Method,* 306.

5. *Wahrheit und Methode,* 309; *Truth and Method,* 304.

6. "On the Very Idea of a Conceptual Scheme," in *Inquiries into Truth and Interpretation* (Oxford: Clarendon Press 1984).

7. Ibid., 198.

8. *Wahrheit und Methode,* 366; *Truth and Method,* 360.

9. *Wahrheit und Methode,* 367; *Truth and Method,* 361.

16

Gadamer and the Problem of Ontology

Gianni Vattimo

"Until now, philosophers thought they were only interpreting the world, yet they were truly changing it." This is how one could rewrite, from the standpoint of a philosophy reconfigured by Gadamer's influence, Marx's famous claim in the *Theses on Feuerbach*. One of the tenets of Gadamer's hermeneutics, one could perhaps say its main tenet, is the identification between the act that interprets the world and the act that changes it (by working historically) while, at the same time, one is first of all changing oneself. If we agree that hermeneutics has been and still is the cultural *koiné* not only of the Western past but also of its twentieth-century present, then we must agree that its current configuration is mostly the result of Gadamer's work. Many of the new philosophical ideas threaded through the renovation of Western philosophy in the period between the nineteenth and twentieth century may be brought back to the aforementioned identification.

One example is provided by the new relationship that Marx tried to establish between theory and praxis, itself an original reelaboration of the classical German idea of history as a history of the spirit. The same observation holds true, of course, for the postpositivistic epistemologies as well as for the artistic avant-gardes of the early twentieth century along with existentialism that represented its philosophical expression. The same identification also lies, although implicitly, behind the renewed assumption of the evangelical motto *veritatem facientes* (the Aristotelian *aletheuein*) *in caritate* that

Gianni Vattimo

lies at the core of several contemporary philosophies (with their attention on social dialogue, on the Levinasian attention to the Other and, more generally, on the constant substitution of ethics for metaphysics).

As years go by and the *Wirkungsgeschichte* of *Wahrheit und Methode* matures, it becomes ever clearer that the meaning of the last section of the book, where Gadamer speaks of an *Ontologische Wendung* of hermeneutics, lies in the direction of an identification between transformation and interpretation of the world. The *Philosophische Hermeneutik* alluded to in the subtitle of the book appears increasingly, and perhaps beyond the intentions of the author, as an *Ontologische Hermeneutik,* or even, and more so, a *Hermeneutische Ontologie.* It is along these lines that I think we should read Richard Bernstein's statement: "if we take Gadamer seriously, and we press his claims, they will bring us beyond philosophical hermeneutics,"[1] because, even leaving aside the ontological preferences of some of his interpreters, the debates around Gadamer's philosophy, in the decades that separate us from the publication of its inaugural text, have been moving precisely in this direction.

Today, both positive receptions and critical rejections of Gadamer's hermeneutics seem to be marked by a basic misunderstanding: namely, the assumption that it may be reduced to a theory of the intrinsically finite and historically bound character of understanding. On the one hand, pragmatist readers start from this basic theme in order to articulate a critique of the hegemonic pretensions of science and technology, while defending a democratic vision based on an ethics of common consciousness or of the *Lebenswelt.* On the other hand, Gadamer's critics find here the reason to impute to him a philosophy that will necessarily end up either in a historicistic relativism or in a vague traditionalism. Indeed, this misunderstanding can only be pushed aside by pressing, as Bernstein recommended, Gadamer's thought beyond the boundaries that traditionally limit it in the usual interpretation. More precisely, the misunderstanding can only be cleared by pressing Gadamer's thought in the direction of that ontological *Wendung* (shift) announced in the third division of *Warheit und Methode.* The pragmatistic reduction of hermeneutics to an appeal to wisdom, and, conversely, its inter-

pretation as a form of historical relativism and acritical traditionalism can only be undermined by a radical reading of Gadamer's
famous claim: "Sein, das verstanden werden kann, ist Sprache" ("Being that can be understood is language").[2] Both readings presuppose
that interpretation, to go back to Marx's claim, does not change the
world, that it is bound to mirror it more or less perfectly, and therefore, that interpretation encounters those "objective" limits that hermeneutics has taught us to acknowledge. As a consequence,
hermeneutics would have brought us to accept that there is no ultimate truth of knowledge, and thus that the only ethical imperative
is the tolerance that befits historically finite beings like us.

But Gadamer's system of thought provides the tools to proceed
well beyond such persistent metaphysical prejudices. As far as *Warheit und Methode* is concerned, the good, correct, appropriate interpretation is never so in virtue of its correspondence to a previously
set truth. Hasty readers of Gadamer may think that this is the case
because human finitude prevents us from knowing things the way
they are. On the contrary, one should rather say that things are what
they truly are, only within the realms of interpretation and language.
In other words, a consistent formulation of hermeneutics requires
a profound ontological revolution, because ontology must bid farewell to the idea of an objectified, external Being to which thought
should strive to adequate itself. It is only by persisting in thinking
being, true being, along these lines, that hermeneutics can be reduced to a simple appeal to wisdom, or to a form of relativism and
traditionalism.

Therefore, I believe that we must provide a radical interpretation
of the thesis according to which the being that can be understood
is language. But let us ask, in the first place: only being that can be
understood? Were it true, Gadamer would be limiting his doctrine
to the domain of the human sciences, and he would imply a sort of
objectivism and metaphysical realism. Certainly, a distinction between natural and human sciences still exists in Gadamer, but only
at a methodological level. In other words, he does not deem it viable
to substitute the rigorous method of scientific inquiry based on the
verification-falsification of propositions with a historical method
based on understanding. In Gadamer's work, however, there are no

arguments that would lead us to consider the experience of truth in the human sciences to be different from the experience of truth in the natural sciences, no matter how truth itself has been reached. In both cases, a true, authentic experience, or the experience of truth, operates a dialectical and thorough modification of the situation of the subject and the situation of the object known. Any theory aspiring to dictate the ultimate difference between natural and human sciences should present itself, in its turn, as a scientific and natural proposition—that is, it should assume the logical status of an "objective" description of the world. In my opinion, Gadamer's hermeneutics is at odds with such a metaphysical stance.

If we take in absolute seriousness the identification between being and language, however, we seem to run into the risk of arbitrariness. If there is no being beyond language, one will not understand the effort, so often stressed by Gadamer, to find the right word. More generally, it looks as if any distinction between truth and falsity, between opinion and science, becomes impossible. The ontological novelty of Gadamer's hermeneutics becomes clear once we realize that the criteria determining the search for the right word as well as the distinction between truth and falsity, between satisfactory and wrong interpretations, are all internal to language itself. Once again, let us remember that the suspicions against the power of these kind of internal criteria to ward off arbitrariness and relativism depend on the persistent metaphysical conviction that determines being as the object, the given. We find a useful approach to this problem in the pages of *Warheit und Methode* where Gadamer, on the basis of Heidegger's doctrine of fore-conception, vindicates the positive function of prejudice. Gadamer quotes §63 of *Sein und Zeit*, which deals among other things with "der methodische Charakter der existenzialen Analytik" (the methodological character of the existential analytics) and the *Seinsinn der Sorge* (the ontological sense of care). Heidegger explicitly asks: "Woher sollen aber die ontologischen Entwürfe die Evidenz der phaenomenalen Angemessenheit für ihre 'Befunde' nehmen?"[3]

Heidegger immediately connects the issue to the distinction between authentic and inauthentic existence. The evidence for the adequacy of the ontological project cannot be found in some comparison between the fore-conception and the things in themselves, but only in the more or less authentic character of the project itself. It is clear that we have now advanced beyond the purely methodological concerns. We are reminded of the most radical aspects of the existential analytics, because the possibility of authentic existence is tied to the resolute anticipation of one's own death.[4] In the pages of *Warheit und Methode* containing the quote from *Sein und Zeit*, Gadamer does not mention the Heideggerian being-toward-death. A little further on,[5] however, he seems to translate Heidegger's thesis in the following terms: "Das Verstehen ist selber nicht so sehr als eine Handlung der Subjektivität zu denken, sondern als Einrücken in ein Ueberlieferungsgeschehen in dem sich Vergangenheit und Gegenwart beständig vermitteln."[6]

We can understand the connection between the resolute anticipation of one's own death and the *Einrücken in ein Überlieferungsgeschehen* (participation in an event of tradition), if we consider that in both cases the authors are reflecting upon the explicit assumption of one's own historicity. Indeed, we must acknowledge that this seemingly "urbanized" reading of Heidegger's being-toward-death clarifies its meaning in a direction most likely unknown to Heidegger himself. These pages by Gadamer teach us better what resolute anticipation of death may mean in Heidegger, even when considered at the existential level. It is well known that in *Sein und Zeit* the past may be understood as *gewesen*—as a possibility still open—and not as *vergangen* only on the basis of the authentic resolution for death. Once translated into Gadamer's terms, this authentic stance entails that the heritage we need to refer to in order to validate the fore-conceptions, and recognize the legitimate and fruitful ones, consists in considering them not as an eternal structure of a metaphysical being (and not even as the objectivity of the "objects" "out there"), but, on the contrary, as pure historical inheritance handed down by mortals to other mortals.

The ontological outcome thus reached—which is neither merely methodological, nor is it confined to the epistemology of the human sciences—is fully contained within the fluidification of objectivity, which gives the measure of the validity of the fore-conception. The effort toward the "true" word, the ever present difficulty of lying in the quietness of a single interpretation, collide with something that cannot be reduced to a *Handlung der Subjektivitaet* (subjective act), and which possesses a normative relevance of its own. This resistance, however, is not the world allegedly lying "out there" but rather the *Überlieferungsgeschehen* (event of tradition) in which the comprehension must *einrücken* (participate) in order to find its validity. It is what Heidegger, using an expression which Gadamer prefers not to use, calls the *Seinsgeschichte* (or the *Seinsgeschick*). In both cases, neither Gadamer's nor Heidegger's word allow any identification with the idea of history as necessity endowed with the features of *Tradition* and *vergangen* more than *Überlieferung* and *gewesen*.

The validity of Gadamer's hermeneutics entails the thesis that things are really what they are only within interpretation. If one pays attention to the dense dialogue between *Warheit und Methode* and *Sein und Zeit* in the important excerpts mentioned, this thesis acquires a precise meaning that may shed light and perhaps even render more acceptable certain Heideggerian theses that have often been perceived as extravagant and "poetic." For instance, the thesis that the thing gives itself authentically only in the *Geviert* (fourfold) of heaven and earth, of mortals and gods. Hermeneutics convincingly shows that the established objectivity of objects, also and especially of the objects of the sciences, can only be obtained within an inherited framework (one would say within a Kuhnian paradigmatic framework), which must be responsibly and explicitly assumed by the interpreter or, as it is more the case in the domain of the scientific experimental research, by the community of interpreters. As Heidegger pointed out in 1920 in his review of Jaspers, the responsible assumption of one's historicity entails the interpretation of the inherited past, not its pedestrian repetition. Gadamer would say that it means to apply the past (see *Applicatio*), that is, to actively include it within a project. The *Überlieferungsgeschehen* (event of tradition) may possess a normative cogency only if it is included in a resolute project that, by keeping itself open to the future, changes the world because it interprets it. The change does not arise out of nothing, but it answers an appeal that, in turn, resonates only in the answer itself. Skipping a few steps, one could say that Gadamer's hermeneutical ontology is grounded on the identification of reality, *Wirklichkeit*, with *Wirkungsgeschichte*.

Since historicity is also, and always, the resolute project of an interpreter, hermeneutics must answer the question about the teleology that sustains and legitimates it. First of all, as a philosophical theory in competition with other theories, hermeneutics cannot claim its validity with allegedly descriptive arguments (arguments describing the structure of being). The identification between *Wirklichkeit* and *Wirkungsgeschichte* is not affirmed by a descriptive proposition: it is the meaning of the project, or rather the meaning of being within whose horizon hermeneutics interprets the experience of the world. Therefore, it is legitimate to think that the sentence "Sein, das verstanden werden kann, ist Sprache" should not be simply read as a statement that clarifies the lexical scope of "*Sein*," or even of that *Sein* that can be understood. On the contrary, it must be considered a teleologic indication, that, I think, we should read next to Heidegger's statement in *Sein und Zeit:* "Sein, nicht Seiendes, 'gibt es' nur sofern Wahrheit ist. Und sie *ist* nur, sofern und solange Dasein ist."[7]

A consistent philosophy of interpretation, if considered as an appeal to transform the objective reality of things "out there" into truth, that is into language and project, truly changes the world. It may introduce itself as that philosophy that, by inheriting the best part of German classic philosophy, answers the summon of an epoch in which science and technology are more and more converging toward a consummation of natural reality into an intersubjectively lived truth. Hermeneutics is more than the *koiné* of the end-of-the-century humanistic culture and of the human sciences in general; it is also a true "ontology of actuality," a philosophy of that late-modern world in which the world really dissolves, and more and more so, into the play of interpretations. Insofar as it is assumed as a responsible historical project, hermeneutics actively grasps being's vocation of giving itself, and increasingly so, as the truth of human language, and not as thing and datum, *Gegenständigkeit*. It is by following this thread that it also finds the ground of ethical choices and it offers

Gianni Vattimo

itself as a true critical theory. And it gives new meaning to Hölder-lin's line: "Voll Verdienst, doch dischterisch wohnet der Mensch auf dieser Erde."[8]

Translated by Stefano Franchi

Notes

1. Richard Bernstein, *Beyond Objectivism and Relativism: Science, Hermeneutics, and Praxis* (Philadelphia: University of Pennsylvania Press, 1983), 150.

2. *Truth and Method,* translated by Joel Weinsheimer and Donald Marshall (New York: Continuum, 2nd rev. ed., 1989), 475.

3. *Being and Time,* translated by Joan Stambaugh (Albany: SUNY, 1996), 288/H312: "Where are ontological projects to get the evidence that their 'findings' are phenomenally adequate?"

4. See *Being and Time,* H309.

5. *Truth and Method,* 274–275.

6. "Understanding is to be thought of less as a subjective act than as participating in an event of tradition, a process of transmission in which past and present are constantly mediated." *Truth and Method,* 290.

7. *Being and Time,* 211/H230: "There is being—not beings—only insofar as truth is. And truth *is* primordial only because and as long as Da-sein is."

8. "Full of merit, yet poetically man dwells on this earth," from the poem that begins "In lovely blueness blooms the steeple with the metal roof," famously quoted by Heidegger as the title for one of the essays in *Vorträge und Aufsätze* (Pfullingen: Neske, 1954), and that appears in English translation as ". . . Poetically Man Dwells" in *Poetry, Language, Thought,* translated by Albert Hofstadter (New York: Harper & Row, 1971), 211–229.

17

Social Identity as Interpretation

Georgia Warnke

How shall we think about the status of our social identities? By social identity I mean the identities we have as blacks, Caucasians, women, Latinos, gays, and so on, identities that we grow up as, assert in struggles for recognition, or try to eliminate and avoid. It has become usual to think of these identities as social constructions, as objective illusions that correspond to no gender, racial or cultural essence and yet create a social reality. In this essay I would like, instead, to explore the implications of conceiving of our social identities as interpretations. While the language of social construction derives from Foucault's work, that of interpretation derives from Gadamer's hermeneutics. I want to argue that recourse to the structure of hermeneutic understanding allows us access to the horizons from which different interpretations arise and, moreover, allows us to reflect on the contexts within which different social identities do and do not make sense. I shall concentrate for the most part on our social identities as women and females, and I shall begin by examining the social constructionist account of these identities in the work of Denise Riley and Judith Butler.[1]

Riley's concerns are the different identities that being women is meant to encompass. Rich and poor women, Anglo and non-Anglo women, women of different religions and backgrounds, black and white women are meant to have some feminine or female essence in common. Moreover, this essence is meant to hold historically so that what the identity of women is at one time coheres with their identity at another. In contrast, Riley argues that what she calls the "arrangement of people under the banners of men and women" is intertwined with the histories of other concepts such as nature, the soul, the social, and the body.[2] Her point is not so much that ideas about women change but, rather, that there is no underlying substance to the category of "women" about which such ideas might change. Instead, that substance is constructed in relation to the constructions of nature, the soul, and so on, and changes with them. Thus, if one wants to get clear on the history of concepts of womanhood or femininity, one has to see the way in which these combine with other concepts to construct different social realities.

One might begin with Aristotle's view of women as misbegotten males. In this view, women's essence lies in their imperfection, in the interruption of a trajectory that most perfectly ends in a man. In medieval theology, this earthly nature on the part of women can still be distinguished from their true identity in the afterlife. They are "the inferior of the male by nature, his equal by grace."[3] Hence women may be composed of "deprived, passive, and material traits, cold and moist dominant humours and a desire for completion by intercourse with men."[4] Still, their souls remain neutral. Indeed, the project sixteenth- and seventeenth-century feminists took up was that of proving and protecting the neutrality of the soul. They sought to prove it through demonstrations of their learning and rationality; they tried to protect it by advocating women's sanctuaries devoted to education and freed from the temptations of sex, which would pollute the soul with the contaminations of the female body. Still, by the eighteenth century, the configuration of the idea of women includes their souls. Sexuality and gender are no longer confined to the body but encompass all aspects of a feminine identity so that Rousseau can write that "the soul of a perfect woman and a perfect man ought to be no more alike than their faces."[5] It is not just that Aristotle thinks that women are imperfect men while Rousseau thinks women are perfect as the helpmate of men. Riley's point is that the substrate here, which is supposed to be imperfect at one point in history and perfect at another is, in each case, a different substrate, a substrate that is constructed in concert with the components of body, soul, humor, and reason that compose it.

The same holds for the introduction of the concept of the social in the nineteenth century. In this instance, the relevant opposition is no longer that between body and soul but rather that between nature and society: what feminists now have to demonstrate is that women are not properly identified with an arational, static nature; nor are they suited by nature only to the domestic domain of raising their children, managing their households and nurturing their husbands. Rather, women are properly identified with the domain of the social that encompasses the nurturing of all. Women's identity is connected to the care for the hygiene, education, sexuality, childbearing, and child rearing of all segments of the population; the proper object for women's activity becomes a philanthropy directed at poverty, immiseration, and delinquency. Women are both the social workers who help the working class care for their families and the objects of instruction who are taught how to care for their families. Most important, however, what they are not, in either case, are political subjects. As the social reconstructs women in its image and dispenses with the constructions of nature, it also delimits women in opposition to a construction of the political sphere that, in turn, becomes the sphere of juridical and government power. To allow women entry into this sphere is unreasonably to pollute important matters of legislation, war, and peace with feminine questions of housing, illness, and care for increasing populations.

In Riley's account, the efforts of women to become political citizens as well as social subjects shows the way in which the category of women is not only "diachronically" but also "synchronically . . . erratic."[6] To deny women the vote in Great Britain, antisuffragists claim that women are different from men in their greater affinity for domestic and social spheres and that their natural talents in these domains would be dissipated by their intrusion into political debates for which they had no talent. But when suffragists argue that women's difference from men indicates just how important their participation in politics might be in adding new perspectives, antisuffragists are just as willing to deny any difference between men and women. "In all . . . respects, the interests of the two sexes are identical. As citizens, therefore they are sufficiently represented already. To give them the franchise would just double the number of voters, without introducing any new interest."[7] Likewise, when suffragists argue that women are affected by the working of the political sphere and therefore should be granted the right to affect it, antisuffragists respond that women's generous but impulsive nature suits them for only an indirect influence. Rather than affecting politics directly, their emotional leanings need to be filtered through the more rational judgments of their husbands and fathers. Yet, when suffragists claim that women are no more impulsive than Irish men,[8] antisuffragists can reply that the impulsiveness of certain sorts of both men and women mean that granting women the vote would lead to domestic dissent and even violence.[9]

If women are historically both equal by grace and thoroughly inferior in body and soul, if they are identified with both nature and the social, if, within one historical period, they can be understood as both the same and different from men and if they differ from one another then, Riley's conclusion is that there is no "there" there, no essence to the feminine gender.[10] She is willing to grant the natural existence of biologically female persons. Yet, gendered women are not the simple expression of the biologically female sex nor are they cultural variations on it. They are rather fictions constructed for different and even competing purposes under different contexts.

Judith Butler takes this claim at least two steps further. In the first place, it is not only the feminine gender that is a social or historical construction but the female sex as well. Moreover, both sex and gender are the product of power, specifically, the hegemonic power of a "compulsory heterosexuality."[11] Here, we might begin by looking to the basis for assigning a particular sex to a particular individual.[12] Although biologists typically equate sex with the presence or absence of a Y chromosome, there are numerous instances in which doctors assign sex to an infant on the basis of its anatomy and in which the sex they assign differs from the sex defined by the infant's chromosomes. In many of these instances the infants' anatomies are ambiguous so that it is unclear whether they should be assigned the male or female sex. Yet, what is interesting to Butler is that such cases do not propel doctors or biologists to rethink their assumption that there are two and only two sexes. Instead, biologists refine their notions of sex determination to account for "mistakes." Thus Dr. David Page pursues what he thinks must be the male sex-determining factor on a chromosome's DNA and investigates the conditions under which it might switch from the Y chromosome, where it belongs, to the X chromosome, where it does not. But in pursuing this research, in Butler's view, he already presumes precisely what we might question: that there are naturally two distinct sexes.[13] Why should we presuppose this "fact" given that many individuals do not conform to the division between male and female? Why not divide human populations into five sexes: males, females, herms or "true" hermaphrodites, merms with "male" chromosomes and "female-like" anatomies, and ferms with "female" chromosomes and "male-like" anatomies.[14] The estimates of the birth numbers of infants born with so-called ambiguous genitalia range from about one in 500 to one in 2,000.[15] Nevertheless, rather than distinguishing between five sexes or giving up on sex categories altogether, doctors are often prepared to intervene surgically.

Suppose, instead, that we question the presumption in favor of two sexes. How does it arise? Butler suggests that we look once more at gender. If gender is not the expression of sex or even a culturally variable expression of sex, and if what women are meant to be changes, what is gender and what is its source? In Butler's view, one can define what the feminine gender is in terms of the gender it is not, as the lack of a masculine gender, or perhaps in terms of a relation between masculine and feminine genders. In either case, it corresponds to nothing substantial in itself but persists only as an opposition between two terms within a specific language. Following Foucault, Butler connects this language to certain disciplinary practices with which it combines to produce a kind of cultural grammar, a grammar that Foucault refers to as a discourse. More specifically, in Butler's view, we are led to the discourse of a compulsory heterosexuality. "The heterosexualization of desire," she writes, "requires and institutes the production of discrete and asymmetrical oppositions between 'feminine' and 'masculine,' where these are understood as expressive attributes of 'male' and 'female.' "[16] Accounting for the distinction between sexes, then, begins with the norm of a reproductive sexuality that imposes a division between two genders and establishes this division as the reflection of a division between two sexes. As Butler puts the point elsewhere, "The category of sex imposes a duality and a uniformity on bodies in order to maintain reproductive sexuality as a compulsory order." Moreover, "this discursive ordering and production of bodies in accord with the category of sex is . . . a material violence."[17]

How can a discursive ordering become a material violence? Butler's suggestion is that the disciplinary practice of maintaining a "normal" heterosexuality creates a binary system in which only two forms of coherent identity are possible. One is either a female sexed subject with a feminine gender who has heterosexual desires or one is a male sexed subject with a masculine gender and heterosexual desires. Other combinations of sex, gender, and desire reflect deviations from the norm and can be investigated and disciplined as such, as deviations for which we must find the cause. Discursive practices thus set up the matrixes of sex, gender and desire within which subjects are socially constituted and in terms of which deviant or ambiguous forms of subjectivity can be identified.

At the root of Butler's explanation for sexed and gendered subjects, then, is power, the power of discursive practices and, specifically, the power of a compulsory heterosexuality. Yet power is also the explanation with which her critics have the most trouble since it seems to deny the possibility of critical reflection, agency, and emancipation from power. If our identities are constructed in terms of the matrixes of specific disciplinary practices and if identities that challenge these matrixes are themselves formed by it, as challenges or deviations from a norm, then it does not appear that we can either reflect on our identities in terms that do not already presuppose these matrixes or liberate ourselves from them. Butler claims that the discursive practices that construct coherent subjects eliminate other possibilities and are thus exclusionary. "Subjects are constituted through exclusion, through the creation of a domain of deauthorized subjects, presubjects, figures of abjection, populations erased from view."[18] Yet, her theoretical apparatus does not seem to allow for criticism of this oppression and exclusion of others. As Seyla Benhabib puts the problem: "the subject that is but another position in language can no longer master and create the distance between itself and the chain of significations in which it is immersed such that it can reflect upon them and creatively alter them."[19]

Butler is, in fact, skeptical of notions of agency and reflection because they presume an Enlightenment idea of the subject at their core, a subject that precedes its actions and characteristics and can reflect on them on this basis. For Butler, however, subjects are constructed as women, men and, indeed, subjects only within specific discourses, as a consequence or effect of a specific grammar of language and practice. For this reason, the subject cannot serve as the starting point for an emancipatory theory. Instead, Butler looks to the Nietzschean notion of genealogy as an antidote to critical reflection and insists that critical reflection simply assumes a conception of rationality that ought itself to be the subject matter of a genealogical investigation. At the same time, she resists the notion that her Foucauldian analysis eliminates all possibilities for reflection, change, or creative alteration. The subject that is produced through discursive practices cannot be the self-originating site of thought or agency. Still, in genealogical investigations we can retrace the route by which we as subjects are constituted. Furthermore, as subjects we are not only produced but also continuously reproduced in practices and discourses, and this constant reproduction opens up the possibility of what Butler calls resignifications. While we cannot separate ourselves from the identities we are in order to reflect on and alter their oppressive and exclusionary aspects, what is possible is "resignification, redeployment, subversive citation from within, and interruption and inadvertent convergences with other [power/ discourse] networks."[20]

In Butler's analysis, then, genealogy replaces critique and resignification replaces agency. Neither genealogy nor resignification, however, has the normative dimension connected to the Enlightenment conception of social criticism or reflectively grounded action. We can undertake genealogical investigations of the route by which we become the identities we are, but any criticism of these identities is already implicated within the networks of discourse and power that produce them. Likewise, we can resignify, redeploy, and subvert, but we cannot appeal to reasons for doing so that transcend the discursive practices within which a given reason counts as a reason. For

Nancy Fraser, these restrictions indicate the limits of Butler's analysis, for they undermine any capacity to indicate why resignification is good.[21] Why should we not be content with the matrixes of sex, gender, and desire that our discursive practices enforce? Why should we criticize various forms of social identity as erratic, oppressive, or exclusionary?

Fraser contends that to answer these sorts of question, Butler must integrate her emphasis on social construction with an analysis that allows for social criticism. Fraser herself gestures toward a Habermasian account of the latter, one that looks to the procedures for rationally justifying norms that are anticipated by the pragmatic structure of communication oriented to understanding. In what follows, I would like to consider an alternative, hermeneutic account. Such an account is suspicious of quasi-transcendental claims to reason in the same way that Butler's Foucauldian account is. Still, while it therefore seems to have the same problems with a normative dimension, I shall try to show that it successfully evades them by introducing distinctions between better and worse interpretations of who we are.

It is worth noting that if the issue at hand is the construction of a sex and gendered subject, then Habermas's procedural analysis of the justification of norms is irrelevant. Habermas sees the justification of norms as a question for the moral employment of practical reason, while issues of identity refer to its ethical employment. Nor is it clear that Habermas has issues of what I am calling social identity in mind here as opposed to the character attributes of an individual or community. Thus, in considering questions of "who I am and who I want to be," he looks to what Charles Taylor calls strong preferences or evaluations, "preferences that concern not merely contingent dispositions and inclinations but the self-understanding of a person, his character and way of life."[22] In considering similar questions of who we are and who we want to be as a collectivity, he introduces such issues as city planning and the protection of cultural or ethnic minorities.

Our decisions on these kinds of issues are not moral decisions about principles or their application but rather determinations and applications of our character as the sort of community we are. Questions of social identity, in contrast, are questions of who we are as blacks or whites, men or women, Quebecois or English Canadians, and whether we want to continue to be these. These distinctions do not amount to a criticism of Fraser's appeal to a Habermasian view since her concern is the possibility of a feminist practice that can recognize the construction of women while nonetheless grounding norms of action guaranteeing their liberty, autonomy, and equality. Still, if our concern is our social identities, then we might pursue Habermas's analysis of the ethical employment of practical reason rather than his analysis of its moral employment and we might, specifically, pursue his suggestion that this ethical employment is hermeneutic in its structure in the way Gadamer's analysis of hermeneutic understanding suggests.

Strong preferences or evaluations are connected to the ways we understand ourselves and are two-directional, according to Taylor. They refer both to our understanding of ourselves and to our ideals of who we would like to be. Yet our self-understanding and ideals depend on the stock of possible descriptions and aspirations available to us through our individual life stories and the history and traditions to which we belong. We can aspire to public service but not to the membership of Knights of the Round Table; we can understand ourselves as good parents or bad spouses but not as heroes in the Greek sense. Understanding and interpretation are linguistic in character, Gadamer argues, and hence necessarily make use of an existing vocabulary of descriptions and identifications. He therefore describes self-understanding in terms that are at least as wary of the subject as a self-evident starting point for reflection as the descriptions Foucault and Butler provide:

Long before we understand ourselves through the process of self-examination, we understand ourselves in a self-evident way in the family, society, and state in which we live. The focus of subjectivity is a distorting mirror. The self-awareness of the individual is only a flickering in the closed circuits of historical life. That is why the prejudices (*Voruteile*) of the individual far more than his judgments (*Urteile*) constitute the historical reality of his being.[23]

By prejudices, Gadamer means the assumptions and expectations that provide our initial orientation to that which we are trying to understand. As such, they take up Heidegger's account of the fore-structure of understanding[24] and situate the conditions of understanding in our being always already oriented toward that which we are trying to understand. We grow up in a tradition or set of traditions that possess their own vocabularies of understanding and evaluation, their own practices, issues, and modes of intelligible behavior. Our understanding of ourselves, then, takes place within a tradition of understanding with specific terms, references, and contrasts. That we take the preservation of cultural or ethnic minorities to be an issue, whichever particular position we take on it, is a consequence of a particular set of historical actions and experiences, the struggles of particular groups as well as our ideals and commitments. Among these are the Holocaust, the Civil Rights Movements, the continuing disappearance of Native American tribes and languages, questions about a possessive individualism and liberalism, and so on. We conceive of ourselves as decent and humane or narcissistic and self-involved rather than, say, heroic or common and do so as the result of a particular history and language of understanding. To be a member of a specific culture at a specific time thus means that our attempts to understand our world and ourselves proceed on the basis of pre-judgments and anticipations of meaning that develop from the historical experiences and traditions of interpretation which we inherit.

The same would seem to hold of our understanding of ourselves in terms of the social identities that are intelligible or coherent for our time. We are heterosexuals or homosexuals in a way that Greeks without sexuality as an identity could not be.[25] We are blacks or whites in a way that a sixteenth-century Xhosa could not be. These identities do not become possible as a result of greater scientific knowledge. Many Greeks and Victorians engaged in similar sexual practices, and common racial distinctions correspond to no genes or internal properties of bodies. Rather, if we are to account for the social identities of races we need to look at a history of Atlantic trade and African slavery. We also need to look at traditions of thought that contrasted civilized Europeans to savages and that, in the late eighteenth and early nineteenth centuries, led to full-blown theories of racial hierarchy.[26] Likewise, we are Hispanic or Latino in ways that we could not be before the twentieth century when certain national policies came to require certain distinctions, which then become ways in which we think about ourselves.

Still, while neither Gadamer nor Butler thus take the subject as an unproblematic starting point for reflection or agency, Gadamer conceives of our identities in terms of traditions of interpretation rather than those of power and in terms of self-understanding rather than those of construction. What is the value of doing so? At first glance, we seem no closer to the possibility of agency or critical reflection. Rather, if Butler argues that the positions "that claim that the subject must be given in advance, that discourse is an instrument of reflection of that subject, are already part of what constitutes me,"[27] Gadamer seems simply to rephrase this view in arguing that the subject is a product of what he calls "effective history" or, in other words, a product of traditions of language, action and practice that compose and delimit the possibilities of identity open to it. "We should learn to understand ourselves better," Gadamer insists, "and recognize that in all understanding, whether we are expressly aware of it or not, the efficacy of history is at work."[28] How do we move from recognizing that history "effects" us or that discourses of power construct us to the possibility that we can consider our effective history or identities critically? How do we know when or in what direction we should change? Shall we be women or females or not, and why or why not?

Gadamer is, himself, wary of the force of an emancipatory reflection, at least to the extent that such reflection is supposed to dissolve prejudices and break free of the weight of history.[29] Our self-understanding is tradition bound. If it criticizes aspects of that tradition, it does so only in the tradition's own terms. Thus Gadamer continues the thought cited above by remarking that "historically effected consciousness (*wirkungsgeschitliches Bewusstsein*) is an element in the act of understanding itself."[30] As Butler puts an analogous point: "Critique . . . always takes place immanent to the regime of discourse/power who claims it seeks to adjudicate, which is to say that the practice of 'critique' is implicated in the very power-relations it seeks to adjudicate."[31] Nevertheless, there is, I think, an important difference between a Gadamerian hermeneutics and Foucauldian analysis. Although Foucault and Gadamer share a suspicion of the subject as a self-evident starting point for reflection, they are also involved in the old dispute between explanation and understanding.

Foucauldians are interested in a genealogical account of the contingent construction of social identities and the subject itself. Instead of taking the social identities we currently possess for granted, genealogies trace their construction through a series of contingent events and convergences. Thus we trace the evolution of sexuality as a characteristic that subjects possess through its final construction in the Victorian age. From a hermeneutic point of view, however, explanation in general is secondary to understanding, and the same would seem to hold for genealogy. Before we can explain why a particular event happens or how a particular identity is constructed, we must first understand what that event is or possess a prior understanding of what the identity or characteristic is. We understand a given natural event to be the eruption of a volcano; we understand a particular social event as a democratic victory; we understand a given action as the expression of a person's sexuality. Having done so, we can look for the causes of the events as we understand them. Yet, in neither the social scientific nor the natural scientific case can we simply disregard the act of understanding the event *as* what we understand it to be; this "as" is rather the starting point for Gadamer's hermeneutics. Understanding is primarily a grasp of "content" or the "subject-matter" and only after we have understood what something is can we explain how it came or comes about.[32]

Furthermore, in taking a particular content to be the particular content we take it to be, in taking an event to be the eruption of a volcano, a democratic victory, or an expression of sexuality, we are already engaged in projecting meaning. In articulating the meaning of that which we are trying to understand, we reveal the linguistic and historical nexus within which we understand. The conditions of understanding are prejudices and projections of meaning that arise within particular traditions of interpretation. Hence we understand an event as an eruption rather than as the wrath of the gods, and in interpreting an event as an electoral victory we understand within a framework that includes intelligible talk of elections, voting, and individual autonomy.

To have overlooked this point is, in Gadamer's view, the problem with "objective" sciences that take both their explanations and *explananda* to be unproblematic. In so doing, they mistake their own prejudices for objective judgments. Yet, there is also a problem with a Foucauldian analysis to the extent that its skirts the question of the conditions for its own investigation. To be sure, as Gadamer does, Foucault and Butler emphasize the discursive practices within which we always operate. They also stress the extent to which both the subject and object of inquiry are constructed: neither the subject of scientific investigation nor his or her object can be viewed as an unconstructed point of origin. Yet, if we take a hermeneutic approach to this situation, we will also be concerned with the conditions for the possibility of the inquiry itself. If we can understand what something is and how it is constructed only in terms of the prejudices developed in traditions of understanding, then we might also ask whether our projections and, indeed, our prejudices are legitimate.

Butler insists that genealogy opens up the possibility of a kind of reflection and political agency. We can inquire into the processes of construction that lead to certain identities through the exclusion and erasure of alternatives, and we can subvert and redeploy those identities. Nevertheless, she avoids the question of the validity of the understanding of the identities available to genealogical investigation and subversion. Our identities are constructed and can be constructed differently in redeploying the effects of power. But why should the constructions of power be subverted or redeployed? We are always constructed one way or another as an effect of discourses of power and it is not clear how a genealogical account of constructed identities can regard one identity as better than another insofar as both are the effect of power. In contrast, if we take up a Gadamerian hermeneutics, the understanding of meaning includes the question of the validity of understanding itself. Once we acknowledge that our projections of meaning are framed in terms of the preunderstandings we possess because of the traditions to which we belong, we can ask whether we ought to rely on these preunderstandings, whether they are of volcanic eruptions, democracy or sexuality. If our understanding of what sexuality is precedes the genealogical explanation of how it is constructed as a characteristic that subjects possess, and if this understanding stems from a projection of meaning that depends on a preunderstanding or set of prejudices, I might also ask whether those prejudices and hence this understanding are valid in the first place. Similarly, if I try to subvert and redeploy an identity, I do so on the basis of an understanding of what that identity is, an understanding that, hermeneutics insists, is open to consideration.

Before tracing the construction or subversion of an identity, then, Gadamer asks us to acknowledge the historical character of our understanding of what that identity is and, moreover, to raise the question of whether that understanding is legitimate or sufficient. Yet, this difference between a Foucauldian and hermeneutic approach simply raises another problem: in terms of what are we to evaluate our understanding's validity or sufficiency? What does it mean to be sufficient and what does it mean to be valid? On a hermeneutic view, as well as on a Foucauldian one, we are embedded in our existing history, vocabulary, and their prejudices. Since we are effected or constructed by them, however, what possible ground can we possess for testing our understandings of meaning and our self-understandings of who we are?

We cannot escape our self-understanding; nevertheless, Gadamer suggests that we can compare it to itself. This point he makes with regard to texts: we project the meaning of a text on the basis of traditions of interpretation and the assumptions or preunderstandings they involve. Hence we may approach Hamlet's "to be or not to be" soliloquy from the point of a tradition for which it exemplifies existential paralysis. At the same time, we test this projection against the text. Since we have access to the text, however, only through our projections of its meaning, we can test our projections only against one another: when our projection of the meaning of one part of the text conflicts with another, we assume that one or the other or both are mistaken and revise them. An interpretation of existential paralysis must cohere with other evidence of Hamlet's confusion and inaction. At work is the hermeneutical circle in which we test our prejudices by retaining only those that allow an understanding of the whole in terms of the parts and the parts in terms of the whole.

"Understanding," Gadamer writes, "is always a movement in this kind of circle, which is why the repeated return from the whole to the parts, and vice versa, is essential."[33]

Riley seems to engage in just this procedure in questioning the coherence of understandings of gender. These understandings are not only "synchronically and diachronically erratic" but also self-contradictory. Indeed, those who insist at the same or different times that women are the same in essence or different from men simply indicate with this incoherence that their interest is not in understanding what women are, if they are anything at all. The same holds of common understandings of race. On one understanding, "race," divides human populations according to skin color and morphological features; on another, a person's "race" is the "race" of his or her parents. Clearly, these accounts are inconsistent with one another. If we hold that a person's color establishes his or her race, we cannot also hold that it depends on his or her ancestry since the two can easily conflict: one might be pinkish in hue and hence "white" according to the first account and, yet, the child of African-American parents and hence "black" according to the second account. Moreover, the accounts are internally incoherent. The first becomes incoherent wherever a person's color fails to fall neatly into pink, black, brown, red, and yellow categories and where morphologies and colors do not either correlate with one another along any definitive lines or divide into definitive patterns. The second account is incoherent if one's parents are of different so-called races. Suppose my mother is Ghanaian and my father is Norwegian. What am I? Indeed, suppose I look like an average Norwegian and my sibling looks like an average Ghanaian.[34] According to the first account, we are of different races; according to the second, we are not. Can my "race" differ from that of my siblings? Or must my siblings and I be of the same race and, if so, which?

From a hermeneutic perspective, if I am interested in understanding race or gender and the understandings my tradition or I possess are self-contradictory, I must revise some or all aspects of them. I must decide what women, blacks, and whites are in a way that allows for self-consistency. Nonetheless, it is not clear that this hermeneutic approach, as thus far elucidated, can provide for the sort of critical reflection for which Fraser calls. There may be a kind of cognitive dissonance in John Locke's view of African chattel slavery, for example; he can both condemn it as "so vile and miserable an estate of man . . . that 'tis hardly conceivable that an Englishman, much less a gentleman should plead for it" and claim in "The Fundamental Constitutions of Carolina" that "Every freeman . . . shall have absolute power and authority over his Negro slave."[35] Yet, this dissonance can be resolved in either of two directions: he can give up his view that freemen in Carolina should have absolute power over their African slaves or he can rescind his condemnation of slavery. In either case, his understanding of Africans and slavery will compose a unified, coherent whole. Interpretations of women's identity are open to the same options for revision: we can determine that they are the same as men in political essentials and grant them suffrage; conversely we can determine that they are inevitably different in the relevant characteristic and deny suffrage.

Gadamer suggests, however, that a hermeneutic approach requires more. The conditions for the possibility of understanding include an assessment of not only the internal coherence of a particular interpretation of meaning but its capacity to make sense out of or illuminate that which it is trying to understand. Thus an explanation or genealogy of an event is not only secondary to understanding what it is, but is often an indication that understanding has failed. In other words, it is often when I have given up on understanding or making sense out of something that I turn to explanations of why someone might have thought to express or do it. Indeed, this recourse to explanation marks the difference between natural and social science for Gadamer, despite their common embeddedness in traditions of interpretation. We no longer try to make sense out of natural events whereas, when we are investigating human events, whether actions, practices, texts or, I want to add, identities, we are interested primarily in precisely what sense they have or what their point is. Thus, if I inquire into an event as the victory of the forces of democratization, I need to be able to make sense out of the way it is this victory or what is democratic about it. This process holds even if I want only to explain the causes of the victory. In understanding it *as* a democratic victory, I see the way and extent to which it is one. If I cannot make sense out of it in this way, then my explanation changes. It is no longer a causal account of the democratic victory but rather an account of the historical or psychological causes through which the victors might mistake their victory as a democratic one.

If, in this strong sense of understanding I am to understand a text rather than only to explain it, I must assume that it has a point to make. Gadamer's suggestion here extends the suggestion he makes about the implications of the hermeneutic circle. If I am to test the validity of my projections of meaning, I must compare them to something. I cannot compare them to the uninterpreted text since I have access to it only through my interpretations. Hence I must rather test my interpretations against one another. If they conflict, moreover, I must reject some or all. But which shall I reject? If I view a text or what we might call a text analogue as wrong or "vile" might it not be my own prejudices, instead, which are inappropriate? If I must revise one of the other of my interpretations of slavery, Africans, race in general, or women, which shall I pick and on what basis? Gadamer suggests that we, again, test our prejudices against one another by assuming the truth of that which we are trying to understand and by considering our views in light of this "truth."

To this end, I involve myself in assessments and evaluations of my beliefs or assumptions in terms of others I hold or in terms of the claims I take a text or a text analogue to make. In effect, Gadamer thinks, I am drawn into a conversation in which I understand the content of the text in terms of the belief and assumptions I possess and rethink those same beliefs and assumptions in terms of those I take the text or text analogue to possess. The endpoint of this conversation is a kind of clarity about the subject matter or issues the text and I address together. The same holds of my understanding of what we might call text analogues such as actions, practices, and identities. As he writes of genuine conversation, "Each person opens himself to the other, truly accepts his point of view as valid and transposes himself into the other to such an extent that he understands not the particular individual but what he says. What is to be grasped is the substantive rightness of his opinion. . . . Thus, we do not relate the other's opinion to him but to our own opinions and views."[36]

But what is the "substantive rightness" of an interpretation of individuals as raced, sexed, or gendered identities? What is its point? Suppose I test each of Locke's conflicting opinions in terms of its substantive rightness. Do I reject his view of authority over African prisoners as chattel and preserve my own beliefs or do I reevaluate those beliefs and reject his view of the vile character of slavery? Gadamer often pursues this sort of question by asking what pertinent or relevant question a text answers, where we can test our views and understandings of the text only to the extent that we see it as an answer to a real question, a question we take seriously. If, in contrast, we can understand a text only in terms of a historical question, a question we no longer take to be serious or relevant, such as the question of how many angels can dance on the head of a pin, then, we cannot understand the sense, point, or "truth" of the answer the text gives. We can understand it as, at most, a response to the question, but we cannot distinguish between plausible and implausible interpretations of the response or between plausible and implausible responses since we have no standard of sense or illumination against which to measure them. But, then, what real question does an understanding of individuals as black or white, male or female, men or women answer? What does this understanding illuminate?

If we ask what question Locke's view of authority over African prisoners answers, I think we can understand the question only as a historical one, one whose sense for us is thankfully lost as a result of the struggles and actions of rebellious slaves, outspoken African-American freemen, "white" abolitionists, and their heirs. In this sense, the question of whether what sort of authority masters ought to have over their slaves is similar to the question of how many angels can dance of the head of a pin. Yet, the issue of what questions our current raced, gendered, and sexed identities answer remains important. If the consequences of these identities are horrific for those who are subject to discrimination, exclusion, and even rape and death because of the identities they are understood to possess, it would seem to be morally imperative to determine whether race and sex or gender possess any point. To be sure, the answer for sex and gender seems quite clear: understanding individuals in these terms facilitates reproduction and, if we follow Butler, even imposes a reproductive sexuality.

Suppose reproduction, however, is ultimately freed from the union of male and female. Suppose couples start to employ cloning or other technologies. Then the question of whether one produces eggs or semen will no longer be any more interesting than the question of whether one is left or right handed. Indeed, even under current technological conditions, we might question the ground reproduction gives to a female or feminine identity. What proportion of our lives or the lives of those in the postindustrial West in any case, is involved in bearing children? If child rearing is an activity in which all adults can participate and if the amount of time we spend in actual childbearing remains minimal, why should our role in reproduction define who we are? If it continues to consume the lives of those in poor nations, does this circumstance ground the identity of women or speak to global policies and traditions that might be rethought through others?

Is there any other, nonreproductive point to dividing understanding of individuals as sexed or gendered? Is there any point at all to understanding ourselves as raced? Doing so may encourage specialized research into nutritional needs and susceptibility to certain diseases and conditions such as research into the dangers of sun exposure for fair-skinned people or screening for sickle-cell anemia in "blacks." It is not clear, however, that we advance research into the dangers of sun exposure by understanding those with fair skin as a separate race. Indeed, the case of "blacks" and sickle cell anemia suggests that interpretive categories of race are simply misleading. If we associate the disease with those we understand as "blacks," we shall overlook the predisposition to the disease in the people of southern India and the Arabian peninsula while looking for it in vain in the Xhosa of South Africa.[37] Do sex and gender identifications do any more to contribute to medical diagnosis and research? Could we not do better by dropping these classifications and concentrating on the diseases to which those with specific characteristics and genetic histories are actually susceptible? Not all those classified as women possess ovaries or need worry about ovarian cancer, while some of those we understand as men may contract breast cancer.

Georgia Warnke

We might be interested in medical research into the causes and risks of being left-handed, for example, but it is not clear that this research would proceed more efficiently by understanding people's left- or right-handedness to be the core of their identity. One can be interested in the diseases associated with certain organs and propensities without these determining who one is.

One last reason for continuing to understand ourselves according to the raced, sexed, and gendered identities we currently possess is that people have suffered under them. How shall we abandon Afghan women or eliminate all remaining affirmative action programs in the United States by simply declaring that neither women nor blacks exist? To do so would seem to declare that we need have no special concern for those who are stoned to death for transgressions of their sexed and gendered identity and that the continuing effects of discrimination require no special consideration for the descendants of slaves. Yet, just as we can condemn the hanging of witches without maintaining that witches exist, we can work for civil, political, and economic justice for women, blacks, and others without retaining the idea that separate races, sexes, or genders exist. We do so by recognizing that the social identities we currently possess are socially effective and that they have consequences for those categorized by them. Still, we need not grant these identities a naturalized existence nor need we abstain from criticizing their adequacy as social identities that make sense.

From a Foucauldian point of view, the social identities we have are the result of power and ones we cannot evade. While we must be one identity or another, we can be them in subversive and redeployed ways. From an interpretive perspective, we can reflect on our identity from the point of view of both its coherence and the questions it is supposed to answer. The coherence of race, gender, and sex categories seems suspect. Further, if we try to make them coherent, we are left with the question of what problems they are meant to resolve and it remains unclear that they resolve any. If we no longer understand race, sex, gender, or sexual preference as social identities, we will still possess certain preferences and act in certain ways; we will still play basketball, raise children, eat too much, and work too hard. But these acts and preferences will no longer divide the way they currently do between those that indicate what we enjoy and those that indicate who we are. Perhaps they will divide in different ways into new social identities that can dispense with discrimination and injustice. Or perhaps all divisions and all identities will become purely individual. The identities we substitute for men and women, blacks and whites and so on will not be substitutions we make independently of the traditions to which we belong. But if we reflect on the sense of our current social identities in terms of the self-understandings and ideals those traditions make available to us, it is not clear that our current social identities make the most sense or remain the best way to understand who we are.

The conclusion to which Foucauldians and Gadamerians come is similar: the need to challenge the reified self-evidence of current categories or interpretations of identity. Gadamerians, however, do so with unabashed reference to grounds and claims to validity. It is because raced and gendered or sexed identities are inconsistent and incoherent, moreover, it is because they answer no meaningful questions, that we might rethink and eliminate them in favor of individualized identities that do better. Our answers to the question of who we are and want to be will appeal to the resources of a tradition that we can reflect upon in hermeneutic ways.

Notes

1. See Denise Riley, *Am I That Name: Feminism and the Category of "Women" in History* (Minneapolis: University of Minnesota Press, 1988) and Judith Butler, *Gender Trouble: Feminism and the Subversion of Identity* (New York: Routledge, 1990). I also compare their work to what I take to be the advantages of a hermeneutic approach in "Hermeneutics and Constructed Identities," forthcoming in *Feminist Interpretations of Hans-Georg Gadamer*, Lorraine Code (ed.), Penn State Press. There I am concerned with the strategic feminism Riley and Butler suggest.

2. Riley, *Am I That Name*, 7.

3. Cited from Ian Maclean, *The Renaissance Notion of Woman: A Study in the Fortunes of Scholasticism and Medical Science in European Intellectual Life*, in Riley, *Am I That Name*, 25.

4. Cited from Maclean in Riley, *Am I That Name*, 24.

5. Cited in Riley, *Am I That Name*, 36.

6. Riley, *Am I That Name*, 2.

7. Cited from anon. in Riley, *Am I That Name*, 71.

8. See speech by Arabella Shore in Riley, *Am I That Name*, 77.

9. See Riley, *Am I That Name*, 67–95. I have somewhat modified that sequences of arguments and replies as she states them.

10. Of course, one might say the same about chairs. They are both armed and unarmed and identified with both form and function; within one historical period, they can be both the same and different from couches, and they manifestly differ from one another. Shall we say we have no justification for calling anything a chair? I owe this question to Martha Burns. Perhaps one difference between chairs and women, however, is that chairs can be anything we humans decide they ought to be, for whatever purposes we or a group of us has. Understood in these terms, the suspicion feminists raise about the category of women is that the purposes groups of individuals have for identifying certain individuals as women are not the purposes those categorized as women would have independently of that group. Chairs have no possibility of having purposes on their own.

11. Butler, *Gender Trouble*, 18.

12. I shall be reconstructing Butler's argument for her claims in a way that differs from her own but hopefully retains its thrust.

13. See Butler, *Gender Trouble*, 106–111.

14. See Geoffrey Cowley, "Gender Limbo" in *Newsweek* (May 19, 1997), 64.

15. Alice Domurat Dreger, "Ambiguous Sex—or Ambivalent Medicine?" *The Hastings Center Report*, May/June 1998, vol. 28, issue 3 (http://www.isna.org/library/dreger-ambivalent.html), 6 of 17 downloaded pages. In *Sexing the Body: Gender Politics and the Construction of Sexuality* (New York: Basic Books, 2000), 51, Anne Fausto-Sterling estimates the frequency as an order of magnitude 1.7 percent of all births.

16. Butler, *Gender Trouble*, 17.

17. Judith Butler, "Contingent Foundations: Feminism and the Question of 'Postmodernism,'" in Seyla Benhabib et al., *Feminist Contentions: A Philosophical Exchange* (New York: Routledge, 1995), 52.

18. Butler, "Contingent Foundations," 47.

19. Seyla Benhabib, "Feminism and Postmodernism: An Uneasy Alliance," in *Feminist Contentions,* 20.

20. Judith Butler, "For a Careful Reading," in *Feminist Contentions,* 135.

21. Nancy Fraser, "False Antitheses: A Response to Seyla Benhabib and Judith Butler," in *Feminist Contentions,* 67–68.

22. Jürgen Habermas, "On the Pragmatic, the Ethical, and the Moral Employments of Practical Reason," in *Justification and Application: Remarks on Discourse Ethics* (Cambridge MA: MIT Press, 1993), 4.

23. Hans-Georg Gadamer, *Truth and Method,* translated by Joel Weinsheimer and (New York: Continuum, 2nd rev. ed., 1994), 276, German added.

24. See Martin Heidegger, *Being and Time,* translated by John Macquarrie and Edward Robinson (New York: Harper & Row, 1962), §32.

25. See David M. Halperin, "Is There a History of Sexuality," in *The Lesbian and Gay Studies Reader,* edited by David M. Halperin (New York: Routledge, 1993).

26. See Thomas McCarthy, "Political Philosophy and Racial Injustice: From Normative to Critical Theory," paper presented at the Central Division Meetings of the American Philosophical Association, April 2000.

27. Butler, "Contingent Foundations," 42.

28. *Truth and Method,* 301.

29. See afterword to *Truth and Method,* 567.

30. *Truth and Method,* 301.

31. Butler, 'For a Careful Reading," 138–139.

32. *Truth and Method,* 383.

33. Ibid., 190.

34. This example is a slight modification of K. Anthony Appiah's in "Race, Culture, Identity: Misunderstood Connections,"in *Color Conscious: The Political Morality of Race* (Princeton: Princeton University Press, 1996), 35.

35. See McCarthy, "Political Philosophy and Racial Injustice," ms. 4.

36. *Truth and Method,* 385.

37. See Amy Gutmann, "Responding to Racial Injustice," in *Color Conscious: The Political Morality of Race* (Princeton: Princeton University Press, 1996), 117.

Bibliography

This bibliography lists only works cited in this book. An exhaustive bibliography of Gadamer's works (circa 1997), including English translations as well as significant secondary literature, has been compiled by Richard E. Palmer and is contained in *The Philosophy of Hans-Georg Gadamer*. Edited by Lewis Edwin Hahn. LaSalle: Open Court, 1997, part III, 555–602.

Adorno, Theodor. *Negative Dialectics*. Translated by E. B. Ashton. London: Routledge and Kegan Paul, 1973.

Adorno, Theodor. "The Valéry Proust Museum." In *Prisms*. Translated by Samuel and Shierry Weber. Cambridge, MA: MIT Press, 1981: 173–185.

Albert, Hans. *Kritik der reinen Erkenntnislehre. Das Erkenntnisproblem in realistischer Perspektive*. Tübingen: J. C. B. Mohr, 1987.

Albert, Hans. *Kritik der reinen Hermeneutik. Der Antirealismus und das Problem des Verstehens*. Tübingen: J. C. B. Mohr, 1994.

Albert, Hans. *Kritischer Rationalismus. Vier Kapitel zur Kritik illusionären Denkens*. Tübingen: J. C. B. Mohr, 2000.

Albert, Hans. *Traktat über kritische Vernunft*. Tübingen: J. C. B. Mohr, 1991. 5th ed. English translation: *Treatise on Critical Reason*. Translated by Mary Rorty. Princeton: Princeton University Press, 1986.

Albert, Hans. *Transzendentale Träumereien*. Hamburg: Hoffmann und Campe, 1975.

Albert, Hans. "Hermeneutics and Economics." *Kyklos* 41, 1988: 573–602.

Albert, Hans. "Kritischer Rationalismus. Vom Positivismusstreit zur Kritik der Hermeneutik." In *Renaissance der Gesellschaftskritik?* Edited by Hans Albert, Herbert Schnädelbach, and Roland Simon-Schäfer. Bamberg: Universitätsverlag, 1999: 15–43.

Albert, Hans. "Der Naturalismus und das Problem des Verstehens." In *Hermeneutik und Naturalismus*. Edited by Bernulf Kanitscheider and Franz Josef Wetz. Tübingen: J. C. B. Mohr, 1999: 3–20.

Anscombe, G. E. M. "The Question of Linguistic Idealism." In Anscombe, *From Parmenides to Wittgenstein, The Collected Philosophical Papers of G. E. M. Anscombe*, vol. 1. Minneapolis: University of Minnesota Press, 1981: 112–133.

Apel, Karl-Otto. *Transformation der Philosophie, Band I: Sprachanalytik, Semiotik, Hermeneutik*. Frankfurt am Main: Suhrkamp, 1973.

Apel, Karl-Otto. "Regulative Ideas or Truth Happening? An Attempt to Answer the Question of the Conditions of the Possibility of Valid Understanding." In Hahn, ed., *The Philosophy of Hans-Georg Gadamer*: 67–94.

Aron, Raymond. *Introduction à la philosophie de l'histoire. Essai sur les limites de l'objectivité historique*. Paris: Gallimard, original publication 1938, revised edition, 1997. English translation: *Introduction to the Philosophy of History. An Essay on the Limits of Historical Objectivity*. Translated by George J. Irwin. London: Weidenfeld and Nicolson, 1961.

Atwell, John E. "Husserl on Signification and Object." In *American Philosophical Quarterly* 6, 1969: 83–93.

Bartley, William Warren. *Unfathomed Knowledge, Unmeasured Wealth. On Universities and the Wealth of Nations*. LaSalle: Open Court, 1990.

Baum, Wilhelm, ed. *Paul Feyerabend—Hans Albert. Briefwechsel*. Frankfurt: Fischer, 1997.

Bauman, Zygmunt. *Intimations of Postmodernity*. London: Routledge, 1992.

Benhabib, Seyla. "Feminism and Postmodernism: An Uneasy Alliance." In *Feminist Contentions: A Philosophical Exchange*. Edited by Seyla Benhabib, Judith Butler, Drucilla Cornell, and Nancy Fraser. New York: Routledge, 1995: 17–34.

Bernasconi, Robert. "The Greatness of the Work of Art." In *Heidegger in Question: The Art of Existing*. Atlantic Highlands, NJ: Humanities Press, 1993: 99–116.

Bernstein, Richard. *Beyond Objectivism and Relativism: Science, Hermeneutics, and Praxis*. Philadelphia: University of Pennsylvania Press, 1983.

Blumenberg, Hans. "An Anthropological Approach to the Contemporary Significance of Rhetoric." In *After Philosophy: End or Transformation*. Edited by Kenneth Baynes, James Bohman, and Thomas McCarthy. Cambridge, MA: MIT Press, 1987: 421–428.

Blumenberg, Hans. "Sophists and Cynics: Antithetical Aspects of the Prometheus Material." In *Work on Myth*. Translated by Robert M. Wallace. Cambridge, Mass.: MIT Press, 1985: 328–349.

Brandom, Robert. *Making It Explicit: Reasoning, Representing, and Discursive Commitment*. Cambridge, MA: Harvard University Press, 1994.

Brandom, Robert. "Exorcising the Philosophical Tradition: Comments on John McDowell's *Mind and World*." *The Philosophical Review* 105, 1996: 427–467.

Braudel, Fernand. *La Méditerranée et le monde méditerranéen à l'époque de Philippe II*, 2 vols. Paris: Colin, 6th ed. 1985. English translation: *The Mediterranean and the Mediterranean World in the Age of Philip II*. Translated by Sian Reynolds. New York: Harper & Row, 1972–1973.

Bibliography

Bubner, Rüdiger. "Kant, Transcendental Arguments and the Problem of Deduction." *Review of Metaphysics* 28, 1975: 453–467.

Bubner, Rüdiger. "On the Ground of Understanding." In *Hermeneutics and Truth*. Edited by Wachterhauser: 68–82.

Burkert, W. *Greek Religion*. Cambridge, MA: Harvard University Press, 1983.

Butler, Judith. "For a Careful Reading." In *Feminist Contentions: A Philosophical Exchange*. Edited by Seyla Benhabib et al. New York: Routledge, 1995: 127–143.

Butler, Judith. "Contingent Foundations: Feminism and the Question of 'Postmodernism.'" In *Feminist Contentions: A Philosophical Exchange*. Edited by Seyla Benhabib et al. New York: Routledge, 1995: 35–57.

Butler, Judith. *Gender Trouble: Feminism and the Subversion of Identity*. New York: Routledge, 1990.

Caputo, John. *Radical Hermeneutics: Repetition, Deconstruction, and the Hermeneutic Project*. Bloomington: Indiana University Press, 1987.

Cavell, Stanley. *Must We Mean What We Say? A Book of Essays*. Cambridge: Cambridge University Press, 1969.

Collingwood, G. R. *The Idea of History*. Oxford: Clarendon, 1946. Reprint 1994.

Coltman, Rod. *The Language of Hermeneutics: Gadamer and Heidegger in Dialogue*. Albany: SUNY Press, 1998.

Connolly, J., and Keutner, T. *Hermeneutics versus Science? Three German Views*. Notre Dame: University of Notre Dame Press, 1988.

Cowley, Geoffrey. "Gender Limbo," *Newsweek*, May 19, 1997.

Danto, Arthur. *The Transfiguration of the Commonplace: A Philosophy of Art*. Cambridge, MA: Harvard University Press, 1981.

Davidson, Donald. "Actions, Reasons, and Causes." In *Essays on Actions and Events*. Oxford: Clarendon Press, 1980: 3–20.

Davidson, Donald. "Communication and Convention." In *Inquiries into Truth and Interpretation*: 265–280.

Davidson, Donald, "Gadamer and Plato's *Philebus*." In *The Philosophy of Hans-Georg Gadamer*. Edited by Hahn: 421–432.

Davidson, Donald. "James Joyce and Humpty Dumpty." In *Midwest Studies in Philosophy* 16. Edited by P. A. French, T. E. Uehling, and H. K. Wettstein. Minneapolis: University of Missesota Press, 1991: 1–12.

Davidson, Donald. "A Nice Derangement of Epitaphs." In *Truth and Interpretation: Perspectives on the Philosophy of Donald Davidson*. Edited by Ernest LePore. Oxford: Blackwell, 1986: 433–446.

Davidson, Donald. "On the Very Idea of a Conceptual Scheme." In *Inquiries into Truth and Interpretation*. Oxford: Clarendon Press, 1984: 183–198.

Davidson, Donald. "Radical Interpretation." In *Inquiries into Truth and Interpretation*. Oxford: Clarendon Press, 1984: 125–140.

Davidson, Donald. "The Social Aspect of Language." In *The Philosophy of Michael Dummett*. Edited by B. McGuinness and G. Oliveri. Dordrecht: Kluwer, 1994: 1–16.

Davidson, Donald. "The Structure and Content of Truth." *Journal of Philosophy* 87, 1990: 279–328.

Davidson, Donald. "Three Varieties of Knowledge." In *A. J. Ayer: Memorial Essays*. Edited by A. Phillips Griffiths. Cambridge: Cambridge University Press, 1991: 153–166.

Davidson, Donald. "Truth and Meaning." In *Inquiries into Truth and Interpretation*. Oxford: Clarendon Press, 1984: 17–36.

de Certeau, Michel. *L'absent de l'histoire*. Paris: Mame, 1973.

de Certeau, Michel. *L'écriture de l'histoire*. Paris: Gallimard, 1975. English translation: *The Writing of History*. Translated by Tom Conley. New York: Columbia University Press, 1988.

de Certeau, Michel. *The Practice of Everyday Life*. Translated by Steven Rendell. Berkeley: University of California Press, 1984.

de Duve, Thierry. *Kant after Duchamp*. Cambridge, MA: MIT Press, 1996.

Deleuze, Gilles and Guattari, Félix. "1933: Micropolitics and Segmentarity." In *A Thousand Plateaus*. Translated by Brian Massumi. Minneapolis: University of Minnesota Press, 1987: 208–231.

Derrida, Jacques. *De la Grammatologie*. Paris: Éditions de Minuit, 1967.

Derrida, Jacques. *La voix et le phénomène. Introduction au problème du signe dans la phénoménologie de Husserl*. Paris: Presses Universitaires de France, 1967.

Derrida, Jacques. "Guter Wille zur Macht (II)." In *Text und Interpretation*. Edited by Philippe Forget. Munich: Fink, 1984: 62–77.

Derrida, Jacques. "Octobiographies: The Teaching of Nietzsche and the Politics of the Proper Name." Translated by Aviatal Ronell. In *The Ear of the Other: Octobiography, Transference, Translation*. New York: Schocken, 1982: 1–38.

Devitt, Michael. *Realism and Truth*. Oxford: Blackwell, 1991.

Dickopp, Karl-Heinz. "Zum Wandel von Nietzsches Selbstverständnis—Afrikan Spir und Gustav Teichmüller." *Zeitschrift für philosophische Forschung* 24, 1970: 50–71.

Dottori, Riccardo. *Die Reflexion des Wirklichen: Zwischen Hegels absoluter Dialektik und der Philosophie der Endlichkeit von M. Heidegger und H.G. Gadamer*. Heidelberg: Carl Winter, 1984.

Dreger, Alice Domurat. "Ambiguous Sex—or Ambivalent Medicine?" *The Hastings Center Report* 28, 1998. (http://www.isna.org/html).

Bibliography

Dummett, Michael. "A Nice Derangement of Epitaphs: Some Comments on Davidson and Hacking." In *Truth and Interpretation: Perspectives on the Philosophy of Donald Davidson.* Edited by Ernest LePore. Oxford: Blackwell, 1986: 433–446.

Eckhart, Meister. *Meister Eckhart Werke I–II, Bibliothek des Mittelalters,* vols. 20–21. Translated by Josef Quint. Edited by Niklaus Largier. Frankfurt: Deutscher Klassiker Verlag, 1993.

Eckhart, Meister. *The Book of the Parables of Genesis.* In *Meister Eckhart: The Essential Sermons, Commentaries, Treatises, and Defense.* Edited by Edmund Colledge and Bernard McGinn. New York: Paulist Press, 1981.

Eckhart, Meister. *Meister Eckhart: Sermons & Treatises,* 2 vols. Edited by M. O'C. Walshe. London & Dulverton: Watkins, 1979 and 1981.

Evnine, Simon. *Donald Davidson.* Cambridge: Polity Press, 1991.

Fausto-Sterling, Anne. *Sexing the Body: Gender Politics and the Construction of Sexuality.* New York: Basic Books, 2000.

Forget, Philippe, ed. *Text und Interpretation.* Munich: Fink, 1984.

Fraser, Nancy. "False Antitheses: A Response to Seyla Benhabib and Judith Butler." In *Feminist Contentions: A Philosophical Exchange.* Edited by Seyla Benhabib et al. New York: Routledge, 1995: 59–74.

Frege, Gottlob. *Die Grundlagen der Arithmetik. Eine logisch-mathematische Untersuchung über den Begriff der Zahl.* Hildesheim: Olms, 1961.

Gadamer, Hans-Georg. *Dialogue and Dialectic: Eight Hermeneutical Studies on Plato.* Translated by P. Christopher Smith. New Haven: Yale University Press, 1980.

Gadamer, Hans-Georg. *Gadamer On Education, Poetry, and History: Applied Hermeneutics.* Translated by Lawrence Schmidt and Monica Reuss. Albany: SUNY Press, 1992.

Gadamer, Hans-Georg. *Gesammelte Werke.* 10 vols. Tübingen: J. C. B. Mohr (Paul Siebeck), 1985–95.

Gadamer, Hans-Georg. *Hegel's Dialectic: Five Hermeneutical Studies.* Translated by P. Christopher Smith. New Haven: Yale University Press, 1976.

Gadamer, Hans-Georg. *Heidegger's Ways.* Translated by John Stanley. Albany: SUNY, 1994.

Gadamer, Hans-Georg. *The Idea of the Good in Platonic-Aristotelian Philosophy.* Translated by P. Christopher Smith. New Haven: Yale University Press, 1986.

Gadamer, Hans-Georg. *Philosophical Hermeneutics.* Translated by David E. Linge. Berkeley: University of California Press, 1976.

Gadamer, Hans-Georg. *Philosophische Lehrjahre: Eine Rückschau.* Frankfurt: Klostermann, 1977. English translation: *Philosophical Apprenticeships.* Cambridge: MIT Press, 1995.

Gadamer, Hans-Georg. *Plato's Dialectical Ethics. Phenomenological Interpretations relating to the "Philebus."* Translated by R. M. Wallace. New Haven: Yale University Press, 1991.

Gadamer, Hans-Georg. *The Relevance of the Beautiful and Other Essays.* Translated by Nicholas Walker. Cambridge: Cambridge University Press, 1986.

Gadamer, Hans-Georg. *Wahrheit und Methode, Gesammelte Werke* 1. Tübingen: J. C. B. Mohr (Paul Siebeck), 1986. English translation: *Truth and Method.* Translated by Joel Weinsheimer and Donald Marshall. New York: Continuum, 2nd rev. ed., 1989.

Gadamer, Hans-Georg. "Bubner zweier Welten." In *Das Erbe Europas.* Frankfurt am Main: Suhrkamp, 1989: 106–125.

Gadamer, Hans-Georg. "Text und Interpretation." In *Gesammelte Werke* 2. Tübingen: Mohr Siebeck, 1986: 330–360.

Gadamer, Hans-Georg. "Und dennoch: Macht des Guten Willens." In *Text und Interpretation.* Edited by Forget: 59–61.

Gadamer, Hans-Georg. "The Hermeneutics of Suspicion." In *Hermeneutics: Questions and Prospects.* Edited by Gary Shapiro and Alan Sica. Amherst: University of Massachusetts Press, 1984: 54–65.

Gadamer, Hans-Georg. "The Philosophical Foundations of the Twentieth Century." In *Philosophical Hermeneutics.* Translated by David E. Linge. Berkeley: University of California Press, 1976: 107–129.

Gadamer, Hans-Georg. "Reflections on My Philosophical Journey." In *The Philosophy of Hans-Georg Gadamer.* Edited by Lewis Edwin Hahn. Chicago: Open Court, 1997: 3–63.

Gadamer, Hans-Georg. "On the Scope and Function of Hermeneutical Reflection." In *Philosophical Hermeneutics.* Translated by David E. Linge. Berkeley: University of California Press, 1976: 18–43.

Gadamer, Hans-Georg. "Truth in the Human Sciences." In *Hermeneutics and Truth.* Edited by Wachterhauser: 25–32.

Gadamer, Hans-Georg. "What Is Practice? The Conditions of Social Reason." In *Reason in the Age of Science.* Translated by Frederick G. Lawrence. Cambridge: MIT Press, 1981: 69–87.

Gadenne, Volker, ed. *Kritischer Rationalismus und Pragmatismus.* Amsterdam/Atlanta: Rodopi, 1998.

Garver, Newton. *This Complicated Form of Life.* Chicago and Lasalle, Illinois: Open Court, 1984.

Goody, Jack. *The Domestication of the Savage Mind.* Cambridge: Cambridge University Press, 1977.

Grondin, Jean. *Hans-Georg Gadamer—eine Biographie.* Tübingen: Mohr Siebeck, 1999.

Grondin, Jean. *Sources of Hermeneutics.* Albany: SUNY, 1995.

Grondin, Jean. "Die Hermeneutik als Konsequenz des kritischen Rationalismus." In *Hermeneutik und Naturalismus.* Edited by Bernulf Kanitscheider and Franz Josef Wetz. Tübingen: J. C. B. Mohr, 1999: 38–46.

Gutmann, Amy. "Responding to Racial Injustice." In *Color Conscious: The Political Morality of Race*. Princeton: Princeton University Press, 1996: 106–178.

Habermas, Jürgen. *The Philosophical Discourse of Modernity*. Translated by Frederick Lawrence. Cambridge: MIT Press, 1987.

Habermas, Jürgen. "On the Pragmatic, the Ethical, and the Moral Employments of Practical Reason." In *Justification and Application: Remarks on Discourse Ethics*. Translated by Ciaran Cronin. Cambridge MA: MIT Press, 1993: 1–18.

Habermas, Jürgen. *Hermeneutik und Ideologiekritik*. Frankfurt: Suhrkamp, 1971.

Habermas, Jürgen. "Erkenntnis und Interesse." *Merkur* 19, 1965: 1139–1153.

Hahn, Lewis Edwin, ed. *The Philosophy of Hans-Georg Gadamer*. Library of Living Philosophers XXIV. Chicago, Open Court, 1997.

Haller, Rudolf. *Questions on Wittgenstein*. London: Routledge, 1988.

Halperin, David M. "Is There a History of Sexuality." In *The Lesbian and Gay Studies Reader*. Edited by David M. Halperin. New York: Routledge, 1993: 416–431.

Hegel, G. W. F. *Die Phänomenologie des Geistes*. Felix Meiner: Hamburg, 1952. English translation: *Phenomenology of Spirit*. Translated by by A. V. Miller. Oxford: Oxford University Press, 1977.

Hegel, G. W. F. *Hegel's Philosophy of Subjective Spirit*. Translated by M. Petry. Dordrecht: Riedel, 1978.

Hegel, G. W. F. *Hegel's Science of Logic*. Translated by A. V. Miller. London: George Allen & Unwin, 1969.

Hegel, G. W. F. *Jenaer Kritische Schriften*. Hamburg: Felix Meiner Verlag, 1979.

Heidegger, Martin. *Poetry, Language, Thought*. Translated by Albert Hofstadter. New York: Harper & Row, 1971.

Heidegger, Martin, *Sein und Zeit*. Tübingen: Niemeyer, 17th ed., 1993. English translation: *Being and Time*. Translated by John Macquarrie and Edward Robinson. New York, Harper & Row, 1962. Also translated by Joan Stambaugh. Albany: SUNY Press, 1996.

Heidegger, Martin. *Vorträge und Aufsätze*. Pfullingen: Neske, 1954.

Heidegger, Martin. *Nietzsche*, 3 and 4 (bound together). Edited by David Farrell Krell. San Francisco: Harper & Row, 1991.

Hoy, David C. "Post-Cartesian Interpretation: Hans-Georg Gadamer and Donald Davidson." In *The Philosophy of Hans-Georg Gadamer*. Edited by Hahn: 110–128.

Husserl, Edmund. *Husserliana, XIX / 1: Logische Untersuchungen, Zweiter Band, Zweiter Teil*. The Hague: Martinus Nijhoff, 1984. English translation: *Logical Investigations*, 1. Translated by J. N. Findlay. London: Routledge and Kegan Paul, 1970.

Janz, Curt Paul. *Friedrich Nietzsche: Biographie in drei Bänden*. Munich: Carl Hanser, 1993, 2nd rev. ed.

Kambartel, Friedrich. "Versuch über das Verstehen." In *"Der Löwe spricht . . . und wir können ihn nicht verstehen." Ein Symposion an der Universität Frankfurt anläßlich des Hundertsten Geburtstags von Ludwig Wittgenstein*. Frankfurt am Main: Suhrkamp, 1991: 121–137.

Kant, Immanuel. *Von einem neuerdings erhobenen vornehmen Ton in er Philosophie*. In *Kants Werke*, 8. Berlin and New York: Akademie Textausgabe, Walter de Gruyter, 1968.

Köbele, S. "*Primo aspectu monstruosa:* Schriftauslegung bei Meister Eckhart," *Zeitschrift für deutsches Altertum und deutsche Literatur* 122, 1, 1993: 62–81.

Kroß, Matthias. *Klarheit als Selbstzweck*. Berlin: Akademie Verlag, 1993.

Kroß, Matthias. "Klarheit als Wahrheit." In *Die ungewisse Evidenz*. Edited by Gary Smith and Matthias Kroß. Berlin: Akademie Verlag, 1998: 139–171.

Lange, Friedrich Albert. *Geschichte des Materialismus und Kritik seiner Bedeutung in der Gegenwart*, vol. 2. Leipzig: J. Baedeker, 1908.

Largier, Niklaus. "*Figurata Locutio:* Hermeneutik und Philosophie bei Eckhart von Hochheim und Heinrich Seuse." In *Meister Eckhart: Lebensstationen—Redesituationen*. Edited by Klaus Jacobi. Berlin: Akademie Verlag, 1997).

Levin, David Michael. "Decline and Fall: Ocularcentrism in Heidegger's Reading of the History of Metaphysics." In *Modernity and the Hegemony of Vision*. Edited by David Michael Levin. Berkeley: University of California Press, 1993: 186–217.

Locke, John. *An Essay Concerning Human Understanding*. Edited by A. S. Pringle-Pattison. Oxford: The Clarendon Press, 1967.

McCarthy, Thomas. "Political Philosophy and Racial Injustice: From Normative to Critical Theory." Paper presented at the central division meetings of the American Philosophical Association, April 2000.

McDowell, John. *Mind and World*. Cambridge, MA: Harvard University Press, 1994.

Malpas, Jeff. *Donald Davidson and the Mirror of Meaning*. Cambridge: Cambridge University Press, 1992.

Malpas, Jeff. *Place and Experience: A Philosophical Topography*. Cambridge: Cambridge University Press, 1999.

Margolis, Joseph. *Life without Principles*. Oxford: Basil Blackwell, 1996.

Michelfelder, Diane P. "Gadamer on Heidegger on Art." In *The Philosophy of Hans-Georg Gadamer*. Edited by Lewis Edwin Hahn. Chicago: Open Court, 1997: 437–456.

Michelfelder, Diane P. and Richard Palmer, eds. *Dialogue and Dialectic*. Albany: SUNY, 1989.

Montaigne, Michel de. *Les Essais*. Edited by Pierre Villey. Paris: Presses Universitaires de France, 1992. English translation: *The Essays of Michel de Montaigne*. Translated by M. A. Screech. Harmondsworth: Penguin, 1991.

Bibliography

Musgrave, Alan. *Essays on Realism and Rationalism*. Amsterdam/Atlanta: Rodopi 1999.

Nancy, Jean-Luc. "The Vestige of Art." In *The Muses*. Translated by Peggy Kamuf. Stanford: Stanford University Press, 1996: 81–100.

Natorp, Paul. *Platos Ideenlehre*. Leipzig: Felix Meiner, 1902.

Nehemas, Alexander. *Nietzsche: Life as Literature*. Cambridge: Harvard University Press, 1985.

Nietzsche, Friedrich. *The Gay Science*. Translated by Walter Kaufmann. New York: Vintage Books, 1974.

Nietzsche, Friedrich. *On the Advantage and Disadvantage of History for Life*. Translated by Peter Preuss. Indianapolis: Hackett, 1980.

Nietzsche, Friedrich. *On the Genealogy of Morals*. Translated by Walter Kaufmann. New York: Vintage, 1969.

Nietzsche, Friedrich. *Sämtliche Briefe*. Berlin: De Gruyter, 1975–1984.

Nietzsche, Friedrich. *Sämtliche Werke, Kritische Studienausgabe*. Edited by Giorgio Colli and Mazzino Montinari. Munich and Berlin: dtv & de Gruyter, 1967–77.

Nietzsche, Friedrich. *Twilight of the Idols*, in *Twilight of the Idols/The Antichrist*. Translated by R. J. Hollingdale. London: Penguin, 1968.

Nietzsche, Friedrich. *Werke. Kritische Gesamtausgabe*. Edited by Giorgio Colli and Mazzino Montinari. Berlin: De Gruyter, 1967.

Nietzsche, Friedrich. *The Will to Power as Art*. Translated by David Farrell Krell. New York: Harper & Row, 1979.

Nohl, Hermann. "Eine historische Quelle zu Nietzsches Perspektivismus: G. Teichmüller, die wirkliche und die scheinbare Welt." *Zeitschrift für Philosophie und philosophische Kritik* 149, 1913: 106–115.

Ong, S.J., Walter J. "System, Space, and Intellect in Renaissance Symbolism." In *The Barbarian Within*. New York: Macmillan, 1962: 68–87.

Orozco, Teresa. *Platonische Gewalt*. Hamburg: Argument Verlag, 1995.

Orsucci, Andrea. *Orient-Okzident: Nietzsches Versuch einer Loslösung vom europäischen Weltbild*. Berlin: Walter de Gruyter, 1996.

Pippin, Robert. *Hegel's Idealism: The Satisfactions of Self-Consciousness*. Cambridge: Cambridge University Press, 1989.

Pippin, Robert. *Kant's Theory of Form*. New Haven: Yale University Press, 1981.

Pippin, Robert. "Fichte's Alleged Subjective, Psychological, One-Sided Idealism." In *The Reception of Kant's Critical Philosophy: Fichte, Schelling, and Hegel*. Edited by Sally Sedgwick. Cambridge: Cambridge University Press, 2000: 147–170.

Bibliography

Pippin, Robert. "Hegel, Freedom, the Will: *The Philosophy of Right*, no. 1–33." In *Hegel: Grundlinien der Philosophie des Rechts*. Edited by Ludwig Siep. Berlin: Akademie Verlag, 1997: 31–53.

Pippin, Robert. "Hegel, Modernity, and Habermas." In *Idealism as Modernism*. Cambridge: Cambridge University Press, 1997: 157–184.

Pippin, Robert. "Naturalism and Mindedness: Hegel's Compatibilism." *The European Journal of Philosophy* 7, 1999: 194–212.

Pippin, Robert. "Negation and Not-Being in Wittgenstein's *Tractatus* and Plato's *Sophist*." *Kant-Studien* 70, 1979: 179–196.

Pippin, Robert. "What Is the Question for Which Hegel's 'Theory of Recognition' is the Answer?" *The European Journal of Philosophy* 8, 2000: 155–172.

Putnam, Hilary. *Realism and Reason*. Cambridge: Cambridge University Press, 1983.

Putnam, Hilary. *Renewing Philosophy*. Cambridge, MA: Harvard University Press, 1992.

Redding, Paul. *Hegel's Hermeneutics*. Ithaca: Cornell University Press, 1996.

Ricœur, Paul. "Appropriation." Translated by John B. Thompson. In *Hermeneutics and the Human Sciences*. Cambridge, MA: MIT Press, 1981: 182–193.

Riley, Denise. *Am I That Name: Feminism and the Category of "Women" in History*. Minneapolis: University of Minnesota Press, 1988.

Risser, James. *Hermeneutics and the Voice of the Other: Re-reading Gadamer's Philosophical Hermeneutics*. Albany: SUNY Press, 1997.

Schantz, Richard. *Wahrheit, Referenz und Realismus. Eine Studie zur Sprachphilosophie und Metaphysik*. Berlin/New York: De Gruyter, 1996.

Schiller, J. Friedrich Von. *On the Aesthetic Education of Man*. Translated by Reginald Snell. New York: Fredrick Unger, 1965.

Schneider, Hans Julius. *Phantasie und Kalkül*. Frankfurt am Main: Suhrkamp, 1992.

Schneider, Hans Julius. "Wittgenstein und die Grammatik." In *Mit Sprache spielen*. Edited by Hans Julius Schneider and Matthias Kroß. Berlin: Akademie Verlag, 1999: 11–29.

Scholz, Oliver R. *Verstehen und Rationalität. Untersuchungen zu den Grundlagen von Hermeneutik und Sprachphilosophie*. Frankfurt: Vittorio Klostermann, 1999.

Smith, Christopher P. *The Hermeneutics of Original Argument*. Evanston, Ill.: Northwestern University Press, 1997.

Smith, Christopher P. "Plato as Impulse and Obstacle in Gadamer's Development of a Hermeneutical Theory." In *Gadamer and Hermeneutics*. Edited by Hugh Silverman. New York: Routledge, 1991: 23–41.

Sonderegger, Ruth. "A Critique of Pure Meaning: Wittgenstein and Derrida." In *European Journal of Philosophy* 5, 1997: 183–209.

Bibliography

Specht, Ernst Konrad. "Literary-Critical Interpretation—Psychoanalytic Interpretation." In *Hermeneutics versus Science?* Edited by J. Connolly and T. Keutner. Notre Dame: University of Notre Dame Press, 1988: 153–169.

Spiekermann, Klaus. *Naturwissenschaft als subjektlose Macht? Nietzsches Kritik physikalischer Grundkonzepte.* Berlin, De Gruyter, 1991.

Strawson, Peter. *Skepticism and Naturalism: Some Varieties.* London: Methuen, 1985.

Strong, Tracy B. *Friedrich Nietzsche and the Politics of Transfiguration.* Berkeley: University of California Press, 1988.

Taylor, Charles. *Hegel.* Cambridge: Cambridge University Press, 1975.

Teichmüller, Gustav. *Die wirkliche und die scheinbare Welt.* Breslau: Wilhelm Koebner, 1882.

Tymoczko, Thomas. "In Defense of Putnam's Brains." *Philosophical Studies* 57, 1989: 281–297.

Vattimo, Gianni. *Beyond Interpretation: The Meaning of Hermeneutics for Philosophy.* Stanford: Stanford University Press, 1997.

Wachterhauser, Brice, ed. *Hermeneutics and Truth.* Evanston, Ill.: Northwestern University Press, 1994.

Warnke, Georgia. *Gadamer: Hermeneutics, Tradition, and Reason.* Stanford: Stanford University Press, 1987.

Warnke, Georgia. "Walzer, Rawls, and Gadamer: Hermeneutics and Political Theory." *Festivals of Interpretation: Essays on Hans-Georg Gadamer's Work.* Edited by Kathleen Wright. Albany: SUNY, 1990: 136–160.

Weiberg, Anja. *"Und die Begründung hat ein Ende"—Die Bedeutung von Religion und Ethik für den Philosophen Ludwig Wittgenstein und das Verständnis seiner Werke.* Wien: WUV-Universitätsverlag, 1998.

Wellmer, Albrecht. "Zur Kritik der hermeneutischen Vernunft." In *Vernunft und Lebenspraxis. Philosophische Studien zu den Bedingungen einer rationalen Kultur.* Edited by Christoph Demmerling, Gottfried Gabriel, and Thomas Rentsch. Frankfurt am Main: Suhrkamp, 1995: 123–156.

Winch, Peter. "Understanding a Primitive Society." In *Rationality.* Edited by Brian Wilson. New York: Harper & Row, 1970: 78–111.

Winkler, Eberhard. *Exegetische Methoden bei Meister Eckhart.* Tübingen: J. C. B. Mohr (Paul Siebeck), 1965.

Wittgenstein, Ludwig. *Tractatus Logico-Philosophicus.* Translated by D. F. Pears and B. F. McGuinness. Routledge and Kegan Paul, London, 1961.

Wittgenstein, Ludwig. *Philosophical Investigations.* Translated by G. E. M. Anscombe. Oxford: Blackwell, 1953.

Bibliography

Wittgenstein, Ludwig. *Philosophical Grammar.* Oxford: Blackwell, 1974.

Wittgenstein, Ludwig. *On Certainty.* Edited by G. E. M. Anscombe and G. H. von Wright. Translated by G. E. M. Anscombe. Oxford: Basil Blackwell, 1969.

Wittgenstein, Ludwig. *Remarks on Colour.* Edited by G. E. M. Anscombe. Translated by Linda L. McAlister and Margarete Schättle. Oxford: Basil Blackwell, 1977.

Wittgenstein, Ludwig. *Remarks on the Foundation of Mathematics.* Edited by G. H. von Wright, R. Rhees, G. E. M. Anscombe. Translated by G. E. M. Anscombe. Oxford: Basil Blackwell, 1956.

Wittgenstein, Ludwig. *Zettel.* Edited by G. E. M. Anscombe and G. H. von Wright. Translated by G. E. M. Anscombe. Oxford: Basil Blackwell, 1967.

Wittgenstein, Ludwig. "Causes and Effect: Intuitive Awareness." *Philosophia* 6, 1976: 409–425.

Contributors

Hans Albert is Professor of Sociology and Scientific Methodology Emeritus at the University of Mannheim.

Ulrich Arnswald teaches at the International University of Germany and is Founding Director of the Institute for International Affairs.

Gerald Bruns is William and Hazel White Professor of English at the University of Notre Dame.

John M. Connolly is Provost and Dean of the Faculty at Smith College.

Jay L. Garfield is Professor of Philosophy at Smith College.

Robert C. Holub is Professor of German at the University of California, Berkeley.

Jens Kertscher teaches at the Technical University of Darmstadt.

Alasdair MacIntyre is Senior Research Professor of Philosophy at the University of Notre Dame.

Jeff Malpas is Professor and Head of the School of Philosophy at the University of Tasmania.

John McDowell is University Professor of Philosophy at the University of Tasmania.

Robert B. Pippin is Raymond W. and Martha Hilpert Gruner Distinguished Service Professor in the Committee on Social Thought, the Department of Philosophy, and the College at the University of Chicago.

Paul Ricœur is Professor Emeritus at the University of Paris X and at the University of Chicago.

Contributors

Stanley Rosen is Borden Parker Bowne Professor of Philosophy at Boston University.

Lawrence Schmidt is Professor of Philosophy at Hendrix College.

Charles Taylor is Professor of Philosophy Emeritus at McGill University.

Gianni Vattimo is Professor of Philosophy at the University of Turin.

Georgia Warnke is Professor of Philosophy at the University of California, Riverside.

Index

Index

Index

Index

Gesammelte Werke, 11, 72n, 76n, 154n
Gesellschaftliches Agens, 67
Geshe Ngawang Samten, 109
Geviert, das. See Fourfold
Gewesenheit. See Past
Gewiese, Emma, 1
Ghost in the machine, 273
Globalization, 41
Goerdeler, Carl, 6, 7
Goethe, J. W., ix, xivn
Goethe Institute, 11
Goodman, Nelson, 269
Goodwill, in dialogue, 38, 56, 57, 113, 181
Goody, Jack, 73n
Grondin, Jean, 5, 6, 12n, 13n, 16, 18, 19, 20, 22n, 23n
Grounding, of understanding, 197, 198, 199, 201, 210
  as derivation, 201, 202, 211
  as hermeneutical and interpretative, 211
  as laying bare, 201, 202
  reciprocity in, 106, 199, 200, 202
  tripartite nature of, 205, 207
Guter Wille zur Macht (II), 113
Gutmann, Amy, 329n

Habermas, Jürgen, ix, xii, 10, 16, 21, 23n, 135, 231, 235n, 238n, 314, 328n
  debate with Gadamer,10, 238n
Haller, Rudolf, 31, 42n
Halperin, David M., 329
Hamann, Richard, 2
Hartmann, Nicolai, influence on Gadamer, 2, 17
Hegel, G. W. F., ix, xii, 5, 9, 16, 61, 65, 66, 120, 169, 195, 198, 217–238, 274, 275, 281
  bad infinite, 222
  dialectic, 234n, 235n, 236n, 237n
  and Gadamer
    solidarity with, 218
    rejection of, 218, 222, 223, 224, 226
  Phenomenology of Spirit, 219, 221
  rehabilitation of Greek thinkers, 220
  revivification of ancient dialectic, 222
  Science of Logic, 221, 227, 238n
  self-sufficiency of the dialectic, 170
  temporality of supercession, 61
  vergangen, 61
Hegel Prize, 11
Hegel Vereinigung, founding of, 10
Heidegger, Martin, ix, xii, 2, 4, 5, 7, 8, 9, 16, 17, 22n, 54, 60, 67, 100, 112, 113,

125, 130, 131n, 132n, 141, 149, 159, 160, 167, 170, 171, 193n, 195, 197, 198, 199, 200, 202, 203, 204, 206, 208, 210, 211, 212, 218, 220, 221, 224, 230, 249, 251, 253, 254n, 270, 275, 302, 304, 305, 316, 329n
  approach toward death, 240–241
  Befindlichkeit (attunement), 54
  Being and Time, 4, 200, 201, 213n, 240, 249, 254n, 255n, 302, 303, 304, 306n
  Being of beings, the, 113
  Being toward death, 240, 241, 244, 302, 303
  death of, 11
  existence, authentic or inauthentic, 302
  fore-conception, 302, 303
  fore-structure of understanding, 316
  fourfold, the *(das Geviert),* 304
  influence on Gadamer, 3, 17, 141
  and National Socialism, 5
  and Nietzsche, 112, 113, 120, 125
  past as *gewesen* not *vergangen,* 302
  rejection of modernism, 67
  personal charisma, 17
  philosophy and religion in, 3
  recuperation of Aristotle, 54
  Stimmung (mood), 54
  totality of being in Nietzsche, 113
  undermining of occidental rationalism, 17
Der Ursprung des Kunstwerkes, 5
Heidegger Society, 11
Heidelberg
  Academy of Sciences, 9
  University of, 1, 6, 9, 10, 11, 41, 212
Heiligen Geist Gymnasium, 2
Hellich, Hedwig, 2
Henrich, Dieter, 8
Heraclitus, 265
Herder, Johann Gottfried, 6, 218
Hermeneutical dialogue, 34
Hermeneutic circle, 83, 87, 107, 202, 320, 321, 323
  whole-part dynamic, 87
Hermeneutic identity, 61, 63
  of art works, 64, 65
Hermeneutic imperative, 97–109
Hermeneutics
  application of, 38
  author intentionalism, 89, 91, 94, 96n
  classical tradition, 19, 22
  Eckhart's, 80, 92, 93

Index

355

Index

Levin, David, 54, 73n
Levin, Susan, 109
Levinas, Emmanuel, 53, 68, 300
Liberation, 231, 238n, 317
Life, human
atomic domain in, 271
definitely contingent, 273
as dreaming, 257, 269, 271
emerging from fragility, 271
extralegal nature of, 273
finitude of, 282
intermediateness of, 273
irreducible to mathematical forms, 261, 273
needs clarification and deepening, 276
spontaneity of, 275
unifying root of science and humanities, 271
Life-world, 218, 231, 270
Limit, within language, 135, 136, 147, 153, 158, 223, 317
Linguistic
context necessary for meaning, 141
expressions as *Ausdrücke*, 137
meaning, as not an object, 135
pragmatism, 197
perspective, 36
relativism, 33, 146
shared practice, 180, 181, 183, 184
Linguisticality, 281, 282
Listening, priority over seeing, 54
Literature, situatedness of, 79
Locke, John, 224, 236n, 322, 324
Logic, 97
Logoi, 52
Logos, 52, 53, 55
Louvain, University of, 9
Löwith, Karl, 3, 5, 8

Marbach, Eduard, 155n
Marburg, 1, 2, 3
"Marburg Demons," 16–17
Marion, Jean-Luc, 160
Mathematics
assimilation into poetry, 269
central role in Socratic philosophy, 260–261
cannot explain human existence, 263
decline into poetic ideology, 264
empties human existence of significance, 263
as ramification of human life, 271

Marx, Karl, 236n, 299, 301
theory and praxis, 299
Theses on Feuerbach, 299
Marx, Werner, 1
McCarthy, Thomas, 329n
McGinn, Bernard, 95n
McMaster University, 10
Meaning
and acts of understanding, 139
born by human beings, 106
collective achievement of community, 100, 304
dependent on intertextuality, 107, 203
derived from context, 100
and difference of expression, 139
as disclosedness, 233
discovery always circular, 106
equally *explicatio* and *applicatio*, 94
expression contingent on, 138
as ideal, 137, 138, 152, 140, 144
identity of, 138, 139, 146
as independent linguistic function, 138
intention, 139
interconnectedness of elements in, 203, 204, 205
of life (*see* Meaning of life)
never exhausted, 91, 220
objectivist theories of, 136
and preunderstanding, 319
and reinterpretation, 160
resistance to elitism, 186
result of normative practices, 233
subject to historical change, 146, 317
universality of, 97
Meaning of life, 97, 104, 105, 107, 258, 264, 265
in Buddhism, 105
as central to Western philosophy, 104
as dependent on human interdependence, 107
as illuminated more by art than rationalism, 264
poetry as correct medium for discussion of, 265
search for as cause of detachment, 258
Mediation, critique of in Plato, 55
Melian dialogues, 59
Memory, as a virtue, 47
Mental acts, 77
Mental event, 144
Messkirch, 1, 16
Metaphor, as basis of language, 53
Metaphysician, the last, 113

Index

Index

Index

Scientific approach (cont.)
errors of, 279
hegemonic pretensions of, 300
historical conditioning of, 158
language of, purged of human meanings, 284
limits of, 27
"Scientism," 21, 196, 196
Scott, Charles, 10
Scripture
fourfold meaning of, 80
interpretation of, 81, 83, 90, 91, 92, 94
Self, other, and world, as precondition for communication, 208, 300
Self-consciousness. *See* Consciousness
Self understanding. *See* Understanding, self
Sellars, Wilfrid, 234
Separation, as negative side of temporal distance, 253
Sex, 310–311
Sexuality, culturally and historically constructed, 316, 317
Simulacra, employed by Nietzsche, 111, 113
Situatedness, 176
Situation relativity of, 137
Skepticism, 225
Skeptics, 104
Skulsky, Harold, 94
Smith, P. Christopher, 47, 53, 54, 55, 57, 58, 71n, 73n, 164, 171n
"Snow is white," 196, 204
Social identity, xii, 307–329
coherence of, 326
as interpretation, 307
limited by tradition, 317
result of power, 326
as social construction, 307, 318, 326
of women, 307–308, 325, 326
Social realm, 26, 32–33, 37
Sociology of knowledge, 21
Socrates, 92, 162, 223, 260, 261, 262, 263, 265
Solipsism, often alias for intersubjectivity, 264
Solomon, 258
Somatic rhetoric, 53
Sonderegger, Ruth, 154n
Sophism, 54, 56
Sophocles, 258
Soteriological nature of philosophy, 109

Soul, human, 261, 262
construction of, 261–262
as having no Platonic Idea, 263, 272
Plato's myths of, 262, 263
as structureless, 263
Space of understanding, 142
Speech
as intentional, 186
partners, 280
as social practice, 48–49
as "speaking-together," 53
Sprachansicht, 36
Spengler, Oswald, 16
Spinoza, Baruch, 241
Stalin, Joseph, 6
Stenzel, Julius, 224
Stoics, 104
Strasbourg, Archbishop of, repression of religieuse, 84
Strauss, Leo, 257
Strawson, Peter, 42n, 213n
Strong, Tracy B., 118, 131n
Structure
as defining and delimiting, 263
formal, 270
translation into, 62
Struggle, 58, 74n, 119
as determiner of knowledge, 119
and heroism, 58, 74n
and rhetoric, in Homer, 58
Stuttgart, 11
Subtilitas applicandi, 77
Subtilitas explicandi, 77
Subtilitas intelligendi, 77
Subjectivity, 112, 114, 130, 226, 229, 230, 232, 264, 267, 268, 270, 273
decay of, into subjectivism, 269, 273
error of, 116, 237n
Sumbouleuesthai, 53, 55, 57
Supercession, temporality of, 61
Suspicion, destructive to dialogue, 57

Taking counsel together, 57
Tarski, Alfred, 204
Techne, 47, 50, 55, 63
Teichmüller, Gustav, 127–128
Die wirkliche and die scheinbare Welt, 127, 129, 133n
Neue Studien zur Geschichte der Begriffe, 127
Temporal distance, 239–255
as changed from empty space to field of energy, 250
as condition for history of effect, 253

Index

Index